The Contract Clause

The Contract Clause

A CONSTITUTIONAL HISTORY

James W. Ely, Jr.

University Press of Kansas

FOR MICKEY, AGAIN

Published by the University Press of Kansas (Lawrence, Kansas 66045), which was organized by the Kansas Board of Regents and is operated and funded by Emporia State University, Fort Hays State University, Kansas State University, Pittsburg State University, the University of Kansas, and Wichita State University

Library of Congress Cataloging-in-Publication Data
Names: Ely, James W., 1938– author.
Title: The contract clause : a constitutional history / James W. Ely., Jr.
Description: Lawrence, Kansas : University Press of Kansas, 2016. | Includes bibliographical references and index.
Identifiers: LCCN 2016023591| ISBN 9780700623075 (hardback) | ISBN 9780700623082 (ebook)
Subjects: LCSH: United States. Constitution—Contract clause. | United States. Supreme Court. | Liberty of contract—United States. | Right of property—United States. | BISAC: LAW / Constitutional. | POLITICAL SCIENCE / Government / National. | POLITICAL SCIENCE / Government / State & Provincial.
Classification: LCC KF4608 .E49 2016 | DDC 346.7302/3—dc23
LC record available at https://lccn.loc.gov/2016023591.

British Library Cataloguing-in-Publication Data is available.

Printed in the United States of America

10 9 8 7 6 5 4 3 2 1

The paper used in this publication is acid free and meets the minimum requirements of the American National Standard for Permanence of Paper for Printed Library Materials Z39.48-1992.

Contents

Acknowledgments

Work on this book has spanned a number of years. In the course of research and writing I have received valuable assistance from many individuals. David J. Bodenhamer, Peter Charles Hoffer, Timothy Huebner, Herbert A. Johnson, Robert Mikos, and Melvin I. Urofsky critiqued all or portions of the manuscript and offered helpful suggestions. I also benefited from comments when I presented parts of the manuscript at the Center of Law and History, Washington and Lee Law School, at the Darlington Foundation Originalism Works-in-Progress Conference, University of San Diego Law School, and at St. Mary's University School of Law. An earlier version of Chapter 1 was published as "The Contract Clause: Origins and Early Development," in *Brigham-Kanner Property Rights Conference Journal* 4 (2015): 199–228.

Institutional support was also important. I am deeply grateful to Stephen Jordan, Carolyn R. Hamilton, and Jason R. Sowards of the Massey Law Library of Vanderbilt University for their skill and patience in locating materials. I thank Dorothy Kuchinski and Renee Hawkins for efficient help in preparing the manuscript.

Editors at the University Press of Kansas were unfailingly supportive despite the length of time it took to complete this project. Michael Briggs was an early enthusiast for a study of the contract clause, and Charles T. Myers, the director, read many of the chapters, offering both encouragement and insightful suggestions. I am, of course, responsible for any shortcomings in this book.

This book is dedicated to my wife, Mickey, in deep appreciation for many years of love, friendship, and support.

Introduction

Few provisions of the Constitution have experienced such a roller-coaster ride through US history as the contract clause. Article I, section 10 provides in part: "No state shall . . . pass any . . . Law impairing the Obligation of Contracts." Inserted into the Constitution without extensive debate, the contract clause was clearly prompted by the sour experience with state debt-relief laws enacted during the Post-Revolutionary Era. It was grounded on the premise that honoring contractual commitments served the public interest by encouraging commerce. The framers, therefore, wished to safeguard the stability of agreements from state legislative abridgment in order to facilitate commercial transactions. Under the leadership of John Marshall, the Supreme Court construed the provision expansively, and it rapidly became the primary vehicle for federal judicial review of state legislation before the adoption of the Fourteenth Amendment. Indeed, the contract clause was one of the most litigated provisions of the Constitution throughout the nineteenth century. Judges in the nineteenth century often extolled the significance of the clause. "There is no more important provision in the Federal Constitution," Justice William Strong observed in 1878, "than the one which prohibits the states from passing laws impairing the obligation of contracts, and it is one of the highest duties of this Court to take care that the prohibition shall neither be evaded or frittered away."[1]

Over time, however, the courts carved out several malleable exceptions to the constitutional protection of contracts—most notably the notion of an inalienable police power—thereby weakening the protection of the contract clause and enhancing state regulatory authority. The exceptions gradually began to swallow the provision, diminishing its importance. An already weakened contract clause received a near-fatal blow in the controversial case of *Home Building and Loan Association v. Blaisdell* (1934), upholding a mortgage moratorium during the Great Depression.[2] As New Deal constitutionalism gained ascendancy in the 1940s, the economic rights of individuals were relegated to secondary status in order to facilitate governmental intervention in the economy. The contract clause was a casualty of this jurisprudential change and largely fell into disuse for several decades. Starting in the 1970s there has been a modest revival of interest in the provision among courts and scholars. Nonetheless, the criteria for invoking the contract clause remain uncertain, and certainly the provision has never regained its former vigor.

Indeed, one scholar has recently taken a dismissive approach to the contract clause, asserting that the provision was buried by New Deal constitutionalism and "is no longer with us."[3] If this pessimistic view is correct, the obvious question arises: Why spend time and energy studying an apparent constitutional relic? Part of the answer, of course, is the undoubted historical significance of the contract clause. Neglect of the provision distorts our understanding of constitutional history. In addition, I will argue that the clause, even if diminished, retains contemporary importance. If no longer central to the leading constitutional issues of the day, the contract clause remains a frequently litigated provision in both federal and state courts. Talk of its demise is exaggerated.

Constitutional questions are not decided in a vacuum. I have endeavored to place evolving contract clause jurisprudence within the broader context of the legal culture, which values contracts as an expression of individualism and a market economy. The book takes account of social, economic, and political developments as they illuminate the role of contracting in US society. Although the contract clause by its terms is binding only on the states, I have given attention to instances in which principles derived from contract clause jurisprudence have been invoked in cases involving contractual impairment by the federal government. I have also treated the question of judicial interference with contracts. The contract clause is seemingly directed against state legislative impairment, but throughout the nineteenth century the Supreme Court intimated that, under some circumstances, a state court ruling altering a prior judicial opinion might run afoul of the Constitution if it undermined contractual stability.

A study of the contract clause provides a window into the shifting concerns and assumptions of Americans. It implicates matters central to US constitutional history, including the protection of economic rights, the growth of judicial review, and the role of federalism. Moreover, it sheds light on attitudinal changes with regard to the sanctity of contracts and private ordering of the economy. Adjudication involving the clause reflects the impact of wars, economic distress, and political currents on reading the Constitution. Issues pertaining to debt relief have been a recurring source of contract clause dispute, particularly in the period before the enactment of a permanent bankruptcy law in 1898. In addition, questions relating to land grants, the status of corporations, grants of tax exemption, regulation of health and morals, municipal debt repudiation, rent control, mortgage moratoria, and franchise arrangements have featured prominently in contract clause litigation. At the time of this writing steps by state and local governments to trim the benefits of public-sector employees have spawned numerous contract clause challenges in both federal and state courts.

Any study of the contract clause must take account of Benjamin F. Wright's classic work *The Contract Clause of the Constitution* (1938). For decades this volume has reigned as the definitive history of the clause and has set the tone for subsequent investigations. I have found Wright's work both informative and balanced but feel that the time is ripe for a fresh look at the history of the contract clause. Nearly eighty years have passed since Wright completed his book. Not only are there subsequent developments and issues to be incorporated in the narrative, but the ensuing decades have opened the way for new perspectives. In some areas, perhaps most notably the understanding of the framers regarding the scope of the contract clause, I have reached different conclusions than those offered by Wright. As the title of Wright's book suggests, his work is almost exclusively focused on interpretations of the clause by the US Supreme Court. He virtually ignores developments at the state level and the construction of parallel contract clauses in state constitutions. I have sought to remedy this omission by blending state and federal court decisions in every time period. I have also considered the extent to which state constitutions might be construed to provide enhanced protection for contracts. It is important to remember that state courts did much of the heavy lifting in interpreting and enforcing the contract clause. They are an integral, if too often overlooked, part of the story.

The book is organized chronologically. Chapter 1 investigates the origins and early evolution of contract clause jurisprudence from the Post-Revolutionary Era to the advent of John Marshall as chief justice in 1801. It points out that the framers felt that a ban on state abridgment of contracts was sufficiently important to be included in the Constitution at the very time they were arguing that a bill of rights was unnecessary. In this connection, it probes the view of the framers of the Constitution and considers contemporary opinion regarding the scope of the contract clause, arguing that, based on admittedly fragmentary evidence, the provision could reasonably be construed to safeguard both private and public agreements from state abridgment. The chapter also considers developments at the state level, noting the widespread adoption of parallel contract clauses in state constitutions. Moreover, I treat the initial federal and state court decisions construing the contract clause and paving the way for a robust reading of the provision in the nineteenth century.

Chapter 2 focuses on the well-known contract clause decisions of the Supreme Court under the guidance of Marshall. Indeed, the provision was a centerpiece of Marshall Court jurisprudence. Although Marshall famously interpreted the clause to encompass public as well as private agreements, he also limited the reach of the provision in several respects. He recognized an opaque distinction between contractual rights and the remedies available to enforce those rights. The right/remedy distinction was elusive and opened the door for lasting confusion as legislators repeatedly sought to modify remedies in such a manner as to hamper the enforcement of contracts. In addition, Marshall determined that there were no implied privileges in corporate charters. The state and lower federal courts heard a large volume of contract clause litigation. They invalidated numerous state debt-relief laws, and in some areas, such as police power and eminent domain, anticipated subsequent rulings by the Supreme Court.

In Chapter 3, I address the impact of the Jacksonian movement and the chief justiceship of Roger B. Taney upon contract clause jurisprudence. These years witnessed a proliferation of contract clause litigation at both the federal and state levels. Despite some differences, the overall picture is one of continuity with the work of the Marshall Court. Taney both limited and strengthened the security of contractual obligations under the contract clause. In *Charles River Bridge v. Warren Bridge* (1837)[4] he established the principle that corporate charters should be strictly construed and that privileges such as monopoly status or tax immunity could never be implied. Similarly, the Supreme Court determined that the contract clause did not prevent the states from exercising the power of eminent domain. On the other hand, under Taney the Court vigorously invoked the provision to safeguard the rights of parties under private agreements and to uphold clearly expressed tax exemptions. Following the lead of the Supreme Court, state courts struck down a host of debt-relief measures. They also grappled with the relationship between the state police power to protect the public health, safety, morals, and the protection afforded agreements by the contract clause. By Taney's death in 1864 the basic contours of contract clause jurisprudence had been established.

Chapter 4 looks at the torrent of contract clause litigation generated during the Civil War and Reconstruction. The Supreme Court confronted a number of novel issues emanating from the sectional conflict, such as the use of Confederate currency as a medium of exchange and the enforcement of contracts for the purchase of slaves. After the war, impoverished southern states enacted a variety of debt-relief laws and enlarged homestead exemptions, prompting contract clause challenges. Other cases raised issues similar to those of the antebellum period. The extent of corporate privileges under their charters remained a much-contested subject. For example, the Supreme Court, as well as numerous state courts, sustained tax exemptions as protected contracts. Moreover, the Court looked with disfavor on legislative attempts to repudiate or evade municipal bonded debt. The decade of the 1870s constituted a high-water mark for the role of the contract clause in constitutional law. Yet the same decade saw an attack on the Marshall Court's application of the contract clause to state contracts, particularly the protection of corporate charters under that provision. Further, state courts began to argue that all contracts were subject to the police power.

Chapter 5 explores a seeming paradox. Even as courts in the late nineteenth century developed a vigorous property-conscious jurisprudence, the contract clause declined in importance. Although both federal and state courts heard a steady stream of contract clause cases, they increasingly relied on other constitutional provisions, notably the due process clause of the Fourteenth Amendment, to protect economic rights. There was a rising barrage of criticism directed against the notion that corporate charters constituted a contract. The Supreme Court embraced the principle that states could not bargain away the police power to preserve public health and safety. Coupled with the doctrine of strict construction of corporate charters, the police power exception did much to undercut the sanctity of corporate charters. The emergence of the public trust doctrine opened another avenue to circumvent the protection of the contract clause. In contrast, courts continued to uphold grants of tax exemption and to invalidate legislative schemes to repudiate municipal debts. They also frequently relied on the contract clause to strike down legislative abridgment of private contracts, including laws that altered foreclosure procedures. The enactment of an enduring bankruptcy law in 1898 reduced the flow of contract clause cases dealing with debtor-creditor relations. This chapter differentiates the contract clause, which protected existing agreements from retroactive impairment, from the emerging liberty of contract doctrine. The liberty of contract doctrine held that the right to make contracts was constitutionally protected by the due process clause.

In Chapter 6, I trace the diminishing place of the contract clause in the constitutional polity from the early decades of the twentieth century until the end of World War II. The chapter is divided into segments, with the first covering the years before the coming of the New Deal in 1933. Both federal and state courts wielded the contract clause to protect contractual arrangements, but there were fewer such cases. Many of the cases presented familiar issues and broke no new ground. Still, in several respects the Supreme Court further confined the reach of the contract clause. It ruled that private agreements as well as public contracts were subject to the police power. It ruled in the rent control cases that a legislative declaration of an economic emergency might provide a basis for legislators to override existing contracts. Finally, after decades of vacillation, it held that the contract clause was directed only at abridgment of agreements by legislation and not the shifting judgements of state courts. The second segment considers the profound impact on thinking about the contract clause that occurred in the wake of the New Deal. The landmark *Blaisdell* decision was a crucial turning point and became the fountainhead of modern contract clause analysis at the federal level. After 1940, as President Franklin D. Roosevelt's appointees gained ascendancy, the Supreme Court jettisoned limitations on state authority over contracts. Left without any meaningful role, the contract clause virtually disappeared from constitutional dialogue for several decades.

Chapter 7 covers the period from the end of World War II to the present. The contract clause received scant attention from judges and scholars until the mid-1970s. Then the Supreme Court, in a pair of rulings, relied on the provision for the first time in more than thirty years to overturn state laws that infringed contracts. These decisions served to revive interest in the contract clause, but the halting and ambiguous opinions did not provide a principled basis on which to rebuild contract clause jurisprudence. To complicate matters, the Court, contrary to historical experience, imposed a higher standard of review when a state impaired its own obligations. In the main, however, the Supreme Court demonstrated only a fleeting interest in the contract clause and devised an amorphous multifactor test for determining violations of the provision. Most of the contract clause litigation in recent decades has taken place in the state courts, spanning a wide variety of disputes. Generalization is difficult, but in a number of cases state courts have invalidated laws as running afoul of the clause in state or federal constitutions. The most vexing contract clause issue at present arises from steps by cash-strapped state and local governments to trim benefits for current and retired employees.[5] I examine this ongoing controversy at length, noting the interplay between the contract clause and federal bankruptcy power.

The place of the contract clause is no longer among the most hotly contested issues in constitutional law. Nonetheless, the provision clearly retains some viability as a constraint on state legislative authority. The conversation over the scope of the contract clause will doubtless continue. I hope that this volume will make a contribution to that debate.

CHAPTER 1

Origins and Early Development

Forrest McDonald remarked that the adoption of the contract clause at the constitutional convention "is shrouded in mystery."[1] To unravel this mystery, one must start by considering the economic changes experienced by the American colonies during the eighteenth century. As the colonies grew and became more prosperous, they gradually rejected the doctrine of mercantilism inherited from Great Britain, with its emphasis upon governmental controls, in favor of an emerging market economy. Wage and price regulations, as well as the system of exclusive public markets, gradually atrophied.[2] Moreover, the law governing real property was revamped little by little to facilitate land transactions, thereby treating landed property increasingly as a market commodity.[3]

As price controls and regulated markets declined, and land speculation quickened, contracts assumed a more prominent role in the growing commercial society of the eighteenth century. In an expanding economy merchants were more likely to trade with or extend credit to persons who were strangers. Under such circumstances, transactions could no longer be grounded in custom or trust. Hence, private bargains in an impersonal market were increasingly determined by written agreements. Parties became accustomed to making deals and looking out for their own interests. Contracts provided a vehicle by which individuals could bargain for their own advantage.[4] The product of private negotiation, not governmental authority, contractual exchanges not only encouraged economic efficiency but also underscored the autonomy of individuals. To achieve these goals, the stability of contracts was essential. It was necessary that bargains be honored and not subject to subsequent legislative interference.

A careful study of Virginia bears out the waxing of contract law and a market economy. William E. Nelson found that "a vibrant market economy" based on tobacco sales developed as early as the mid-seventeenth century. This robust economy "gave rise to complex commercial transactions and commercial litigation." Nelson concluded that in Virginia by the 1640s "the hallmark doctrine of market capitalism, that individuals should be free to enter into contracts which courts would then enforce, was firmly in place."[5]

POST-REVOLUTIONARY ERA

The troubled conditions of post-Revolutionary America, however, presented serious challenges to an economy based on private bargaining. Independence from Great Britain caused considerable economic dislocation. It ended the trade restrictions imposed by the British Navigation Acts but also brought about the loss of markets with Great Britain and its other colonies. In addition, the Revolution caused wholesale interference with private economic relationships by state legislatures. Reacting to the depressed economic climate in the wake of independence, state lawmakers enacted a variety of debt-relief laws to assist debtors at the expense of creditors. They passed laws staying the collection of debts, allowing the payment of debts in installments, and authorizing the payment of debts in commodities.[6] South Carolina's Pine Barren Act of 1785 was a particularly egregious measure. Under this act debtors could tender distant property or worthless pineland to satisfy outstanding obligations.[7] State lawmakers also issued quantities of paper money and made such paper currency legal tender for the payment of debts. These measures not only hampered commerce by frustrating the enforcement of contracts but seemingly portended threats to the security of property generally. Creditors and merchants saw these laws as little more than a confiscation of their property interests.

Although popular in some quarters, legislative tampering with agreements aroused intense criticism. In 1786, for example, Noah Webster, later the author of a famous dictionary, declared, "But remember that past contracts are sacred things; that Legislatures have no right to interfere with them; they have no right to say, a debt shall be paid at a discount, or in any manner which the parties never intended. It is the business of justice to fulfil the intention of parties in contracts, not to defeat them."[8] Alexander Hamilton, while secretary of the Treasury, pictured state legislative interference with contracts as rendering commerce uncertain and as weakening the security of property.[9] Likewise, Chief Justice John Marshall later recalled the deleterious impact on society of laws meddling with contracts in the newly independent United States:

> The power of changing the relative situation of debtor and creditor, of interfering with contracts, a power which comes home to every man, touches the interest of all, and controls the conduct of every individual in those things which he supposes to be proper for his own exclusive management, had been used to such an excess by the State legislatures, as to break in upon the ordinary intercourse of society, and destroy all confidence between man and man. The

> mischief had become so great, so alarming, as not only to impair commercial intercourse, and threaten the existence of credit, but to sap the morals of the people, and destroy the sanctity of private faith. To guard against the continuance of the evil was an object of deep interest with all the truly wise, as well as the virtuous, of this great community, and was one of the important benefits expected from the reform of the government.[10]

Legislative interference with contractual arrangements was not confined to debt-relief laws. Consider the controversy over the revocation of the charter of the Bank of North America. The first incorporated bank in the United States, the Bank of North America received charters from the Continental Congress in 1781 and the Pennsylvania legislature the following year. Given doubts about the authority of Congress to grant charters of incorporation, the Bank was generally regarded as a Pennsylvania institution. In 1785 the Pennsylvania legislature, responding to pressure from radicals and agrarians, moved to annul the charter. Critics maintained that the bank encouraged the accumulation of capital and hampered the issuance of paper money by the state. The repeal proposal triggered a bitter debate in the state.[11] James Wilson, a prominent lawyer and later a member of the constitutional convention and a Supreme Court justice, took the lead in defending the bank. Wilson had borrowed heavily from the bank, and thus he may have been as concerned with his personal economic advantage as with the security of charters. Whatever his motives, Wilson's arguments in support of the bank were prescient. In a widely circulated pamphlet, *Considerations on the Bank of North America,* Wilson attacked repeal as economic folly. More important for our purposes, he argued that the act incorporating the bank amounted to a contract between the state and the corporation that the legislature was bound to respect. Wilson insisted that "while the terms are observed on one side, the compact cannot, consistently with the rules of good faith, be departed from on the other." Noting the practical significance of corporate charters, he added, "To receive the legislative stamp of stability and permanency, acts of incorporation are applied for from the legislature. If these acts may be repealed without notice, without accusation, without hearing, without proof, without forfeiture; where is the stamp of their stability?"[12] In a nutshell, Wilson contended that a state was obligated to honor its own undertakings and that stability in regard to corporate charters was essential for successful enterprise. As Jennifer Nedelsky pointed out, "Not only did [Wilson] think that upholding contracts was extremely important economically, he saw the obligation of contract as part of the fundamental obligation to fulfill promises which makes society possible."[13]

James Wilson argued in 1785 that legislative grants of corporate charters amounted to contracts, and he subsequently championed adoption of the contract clause as part of the Constitution. (Courtesy of National Portrait Gallery, Smithsonian Institution/Art Resource, NY)

Other legislators echoed Wilson, with one insisting that "charters are a species of property."[14]

These arguments did not prevail in 1785. Defenders of the repeal law denied that a corporate charter should be treated as a contract and stressed the power of the legislature to revoke charters.[15] Although the charter was rescinded, Wilson had anticipated much constitutional jurisprudence. Indeed, one scholar has contended that the contract clause "was an outgrowth of the arguments about Pennsylvania's authority to breach its own contract."[16]

Wilson was not alone in advancing these views. In 1786 Pelatiah Webster, a Philadelphia merchant and author of several pamphlets on finance and government, reiterated the points stressed by Wilson. Maintaining that "charters (or rights of individuals or companies, secured by the State) *have ever been considered as a kind of sacred things*," he denied that legislatures could repeal the grant and destroy the rights of the grantee. Webster even argued that "the sacred force of contracts *binds stronger in an act of state*, than in the *act of an individual*, because *the whole government is injured and weakened by a violation of the public faith*."[17]

As these comments indicate, state interference with the rights of creditors, when coupled with the revocation of an important corporate charter, bitterly disappointed many political leaders of the Post-Revolutionary Era. They became convinced that state protection of economic rights was inadequate. Historians generally agree that the establishment of safeguards for private property was one of the principal objectives of the constitutional convention of 1787. "Perhaps the most important value of the Founding Fathers of the American constitutional period," Stuart Bruchey has cogently pointed out, "was their belief in the necessity of securing property rights."[18] Delegates repeatedly stressed this theme during the convention. For instance, James Madison asserted at the Philadelphia convention that "the primary objects of civil society are the security of property and public safety."[19]

The first provision protective of contractual rights was part of the Northwest Ordinance of July 1787. Passed by the Confederation Congress while the constitutional convention was meeting in Philadelphia, the Northwest Ordinance established a framework for territorial governance in the Old Northwest. Articulating a number of fundamental principles, the Northwest Ordinance had much of the character of a constitutional document.[20] The Northwest Ordinance contained several important provisions regarding the rights of property owners, including one ensuring the sanctity of private contracts. Article 2 of the Northwest Ordinance stated, "And, in the just preservation of rights and property, it is understood and declared, that no law ought ever to be made or have force in the said territory, that shall, in any manner whatever, interfere with or affect private contracts, or engagements, bona fide, and without fraud previously formed."[21] This language may have been inserted in response to Shays's Rebellion in Massachusetts, which sought to prevent the collection of debts. It has also been seen as part of a larger scheme to encourage commercial development in the largely unsettled territories. Viewed in this light, the protection of agreements was a crucial step in attracting eastern investors. The territorial government was prevented from abridging private economic deals, creating a hospitable climate for outside capital.[22] The contract clause in the Northwest Ordinance foreshadowed the step to forge a constitutional guarantee of existing contracts.

THE CONSTITUTIONAL CONVENTION

Given the concern shared by many delegates to the constitutional convention that state governments were invading property and contractual rights and hampering commerce, it is hardly a surprise that the new Constitution contained a cluster of provisions designed to rectify the abuses at the state level. Thus, the Constitution prevented the states from enacting bills of attainder and from making anything but gold or silver legal tender for the payment of debts.

A provision barring the states from impairing contracts was added late in the convention's deliberations, and with surprisingly little debate given its subsequent significance in US constitutionalism. On August 28, 1787, the delegates were considering constitutional limitations upon the authority of the states. Rufus King of Massachusetts moved to insert into the Constitution language "in the words used in the Ordinance of Cong[ress] establishing new States, a prohibition on the States to interfere in private contracts."[23] King's proposal faced a cool reception. Gouverneur Morris declared his opposition, observing, "This would be going too far. There are a thousand laws relating to bringing actions—limitations of actions & which affect contracts—The Judicial power of the US—will be a protection in cases within their jurisdiction; and within the State itself a majority must rule, whatever may be the mischief done among themselves."[24] James Wilson supported King's motion. James Madison was somewhat ambivalent, but was generally favorable. He "admitted that inconvenience might arise from such a prohibition but thought on the whole it would be overbalanced by the utility of it." Anticipating later issues, Madison added, "Evasions might and would be devised by the ingenuity of the legislatures."[25] George Mason joined Morris in resisting King's proposal. He stated, "This is carrying the restraint too far. Cases will happen that cannot be foreseen, where some kind of interference will be proper & essential—He mentioned the case of limiting the period for bringing actions on account—that of bonds after a certain (lapse of time)—asking whether it was proper to tie the hands of the States from making provision in such cases?"[26] In response,

Wilson argued that only retrospective interferences with contracts would be prohibited by the proposed ban. This comment interjected a note of confusion into the deliberations. It prompted Madison to ask, "Is not that already done by the prohibition of ex post facto laws, which will oblige the Judges to declare such interferences null & void?"[27] John Rutledge moved to substitute for King's motion the words "nor pass bills of attainder nor ex post facto laws." This motion carried by a vote of seven to three, and the suggested contract clause was shelved.[28]

A day later John Dickinson declared that he had examined William Blackstone's *Commentaries on the Laws of England* and had "found that the terms 'ex post facto' related to criminal cases only; that they would not consequently restrain the States from retrospective laws in civil cases, and that some further provision for this purpose would be requisite."[29] But the convention never debated the question of a contract clause again. Nonetheless, the Committee of Style and Arrangement, charged with preparing a final document, placed a differently worded contract clause into Article I, section 10, that contained various restrictions on state power. The proposed language barred the states from "altering or impairing the obligation of contracts." The convention deleted the words "altering or" without recorded discussion, and the contract clause was adopted as part of the Constitution.[30] The clause could be seen as an extension of the ban on ex post facto laws to measures involving contracts.[31]

Authorship of the clause is uncertain. The committee was composed of Hamilton, William S. Johnson, King, Madison, and Morris. Only Morris had spoken in opposition to a provision protecting contractual rights. King had initially proposed a qualified clause limited to private contracts, and Madison had offered a guarded endorsement. Neither, however, seems a likely source for a broad restriction on state power over contracts.[32] McDonald persuasively speculates that Hamilton, with his modern understanding of contracts, was the probable author.[33] Other scholars have suggested that Wilson, who was not a committee member but who was a close friend of Hamilton, may have proposed the final wording.[34] Thus, Nedelsky has concluded, "It seems entirely likely that Wilson would have inserted such a clause."[35]

In any event, the convention as a whole did not revisit this issue. Elbridge Gerry of Massachusetts warmly endorsed the principle behind the contract clause. He "entered into observations inculcating the importance of public faith, and the propriety of the restraint put on the States from impairing the obligation of contracts." Gerry sought to apply the contract clause to the new federal government, but his motion to this effect failed for lack of a second.[36] This underscores the fact that the ban on contractual interference was deliberately applied just to the states.[37] The framers seemingly realized that laws violative of contracts might be necessary in some circumstances but felt that such measures should only be enacted by Congress. To that end, Congress was empowered to "establish . . . uniform Laws on the subject of Bankruptcies throughout the United States." Congress, the framers felt, could better assess public need and was less likely to be influenced by local considerations and particular interest groups. Moreover, it is striking that, despite its circuitous path into the Constitution, the framers thought a specific ban on state impairment of contracts was sufficiently vital to include at the very time they were arguing that a bill of rights was unnecessary.[38]

The contract clause fit comfortably into the larger scheme of the Federalists to foster a commercial society. "Federalists proposed, in sum," two scholars have concluded, "to place the new land in the mainstream of acquisitive capitalism."[39] As we have seen, by the late eighteenth century contracts played a critical role in a growing market economy. The reliability of agreements was essential. Roger Sherman and Oliver Ellsworth, delegates from Connecticut to the constitutional convention, explained in September of 1787 that the convention thought the contract clause was "necessary as a security to commerce, in which the interests of foreigners, as well as the citizens of other states, may be affected."[40] Echoing that sentiment, Lawrence M. Friedman has pointed out that "business had to be able to rely on the stability of arrangements legally made, at least in the short and middle run."[41] The contract clause was designed to provide that stability. Analyzing the purpose of the contract clause, Charles A. Beard tellingly observed, "Contracts are to be safe, and whoever engages in a financial operation, public or private, may know that state legislatures cannot destroy overnight the rules by which the game is played."[42]

RATIFICATION DEBATES

Consistent with republican theory that political authority rested on the sovereignty of the people, the framers submitted the proposed Constitution for ratification by popularly elected state conventions. During the ensuing ratification debates the proponents of the Constitution termed themselves Federalists and dubbed critics of the Constitution as Anti-Federalists. The ratification debates primarily turned upon far-ranging political and constitutional issues in which the contract clause did not figure prominently. The Federalists tended to be commercially minded individuals, such as merchants and planters producing crops for export, who looked with favor on the contract clause. A writer in the *New Hampshire Spy* in November of 1787 expressed the Federalist viewpoint, observing that the Constitution "also expressly prohibits those destructive laws in the several states which alter or impair the obligation of contracts; so that in future anyone may be certain of an exact fulfilment of any contract that may be entered into or the penalty that may be stipulated for in case of failure."[43]

It is useful to review the arguments of both proponents and critics of the Constitution as they pertain to the contract clause. The various restrictions on state power contained in Article I, section 10, including the contract clause as well as the prohibition of paper money and ex post facto laws, were often linked for the purposes of debate. Leading Federalists pictured this cluster of restrictions as essential for preserving credit and encouraging commerce. Writing in the *Federalist,* Hamilton assailed state infringement of contracts as "atrocious breaches of moral obligation and social justice." Still, he focused on the dire implications for trade among the states posed by laws abridging agreements. "Laws in violation of private contracts," Hamilton warned, "as they amount to aggressions on the rights of those states, whose citizens are injured by them, may be considered as another probable source of hostility."[44] He expressed concern that such contractual infringements would invite retaliation by other states, undercutting the goal of a commercial union. Similarly, Charles Pinckney of South Carolina, also a delegate to the constitutional convention, characterized Article I, section 10 as "the soul of the Constitution" at the South Carolina ratifying convention. Echoing Hamilton, Pinckney explained, "Henceforth, the citizens of the states may trade with each other without fear of tender-laws or laws impairing the nature of contracts." Moreover, he anticipated that these limitations on the states would restore American credit in foreign markets. "No more shall paper money, no more shall tender-laws," Pinckney declared, "drive their commerce from our shores, and darken the American name in every country where it is known."[45] Wilson, addressing the Pennsylvania ratifying convention, likewise emphasized the interstate dimensions of contracts. He insisted that Article I, section 10, alone "would be worth our adoption."[46]

Other prominent Federalists saw Article I, section 10, as a vehicle to bar state debt-relief legislation. David Ramsay of South Carolina, for example, observed that this provision "will doubtless bear hard on debtors who wish to defraud their creditors, but it will be a real service to the honest part of the community."[47] Likewise, William R. Davie of North Carolina, who had served in the military during the Revolutionary War and represented North Carolina at the constitutional convention, championed the contract clause as a curb on irresponsible state relief measures. Picturing the provision as essential for the interests of both agriculture and commerce, he warned that South Carolina "might in the future, as they have already done make pine barren acts to discharge their debts. They might say that our citizens shall be paid in sterile, inarable lands, at an extravagant price. They might pass the most iniquitous installment laws, procrastinating the payment of debts due from their citizens for years, nay, for ages."[48]

James Madison in the *Federalist* defended Article I, section 10, in different terms, stressing broad considerations of justice. He pictured bills of attainder, ex post facto laws, and laws abridging contracts as "contrary to the first principles of the social compact, and to every principle of sound legislation." Madison described the restrictions in this section as a "constitutional bulwark in favor of personal security and private rights." With the contract clause evidently in mind, he added:

> The sober people of America are weary of the fluctuating policy which has directed the public councils. They have seen with regret and with indignation, that sudden changes, and legislative interferences, in cases affecting personal rights, become jobs in the hands of enterprising and influential speculators; and snares to the more industrious and less informed part of the community. They have seen too, that one legislative interference is but the first link of a long chain of repetitions; every subsequent interference being naturally produced by the effects of the preceding.[49]

This sketchy record makes clear that leading Federalists, despite differing explanations of the contract clause, saw the provision to be of crucial importance. At the same time, their brief and ambiguous comments give little guidance as to the intended scope of the clause. Indeed, there was a range of opinion about the meaning of the contract clause, and the framers did not all share a common understanding. "The clause meant different things to different men in 1787–1788," Steven R. Boyd aptly concluded, "and throughout the early national period."[50]

Several proponents of the Constitution expressed the opinion that the limitations on state authority found in Article I, section 10, generated much of the opposition to ratification.[51] There is little evidence, however, to support this position with respect to the contract clause. Anti-Federalists rarely focused on the clause in urging rejection of the proposed new government. In fact, several Anti-Federalists admitted that the states had often acted irresponsibly regarding contracts. Thus, in February of 1788 James Winthrop of Massachusetts suggested amendments as a basis for accepting the Constitution. One proposal declared, "It shall be left to every state to make and execute its own laws, except laws impairing contracts, which shall not be made at all."[52] Another Anti-Federalist endorsed the restraints of Article I, section 10: "These prohibitions give the most perfect security against those attacks upon property which I am sorry to say some of the states have but too wantonly made, by passing laws sanctioning fraud in the debtor against his creditor."[53] His concern was not with the contract clause itself but with the means of enforcement. This writer insisted that state, not federal, courts should be trusted with deciding cases arising under this section.

Although discussion of the contract clause by those opposed to the Constitution was infrequent, one prominent Anti-Federalist, Luther Martin of Maryland, vigorously attacked the denial of state power to interfere with contracts. Speaking before the Maryland House of Delegates in November of 1787, Martin recognized that the contract clause might have a broad reach. In often-quoted language he asserted:

> I considered, Sir, that there might be times of such great public *calamities* and *distress* and of such *extreme scarcity of specie,* as should render it the *duty* of a government, for the *preservation* of even *the most valuable part* of its citizens, in some measure to interfere in their favor, by passing laws *totally or partially stopping* the courts of justice, or authorizing the debtor to pay by installments, or delivering up his property to his creditors at a *reasonable* and *honest* valuation. The times have been such as to render regulations of this kind necessary in most or all of the States, to prevent the *wealthy creditor* and the *monied* man from *totally* destroying the *poor* though even industrious debtor. *Such times* may *again* arise. I therefore voted against depriving the States of this power, a power which I am decided they ought to possess, but which, I admit, ought only to be exercised on very important and urgent occasions.[54]

Focusing on debtor-creditor relationships, Martin stressed his belief that the states should retain the power to abridge contracts in periods of economic emergency. This view, of course, was squarely opposed to that of the Federalists.

SCOPE OF THE CONTRACT CLAUSE

With the ratification of the Constitution, debate over the contract clause shifted to ascertaining the scope of its ban on state contractual impairments.

No doubt the immediate impetus for the inclusion of the clause was to curtail state debt-relief measures that weakened the security of private agreements. This has caused some scholars to reach the dubious conclusion that the framers expected the contract clause to be confined to debtor-creditor relationships.[55] One cannot infer the extent of the contract clause, however, solely from the necessities of the moment. There is no evidence that the clause was directed solely at creditor-debtor legislation. It is phrased in general terms and appears calculated to safeguard all contractual rights from legislative interference.[56]

Perhaps the most vexing question for historians is whether the contract clause was expected to reach contracts made by the states as well as agreements among private parties. Starting in the 1870s a number of commentators expressed doubt that the framers anticipated inclusion of public contracts within the ambit of the clause. As a corollary, these scholars maintained that the Supreme Court under the leadership of Chief Justice John Marshall expanded the scope of the contract clause beyond the limited objectives of the framers to safeguard private arrangements.[57] In a 1919 study, for example, Warren B. Hunting reviewed some of the evidence pertaining to the meaning of the clause and concluded without explanation that the convention "had in mind only the contracts of private individuals."[58] The growing tendency during the Gilded Age to question the application of the contract clause to public agreements is explored more fully in a later chapter.

This narrow interpretation of the contract clause, which gradually gained currency, was endorsed by Benjamin F. Wright in his leading study, *The Contract Clause of the Constitution* (1938). "The men of 1787–1788," he declared, "discussed the clause only in relation to private contracts, i.e., contracts between individuals." Wright added, "A careful search has failed to unearth any other statements even suggesting that the contract clause was intended to apply to other than private contracts."[59] Writing at a time when New Deal constitutionalism was gathering strength, Wright reflected the tradition of the Progressive historians who were deeply skeptical about the traditional role of the federal judiciary as a safeguard of the rights of property owners and who celebrated the growth of governmental powers over the economy. "Surely it is significant," Wallace Mendelson cogently noted, "that he produced *The Contract Clause* during the Great Depression . . . when the Progressive Movement's disdain for 'government by judges' was still a rampant force in liberal circles."[60] It became an article of faith that Marshall took an expansive view of the contract clause in order to protect vested property interests. This Progressive attitude might have led Wright to downplay contrary evidence. Nonetheless, Wright's work has been highly influential. Although his interpretation has been increasingly called into question, it is still common for scholars to assert that the framers expected the contract clause to cover only private agreements.[61]

I wish to challenge this conventional wisdom and to propose a contrary thesis—that the contract clause could fairly be construed to safeguard both private and public contracts from state abridgment, and that the contract clause decisions of the Marshall Court, treated in the next chapter, were well grounded. As we have seen, the framers of the Constitution and the delegates to the state ratifying conventions did not focus to any great extent on the nature of the prohibition contained in the clause. Given the sketchy record, I recognize that it is difficult to establish with certainty what the contract clause was expected to accomplish. Further, it is unlikely that all who supported the clause had the same anticipation as to its impact. Still, I contend that a conscientious review of the admittedly fragmentary evidence fails to support the frequent statement that the contract clause was confined to private agreements.

We should start by examining the wording of the contract clause. Wright and others appear to proceed on the problematic assumption that the clause was simply intended to replicate the earlier provision in the Northwest Ordinance. However, King's motion to that effect was defeated, and the Committee of Style markedly changed the wording of the clause as finally adopted. Specifically, the committee deleted the words "private" as well as "bona fide, and without fraud previously formed," which appear in the Northwest Ordinance. Wright never really comes to grips with this changed wording, which on its face gives the contract clause a much broader scope. It is curious, to say the least, to maintain that the language as adopted was the equivalent of wording that was explicitly rejected. Instead of this reasoning, I submit that the best evidence of what the framers intended is what was written and adopted. We should be skeptical about the notion that the unqualified language of the contract clause was somehow thought to reach only a limited range of contracts. As Mendelson has pointed out, "If the Constitutional Convention had wanted the clause to cover only private contracts, it could have easily said so."[62] The model of the Northwest Ordinance was immediately before the convention. Instead of following the private-contract approach of the Northwest Ordinance, the framers adopted more general wording. This significant change went unchallenged by any delegate, strongly indicating that it reflected the sense of the convention. As Robert L. Clinton has cogently observed, "The proceedings at Philadelphia offer no basis for believing that the Founders intended to make a sharp distinction between public and private contracts."[63]

The debates at the state ratifying conventions lend little support for confining the protective reach of the contract clause to private agreements. Only one Federalist unequivocally affirmed that the contract clause would apply solely to private obligations. At the first North Carolina ratifying convention, held in July of 1788, Anti-Federalists warned that the various provisions in Article I, section 10, particularly the contract clause, would compel the state to redeem its depreciated securities at face value. William R. Davie responded:

> Mr. Chairman, I believe neither the 10th section, cited by the gentleman, nor any other part of the Constitution, has vested the general government with power to interfere with the public securities of any state. I will venture to say that the last thing which the general government will attempt to do will be this. They have nothing to do with it. The clause merely refers to contracts between individuals. That section is the best in the Constitution. It is founded on the strongest principles of justice.[64]

It goes without saying that a single statement, made in the course of a debate, is a slender basis for generalizations about the thoughts of the framers regarding the scope of the contract clause.

Other infrequent references to the contract clause by Federalists are too discursive to cast light on the subject. Discussing the monetary clauses of Article I, section 10, Charles Pinckney told the South Carolina ratifying convention that the states should not be "intrusted with the power of emitting money, or interfering with private contracts; or, by means of tender-laws, impairing the obligation of contracts."[65] This observation tells us little because the contracts affected by debt-relief laws were invariably private. Moreover, Pinckney does not purport to be addressing the meaning of the contract clause.

More telling is the exchange between Patrick Henry, a leading Anti-Federalist, and Governor Edmund Randolph, who had served as a delegate to the constitutional convention. At the Virginia ratifying convention Henry insisted that the clause would require states to redeem paper money at face value:

> How will this thing operate, when ten or twenty millions are demanded as the quota of this state? You will cry out that speculators have got it at one for a thousand, and they ought to be paid so. Will you then have recourse, for relief,

> to legislative interference? They cannot relieve you, because of that clause. The expression includes public contracts, as well as private contracts between individuals. Notwithstanding the sagacity of the gentleman, he cannot prove its exclusive relation to private contracts.[66]

Henry clearly saw the potential sweep of the contract clause. Equally revealing is the response by Randolph. He correctly maintained that Congress, which had issued a good deal of paper money, was not bound by the contract clause. Randolph continued:

> I am still a warm friend to the prohibition, because it must be promotive of virtue and justice, and preventive of injustice and fraud. If we take a review of the calamities which have befallen our reputation as a people, we shall find they have been produced by frequent interferences of the state legislatures with private contracts. If you inspect the great corner-stone of republicanism, you will find it to be justice and fairness.[67]

Although Randolph indeed mentioned state interference with private contracts as a particular mischief, he does not contradict Henry or in any way suggest that the protection of the clause was restricted to private agreements.[68]

The observations of other participants in the ratification debates do not draw a distinction between public and private contracts. Martin flatly opposed any limitation on state authority over contracts, and consequently had no reason to address the issue. In the *Federalist* Madison defended the clause in terms of the unfairness of violating agreements. Because he invoked "principles of the social contract" and was anxious to safeguard "personal security and private rights," it seems unlikely that he thought states were free under the contract clause to dishonor their own obligations.[69] It bears emphasis that in most situations state impairment of public contracts would negatively affect the very "private rights" that Madison sought to protect.

Lastly, the views of Wilson and Hamilton deserve particular attention because both have been identified as probable authors of the contract clause. Wilson, it will be recalled, was already on record as believing that state legislatures could not abridge their own agreements. It therefore seems highly likely that Wilson fully expected the contract clause to reach public contracts. Likewise, Hamilton was a strong supporter of a comprehensive reading of the provision, a point discussed later in this chapter.

My purpose is not to demonstrate that the collective intent of the framers was to embrace both public and private contracts within the constitutional ban on impairment. The fragmentary nature of the extant evidence makes it impossible to establish conclusively the thinking of the various framers, who might well have harbored somewhat different ideas as to the extent of protection afforded agreements. But historians have leaped too quickly to the conclusion that the clause was meant to govern only private agreement, virtually ignoring a good deal of contrary evidence. There is certainly room to doubt that the framers drew a bright line between public and private contracts.

INITIAL INTERPRETATIONS

Courts, legislators, and interested parties early grappled with the meaning of the contract clause. Despite the apparent clarity of its language, the contract clause posed a number of interpretative issues. When did the clause take effect? Did it apply to already existing agreements? What agreements amounted to a contract for purposes of protection under the clause? Did the clause prevent state lawmakers from making any adjustments to the rights and obligations of contracting parties?

As would be expected, the initial invocation of the provision concerned a debt-relief measure. In November of 1788, just months after ratification of the Constitution but before the new federal government was organized, the South Carolina legislature passed a revised installment law allowing debtors to pay their obligations over five years. Several South Carolinians protested that the statute was an unconstitutional impairment of contract. Despite some expressed reservations, most legislators felt that laws enacted before the effective date of government under the Constitution were not affected by the clause.[70] This position was eventually ratified by the Supreme Court.[71]

The first-known federal court decision invalidating a state statute was grounded on the contract clause. At issue in *Champion and Dickason v. Casey* (1792) was a 1791 Rhode Island private act extending for three years the time in which the debtor, Silas Casey, could settle his accounts with his creditors. The act also exempted Casey from all arrests and attachments for three years. Casey was a prominent Rhode Island merchant who suffered business reversals during the Revolutionary War. He used his political connections to win passage of the stay law. Two British merchants brought suit in the US Circuit Court for Rhode Island against Casey to recover unpaid debts of nearly $20,000. In defense, Casey raised the Rhode Island act as a bar to the suit.[72] The case was heard by Chief Justice John Jay, Justice William Cushing, and District Judge Henry Marchant. They dismissed Casey's defense as legally insufficient. Although the decision was never officially reported, newspaper accounts explained the outcome: "The Judges were unanimously of Opinion, that, as by the Constitution of the United States, the individual states are prohibited from making laws which shall impair the Obligation of Contracts, and as the resolution in question, if operative would impair the Obligation of the Contract in question, therefore it could not be admitted to bar the action."[73] Most of the historical assessment of this case has emphasized its importance in the emergence of federal judicial review. Yet the opinion also demonstrates the high standing of the contract clause in the law of the early Republic and the willingness of federal judges to enforce it. Not only did the decision arouse no opposition, but the Rhode Island legislature adopted a resolution that it would not grant any more individual exemptions for private debts.

These early harbingers of a muscular contract clause doctrine did not address the scope of the clause. Two members of the Supreme Court, as well as other leading commentators, however, squarely took the position that a state could not repudiate its own agreements. Wilson advanced this view in his separate opinion in *Chisholm v. Georgia* (1793).[74] At issue was the authority of the federal judiciary to hear suits brought against states without their consent. In *Chisholm* a citizen of South Carolina, acting as the executor of a deceased creditor, instituted a suit against Georgia to recover for supplies delivered during the Revolution. The Supreme Court asserted the right of the federal courts to adjudicate this claim, igniting a political firestorm that resulted in the adoption of the Eleventh Amendment.[75] In his separate opinion, Wilson analyzed the nature of sovereignty and the federal union. Turning to the contract clause, Wilson made his interpretation plain:

> Another declared object is, "to establish justice." This points, in a particular manner, to the Judicial authority. And when we view this object in conjunction with the declaration "that no State shall pass a law impairing the obligation of contracts"; we shall probably think that this object points, in a particular manner, to the jurisdiction of the Court over the several States. What good purpose could this Constitutional provision secure, if a State might pass a law impairing the obligation of its own contracts; and be amenable, for such a violation of right, as to no controlling judiciary power? We have seen, that on the principles of general jurisprudence, a State, for the breach of a contract, may be liable for damages.[76]

In this language Wilson emphatically linked his view, first suggested in his remarks on the repeal of the Bank of North America charter, that a state could not abridge its own obligations under the contract clause.

Going a step further, Justice William Paterson, in the well-known case of *Vanhorne's Lessee v. Dorrance* (1795), ruled that a Pennsylvania statute that sought to resolve conflicting land claims in the Wyoming Valley of the Susquehanna River by vesting title in one group of settlers impaired the state's contract.[77] The conflict originated in an interstate dispute over the settlement of these territories. During the colonial era a group of settlers from Connecticut acquired title to the disputed tract from Connecticut and from Indians rather than from the proprietors of Pennsylvania. The heirs of the proprietors, however, sold the land in question to Pennsylvania speculators and farmers. This gave rise to a bitter dispute as Pennsylvania and Connecticut settlers both claimed the same land. In the mid-1780s some of the settlers from Connecticut talked of creating a separate state, which could resolve any question as to the validity of their land titles. In order to secure the allegiance of the Connecticut settlers, the Pennsylvania legislature in 1787 enacted a law confirming the title to all land actually settled.[78] Under the statute, the Pennsylvania claimants were to receive other vacant land by way of compensation for being divested of their property. But a year later the Pennsylvania legislature suspended the confirming act and repealed it in 1790. The validity of the confirming act was challenged in a test case. The plaintiff, who grounded his claim on a chain of title from proprietors of Pennsylvania, brought an ejectment action to in effect quiet title to the land. The defendant sought to demonstrate a superior title. His claim rested upon the 1787 confirming act, which purported to vest title in the settlers from Connecticut.

Paterson had been a leading member of the constitutional convention and later a senator before being named to the Supreme Court.[79] He played a key role in a number of the important decisions of the 1790s and emerged as a champion of judicial review. In *Vanhorne's Lessee* he presided with Judge Richard Peters in the US Circuit Court for Pennsylvania. In his extensive charge to the jury, which has the character of a philosophical address on the nature of constitutional government, Paterson found infirmities with the confirming act. First, he asserted that the measure amounted to an unconstitutional taking of property because it failed to provide just compensation. Constitutional principles, he insisted, required that just compensation must be in money. Second, and more important for our purposes, Paterson determined that the confirming act ran afoul of the contract clause.

Although he recognized that the confirming act and the suspending act were enacted prior to adoption of the US Constitution and were not affected by it, Paterson evidently reasoned that the 1790 repealing act was subject to the new Constitution and thus afforded him an opportunity to consider the larger issue of state legislative authority over land grants. With respect to the confirming act, Paterson told the jury:

> It impairs the obligation of a contract, and is therefore void. . . . But if the confirming act be a contract between the Legislature of Pennsylvania and the Connecticut settlers, it must be regulated by the rules and principles, which pervade and govern all cases of contracts; and if so, it is clearly void, because it tends, in its operation and consequences, to defraud the Pennsylvania claimants, who are third persons, of their just rights; rights ascertained, protected, and secured by the Constitution and known laws of the land. The plaintiff's title to the land in question, is legally derived from Pennsylvania; how then, on the principles of contract, could Pennsylvania lawfully dispose of it to another? As a contract, it could convey no right, with the owner's consent; without that, it was fraudulent and void.[80]

In this jury charge Paterson treated a land grant as a type of contract and maintained that Pennsylvania could not abrogate its first disposition of land to the Pennsylvania claimants. Not surprisingly given this instruction, the jury returned a verdict for the plaintiff.[81]

Other historical evidence is also consistent with interpretation of the contract clause as protective of both private and public agreements. The 1795 sale by Georgia of vast western public lands known as the Yazoo to four land companies set the stage for the most famous pre-Marshall explication of the contract clause. The Yazoo land grants constituted a large part of the present states of Alabama and Mississippi. Amid allegations of widespread fraud and bribery, anti-Yazoo forces gained control of the legislature in November of that year. They promptly enacted a law nullifying the Yazoo land sale. By this time, however, much of the land had been resold by the original grantees to parties who claimed to be bona fide purchasers. For example, millions of acres were acquired by a group of Boston investors organized as the New England Mississippi Land Company. This tangled situation raised the fundamental issue of whether the Georgia legislature could legally declare its prior action void and annul the land titles under the 1795 grant. The investors sought compensation for the land they had purchased, and a protracted controversy ensued over the validity of Georgia's actions. It eventually gave rise to the first Supreme Court decision pertaining to the contract clause, *Fletcher v. Peck* (1810). Our focus at this point, however, is on the earlier stages of the dispute.[82]

William Constable, a New York merchant and land speculator, sought a legal opinion from Hamilton, who was then practicing law in New York City, concerning the title of the grantees and their assigns.[83] In a famous opinion, dated March 25, 1796, Hamilton argued that the Georgia rescinding act was unconstitutional. He reasoned:

> In addition to these general considerations, placing the revocation in a very unfavorable light, the constitution of the United States, article first, section tenth, declares that no state shall pass a law impairing the obligation of contract. This must be the equivalent to saying, no state shall pass a law revoking, invalidating, or altering a contract. Every grant from one to another, whether the grantor shall be a state or an individual, is virtually a contract that the grantee shall hold and enjoy the thing granted against the grantor, and his representatives. It, therefore, appears to me, that taking the terms of the constitution in their large sense, and giving them effect according to the general spirit and policy of the provisions, the revocation of the grant by the legislature of Georgia, may justly be considered as contrary to the constitution of the United States, and, therefore, null; and that the courts of the United States, in cases within their jurisdiction, will be likely to pronounce it so.[84]

For Hamilton, then, the contract clause covered agreements to which a state was a party. Moreover, grants of land by a state constituted a contract with the original grantees. Hamilton's opinion letter was incorporated into a pamphlet and widely circulated, providing valuable ammunition for defenders of the Yazoo claimants.[85]

Similarly, in August of 1796 Robert Goodloe Harper, a prominent South Carolina attorney and then a member of the House of Representatives, rendered a formal opinion declaring that the attempted nullification of the land sale by the Georgia legislature was void. He emphasized the contractual nature of the transaction, observing:

> These sales moreover were contracts, made with the utmost solemnity, for a valuable consideration, and carried deliberately into execution. It is an invariable maxim of law, and of natural justice, that one of the parties to a contract cannot by his own act, exempt himself, from its obligations. A contrary principle would break down all the ramparts of right, dissolve the bonds of property, and render good faith, to enforce the observance of which, is the great object of civil institutions, subservient to the partiality, the selfishness, and unjust caprices of every individual. There is no reason why governments, more than private persons, should be exempt from the operation of this maxim; nor are they considered as exempt by our constitution or our laws. The state of Georgia, being a party to this contract, could no more relieve itself from the obligation,

> by any act of its own, than an individual, who had signed a bond, could relieve himself from the necessity of payment.[86]

Thus, Harper joined Hamilton in concluding both that the Yazoo land grant amounted to a contract and that the Constitution barred abrogation by a state of its obligations.

The precepts of natural law also informed the emerging contract clause jurisprudence. Belief in the existence of fundamental rights derived from natural law philosophy was widely shared by late-eighteenth-century jurists. Under natural rights theory certain rights were deemed so basic as to be beyond the reach of governmental authority. Written constitutions, state or federal, did not encompass the full range of individual liberties. In the famous case of *Calder v. Bull* (1798) Justice Samuel Chase famously invoked natural law: "There are certain vital principles in our free republican governments, which, will determine and overrule an apparent and flagrant abuse of legislative power." Giving examples of prohibited legislative actions, he maintained that state legislatures could not "violate the right of an antecedent lawful private contract; or the right of private property."[87] Chase explained that lawmakers could not abridge agreements even if there had been no explicit provision barring such interference in the Constitution. In other words, he saw the contract clause as an additional guarantee of the rights of contracting parties, which deserved protection under natural law. As we shall see, the Supreme Court looked to natural law concepts as a basis to interpret or supplement the protection afforded by the contract clause.

STATE DEVELOPMENTS

Developments at the state level also attested to the importance of contractual rights in the constitutional order. As they revised their own fundamental laws, many states included a contract clause based on the federal model. In 1790, for example, Pennsylvania and South Carolina added a contract clause to their new constitutions. The Pennsylvania Constitution stated, "That no ex post facto law, nor any law impairing contracts, shall be made." The newer states typically followed suit. The Kentucky Constitution of 1792, the Tennessee Constitution of 1796, the Mississippi Constitution of 1817, and the Illinois Constitution of 1818 each contained a contract clause. Such widespread adoption of constitutional provisions supporting contractual rights at the state level strongly indicates broad acceptance of the principle of contractual stability in the face of legislative interference. It also meant that a state constitution could serve as an independent basis on which to challenge infringements of agreements. Further, it is noteworthy that no state differentiated between private and public contracts in framing its ban. Clearly state constitution makers were not sufficiently concerned about the Wilson-Hamilton-Harper interpretation of the federal contract clause to make a move to limit the range of protection afforded by similar state provisions.

Moreover, in 1799 the Supreme Judicial Court of Massachusetts became the first state court to invalidate a state law as a violation of the federal Constitution. The case, involving a suit to enforce a promissory note, arose from the 1795 Yazoo grant, discussed above. In a decision that anticipated the jurisprudence of John Marshall, the Massachusetts court ruled that the Georgia repeal act was void as an infringement of the obligation of contract under Article 1, section 10. It found that title to the land was legally conveyed by the Georgia grant.[88]

The failure of Congress to enact a permanent bankruptcy law until 1898 gave rise to constitutional problems. The absence of federal legislation left open questions as to the authority of the states to pass bankruptcy or other debt-relief measures without running afoul of the contract clause. Notwithstanding early federal and state court decisions enforcing the contract clause, state legislatures initially did much to define the scope of the provision in the late eighteenth century. They compiled a mixed record. A number of states, such as South Carolina, continued to enforce debt-relief measures adopted before the effective date of the Constitution. In addition, some states, including New York and Maryland, experimented with bankruptcy laws. Moreover, a number of jurisdictions gradually curtailed imprisonment for debt.[89] All of this legislation potentially weakened the rights of creditors under existing contracts.

Of greater long-term significance, some legislators and commentators took the position that legislatures remained free to alter the means of enforcing contracts without impairing the underlying obligations. For example, Joseph Jones, a Virginia legislator and judge who was also a member of the state ratifying convention, wrote Madison in December of 1787 that the legislature was considering a debt relief measure that would postpone execution sales for a year unless the property was to be sold at three-fourth of its value. To gain this relief the debtor was required to post a bond to secure payment at the end of the one year. Jones explained that the execution law was seen as "calculated to give some relief to Debtors, without any direct interference with private contracts."[90] This elusive distinction between contractual rights and remedies found expression in other states and would vex contract clause jurisprudence for more than a century.

Nonetheless, the contract clause apparently had some immediate impact on legislative behavior. State lawmakers interfered with contracts less frequently and in more restrained ways than before adoption of the Constitution.[91]

PROSPECTS FOR A ROBUST CONTRACT CLAUSE

Uncertainty over the protection given contractual arrangements under the contract clause was widespread in the years immediately following the adoption of the Constitution. Clearly the provision was not generally understood as barring any state legislation affecting contracts. Probably few would have anticipated the emergence of the contract clause into one of the most important provisions of the Constitution during the nineteenth century.

At the same time, the potential for a muscular reading of the contract clause was established well before the Supreme Court first addressed the question in 1810. The very inclusion of the contract clause in the Constitution demonstrated the commitment of the framers to contractual stability. As J. Willard Hurst observed, the contract clause represented "a striking intervention of national law into fields of policy that would ordinarily be the domain of the states."[92] Moreover, not only had federal courts invoked the clause to strike down state laws infringing contracts, but key figures had endorsed a far-ranging application of the provision as a shield for agreements. Changes in the economy also underscored the pivotal place of contracts and consequently for the contract clause. The principal engine of economic growth was the expanding national market. The constitutional text protecting agreements from legislative adjustment by the states harmonized easily with a public policy promoting national economic development. The language of the contract clause thus proved a base for the courts to safeguard the rights of contracting parties as a means of encouraging the ascendancy of market forces.[93]

CHAPTER 2

The Era of John Marshall, 1801–1835

When John Marshall became chief justice in 1801 he assumed leadership of a Supreme Court that had little prestige and uncertain authority. Marshall's achievement in transforming the Court into a significant institution in US public life has been treated extensively elsewhere. Our focus will be on how Marshall construed the contract clause to safeguard economic rights and foster the growth of enterprise. Because a great deal of contract clause litigation took place in the state and lower federal courts and never reached the Supreme Court, we will also consider how these tribunals reacted to Marshall's contract clause rulings.

Of course, Marshall was not writing on an entirely fresh slate. As we have seen in Chapter 1, state and lower federal courts were wrestling with the meaning of the contract clause in the late eighteenth century. During the first decade of the nineteenth century, state legislatures continued the practice of enacting a variety of stay and other debt-relief measures, over the objection that such laws were unconstitutional. In fact, a new wave of such laws was enacted in the wake of the economic distress caused by President Thomas Jefferson's trade embargo in 1807. Most of these measures were never challenged in court. Indeed, the Supreme Court only decided its first contract clause case in 1810, more than twenty years after the adoption of the Constitution. This left ample room for divergent interpretations of the provision to flourish.[1]

Some state judges were inclined to sustain relief laws, implying that some legislative interference with contractual rights was constitutional, especially in times of economic distress. A pair of Georgia judicial opinions in 1808 is instructive. In the first case a Georgia planter petitioned the Superior Court of Georgia to halt an execution sale of his property to satisfy a judgment. He alleged that the sale "would prove ruinous" because a fair price could not be obtained in view of "the pecuniary embarrassments, occasioned by the embargo acts." Invoking the equity powers of the court, Judge Thomas Charlton observed "that cases of this description involve hardship and oppression; that they are against equity and conscience; that they are promotive of injury to the public; that they enable monied men to accumulate usurious wealth." He then temporarily enjoined the execution sale on condition that the petitioner pledge "sufficient property" as security for the debt.[2] Although this case did not turn upon the contract clause, Charlton's reasoning suggests judicial sympathy for the notion that the state could modify agreements in extraordinary situations.

Another decision by the same judge was even more revealing. In May of 1808 the Georgia legislature enacted a law staying the collection of debts until December of that year, provided that the debtors posted security for ultimate payments of the debt and interest.[3] Judge Charlton brushed aside an argument that the stay law infringed the obligation of contract. He ruled that an impairment of contract encompassed any measure that "lessens the value of contracts, that gives them a diminished value, takes from them any of the essential properties of contracts, or which divests them of that priority of lien, obligation, or recovery, which they would otherwise possess." Charlton reasoned that the stay law suspended enforcement of the agreement but did not destroy "any of the properties of contracts" and that the contract remained as valuable as before passage of the stay law.[4] Such debt-relief laws were a persistent source of contract clause litigation throughout the nineteenth century. Charlton's ruling anticipated a recurring question of how far state legislators could alter remedies without running afoul of the constitutional ban on the impairment of contracts.

Other developments in the early nineteenth century clearly foreshadowed the Marshall Court's contract clause jurisprudence. Despite lingering suspicion of corporations, the number of corporate charters proliferated in the late eighteenth and early nineteenth centuries. These charters were increasingly viewed as a form of private property immune from legislative tampering.[5] In 1806 Chief Justice Theophilus Parsons, speaking for the Supreme Judicial Court of Massachusetts, held that under common law principles the legislature could not alter or revoke the charter of a turnpike company unless such power was reserved in the act of incorporation. Parsons did not ground his conclusion on the contract clause, but his thinking casts light on judicial attitudes toward the sanctity of corporate charters.[6] A year later the New York Council of Revision, which included the distinguished jurist James Kent, vetoed a bill that sought to alter the mode of selecting the trustees for Columbia University.[7] The veto message, although making no mention of the contract clause, declared, "It is a sound principle in free governments, and one which has received frequent confirmation by acts of the Legislature, that charters of incorporation, whether granted for private or local, or charitable, or literary or religious purposes, were not to be affected without due process of law, or without the consent of the parties."[8] The message stressed the security of the rights granted by corporate charters from legislative interference.

Similarly, a series of legislative committee reports in New Jersey insisted that the lawmakers could not repeal charters at pleasure. For example, an 1806 report declared, "In the opinion of the committee the constitution of this state will not justify any measure which will go to destroy a charter right which has been granted to an incorporate body for a term of years without their consent."[9] In legislative debates corporate charters were increasingly likened to contracts, which could not be rescinded. As one scholar has pointed out, "The doctrine that corporate charters were not subject to alteration or repeal at the discretion of the legislature was widely enough accepted in New Jersey during the first two decades of the nineteenth century to cause the defeat of several attempts to rescind or alter corporate privileges once they had been granted."[10] After the understanding that corporate charters were in the nature of contracts gained currency, it would be an easy step to shelter such charters under the contract clause.

By the time the Supreme Court first examined the contract clause, considerable authority existed for a muscular reading of the provision. Of course, the justices did not necessarily have to follow this path, but the ground had been laid to put teeth into the clause.

PUBLIC CONTRACTS

Marshall articulated his conception of the contract clause in a series of famous decisions, starting with *Fletcher v. Peck* (1810).[11] This case originated in the vast Yazoo land sales made by the Georgia legislature in 1795 to four private land companies. The tangled background of the resulting dispute was treated in Chapter 1. Controversy over the Yazoo land dragged on for years. In 1802 Georgia ceded the territory to the United States. After repeated attempts to secure payments from Congress to settle the contested Yazoo claims, some claimants arranged a friendly suit in federal court based on diversity of citizenship jurisdiction. John Peck of Boston sold a small tract of Yazoo land to Robert Fletcher, a resident of New Hampshire. Fletcher thereafter brought suit for breach of the title covenants in the deed against Peck, asserting that Peck's title was invalid.

Fletcher v. Peck presented a number of vexing issues for the Supreme Court. Much of the literature has focused on *Fletcher* as an early instance of

As chief justice, John Marshall fashioned the contract clause into a bulwark for public as well as private agreements. (Library of Congress)

judicial review of a state law and has questioned the propriety of the Court deciding a collusive case. These important issues will not be examined here. Writing for the Court, Marshall refused to consider alleged legislative corruption as a basis to strike down the original sale by the legislature, reasoning that the judiciary could not investigate legislative motives. He then sustained the 1795 transaction, making three crucial points: (1) that a grant of land was an executed contract, binding on the parties and within the purview of the contract clause, (2) that the contract clause prevents states from impairing contracts between states and individuals and is not limited to protecting contracts between private parties, and (3) that the Georgia act rescinding the Yazoo sale was void either because it violated "the general principles which are common to our free institutions" or the constitutional ban against impairing the obligation of contracts.[12] Marshall's opinion is significant because it established the fundamental rule that the contract clause guarded public as well as private contracts against state abridgment. Viewing the provision literally, the chief justice observed that the words of the contract clause "are general, and are applicable to contracts of every description."[13]

Several aspects of this landmark decision warrant exploration. First, Marshall's opinion was not especially innovative. As we have seen, leading jurists had long maintained that a state grant was a contract whose obligation was binding on that state. Squarely in point were the legal opinions of Alexander Hamilton and Robert Goodloe Harper, arguing that the Georgia rescission act ran afoul of the contract clause. These letters anticipated much of the Supreme Court's reasoning. Moreover, the Court had intimated in *Huidekoper's Lessees v. Douglass* (1805) that a state land grant was "a contract; and although a state is a party, it ought to be construed according to those well-established principles, which regulate contracts generally."[14] In other words, Marshall in *Fletcher* did not break much new ground.

Second, the opinion in *Fletcher* makes plain the high standing of the contract clause in Marshall's thinking. Marshall insisted that, by adopting the Constitution, the people "manifested a determination to shield themselves and their property from the effects of those sudden and strong passions to which men are exposed." He then characterized Article 10, section 1, which included the contract clause and other restraints on state power as being a "bill of rights for the people of each state."[15]

Third, by invoking "general principles which are common to our free institutions" as well as the contract clause Marshall left the basis of his opinion rather ambiguous. Was he simply appealing to unwritten principles to bolster his reliance on the clause, or was he suggesting that courts might invalidate statutes contrary to the fundamental premises of legitimate government? Benjamin F. Wright maintained that Marshall's *Fletcher* opinion "wavers between reliance upon the contract clause and upon the principle of justice."[16] "Marshall," Suzanna Sherry concluded, "ultimately relied on some unfathomable combination of unwritten law and the written Constitution."[17] One must remember that Marshall, like many of his contemporaries, believed in natural law, which preexisted the organization of government. His reference to natural rights was not necessarily inconsistent with reliance on an express constitutional provision. Marshall might well have meant to indicate that fixed principles of natural law were incorporated into the contract clause.[18] Yet, as we shall see, in a later case pertaining to the contract clause, Marshall affirmed his belief in natural rights.

Further, in assessing Marshall's position, it is important to keep in mind the concurring opinion of Justice William Johnson.[19] He declared, "A state does not possess the power of revoking its own grants. But I do it on a general principle, on the reason and nature of things: a principle which will impose laws even on the deity."[20] Johnson stressed that his opinion "was not founded on the provision in the constitution of the United States, relative to impairing the obligation of contracts."[21] He found the wording of the contract clause equivocal and predicted that construing the phrase "the obligation of contracts" would prove difficult. Johnson pointed out that the states "are continually legislating on the subject of contracts" and doubted that statutes of limitations were intended to be covered by the provision.[22] Indeed, he insisted that an executed grant of land was not a contract. Given his explicit rejection of Marshall's reading of the contract clause, Johnson had to identify some other basis for striking down the Georgia law. One scholar has asserted, "It is likely that Johnson's reliance on natural law in the *Fletcher* case grew out of his hostility to the retrospective character of the state action and the total absence of compensation to the grantees."[23] Hence, Marshall's reference to "general principles" may have served in part to encompass Johnson's analysis in a unanimous finding that the rescission act was invalid.

Lastly, it is noteworthy that, aside from representatives of Georgia, the decision in *Fletcher* aroused little controversy. "The decision in *Fletcher v. Peck*, reflecting a bias in favor of vested property rights," a leading scholar has concluded, "was in near perfect harmony with the attitudes and values of most politically conscious Americans."[24] William E. Nelson similarly found that *Fletcher* "defused a heated political controversy that had long been raging in Georgia and in the Congress of the United States and resolved the case with little negative comment."[25] He explained that Marshall achieved this result by appealing to widely shared beliefs that a legislature could not reclaim land it had previously granted. As a practical matter, the decision in *Fletcher* was instrumental in persuading Congress in 1814 to appropriate funds to compensate the Yazoo claimants, a consequence that would have been unthinkable if Marshall's reading of the contract clause was at odds with dominant national opinion.

Two years later Marshall reaffirmed the principle that the contract clause protected agreements to which a state was a party. At issue in *New Jersey v. Wilson* (1812) was the continuing validity of a tax exemption on certain lands purchased by the New Jersey colonial legislature in 1758 and granted to the Delaware Indians.[26] In exchange for this grant the Indians relinquished their claims to other lands in New Jersey. The Indians occupied the land until 1803, when they relocated, and the land, with legislative permission, was sold to private parties. The following year the legislature repealed the tax exemption, setting the stage for litigation charging that the repeal amounted to an impairment of contract.

Citing *Fletcher*, Marshall insisted that the arrangement between New Jersey and the Indians contained "every requisite to the formation of a contract." He pointed out that the "privilege, though for the benefit of the Indians, is annexed, by the terms which create it, to the land itself, and not to their persons."[27] This privilege, Marshall reasoned, would increase the value of the land in the event of a sale. Because the purchasers succeeded to all the rights of the Indians and have the benefit of their contract, the 1804 repeal act impaired "this essential part" of the contract.

The outcome in *Wilson* was not as obvious as Marshall made it appear. He did not consider, for example, whether a colonial legislature operating under the British crown could enact a law that would forever curtail the state's power of taxation.[28] Nonetheless, *Wilson* became the fountainhead of a long line of Supreme Court decisions invoking the contract clause to uphold state grants of tax immunity against attempted repeal. As discussed later, over time some justices took the position that a state could not permanently bargain away its taxing power, but *Wilson* has never been overruled.

Another far-reaching application of the contract clause occurred in the landmark case of *Dartmouth College v. Woodward* (1819), which determined that a corporate charter was a constitutionally protected contract.[29] There were only a handful of corporations in the United States before 1800, and most of these were municipal or charitable in character. During the early nineteenth century, however, the corporation evolved into an advantageous form of business organization. Most business corporations in this period were chartered by special act of the state legislature. As the number and size of business corporations grew, some observers began to express concern over the concentration of power in private hands. The perception that corporations received special, state-conferred privileges meant that they were often loosely equated with monopolies in the public mind. Public supervision of corporations became an issue, and the power of the states to repeal or alter charters of incorporation seemed to provide an avenue to impose regulation.

The *Dartmouth College* case arose from a move by the New Hampshire legislature to amend the charter of the college.[30] In 1769 the British crown granted the application of the Reverend Eleazor Wheelock for a corporate charter for a religious and educational institution. Wheelock raised funds from private sources to finance the college. The corporation was to have "continuance forever," and to that end the charter created a self-perpetuating

Legislative efforts to overhaul the charter of Dartmouth College and impose state control of the institution set the stage for an important Supreme Court decision declaring that corporate charters were contracts protected by the contract clause. (Courtesy of Dartmouth College Library)

board of twelve trustees. A quarrel later erupted between the founder's son and then-president of the college, John Wheelock, and the trustees. As a result Wheelock was removed as president. By 1815 this dispute generated a statewide political controversy. The following year the legislature changed the charter of the college in material respects with legislation that (1) enlarged the board of trustees from twelve to twenty-one members and empowered the governor to appoint the new trustees, (2) created a board of overseers also appointed by the governor with veto power over the trustees, and (3) changed the name of the institution to Dartmouth University. The old trustees challenged the legislation and brought suit to recover certain corporate property. They argued, among other things, that the law violated the contract clause. Rejecting this claim, the New Hampshire Court of Appeals maintained that Dartmouth College was a public corporation, and that the contract clause "was obviously intended to protect private rights of property, and embrace all contracts relating to private property, whether executed or executory, and whether between individuals, between states, or between states and individuals."[31] The court seemingly agreed that the contract clause applied to private corporations[32] but ruled that Dartmouth was an institution devoted to the public purpose of education. The trustees carried the case to the Supreme Court.

In his opinion Marshall first focused on the types of agreements that came within the ambit of the contract clause. He broadly insisted that the provision was intended to curb "the legislature in future from violating the right to property." The chief justice observed that the contract clause was confined to "contracts respecting property, under which some individual could claim a right to something beneficial to himself."[33] Marshall stressed that the clause did not restrict state power over public corporations that served the functions of government. To his mind the case turned upon the application of this principle to the college. Marshall considered at length the distinction between public and private corporations in the factual context of this case, concluding that Dartmouth College was a private eleemosynary corporation endowed by private funds.[34] He then found that the 1769 charter amounted to a contract for constitutional purposes.[35] As we have seen, this was not a novel point. Instead, Marshall simply affirmed widely accepted attitudes regarding corporate enterprise. Stephen A. Siegel has observed, "There is no doubt that the norm that state-granted franchises were entitled to some degree of sanctity was widely held at the time the Constitution was adopted and throughout the early republic period."[36] With that settled, Marshall readily decided that the 1816 New Hampshire act impaired the charter of Dartmouth College and was void under the contract clause. He correctly pointed out that the effect of the law was to transfer the governance of Dartmouth College from the trustees to the governor, totally changing the system of government set forth in the charter.

Marshall spoke entirely in terms of charitable institutions. Much of the lasting significance of the *Dartmouth College* doctrine that the charter of a private corporation was a contract safeguarded by the Constitution from legislative abridgment, however, relates to its application to business corporations. Historians have pondered inconclusively whether Marshall had business corporations in mind.[37] It has been argued that, given his stress on private property and his conviction that secure corporate rights would promote economic growth, Marshall just assumed that the contract clause safeguarded business enterprises.[38] But such a reading of the decision need not rest on inferences. In a lengthy and learned concurring opinion, Justice Joseph Story agreed with Marshall's reasoning but moved beyond the facts of the case to expound a comprehensive reading of the contract clause. Indeed, this was likely his purpose in writing a concurrence. Amplifying the public-private dichotomy, Story explicitly linked the contract clause to emerging business ventures. He gave examples of private corporations, including "a bank, whose stock is owned by private parties" and "insurance, canal, bridge, and turnpike companies."[39] Story was clear that the charters of such enterprises were protected by the contract clause. "In respect to franchises, whether corporate or not," he wrote, "which include a pernancy of profits, such as a right of fishery, or to hold a ferry, a market, or a fair, or to erect a turnpike, bank, or bridge, there is no pretence to say that grants of them are not within the constitution."[40] Thus, Story sought to broaden the reach of *Dartmouth College*.[41]

Although the *Dartmouth College* decision aroused little public interest or newspaper comment at the time, historians have long emphasized the impact of the case on the rapid growth of business corporations in the Antebellum Era. Charles Warren, for example, noted "the immense effect of this case upon future jurisprudence and the future development of corporate interests in this country."[42] Herbert A. Johnson characterized *Dartmouth College* as "what may be the most important Supreme Court opinion concerning the clause and the nature of property rights in the United States."[43] No doubt the decision gave a secure legal foundation to corporate enterprise and thus encouraged investors. Indeed, a number of state courts invoked *Dartmouth College* and ruled that a state legislature could not abridge a corporate charter.[44]

Still, the long-term significance of *Dartmouth College* should not be overstated. Story himself suggested a means by which states could circumvent the ruling. He declared that a state could not alter or revoke a charter of incorporation unless "a power be reserved for this purpose."[45] Lawmakers merely had to reserve such a right in order to take future steps concerning corporate charters. In this way the legislative power to change the charter was part of the original contract, and there would be no impairment. Observers were quick to see the potential to preserve state authority created by this comment. Weeks after the decision was announced a Kentucky newspaper opined, "We hope our Legislature will not hereafter grant any charter whatever, without reserving the right to alter, amend or repeal as the public interest may require."[46] Over time it became common for legislatures to insert such language in individual charters and general incorporation laws, thus diluting the protection afforded corporations by *Dartmouth College*.[47] In 1831 Delaware incorporated a reservation clause in its constitution, and eventually the authority to alter or repeal corporate charters was included in many state constitutions.

In addition to the spread of reservation clauses, Marshall later limited the potential scope of *Dartmouth College*. In *Providence Bank v. Billings*, discussed below, he ruled that state corporate charters did not imply an exemption from taxation. Consequently, as Michael J. Klarman has cogently noted, "Extravagant claims about the significance of *Dartmouth College* seem dubious."[48]

A history of disputed land titles in Kentucky presented the Marshall Court another opportunity to apply the contract clause to the public acts of states. In 1789 the Virginia legislature, as part of the process of separating Kentucky from Virginia, enacted a compact that provided in part that "all private rights and interests of land . . . shall remain valid and secure under the laws of the proposed state, and shall be determined by the laws now existing in this state."[49] The evident purpose of such language was to secure the land ownership of persons who derived their titles under Virginia law. The compact became part of the 1792 Kentucky Constitution.

Given duplicate and overlapping land grants, inadequate surveys, and outright fraud, there was extensive title confusion in Kentucky. Much of the land, moreover, was claimed by absentee owners in Virginia. Under these uncertain circumstances, many settlers in Kentucky found that they had occupied and improved land actually owned by others. Efforts by settlers to secure title entailed extensive litigation and were often unsuccessful.[50] Yet the common law, in effect in Virginia, treated occupants harshly. The legal owner could not only recover possession from occupants but was not obligated to pay compensation for any improvements. In addition, the occupant was liable for rent and waste during his period of possession. To protect settlers, the Kentucky legislature in 1797 and 1812 enacted occupying claimants' laws. Under this legislation settlers with color of title could recover the value of their improvements, as determined by a jury, to be offset against rent. The laws also limited the occupant's liability for rent. Further, if the value of improvements exceeded three-fourths of the value of the land without improvements, the occupant had a choice of a judgment for the improvements against the owner or could acquire a right to the title by agreeing to pay the value of the unimproved land. The Kentucky occupying claimants' laws clearly changed the common laws rules to the disadvantage of nonoccupying owners. Virginia landowners, joined by some in Kentucky, alleged that these laws violated the Virginia-Kentucky compact governing the security of interests in land.

The controversy over the constitutionality of the occupying claimants' laws reached the Supreme Court in 1821 in a suit by John Green of Virginia to recover land in Kentucky. No representative of the occupying claimants participated in the argument before the Court. Justice Story spoke for a unanimous bench in the first of two opinions in *Green v. Biddle*.[51] Apparently assuming that a compact between states was a contract, Story held in a brief opinion that under the 1789 compact, property rights and interests derived from Virginia were to be exclusively determined by the laws of that state. Reviewing the 1797 and 1812 Kentucky legislation, he concluded that the measures "materially impair the rights and interests of the rightful owner in the land itself. They are parts of a system, the object of which is to compel the rightful owner to relinquish his lands, or pay for all lasting improvements made upon them, without his consent or default; and in many cases those improvements may greatly exceed the original cost and value of the lands in his hands." Story added, "It requires no reasoning to show, that such laws necessarily diminish the beneficial interests of the rightful owner in the lands."[52] The Kentucky legislature expressed strong opposition to Story's opinion, and, upon motion of Henry Clay, the Court granted a rehearing.

Only four justices participated in the second *Green* opinion. Writing for a plurality of three in 1823, Justice Bushrod Washington reaffirmed the ruling by Story. Washington found that the Kentucky occupying claimants' laws rendered the rights of owners less secure than under Virginia law and thus amounted to an impairment of the obligation of contract. He expressly insisted that a compact between states was a contract within the meaning of the Constitution. Washington observed, "A State has no more power to impair an obligation into which she herself has entered, than she can the contracts of individuals."[53] Washington's opinion in *Green* underscored what one scholar termed "his uncompromising voice on the Court for the adherence to contract."[54] Critics stressed that only three justices joined this opinion, but the absent justices had subscribed to the 1821 opinion. It seems reasonable to conclude that a majority of the Court supported the Washington/Story position.[55]

Justice Johnson, who had joined Story's earlier opinion in this case, now dissented. As this behavior suggests, it is not easy to ascertain Johnson's views in relation to the contract clause. He pursued a seemingly inconsistent course. After his separate opinion in *Fletcher,* Johnson voted with the other justices in *Wilson*, *Dartmouth College*, and *Sturges*. But in *Green* he reversed direction and thereafter resisted a broad reading of the clause. Declining to address the contract clause in *Green*, Johnson felt that the Court's construction of the compact unduly restricted the sovereign power of Kentucky to govern its own territory.[56]

As a practical matter, the *Green* opinions had little immediate impact. Kentucky lawmakers and judges largely ignored the decisions and continued to enforce the occupying claimants' law. Indeed, similar measures were widely enacted by states before the Civil War.[57] The Supreme Court later backed away from a robust reading of the 1789 compact, upholding a Kentucky law that aided occupiers by reducing the period to acquire an adverse possession title.[58] Likewise, *Green v. Biddle* had limited influence on the evolution of contract clause jurisprudence. The Court reinforced the principle that states are bound by their own agreements, but the extension of this norm to contracts between states was problematic. Although an agreement between two states could plausibly be viewed as a contract, the contract clause was most likely crafted to safeguard the economic rights of individuals, not to protect one coequal state from the claims of another. Yet *Green* rests on the premise that states may enter into compacts that surrender part of their sovereignty. The contract clause was an awkward constitutional vehicle to police interstate agreements, which might have been better analyzed under the compact clause of the Constitution. As Herbert A. Johnson has aptly commented, "The contract clause was perhaps stretched to its logical limit in applying it to an agreement between two states."[59] In any event, with *Green* the Supreme Court had completed the framework for the public branch of contract clause jurisprudence. Much of the enforcement of the Court's decisions would fall to the lower federal courts and the state judiciaries.

Story gave a new force to *Dartmouth College* with his circuit court opinion in *Allen v. McKean* (1833).[60] At issue was an 1831 Maine law altering the tenure in office of the president of Bowdoin College, who previously held office during good behavior. The president brought suit to recover his salary despite being removed from his post. Relying heavily on *Dartmouth College*, Story found that Bowdoin College was a private corporation. He again emphasized that the *Dartmouth College* doctrine applied to businesses as well as educational corporations. Story concluded that the 1831 law impaired the obligation of the president's contract with the college.

Likewise, state courts also invoked the contract clause to hold states to their agreements. The Supreme Court of Errors of Connecticut, for example, relied on *New Jersey v. Wilson* to sustain a tax exemption on land granted for maintenance for ministry of the gospel against a legislative attempt to repeal the exemption.[61] Charters were often the subject of litigation. Characterizing the contract clause as "a most valuable provision of the Constitution," the Connecticut court ruled that the legislature impaired the contractual rights of a turnpike company when it attempted to repeal a toll law treated as part of the original charter grant.[62] In 1834 the New Hampshire Supreme Court held that a charter granting an exclusive right to maintain a bridge was a contract. It added that the contract was "inviolable" and insisted that the legislature "cannot annul that contract, or in any way impair its obligation."[63] By contrast, the Supreme Court of Alabama anticipated future developments when it brushed aside a contract clause argument and declared that a grant of a ferry over a public watercourse did not confer an exclusive privilege that barred the subsequent erection of a toll bridge.[64]

PRIVATE CONTRACTS

Although the framers were clearly concerned about state legislative abridgment of agreements between private individuals, the Supreme Court, as we have seen, initially addressed contracts between individuals and states. The first national bankruptcy law, which lasted only from 1800 to 1803, proved unpopular in agricultural regions and was not heavily utilized.[65] Absent federal legislation, many states continued the time-honored practice of enacting a variety of debt-relief measures.[66] These included laws staying the execution of judgments and laws authorizing the payment of debts in installments. The commercial disturbances in the wake of the War of 1812 stimulated a fresh round of such laws. It is revealing that a number of such debt-relief measures were never challenged, suggesting broad acceptance.

State and lower federal courts took the lead in assessing the validity of debt-relief laws. At issue in *Jones v. Crittenden* (1814) was a North Carolina measure staying the enforcement of judgments for debt for as long as a year.[67] The Supreme Court of North Carolina found that the suspension act ran afoul of the contract clause. Declaring that the "obligation of a contract may be impaired by various modes and in different degrees," the court explained that a law that released a party from a stipulation or compelled a party to do more than promised constituted an impairment. The court pictured dire consequences from stay laws. "The right to suspend the recovery of a debt for one period," it observed, "implies the right of suspending it for another; and as the state of things which called for the first delay, may continue for a series of years, the consequence may be a total stagnation of the business of society, by destroying confidence and credit amongst the citizens." Nor was the court impressed with the argument that the stay law applied only to the remedy and not to the underlying contractual right. "It is difficult to conceive," it declared, "how a law could otherwise impair an existing right than by withholding the remedy, which is in effect to suspend the right."[68] Thus, the North Carolina court early articulated two key themes in emerging contract clause jurisprudence—the importance of contractual stability to the economy and recognition of the difficulty of differentiating between the right and the available remedy to enforce that right. The latter point was crucial because much debt-relief legislation purported to change only the remedy available to enforce contractual rights.

At the same time, the *Jones* case illustrates a central problem with judicial enforcement of the contract clause in the context of debt-relief laws. The 1812 stay law was in effect for two years before being invalidated, thus providing temporary relief for debtors during an economically difficult period.[69] Contemporaries noted the Sisyphean character of judicial efforts to curb state relief laws. In 1829 Samuel E. Sewall observed, "Until these statutes have been declared unconstitutional by some competent tribunal, their operation is the same as if their validity were unimpeachable. Many years must elapse before all the classes of these laws can be brought to the examination of the highest national tribunal. And new statutes can be passed much faster than the old ones can be declared unconstitutional."[70]

Notwithstanding the contract clause, then, debt-relief laws often achieved their purpose of giving debtors some breathing room. A number of states moved beyond stay laws, which temporarily delayed enforcement of contracts, and enacted insolvency or bankruptcy measures. The distinction between bankruptcy and insolvency was never clearly articulated, and the terms were often employed interchangeably.[71] Under such legislation an insolvent debtor who assigned his property for the benefit of his creditors was discharged of liability for all debts. Lower federal courts reached different conclusions with respect to the validity of state insolvency laws. In the US Circuit Court for Pennsylvania, Justice Washington found the Pennsylvania insolvency law as applied to a preexisting agreement to be invalid under the contract clause. "The old contract," he wrote, "is completely annulled, and a legislative contract imposed upon the parties in lieu of it."[72] He agreed, nonetheless, that a prospective law, operating on subsequent contracts, "would clearly be constitutional." On the other hand, in 1817 Justice Brockholst Livingston upheld New York's 1811 insolvency law, as applied to debts incurred prior to the enactment of the measure, against a contract clause challenge. He maintained that there was no provision in the Constitution "of more ambiguous import, or which has occasioned, and will continue to occasion, more discussion and disagreement" than the contract clause.[73] Livingston seemingly agreed that stay laws and installment payment laws were invalid under that provision. However, he distinguished insolvency laws, pointing out that many states, including New York, had insolvency systems in force for decades without controversy. Consequently, Livingston felt that insolvency laws must be presumed constitutional. Moreover, Livingston reasoned, insolvency laws encouraged trade and were not within the purview of the contract clause.[74] These inconsistent opinions left the commercial community in a quandary as to the validity of insolvency legislation.

The Supreme Court tackled the validity of state insolvency laws in *Sturges v. Crowninshield* (1819), its first case dealing with the constitutional protection afforded private contracts.[75] In March of 1811 Richard Crowninshield gave two promissory notes to Josiah Sturgis, but he soon thereafter became insolvent and sought a discharge of his debts under New York's insolvency law, enacted in April of 1811. Notwithstanding the discharge, Sturgis brought suit to recover on the notes. Speaking for a unanimous court, Marshall took the position that, in the absence of congressional exercise of its bankruptcy power, the states remained free to provide relief for insolvent debtors. Turning to the contract clause, he declared, "A contract is an agreement, in which a party undertakes to do, or not to do, a particular thing. The law binds him to perform his undertaking, and this is, of course, the obligation of his contract. . . . Any law which releases a part of this obligation, must, in the literal sense of the word, impair it."[76]

Marshall was clear that the clause was directed not solely against those specific laws controversial at the time of the framing of the Constitution in 1787 but also prohibited "the use of any means by which the same mischief might be produced." He added, "The convention appears to have intended to establish a great principle, that contracts should be inviolate."[77] Marshall did not explicitly confine the reach of the contract clause to retrospective laws, but the law at issue had been passed after the contracts were made. Thus, *Sturges* clearly invalidated statutes purporting to discharge prior debts, but the application of the contract clause to subsequent contracts was left open.

In the course of his opinion Marshall complicated emerging contract clause jurisprudence by recognizing a cloudy distinction between contractual rights and the remedies available to enforce those rights. "The distinction between the obligation of a contract, and the remedy given by the legislature to enforce that obligation," he wrote, "has been taken at the bar, and exists in the nature of things. Without impairing the obligation of the contract, the remedy may certainly be modified as the wisdom of the nation shall direct."[78] For example, Marshall declared that a state could abolish imprisonment for debt without impairing the contract. Perhaps unwittingly the chief justice opened the door to considerable confusion. State legislatures pointed to Marshall's language as they altered enforcement procedures in ways that made the enforcement of contractual obligations more difficult. As we shall see, the distinction between infringement of a contract and modification of remedies was elusive and proved a fertile source of litigation throughout the nineteenth century. James Kent, usually a champion of Marshall's jurisprudence, criticized Marshall's wording in *Sturges* as "latitudinary" and "rather hazardous" and declared, "It seems, however, to me, that to lessen or take away from the extent and efficacy of the remedy to enforce the contract, legally existing when the contract was made, impairs its value and obligation."[79]

The Supreme Court increased the uncertainty about the scope of *Sturges* when it decided *McMillan v. McNeil* (1819) the next day. In a brief opinion Marshall apparently applied *Sturges* to strike down application of a Louisiana insolvency law when the debt had been incurred after the enactment of the law. He declared that this fact "made no difference in the application of the principle."[80] This implied that any insolvency law, with respect to either prior or future agreements, violated the contract clause. The Supreme Court did not revisit this issue for almost a decade, but the state and lower federal courts heard a stream of challenges to debt-relief legislation. Indeed, the panic of 1819 produced a new round of laws seeking to protect debtors.

During the 1820s state and lower federal courts declared a number of debt-relief laws void and explored the question of when and how legislatures could change remedies. At issue in *Townsend v. Townsend* (1821) was a state law suspending execution upon any judgment for two years unless the plaintiff agreed to accept the notes of certain state banks in satisfaction of the judgment.[81] The Supreme Court of Tennessee expressed concern that if the legislature could suspend execution for two years, it could extend the suspension indefinitely. The court ruled that a legislative change in the law governing execution in effect at the date of the contract would impair the obligation of the contract. "The Legislature may alter remedies," it explained, "but they must not, so far as regards antecedent contracts, be rendered less efficacious or more dilatory than those ordained by the law in being when the contract was made." Distinguishing retrospective and prospective laws, the court pointed out that the legislature "may regulate contracts of all sorts, but the regulation must be before, not after, the time when the contracts are made."[82] Having thus limited the power of lawmakers to modify contractual remedies, the court found that the suspension violated the contract clause in both federal and state constitutions.

Two years later the Supreme Court of Kentucky struck down a similar statute suspending execution upon judgments.[83] The court considered at length the meaning of the phrase "the obligation of contracts," concluding that it referred to a legal obligation, not a duty binding only in conscience. The remedy in law to enforce an agreement, the court explained, constituted the legal obligation. Declining to follow the *McMillan* decision on the ground that the rationale for the result was unclear, it ruled that the application of relief laws to contracts made thereafter did not run afoul of the contract clause. However, the contracts at issue were made before the suspension act was passed and therefore impaired the obligation of existing agreements.

Other courts also looked skeptically at debt-relief measures. In 1821 the US Circuit Court for Pennsylvania found that a law authorizing the majority of the creditors of a discharged debtor to agree that he be released from liability for seven years on any property thereafter acquired, as applied to debts contracted prior to such discharge, destroyed a creditor's remedy for seven years and ran afoul of the contract clause.[84] Another application of the clause occurred in *Baily v. Gentry* (1822), in which the Supreme Court of Missouri held that a law granting a stay of execution on judgments for two-and-a-half years unless the plaintiff agreed to accept property at two-thirds of its appraised value in satisfaction of the judgment was void under both federal and state constitutions.[85] "To impair," the court remarked, "in the sense in which it was used in both the Constitutions, means to alter so as to make the contract more beneficial to one party, and less so to the other, than by its terms it purported to be." Conceding a distinction between the remedy and the contract, the court nonetheless insisted that the legislature "cannot constitutionally take away all remedy."[86] To the court, legislative postponement of the plaintiff's right to enjoy his monetary award for two-and-a-half years destroyed any remedy for that period. This line of decisions foreshadowed the position eventually reached by the Supreme Court regarding the right/remedy distinction.

In another area of contention, there was authority that a state was free to apply debt-relief laws prospectively. As early as 1816 the Supreme Judicial Court of Massachusetts ruled that a law in effect when a contract is made cannot be said to impair it. The court reasoned, "For the contract, being made under the law, is presumed to be made with reference to it, and the parties are legally conusant of it at the time. The contract in such case is not impaired by the law: for the law is part of the contract."[87] The view was echoed by the *Townsend* opinion and by the Supreme Court of Ohio.[88] Thus, a number of state and lower federal courts had adopted the prospective-retrospection distinction before the Supreme Court returned to the issue of state insolvency laws and the questions left unresolved by *Sturges.*

In *Ogden v. Saunders* (1827), a fragmented Supreme Court, by a vote of four to three, upheld application of a New York bankruptcy law to debts contracted after the time of enactment.[89] *Ogden* involved a suit by a Louisiana resident on a bill of exchange. The defendant raised a discharge of all debts under the New York statute as a defense. Although each of the four justices in the majority wrote a separate opinion, they agreed on certain main points. First, the availability of enforcement remedies under state law in effect when the contract was made constituted the obligation of a contract. Washington endorsed the definition given by Marshall in *Sturges,* ruling that the "obligation of contract" was "the law which binds the parties to perform their agreement."[90] Second, the contract clause was directed against retroactive legislation that impaired existing contracts and did not bar state laws relating to agreements made in the future. The majority justices expressed concern that giving a prospective reading to the contract clause would deprive the states of virtually all their traditional authority over contracts. As Justice Robert Trimble argued, such a construction would "transform a special limitation upon the general powers of the states, into a general restriction."[91] Trimble insisted that the contract clause left the states "full liberty to legislate upon the subject of all future contracts."[92] The upshot was that the contract clause did not raise an absolute barrier to state insolvency laws, a significant result because Congress was unable to pass lasting bankruptcy legislation. Moreover, the majority justices reached a conclusion likely congruent with the expectation of the framers. Recall that James Wilson at the constitutional convention declared that the contract clause would only prohibit retrospective interference with agreements.

During Marshall's tenure the Supreme Court never carefully analyzed the extent to which states remained free to alter contractual remedies. In fact, it appears that the justices were quite divided. Johnson, for instance, took the position that the enforcement of contracts was a "public duty" of the states. He reasoned that the states had virtually unlimited authority to alter remedies and that parties entered contracts with this background knowledge. Johnson dismissed the notion that "the remedy is grafted into the contract."[93] In contrast, Washington asserted that the states had virtually no room to alter remedies existing when a contract was made.[94] Several jurists sought a middle ground, maintaining that there were limits to what remedial changes were allowable under the contract clause. Trimble, for example, sought to cabin Marshall's observation in *Sturges* that states could modify the remedies available for breach of contract. Echoing earlier state court opinions, he declared, "I do not mean to say that every alteration of the existing remedies would impair the obligation of contracts; but I do say, with great confidence, that a law taking away all remedy from existing contracts, would be, manifestly, a law impairing the obligation of contracts."[95] This often-quoted language was an attempt to curtail state authority over remedies and proved influential.[96] Justice Smith Thompson agreed.[97] In his influential 1833 treatise, *Commentaries on the Constitution of the United States*, Story also adopted this view. He defined "the obligation of contract" in terms of the means of enforcement provided by state law. Story concluded, "If there are certain remedies existing at the time, when it is made, all of which are afterwards wholly extinguished by new laws, so that there remains no means of enforcing its obligation, and no redress; such an abolition of remedies, operating *in presenti*, is also an impairment of the obligation of such contract." The legislature may vary the extent of remedies, he explained, "so always, that some substantial remedy be in fact left."[98] Thus, the Supreme Court arrived at a position similar to that articulated by state courts in the 1820s, which maintained that state legislatures could modify but not eliminate all effective contractual remedies.

Marshall, authoring his only dissent in a major constitutional case, reiterated his view of the sweeping nature of the prohibition imposed by the contract clause. Significantly, he grounded contractual rights in preexisting natural law rather than state law, reasoning that the right to contract existed "anterior to, and independent of society."[99] Marshall asserted, "Individuals do not derive from government their right to contract, but bring that right with them into society; that obligation is not conferred on contracts by positive law, but is intrinsic, and is conferred by the act of the parties."[100] He thus sought to distinguish the "obligation" of contract from the remedy, a position seemingly inconsistent with his view in *Sturges*. There he defined obligation in terms of legal mechanisms to enforce performance. Curiously Marshall observed that the contract clause "is the language of restraint. It prohibits the States from passing any law impairing the obligation of contracts; it does not enjoin them to enforce contracts." He continued, "The constitution contemplates restraint as to the obligation of contracts, not as to the application of remedy."[101] Marshall acknowledged that this construction of the contract clause had the potential to effectively undercut the enforcement of contracts, a position at sharp odds with the security of agreements he was at such pains to champion.

Marshall also made the powerful argument that, if state law governed contractual expectations, a legislative act "declaring that all contracts should be subject to legislative control, and should be discharged as the legislature might prescribe, would become a component part of every contract."[102] Parties in effect would enjoy only those contractual rights that lawmakers chose to recognize. Such a result, Marshall contended, would drastically undermine the sanctity of contract and the protective function of the contract clause.[103] Further, he pointed out that under the majority's analysis, lawmakers could not repeal or modify bankruptcy laws because the law at the time of making a contract constituted part of the agreement. Marshall concluded by insisting that the contract clause was not limited to retrospective legislation but was intended to cover laws that were "prospective as well as retrospective in their operation."[104] Herbert A. Johnson has cogently noted that Marshall's dissenting opinion, grounded in natural-law reasoning, adopted "what may be considered an extremely theoretical view of contractual rights."[105]

Probably Marshall received little solace when a majority of the justices ruled against the validity of the New York discharge in the immediate case. In addition to the three dissenters, Justice Johnson, who joined the majority on the contract clause issue, took the position that a state bankruptcy statute could not be applied to a debt owed to creditors from another state. The reasoning behind Johnson's opinion is opaque, but his conclusion dovetails with one interpretation of the contract clause as a vehicle to prevent parochial legislation from interfering with the national credit market.

The result of these state bankruptcy law cases was something of an untidy compromise. A state could validly discharge the debts insolvents incurred after passage of a bankruptcy law, but retroactive application of such laws to agreements entered into before enactment unconstitutionally impaired the obligation of contract. Further, state bankruptcy laws could not discharge obligations payable to residents of other states. The obvious solution to this confused situation was for Congress to enact a uniform bankruptcy scheme. However, this step, of course, was delayed until long after Marshall's death. It also bears emphasis that *Ogden* marked a sea change in the Marshall Court's contract clause jurisprudence. Thereafter, the Court was more cautious in applying the clause and was inclined to uphold state legislation dealing with contractual matters.

Although now clearly confined to retrospective modifications of existing contractual obligations, the contract clause still played an important role in the constitutional order. "Most Contract Clause challenges," Klarman has point out, "were heard only in state court."[106] After *Ogden* many state courts continued to look askance at debtor relief statutes.[107]

LIMITS TO THE REACH OF THE CONTRACT CLAUSE

The Marshall Court was instrumental in formulating a robust contract clause jurisprudence, but it is important to keep this development in perspective. As was made clear in *Ogden*, the justices never displaced all state authority over contracts or established exclusive federal hegemony. Indeed, in numerous cases the Supreme Court and state courts recognized limits to the scope of contract clause protection.

Some contractual arrangements, for instance, were deemed not to be within the purview of the contract clause. Although the Court under Marshall never squarely addressed the issue, there was authority that marriage was not a contract within the meaning of the clause. As discussed above, Marshall in *Dartmouth College* declared the provision only embraced agreements that "respect property, or some object of value." He added that the contract clause "never has been understood to restrict the general right of the legislature to legislate on the subject of divorces."[108] Prominent jurist and treatise writer James Kent agreed that divorce for cause did not impair a marriage contract.[109] In line with these comments, the Supreme Court of Connecticut early upheld a legislative divorce against a contract clause challenge.[110] Likewise, contracts illegal when made conferred no legal rights. Thus, usurious agreements were outside the scope of the clause. Marshall took the position that contracts made in violation of existing usury laws were void *ab initio*, and consequently there was no contract to be impaired.[111]

In addition, time-honored remedies could be eliminated. Imprisonment for debt had long been available under English and colonial law to coerce payment of contractual debts by defaulting parties. Yet attitudes toward imprisonment for debt began to change by the end of the eighteenth century for both humanitarian and practical reasons. States gradually limited or abolished this device over the objection of some creditors who saw such steps as the elimination of an often-efficacious remedy and an impairment of contract.[112] Courts, however, were not receptive to this argument. As early as 1802 Kent ruled that a New York law allowing imprisoned debtors to go outside the prison walls but remain within certain assigned bounds did not violate the contract clause. Picturing the law as a regulation regarding jails, he declared, "The constitution could not have an eye to such details, so long as contracts were submitted, without legislative interference, to the ordinary and regular course of justice, and the existing remedies were preserved in substance, and with integrity."[113]

In time the Supreme Court put its stamp of approval on laws abolishing imprisonment for debt. In *Sturges* Marshall, in the course of distinguishing remedies from contractual obligations, remarked, "Imprisonment is no part of the contract, and simply to release the prisoner does not impair its obligation."[114] The Court affirmed Marshall's comment in *Mason v. Haile* (1827). "Can it be doubted," Justice Smith Thompson queried, "but the legislatures of the States, so far as relates to their own process, have a right to abolish imprisonment for debt altogether, and that such law might extend to present, as well as future imprisonment?" He continued, "[Imprisonment] is a measure which must be regulated by the views of policy and expediency entertained by the State legislatures. Such laws act merely upon the remedy, and that only in part. They do not take away the entire remedy, but only so far as imprisonment forms part of such remedy."[115] Story, writing for the Court, reiterated this point in 1835, pointing out that abolition of imprisonment "does not impair the obligation of the contract, but leaves it in full force against his property and effects."[116] Thus, the Court could accommodate the reform movement to eliminate imprisonment for debt while protecting contracts by insisting upon other forms of enforcement.

Statutes of limitations, restricting the time within which actions could be brought, were also seen as remedial in nature and consequently were subject to a large amount of state discretion in setting the appropriate limits. As early as 1812 the Supreme Judicial Court of Massachusetts decided statutes of limitations that allowed a reasonable time for the commencement of suits on preexisting contracts were useful regulations that did not amount to an impairment of contract.[117] Subsequently, in *Sturges*, Marshall, without much analysis, opined that statutes of limitations related to the availability of judicial remedies.[118] Thus, a legislature could retroactively shorten the time to begin actions on preexisting agreements as long as a reasonable period was permitted before suit was barred.[119]

Moreover, the Supreme Court allowed the states considerable leeway by finding that there was no contract at issue. In *Goszler v. Corporation of*

Georgetown (1821) the Court demonstrated its willingness to uphold municipal control of streets even if adjacent landowners were harmed.[120] An owner in Georgetown made improvements to a lot on a street graded according to a 1799 ordinance. Subsequently the municipal corporation passed another ordinance altering the level and graduation of the street, and the owner brought suit to halt the project. Speaking for the Court, Marshall held that the 1799 ordinance was not in the nature of an unalterable compact. Therefore the city could enact later laws changing the level of streets. Marshall expressed doubt about the power of local government "to make a contract which should so operate as to bind its legislative capacities forever thereafter."[121]

Employing similar reasoning, the Supreme Court brushed aside a contract clause attack on a New York recording act that gave priority to a subsequent purchaser when a prior deed was not recorded. The effect of the law was to render the prior deed void as against the subsequent purchaser. The Court found no contract by the state that the priority of title should depend on common law principles or that the state would never require recording to give legal operation to a deed. "It is within the undoubted power of state legislatures," the Court declared, "to pass recording acts, which the elder grantee shall be postponed to a younger, if the prior deed is not recorded within a limited time; and the power is the same whether the deed is dated before or after the passage of the recording act."[122] Nor did the Court raise any contract clause objection to state laws modifying land law or curing technical defects in deeds.[123]

The leading decision of the Supreme Court under Marshall limiting the reach of the contract clause was *Providence Bank v. Billings* (1830).[124] The case arose when Rhode Island levied a tax on the capital stock of corporations in the state. Although there was no express tax exemption in its charter, Providence Bank maintained that by granting a corporate charter, the state implied a promise not to tax the bank. Writing for the Court, Marshall affirmed the principle that the bank charter was a contract within the protection of the Constitution. He stressed, however, that the taxing power was of vital importance to the capacity of government to provide for the needs of the community and that "the relinquishment of such a power is never to be assumed."[125] Absent express tax immunity, then, individuals and institutions must bear a portion of the public burden. It followed that the Rhode Island tax law did not impair the obligation of contract created by the bank charter. Acknowledging a reservoir of state power, Marshall tellingly insisted, "The constitution of the United States was not intended to furnish the corrective for every abuse of power which may be committed by the state governments."[126] He distinguished the *Wilson* decision by pointing out that the tax immunity in that case was an express stipulation. *Providence Bank* highlighted the tendency of the Marshall Court after 1827 to confine the breadth of the contract clause and anticipated the contract clause jurisprudence of the Supreme Court during the tenure of Chief Justice Roger B. Taney, which stressed strict construction of corporate charters.

During Marshall's tenure as chief justice, state courts developed several doctrines that also imposed constraints on the extent of protection afforded by the contract clause. At issue in *Coates v. Mayor, Alderman, and Commonalty of the City of New York* (1827) was a state law authorizing New York City to regulate or prevent interment of the dead within the city.[127] Pursuant to this statute, the city adopted an ordinance in 1823 that barred any interment in certain areas. The statute and ordinance were assailed in part as an infringement of a royal charter confirming in a church land for a yard and burying ground. Viewing the law as a means to protect the public health and safety by suppressing a nuisance, the New York court declared, "There is nothing impairing the obligation of contracts, within the sense of the Constitution of the U.S."[128] This was an early expression of the notion that the state police power could override previous agreements.

Another limit on the scope of the contract clause recognized by state courts was the power of eminent domain. As noted above, in 1834 the New Hampshire Supreme Court upheld an exclusive bridge franchise under the contract clause against a legislative effort to authorize a second bridge in the same area. However, the court significantly added, "It does not impair that contract to hold that the property acquired under it may be taken for public use—that it is liable to be subjected to the public servitude and the public burdens." The court added that the exclusive right conferred by the grant could not be taken from the grantees "except for public use, and upon adequate compensation being made."[129] This was a forerunner of a ruling by the Supreme Court under Taney that contracts were subject to the exercise of eminent domain by the states and that the use of such power did not run afoul of the contract clause.[130]

CONTRACT CLAUSE AND NATURAL LAW

Scholars have long debated the role of natural law in the jurisprudence of the New Republic. Under natural law theory certain rights were regarded as so basic as to be beyond the reach of government. In other words, the rights enumerated in state and federal constitutions were not an exclusive inventory of personal liberties. Yet the relationship between natural law and written constitutional texts was elusive and raised a number of questions. Was it appropriate for judges to go beyond the language of constitutions and rely on fundamental principles not expressly set forth in such documents? Or was the invocation of natural law confined to guiding judicial construction of constitutional and statutory provisions? Could natural law override constitutional provisions? There was also doubt as to which individual rights were protected under natural law, although Americans of the founding generation tended to conflate natural law with the traditional "rights of Englishmen" and common-law guarantees.[131]

Notwithstanding this lack of certainty, the notion that individuals possessed certain rights that predated government found repeated expression in early American jurisprudence. "Judges and lawyers throughout the new nation," Sherry concluded, shared a common belief that both written and unwritten rights should be enforced by courts."[132] As this comment suggests, in the late eighteenth and early nineteenth centuries both federal and state courts cited fundamental natural rights as a basis for constitutional decisions, especially to safeguard the rights of property owners.[133] Marshall and his colleagues were certainly conversant with the prevalent natural rights philosophy. Nelson has described the chief justice as "a traditionalist who believed in natural rights that pre-existed government and legislation."[134] It is hardly surprising, therefore, that the Supreme Court under Marshall's leadership sometimes employed natural law rhetoric.

Our concern, of course, is not with the larger issue of the role of natural law in the emerging constitutional order but with the more focused question of the relationship between natural law and the contract clause. As we have seen, both Marshall and Johnson demonstrated a propensity to invoke principles of natural law in contract clause cases. Yet the pattern was hardly consistent. In *Dartmouth College,* for example, Marshall made no reference to natural law. His attempt to fashion a natural law understanding of the contract clause in *Ogden* was rejected by the Court majority and never resurfaced. By the 1820s, moreover, Johnson moved away from his earlier reliance on natural law.[135] In fact, the textual basis of the contract clause was likely more dispositive in cases concerned with state abridgment of agreements than occasional references to natural law principles.[136] The same holds true for state court adjudications. State judges sometimes linked the text of the contract clause with natural law. The Supreme Court of Connecticut, for example, declared that the grant of a corporate charter could not be revoked by the legislature. "Both the letter and the spirit of the constitution of the United States are violated, by such a proceeding," it proclaimed, "as well as the fundamental principles of natural justice and of the social compact."[137]

The most significant decision in which the Marshall Court utilized natural law to restrain legislative authority over private property was *Terrett v. Taylor* (1815).[138] Because scholars have had difficulty in coming to grips with this case, and some have even characterized it as a contract clause ruling, *Terrett* warrants careful examination. The case involved land purchased by the Protestant Episcopal Church in Alexandria, Virginia, from private parties during the colonial era. In 1776 the state legislature confirmed all the church's land titles. More than twenty years later, however, the lawmakers repealed the 1776 law, asserted the power to sell all Episcopal church property, and directed the parish overseers of the poor to sell any vacant glebe lands and use the proceeds to assist the poor. This measure was the result of a popular campaign to confiscate land owned by the formerly established church.[139] At this time the Alexandria Parish was located in the District of Columbia, established in 1801. Taylor, an official of the Episcopal Church of Alexandria, brought suit against Terrett, an overseer of the poor, to quiet title and enjoin the overseers from claiming the disputed land. Invoking natural law principles repeatedly throughout his opinion, Story struck down Virginia's attempt to retroactively revoke the church's title. "Such a doctrine," he lectured, "would uproot the very foundations of almost all the land-titles in Virginia, and is utterly inconsistent with a great and fundamental principle of republican government, the right of the citizens to the free enjoyment of their property legally acquired."[140] He also invalidated another law repealing an act that incorporated the Episcopal churches, explaining that a law abolishing private corporations and disposing of their property was inconsistent with natural law. "We think ourselves standing upon the principles of natural justice," Story declared, "upon the fundamental laws of every free government, upon the spirit and letter of the constitution of the United States, and upon the decisions of most respectable judicial tribunals in resisting such a doctrine."[141] Story made reference to multiple sources to support his decision but never mentioned the contract clause or any other provision of the Constitution.

Terrett has puzzled historians, who have reached diverse conclusions regarding the rationale for the decision. Despite the fact that the provision is never invoked, a number of historians have treated *Terrett* as a contract clause case.[142] Yet there is a fundamental problem with this assessment. Was there a contract? None of the state laws struck down by the Supreme Court was like a contract. As G. Edward White pointed out, "It is hard from the case's facts, to know just what contract a state had impaired."[143] I contend that *Terrett* is not properly seen as an application of the contract clause. Wright is correct when he asserts that in *Terrett* "the Court does not apply the contract clause."[144] The matter in dispute was not state abridgment of a contract but an effort by the state to confiscate church property. It was analogous to taking property without payment of just compensation. Story, however, could not rely on the takings clause of the Fifth Amendment because that provision pertained only to actions by the federal government.[145] Outraged by Virginia's interference with property rights but unable to identify an express constitutional provision that seemed applicable, he turned to natural law principles to restrain legislative authority.[146] There is no need for scholars to hunt for some tenuous link to the contract clause.

Story's opinion in *Terrett* illustrates the tendency of the Supreme Court to occasionally rely on natural law precepts, either alone or as an alternative holding, before approximately 1820.[147] It can perhaps best be pictured as a parting gesture to the natural law tradition, which by then was gradually fading. The case, however, sheds no light on the construction of the contract clause. The holding simply does not support Kent Newmyer's sweeping conclusion that, by virtue of Story's opinion, "the Contract Clause was well on its way to becoming an all-purpose instrument for protecting private property from state regulation, even when no contract was involved."[148] Not only did Story fail to invoke the contract clause but the provision never served as such a broad check on state economic regulations.

END OF AN ERA

By the time of Marshall's death in July of 1835 the contract clause had been fashioned into a secure base for the protection of existing contractual rights against retroactive state legislative abridgment. The provision had been construed to cover public as well as private agreements. It was generally agreed that states could not alter in any way the terms of contracts, although there was lingering uncertainty as to how far states were free to modify enforcement remedies. The contract clause was the centerpiece of Marshall Court jurisprudence and became the principal vehicle by which the justices could police state economic regulations. Much of the credit for these developments belongs to the chief justice, but the work of Story and Washington also deserves mention. Nor should we overlook the important decisions by state courts that demonstrated a willingness to uphold contracts under state constitutional provisions, sometimes in conjunction with the federal contract clause. Indeed, in some respects state courts anticipated later results at the federal level. Because most contract clause cases were heard in state courts, their role, if often overlooked, was crucial. Still, few in 1835 would have predicted that the clause would have profound influence throughout the nineteenth century and would be among the most litigated provisions of the Constitution.

CHAPTER 3

The Taney Era

By the time of John Marshall's death in July of 1835 Jacksonian democracy had become the dominant political force in the United States. Dedicated to popular democracy, Jacksonians favored broad suffrage for white males. They were suspicious of the power of the national government and supported a large measure of state sovereignty. In particular, Jacksonian Democrats were hostile to any arrangements that smacked of special privilege. They were generally not opposed to business enterprise and the market economy but insisted that government should remain neutral and not be used by particular groups to secure advantages not available to others. Thus, Jacksonians viewed state-conferred monopolies as threats to democracy.[1] It is important to recall that a sizeable portion of the public did not support Andrew Jackson as president or endorse the tenets of Jacksonian democracy. Nonetheless, the Democrats controlled the national government for most of the time before the Civil War, and Jacksonian ideology set the tenor of political dialogue throughout the remainder of the antebellum years.

President Jackson named Roger B. Taney to replace Marshall as chief justice. Taney had served in Jackson's cabinet as attorney general and secretary of the Treasury. The nomination was highly controversial, in part because as secretary of the Treasury he had implemented the president's policy of removing the federal deposits from the Second Bank of the United States and transferring them to state banks. In addition, Jackson made a number of other appointments to the Court that substantially altered the complexion of the bench.[2] Contrary to the fears of many, including Justice Joseph Story,[3] Taney proved to be a champion of economic growth and was protective of property and contractual rights. "On the Supreme Court," Daniel Walker Howe has pointed out, "Taney did not implement an antimarket agenda."[4] Although his views regarding the contract clause were colored by Jacksonian ideology, Taney paradoxically both strengthened and confined the security of contractual obligations under the clause. In many respects he built upon Marshall's jurisprudence, especially with respect to debtor-creditor relations. Although Taney tempered the protection afforded corporations under the contract clause, the overall picture was one of continuity, not change. Indeed, the Taney years witnessed a proliferation of contract clause litigation at both the federal and state levels. In many

Chief Justice Roger B. Taney limited application of the contract clause to corporate charters with the doctrine of strict construction but otherwise vigorously enforced the provision. (Library of Congress)

respects the Supreme Court enforced the clause vigorously, and the provision was the primary basis for decisions invalidating state laws during the Taney era. As Benjamin F. Wright convincingly pointed out, "The simple fact is that the contract clause was a more secure and a broader base for the defense of property rights in 1864 than it had been in 1835."[5]

DOMINANCE OF CONTRACTS

Contracts set the legal framework for the expanding world of economic dealings in the nineteenth century.[6] "Nearly all the business transactions of life," Timothy Walker, a prominent Ohio lawyer, declared in 1837, "have some connection with contracts." He added, "A large proportion of the wealth of every man consists of contracts."[7] In his 1857 treatise Theophilus Parsons proclaimed, "The law of contracts in its widest extent may be regarded as including all the law which regulates the relations of human life. Indeed, it may be looked upon as the basis of human society."[8] The law of contracts allowed private parties wide latitude to arrange their own bargains in a growing market economy and was an expression of individual autonomy. This extensive reliance on voluntary agreements led James Willard Hurst to characterize this era as "above all, the years of contract in our law."[9]

Given the central place of contracting in US society during the nineteenth century, it is not surprising that the constitutional protection of contracts received broad support. Both federal and state courts repeatedly extolled the importance of the contract clause. Taney, for example, explained in 1843 that the provision "was undoubtedly adopted as a part of the Constitution for a great and useful purpose. It was to maintain the integrity of contracts, and to secure their faithful execution throughout this Union, by placing them under the protection of the Constitution of the United States."[10] State courts echoed this beneficial understanding of the clause. A New York judge praised the contract clause "and the series of wise and salutary conditions under it, as forming the most important safeguard of the rights of industry and labor possessed by the American citizen."[11] The Supreme Court of Arkansas similarly declared in 1858 that the contract clause "is justly ranked among the wisest in the Federal Constitution. Without it—private rights would, at all times, be liable to invasion by the enactment of laws consequent upon fluctuating policy, strong passions, and sudden changes."[12]

State constitution makers also affirmed this commitment to contractual stability by generally placing a contract clause in their constitutions. During Taney's tenure as chief justice, fourteen additional states, including Arkansas, California, Florida, Texas, and Wisconsin, adopted constitutional language barring the impairment of contracts. These provisions established a separate basis to challenge legislation on state grounds but raised the vexing question of whether, and to what extent, the protection afforded agreements under state constitutions varied from the federal provision. At the same time, it should be noted that some of the older states, such as Connecticut and North Carolina, had not adopted a contract clause by the end of the Taney period.

OBLIGATION OF CONTRACT AND REMEDIES

Courts continued to wrestle with the baffling inquiry of what the "obligation of contract" was and how the obligation differed from the remedy for nonperformance. Both courts and commentators expressed frustration with this inquiry. Reflecting this attitude, Justice Robert G. Grier, while presiding in a federal circuit court, declined to attempt "any metaphysical definition of what constitutes the 'obligation of a contract.'"[13] Nonetheless, courts increasingly defined the obligation of a contract in terms of the available remedy. In 1853 Justice Benjamin R. Curtis articulated this view: "The obligation of a contract, in the sense in which those words are used in the Constitution, is that duty of performing it, which is recognized and enforced by the laws. And if the law is so changed that the means of legally enforcing this duty are materially impaired, the obligation of the contract no longer remains the same."[14] In the same vein, the Supreme Court of Pennsylvania concluded

> that the law existing when a contract is made enters into it and necessarily forms a part of it. The remedies prescribed for enforcing performance, are regarded by the parties as constituting that 'obligation' of contract which is within the protection of the constitution. If the remedies were taken away, there would be nothing but the moral obligation left, and it is absurd to suppose that this was the "obligation of the contract" which the legislature was prohibited from impairing.[15]

The important legal scholar Theodore Sedgwick aptly summarized the emerging position when he admitted his "entire inability to distinguish between the *obligation* and the *remedy* of a contract. Obligation, I suppose, means binding force, the force or constraint which binds the party to perform his agreement." He contended that "obligation and remedy are strictly convertible terms."[16]

If the obligation and remedy were in effect treated as one and the same, the question remained as to which alterations of existing remedies amounted to impairment of the rights created by the contract. The Marshall

Court had grappled inconclusively with this issue, and courts in the Taney period were frequently called upon to determine how far state legislatures could modify available remedies. Taney, like his predecessor as chief justice, was unable to formulate a bright-line test. In *Bronson v. Kinzie* (1843) he pointed out that the states were free to change judicial procedures and could exempt such items as agricultural implements, tools, and "articles of necessity in household furniture" from execution on judgments according to their "own views of policy and humanity." He even agreed that states could adopt new remedies that might "render the recovery of debts more tardy and difficult."[17] But Taney also sought to establish an outer limit to state control over remedies, declaring:

> It is difficult, perhaps, to draw a line that would be applicable, in all cases, between legitimate alterations of the remedy and provisions which, in the form of remedy, impair the right. But it is manifest that the obligation of the contract, and the rights of a party under it, may in effect be destroyed by denying a remedy altogether; or may be seriously impaired by burdening the proceedings with new conditions and restrictions, so as to make the remedy hardly worth pursuing. And no one, we presume, would say that there is any substantial difference between a retrospective law declaring a particular contract or class of contracts to be abrogated and void, and one which took away all remedy to enforce them, or encumbered it with conditions that rendered it useless or impracticable to pursue it.[18]

Recall that a number of justices in the Marshall era insisted that a state law foreclosing any means of enforcing a contract was clearly unconstitutional. Their successors reached the same conclusion. "When every form of redress on a contract is taken away," Justice Levi Woodbury explained in 1848, "it will be difficult to see how the obligation of it is not impaired."[19] Beyond this point, however, there was little agreement. Taney's balancing test provided inadequate guidance for many situations and compounded the lingering confusion. A decade after *Bronson* Justice Curtis acknowledged the "difficulty of determining, in some cases, whether the change in remedy has materially impaired the rights and interests of the creditor."[20]

State courts also found the distinction between contractual rights and remedies elusive. After recognizing that legislators could alter the remedy as long as they did not "materially" impair the rights of the contracting parties, the Supreme Court of Wisconsin made clear its unhappiness with this rule. "Practically this rule may seem vague and unsatisfactory," the court observed, "but it is the most certain *general* one of which the nature of the subject admits. The difficulty of applying its doctrines to particular cases, and of distinguishing between what are legitimate changes of the remedy, and those changes which, in the form of remedy, impair the right has often suggested itself to the mind of courts when dealing with it."[21] Some state judges even questioned the viability of this inquiry, expressing doubt that there was a meaningful difference between the rights created by a contract and the remedies to enforce those rights. In 1858, for example, the Supreme Court of Pennsylvania broadly insisted, "Plain common sense, responding to the demands of justice, has scattered to the winds the flimsy distinction between the *right* and *remedy*, so far as to declare that any change of the nature or extent of the latter, so far as to impair the former, is just as much a violation of the compact as if the right itself was destroyed."[22]

Dissatisfaction with the right/remedy distinction found expression in one state constitution. When New Jersey adopted a constitution in 1844 the delegates were mindful of the uncertainty over the authority of the legislature to alter the remedies available when an agreement was made and sought to clarify the rights of the parties. The delegates inserted language that provided, "The legislature shall not pass any . . . law impairing the obligation of contracts, or depriving a party of any remedy for enforcing a contract which existed when the contract was made."[23] The delegates were aware that this was a unique provision with broader language than the contract clause in the federal Constitution. As one delegate elaborated, "It should be understood when a contract is made what the remedy is, and the law should not be allowed to step in and take away the remedy—thus laughing to scorn the principle that 'you shall not impair the obligation of contracts,' when you may destroy its value, or take away his remedy." Creditors, he continued, must be able to depend on the same remedies as when the contract was entered.[24] Other delegates argued that the provision unduly restricted legislative authority over remedies, but the proposal carried by a wide margin. Leading commentators applauded the New Jersey constitutional clause, with Sedgwick declaring, "This provision is evidently drawn to obviate the difficulties and answer the objections growing out of the subtle distinction taken between the obligation and the remedy." The stipulation, he added, "seems to me every way worthy of commendation for its vigorous justice and sound judgment."[25] Apparently the New Jersey courts had no opportunity to construe this constitutional provision before the Civil War, but a federal circuit court relied on the state constitution to strike down a law that altered a remedy expressly given to a mortgagee by the contract itself.[26]

The Supreme Court of New Jersey in the late nineteenth century acknowledged, "This provision is peculiar to the constitution of this state and is regarded as having an important effect in restriction of the power of the legislature over remedies."[27] As we shall see, however, it is unclear that this language was treated by the state courts as the kind of robust limitation on legislative power that the constitutional delegates expected.

Notwithstanding this litany of complaints, the right/remedy distinction proved durable. Because precise lines proved impossible to draw, the result was to create some wiggle room for legislators, who invariably maintained that laws pertaining to contracts related only to remedies and left the rights untouched. Consequently, the right/remedy distinction featured prominently in contract clause litigation throughout the nineteenth century.

PUBLIC CONTRACTS

Following the lead of Marshall, Taney and his colleagues continued to insist that the contract clause reached contracts by the states as well as between private parties. "A State," the Supreme Court ruled in 1851, "can no more impair, by legislation, the obligation of its own contracts, than it can impair the obligation of the contracts of individuals. We naturally look to the action of a sovereign State, to be characterized by a more scrupulous regard to justice, and a higher morality, than belong to the ordinary transactions of individuals."[28] A year later the Supreme Court of Georgia likewise observed, "It is well settled, that a contract entered into between the State and an individual, is as fully protected by this prohibition, as a contract between two individuals; that the contracting parties whoever they may be, stand in this respect, upon the same ground."[29]

Yet this reading of the contract clause begged the question of what amounted to a public contract. During Marshall's tenure the Supreme Court had decided that land grants, corporate charters, and tax exemptions were contracts, but it certainly did not follow that every legislative enactment was a contract that could not subsequently be altered or repealed. Indeed, generally a legislative body was free to undo the work of its predecessors and change policies. It was settled, for example, that appointment to a public office did not amount to a contract, and hence lawmakers could alter the terms and tenure of such offices in their discretion without violating the Constitution.[30] Parties frequently contended that there was no contract but merely legislation subject to revision under the sovereign power of the state. The test for ascertaining which particular legislative act amounted to a contract remained hazy. Sedgwick, for instance, noted that "much more serious embarrassments present themselves in regard to rights or interests created by or under legislation" and maintained that "in the term contracts are not included rights, or rather interests, growing out of measures of public policy."[31] The crucial distinction appeared to be whether the legislation conferred fixed private property rights or was merely a general policy for the public good.[32] This standard, however, was not easy to apply in different factual settings.

Allied to this inquiry was another question: Who was to determine whether a state had entered into a contract? Normally the federal courts adhered to the construction given by state courts to their own constitutions and laws. But this rule, the Supreme Court explained in 1854, applies only to ordinary acts of legislation and "does not extend to contracts of the State, although they should be made in the form of law." Speaking for the Court, Taney declared:

> For it would be impossible for this court to exercise any appellate power in a case of this kind, unless it was at liberty to interpret for itself the instrument relied on as the contract between the parties. It must necessarily decide whether the words used are words of contract, and what is their true meaning before it can determine whether the obligation the instrument created has or has not been impaired by the law complained of.[33]

The Supreme Court, then, would make an independent judgment as to whether a contract existed and whether the state impaired its obligations. Otherwise a state court could evade application of the contract clause by the simple expedient of denying that arrangements made by the state constituted a contract. Recognizing this problem, Justice James M. Wayne asked:

> Of what use would the appellate power be to the litigant who feels himself aggrieved by some particular State legislation, if this court could not decide, independently of all adjudication by the Supreme Court of a State, whether or not the phraseology of the instrument in controversy was expressive of a contract and within the protection of the Constitution of the United States, and that its obligation should be enforced, notwithstanding a contrary conclusion by the Supreme Court of a State?[34]

This rule of construction governed regardless of whether the claimed contract arose under the form of state legislation or by an agreement to which the state was a party.

CORPORATE CHARTERS

Although many Jacksonian Democrats were suspicious of business corporations, the Supreme Court under Taney did not reject the *Dartmouth College* doctrine and repeatedly ruled that state-granted corporate charters were within the scope of the contract clause. Still, Taney was prepared to allow the states greater latitude to regulate corporate activity and fashion economic policy by insisting that corporate grants should be strictly construed. Taney's approach is best illustrated by the famous case of *Charles River Bridge v. Warren Bridge* (1837),[35] decided early in his tenure as chief justice.

The *Charles River Bridge* case reached the Supreme Court as the transportation revolution was transforming the antebellum United States. New modes of transportation—turnpikes, canals, steamboats, railroads—rapidly appeared and competed for public favor. This transportation boom put legislators in a difficult position. The long-range public interest was best served by encouraging improved transportation. Yet it also appeared essential to protect investors who would risk capital in often-speculative ventures. Many of the legal issues implicit in the transportation revolution, such as the extent of corporate privilege, the impact of changing technology, and the conflict between economic competition and vested rights, were presented in *Charles River Bridge.*

Incorporated in 1785 by the Massachusetts legislature, the Charles River Bridge Company was empowered to operate a toll bridge over the Charles River between Charlestown and Boston. The initial franchise was for forty years, but it was extended in 1792 for an additional thirty years. In response to calls for cheaper and easier means to cross the river, and anxiety about monopoly privilege, the legislature in 1828 granted a charter to the Warren Bridge Corporation for the purpose of erecting a second bridge parallel to the original structure. The charter of the Warren Bridge provided that as soon as the cost of construction was paid the bridge would revert to the state as a free bridge. Because a toll bridge could not successfully compete with a free bridge, the Warren grant threatened to significantly reduce the value of the initial franchise. Nothing in the Charles River Bridge charter explicitly prevented the state from creating a second bridge, but the company contended that its charter impliedly conferred the exclusive right to maintain a bridge for the seventy-year life of the extended grant. Appearing for the old bridge company, Daniel Webster maintained that the 1828 act infringed the obligation of contract because it effectively destroyed

The Charles River Bridge was at the center of a dispute over implied corporate privilege when the Massachusetts legislature established a rival bridge. (Library of Congress)

this implied exclusive privilege. He also warned that entrepreneurs would not invest in projects unless they could rely on government not to act in ways fundamentally inconsistent with existing charters. If contracts were not protected, economic growth would be hampered. The attorneys for the Warren Bridge countered that the old bridge had never been given an exclusive right to a line of travel.[36]

The case was first heard by the Supreme Court in 1831, but final disposition was delayed until 1837. By then Taney had replaced Marshall as chief justice. Rejecting the contract clause argument, Taney established the principle that corporate grants should be strictly construed in favor of the public. Building upon Marshall's opinion in *Providence Bank v. Billings* (1830), he insisted that governments cannot be assumed to have relinquished power by implication. "While the rights of private property are sacredly guarded," Taney explained, "we must not forget that the community also have rights, and that the happiness and well-being of every citizen depends on their faithful preservation."[37] He stressed that nothing in the 1785 charter contained an undertaking by the state that no other bridge would be erected. In interpreting corporate charters, Taney continued, "no rights are taken from the public, or given to the corporation, beyond those which the words of the charter, by their natural and proper construction, purport to convey."[38] He refused to extend the reach of *Dartmouth College* by implication. Further, the chief justice voiced concern at the negative practical impact of the doctrine of implied corporate powers for advancing technology:

> If this court should establish the principles now contended for, what is to become of the numerous rail roads established on the same line of travel with turnpike companies; and which have rendered the franchises of the turnpike corporations of no value? Let it once be understood that such charters carry with them these implied contracts, and give this unknown and undefined property in a line of travelling; and you will soon find the old turnpike corporations awakening from their sleep, and calling upon this court to put down the improvements which have taken their place. The millions of property which have been invested in railroads and canals upon lines of travel which had been before occupied by turnpike corporations, will be put in jeopardy. We shall be thrown back to the improvements of the last century, and obliged to stand still, until the claims of the old turnpike corporations shall be satisfied; and they shall consent to permit these states to avail themselves of the lights of modern science, and to partake of the benefits of those improvements which are now adding to the wealth and prosperity, and the convenience and comfort, of every other part of the civilized world.[39]

The upshot of *Charles River Bridge* was to afford the states, unless restrained by express language in a charter, wide range to regulate corporations under the police power and to sponsor new projects. It also created room for dynamic capital and technological innovation free of claims resting on obsolete charters. In fact, fledgling railroads were prime beneficiaries of *Charles River Bridge.* "The touchstone of Taney's opinion," Stanley I. Kutler has observed, "was its practicality, its responsiveness to contemporary reality—in short, it was a document of public policy."[40] Yet nothing in the opinion barred states from explicitly granting monopoly privilege, and in fact, as discussed below, a number of monopoly charters were subsequently granted by legislatures and enforced by state and federal courts.

Story, joined by Thompson, authored a forceful dissent that raised legal and practical objections to the majority opinion. He insisted that corporate grants should be construed liberally to effectuate the intention of the legislature to promote projects and vindicate the reasonable expectation of the investors. Stressing that construction of a bridge over the Charles River was a risky enterprise in 1785 and that the grant of an exclusive privilege for a term of years served the public interest by encouraging investment, Story argued that a narrow reading of the corporate charter would discourage future commitments of capital. "I can conceive of no surer plan to arrest all public improvements, founded on private capital and enterprise," he observed, "than to make the outlay of that capital uncertain, and questionable both as to security, and as to productiveness."[41] Common sense, in his mind, dictated that the grant "carries with it an exclusive franchise to a reasonable distance on the river; so that the ordinary travel to the bridge shall not be diverted by any new bridge to the injury or ruin of the franchise."[42] He asked why, if the legislature could not revoke the charter by virtue of the contract clause, lawmakers could in effect destroy its value and substance. Story insisted that if public exigencies required the erection of a new bridge, the proper course was to treat this as a taking of property of the Charles River Bridge and pay just compensation.[43] He found that the act incorporating the Warren Bridge impaired the obligation of the prior contract of the Charles River Bridge Company.

Both Taney and Story focused on the importance of encouraging economic growth but differed sharply as to how to achieve this goal. Story was legitimately concerned about contractual stability and the rights of investors, but he proved to be a poor prophet. Notwithstanding his dire warnings, the years after 1837 witnessed steady economic development. New avenues of commerce were attractive to investors as well as the public. "The real effect of the *Charles River Bridge* case," Herbert Hovenkamp has written, "was to give entrepreneurs what they bargained for."[44] Moreover, leading legal commentators generally applauded the strict construction principle. Sedgwick, for example, declared that the doctrine "has commended itself to the general good sense no less than the sound legal judgment of the country."[45]

The Court under Taney consistently affirmed the rule of strict constructions of legislative grants, and some of the justices even offered additional rationales for this principle. In 1854 Taney pointed out that nearly every charter of incorporation "is drawn originally by the parties who are personally interested in obtaining the charter" and were typically passed at the end of a legislative session "in a hurried manner." It was therefore appropriate, he reasoned, that "any right or exemption" the corporation claimed should be expressed in "clear and unambiguous language."[46]

Indeed, some justices felt the strict construction doctrine was inadequate and preferred a more categorical rule that states could not make irrevocable grants of monopoly status or tax concessions. A stalwart Jacksonian and champion of states' rights, Justice John Catron was a frequent dissenter when the Court invoked the contract clause. He dismissed the strict construction rule of *Charles River Bridge* as "illusory and nearly useless." Catron decried "the unparalleled increase of corporations throughout the Union within the last few years, and the ease with which charters containing exclusive privileges and exemptions are obtained."[47] Justice Peter V. Daniel had much the same attitude and was highly solicitous of state authority. "Daniel," one scholar has observed, "was a consistent and inveterate foe of the application of the contract clause to corporate charters."[48] Although their views were never adopted by the Taney Court, they were harbingers of gradually increased criticism of the scope of contract clause protection as the nineteenth century progressed.

As with *Charles River Bridge*, many applications of the strict construction doctrine in the Antebellum Era concerned competing modes of transportation, and the Supreme Court invariably rejected the contention that subsequent grants infringed the contractual rights of the original grantee. Not all such cases involved claims by corporations. In two cases individuals asserted an exclusive privilege of ferriage over rivers. The Supreme Court easily brushed aside both claims, relying in part on a strict construction of the legislative grant of ferriage rights.[49]

A more challenging case arose from competition between railroads. States often granted monopolies to early railroads for limited periods as an inducement to attract private capital. At issue in *Richmond, Fredericksburg, and Potomac Railroad Company v. Louisa Railroad Company* (1852) was language in an 1834 Virginia charter that the legislature would not for thirty years "allow any other railroad to be constructed" between Richmond and Washington, "or for any portion of the said distance, the probable effect of which would be to diminish the number of passengers" travelling between the designated cities on the grantee railroad.[50] Despite this provision, lawmakers in 1848 authorized another carrier to extend its track into Richmond. Charging that the 1848 act impaired its contract with the state, the Richmond, Fredericksburg, and Potomac Railroad sued to enjoin its rival from construction of a line into Richmond. The issue was the extent, not the existence, of an exclusive privilege. Invoking the rule that any ambiguity in a contract must be construed against the corporation and in favor of the state, the Court majority insisted that the state granted a monopoly only of transporting passengers on the route between Richmond and Washington, and that the 1836 charter did not pertain to freight traffic or bar construction of another carrier parallel to any portion of the route. Consequently, the Court found no impairment of the original charter. The three dissenters read the charter differently, illustrating that the strict construction rule did not resolve all interpretative problems. They concluded that the 1848 charter was not confined to freight traffic and that "this extension act impairs the obligation of the contract, by authorizing another road to be built, the probable effect of which would be to diminish the number of passengers travelling on the complainants' road."[51]

Late in Taney's tenure as chief justice another case presented some of the same issues as *Charles River Bridge*, and the Court again applied the strict construction doctrine. In 1790 New Jersey empowered commissioners to enter a contract for constructing a bridge over the Hackensack River. The statute provided that the bridge owners had a right to collect tolls from persons crossing the bridge and that it was unlawful to erect another bridge for ninety-nine years. In 1860, however, the legislature authorized another company to build a railroad bridge over the river, and the original bridge company complained that the 1860 act impaired the obligation of its contract. Speaking for the Court in *Bridge Proprietors v. Hoboken Company* (1864), Justice Samuel F. Miller readily concluded that the legislative act was a contract that granted a monopoly to secure the payment of tolls.[52] The more vexing question, he noted, was whether the railroad structure abridged the exclusive privilege as understood in 1790. Taking a page from Taney's analysis in *Charles River Bridge*, Miller stressed the swift advance of technology in the years since the original grant was made. "In no department of human enterprise," he observed, "have more rapid changes been made, than in that which relates to the means of transportation of persons and property from one point to another, including the means of crossing water courses, large and small." He added that the 1790 act was passed "before a steam engine or railroad was thought of."[53] Miller reasoned that the railroad bridge did not serve the same function as the original bridge because passengers on foot and vehicles could not pass over it, and therefore the new structure would not interfere with the right of the proprietors to collect tolls. Stressing the different role of the railroad bridge, he found that the subsequent measure authorizing the second bridge did not impair the obligation of the 1790 contract. Not only were exclusive privileges never to be implied, but the Supreme Court carefully parsed even express grants of privilege.

State courts heard numerous cases arising from subsequent legislation authorizing competing modes of transportation and frequently invoked the strict construction doctrine to dismiss claims alleging a violation of the contract clause. "Ever since the decision of the Charles River Bridge case," the Supreme Court of Connecticut explained in 1860, "it has been held to be the settled law throughout the country, that charters are to be construed most favorably for the state."[54] Similarly, Joseph Henry Lumpkin, chief justice of the Georgia Supreme Court, emphatically rejected the notion of implied monopoly right, declaring, "Such a doctrine, in my opinion, is at war with the universally recognized principles of American constitutional law, and totally inapplicable to our local situation and change of circumstances. For if there be one principle settled in the country beyond the hazard of change, it is, that in grants by the public, nothing passes by implication."[55] Committed to a competitive economic environment, Lumpkin pictured the dire consequences of stagnation and litigation that would flow from allowing the mere existence of an earlier charter to bar rival enterprise.[56]

There was a variety of clashes between different forms of transportation. The advent of railroads raised recurring contract clause issues. State courts repeatedly found that there was no implied exclusive privilege in turnpike, canal, or bridge company charters and that such documents were not impaired by subsequent legislation authorizing the construction of railroads that threatened to divert traffic.[57] Enthusiastically endorsing *Charles River Bridge*, the Supreme Court of Appeals of Virginia held that exclusive privilege must be established by express provision in a legislative grant. The court not only upheld the power of lawmakers to authorize construction of a railroad alongside a canal but also ruled that the railroad could erect bridges over the canal.[58] Nor was the grant of ferry rights across a river infringed by the erection of a bridge or authorization of another ferry.[59] Likewise, a bridge company charter was not impaired by the later establishment of a ferry,[60] the operation of which diminished the amount of bridge tolls, or by the erection of another bridge.[61]

As states began to enact railroad safety laws in the mid-nineteenth century, carriers argued that such regulations violated their corporate charters. State courts easily brushed aside this contention, emphasizing that nothing in the corporate charters precluded the legislatures from subsequently requiring safety measures.[62] For example, laws requiring that railroads fence their tracks, and imposing strict liability on carriers for failure to comply, were held not to abridge the charter rights of rail companies. Absent express language, courts insisted that lawmakers were free to mandate the adoption of new improvements necessary for public safety under the police power.[63]

As noted above, some states expressly granted monopoly status to certain carriers for limited periods. Where the grant of monopoly status was clear, courts displayed little hesitation in upholding the express exemption. The 1830 Massachusetts charter of the Boston and Lowell Railroad provided that no other railroad would be authorized between Boston and Lowell for thirty years. Invoking an 1852 state statute, two rival lines maintained that they had a right to combine operations and carry passengers and freight by a different route from Boston to Lowell. Alleging a breach of its exclusive franchise, the Boston and Lowell Railroad brought suit for an injunction against such operations and an accounting for lost revenue. Finding that the 1830 charter amounted to a contract binding upon the state, Lemuel Shaw, chief justice of Massachusetts and a prominent jurist, insisted that nothing in *Charles River Bridge* indicated that an express grant of an exclusive right was invalid. He observed that the conferral of monopoly privilege was a matter of legislative policy. It followed that the rival railroads had no right to combine operations and infringe the monopoly of the Boston and Lowell.[64] The most important and durable of such monopolies was granted to the Camden and Amboy Railroad by the New Jersey legislature in 1832. The charter contained a provision that no other railroad would be allowed to carry passengers or goods across New Jersey between New York City and Philadelphia. With the appearance of potential rival lines, the extent of this privilege was called into question. Applying the strict construction principle, the New Jersey Court of Chancery ruled that the privilege only concerned through traffic between New York City and Philadelphia and did not pertain to local traffic between intermediate points over the route.[65] In other words, the monopoly exclusively covered through traffic. Yet the court enjoined the other carriers from joining their services in such a way as to provide a continuous line of transportation between the terminal cities.[66]

Aside from the monopoly cases, state courts relied on the contract clause to enforce express provisions in various charters. In a line of decisions in the 1840s the Supreme Court of Connecticut upheld exclusive rights in bridge charters against legislative attempts to revive a competing ferry[67] and struck down a law mandating an increase in the draw of a bridge.[68] In *Enfield Toll Bridge Company v. Hartford and New Haven Rail-Road Company* (1845) the court invalidated a law authorizing a railroad to erect a bridge within an area reserved for the toll bridge under 1798 legislation.[69] Although the new bridge was suitable only for rail traffic, the court determined that the railroad structure was still a bridge and impaired the 1798 charter. Nor was the court impressed with the fact that railroads were unknown when the original grant was made. This case is striking because it makes no allowance for advancing technology and appears to reach a conclusion opposite not only to that of other state courts but also to the later decision by the Supreme Court in *Bridge Proprietors.* Legislative efforts to modify the operation of trains at a crossing also ran afoul of the contract clause. The Supreme Judicial Court of Maine found that a statute requiring a wait at such crossing interfered with the authority of company directors and this infringed the privileges granted in the corporate charter.[70]

Clearly state courts generally embraced the strict construction principle of *Charles River Bridge*. They were adverse to implied claims of special privilege, and even where an exclusive privilege was expressly granted, they tended to read the privilege narrowly. Yet it would be a mistake to conclude that state courts were not mindful of the contract clause as a restraint on state power over charters. They repeatedly stressed that lawmakers could not revoke or amend charters absent a reservation of such authority. Moreover, state judges were prepared to enforce the explicit terms of state grants under the contract clause.

OTHER LIMITATIONS ON CHARTERS

Continuing the pattern established before Taney became chief justice, by the 1840s it was the prevalent practice for state legislatures to insert clauses in corporate charters reserving the power to alter or repeal such charters. A charter of incorporation was still a contract under *Dartmouth College*, but legislators could effectively circumvent that ruling. As the Georgia Supreme Court explained in 1857, "It has become the practice in many of the States for the Legislatures, in granting charters, to reserve the power to alter or repeal them at pleasure, thus putting them on the footing they were before the decision [in *Dartmouth College*]."[71] Not only were reservation clauses placed in individual charter grants[72] but general incorporation laws provided that every charter was subject to the reserved power of alteration or repeal by the legislature.[73] A number of states even placed such reservation clauses in their constitutions. State courts repeatedly sustained these reservations, reasoning that exercise of such power was consistent with the terms of the contract.[74] Hence there was no violation of the contract clause with respect to corporations chartered after the reservation was enacted. Because newer states often adopted reservation language at the time of admission to the Union, the issue of irrevocable monopoly privilege never arose in these jurisdictions.

The protection afforded charters under the contract clause was further diluted by the power of eminent domain. Recall that Story, dissenting in *Charles River Bridge*, recognized that a state could acquire a corporate franchise on payment of compensation. In the pioneering case of *Boston Water Power Company v. Boston and Worcester Rail Road* (1839), a railroad company to which the power of eminent domain had been delegated by the Massachusetts legislature planned to build its line through water basins owned by a water power company operating under a prior grant.[75] Chief Justice Shaw dismissed the contention that such an exercise of eminent domain impaired the obligation of contract with the water power company, pointing out that all land was subject to being taken upon payment of compensation. Other state courts agreed that the exercise of eminent domain was not confined by the contract clause. In 1843 the Supreme Court of Vermont upheld a statute authorizing the acquisition of the franchise of any turnpike company. Acknowledging that grants constitute inviolable contracts, the court nonetheless declared that the power of eminent domain was an implied reservation in all grants of land or of corporate franchises. It ruled, "This right of eminent domain will always enable the legislature to take the benefit of the grant from the grantees, for public use."[76]

These state court decisions anticipated a ruling by the Supreme Court in *West River Bridge Company v. Dix* (1848) that the contract clause did not prevent states from exercising certain essential attributes of sovereignty, such as eminent domain.[77] In 1793 Vermont granted the company the right to maintain a toll bridge for 100 years. In 1843, as part of a road improvement scheme, the state planned to convert the toll bridge into a free bridge upon payment of compensation to the company for its land and franchise. Webster, arguing for the bridge company, maintained that Vermont was destroying the force of a contract and that the power of eminent domain was subject to the contract clause. If the contract clause, he warned, "does not extend to the contracts of the State governments, and they are left to be destroyed by the eminent domain, then there is an end of public faith."[78] Rejecting Webster's contention, Justice Daniel, writing for the Court, concluded that eminent domain was "paramount to all private rights vested under the government, and these last are, by necessary implication, held in subordination to this power, and must yield in every instance to its proper exercise."[79] Eminent domain, he continued, does not interfere with "the inviolability of contracts" because all contracts are subordinate to preexisting conditions inherent in sovereignty. The contract clause, Daniel explained, was designed to prevent "the interpolation of some new term or condition foreign to the original agreement," not the exercise of inherent state authority to acquire property.[80] "A franchise," he insisted, "is property, and nothing more."[81] Consequently, a state could extricate itself from an ill-considered or outmoded corporate franchise without running afoul of the contract clause by payment of compensation. Although Daniel did not expressly address this point, commentators generally agreed that a state legislature could not enter a contract to relinquish the power of eminent domain.[82]

The spread of reservation clauses and the ruling in *West River Bridge*, coupled with the strict construction doctrine, reflected Jacksonian hostility toward corporate monopoly privilege.[83] But Taney and the majority of his colleagues were not adverse to corporate enterprise and continued to shelter express grants under the contract clause. This point becomes clear when we turn our attention to how the Court handled bank regulations and corporate tax exemptions.

POLICE POWER

Notwithstanding the increased discretion the developments discussed above allowed state lawmakers to control corporations, state courts sometimes voiced concern that the interpretation of the contract clause by the Supreme Court stifled state authority over corporate charters. Taking aim at *Dartmouth College*, the Georgia Supreme Court warned in 1857, "It is not quite certain that a period may not arrive, when there shall be cause of regret that that Court placed a construction on the constitutional powers of the States which restrict them from repealing or modifying Acts of incorporation of any sort passed by them."[84] In the same vein, a few years later Judge Byron Paine of the Wisconsin Supreme Court complained that the contract clause had "been extended to matters not within its intention, so as unwarrantably to cripple and restrict the legislative power of the States."[85]

In this context several state courts moved beyond the strict construction of corporate grants and grappled with the notion that legislators could not contract away the police power to safeguard the public health, safety, and morals. The police power was deemed inalienable and trumped the terms of any contract between the state and individuals. As the Supreme Court of Indiana stated in 1861, the legislative authority to impose safety regulations on railroads "was a police power, which resides in the law-making power in all free states, and of which the Legislature cannot divest itself even by an express grant to any private or public corporation."[86]

Courts readily sustained railroad fencing laws, brushing aside allegations that such regulations amounted to alteration of prior charters.[87] The Supreme Court of Missouri explained, "But while private charters are thus protected, it is also true that corporations, like natural persons, are subject to those regulations which the state may prescribe for the good government of the community. There is no reason why corporations should not be subject to police regulations as natural persons."[88] Application of the police power was by no means confined to railroad safety. As the antebellum prohibition movement gained momentum, courts had to address the impact of prohibition laws on antecedent contractual arrangements. The Supreme Court of Michigan held that a law prohibiting the manufacture and sale of alcoholic beverages was within the police power and did not impair preexisting contracts to sell such beverages. It declared that a party could not by means of a contract escape state regulatory authority to protect the community from injurious trades.[89] Courts were also called upon to determine the legal status of licenses to sell liquor. The Supreme Judicial Court of Massachusetts concluded that a license to sell alcoholic beverages did not constitute a contract. Declaring that a liquor license "bears no resemblance to an act of incorporation," the court viewed the license as mere permission to carry on a trade under regulation.[90] Therefore, it reasoned that a license could be modified or repealed if the legislature decided to ban all sales of such beverages.

Lotteries were also a source of contract clause litigation as states fluctuated between authorizing private parties to conduct lotteries for a variety of purposes and then seeking to suppress lotteries as a nuisance. In *Phalen v. Virginia* (1850) the Supreme Court expressed doubt that a license to operate a lottery amounted to a contract.[91] In any event the Court insisted that the state police power trumped a license to raise money by means of a lottery. It emphatically declared, "The suppression of nuisances injurious to public health or morality is among the most important duties of government. Experience has shown that the common forms of gambling are comparatively innocuous when placed in contrast with the wide-spread pestilence of lotteries."[92] Hence, even if a lottery license was viewed as a contract, a state law could retroactively limit the time within which an existing lottery must be conducted.

The embryonic concept that the contract clause did not bar an exercise of state police power would gradually evolve into a significant limit on the protection afforded agreements by the Constitution. But as long as the general understanding of the police power was confined to health, safety, and public morals there was little danger that this exception would undermine the function of the contract clause to safeguard the stability of agreements. Moreover, the cases that first developed the police power as a limitation on the contract clause involved claimed abridgments of corporate charters or legislative grants of special privileges. Not until the early twentieth century was the police power exception extended to agreements between private parties.

STATE BANK REGULATIONS

The ruling in *Charles River Bridge* did not herald an anticorporation outlook by the Taney Court or suggest a reluctance to defend corporate privileges clearly contained in their charters under the contract clause. This was demonstrated by a line of cases in which the Court, albeit by a divided vote, voided laws regulating state-charted banks as violative of the Constitution. These were the first decisions to determine that regulation of business enterprises ran afoul of the contract clause.

Banking was essential to fuel economic growth in the Antebellum Era. In the absence of a national bank or currency, state-charted banks issued notes that circulated as a kind of currency and helped to mobilize capital. Yet outspoken critics pictured banks as little better than swindlers and warned that unsound banks threatened financial ruin. So banking remained a highly contentious issue. The grants of bank charters and the enactment of laws defining their functions stirred strong emotions. Despite widespread suspicion of banks and misunderstanding of their role in the economy, state legislatures liberally created banks, often with inadequate supervision. In addition, a number of states established state-owned banks. Shifting state policies and a climate of suspicion triggered a number of cases regarding oversight of banks.

A good example of the litigation emanating out of changing bank regulations was *Planters' Bank of Mississippi v. Sharp* (1848).[93] At issue was an 1830 Mississippi charter that gave the bank authority "to receive money on deposit, and pay away the same free of expense, discount bills of exchange and notes." Ten years later the Mississippi legislature enacted a law making it unlawful for any bank to transfer any note or bill and providing that any action upon such note or bill should abate. The 1840 statute, Charles Warren explained, "was illustrative of the unsettled conditions of State banking and of the extreme hostility felt at this time towards banking corporations."[94] The Supreme Court of Mississippi warmly endorsed *Dartmouth College* and agreed that bank charters were contracts protected by the Constitution. However, it narrowly construed the charter at issue as not to encompass the power to negotiate notes.[95] Pointing out that the power to transfer notes was plainly conferred in the original charter and that such right was an "incident to its business as a bank," the Supreme Court by a vote of six to three overturned the state court decision. It determined that the 1840 measure impaired both the contract between the state and the bank and the contract between the maker of the note and the bank. "One of the tests that a contract has been impaired is," the Court observed, "that its value has by legislation been diminished. It is not by the Constitution, to be impaired at all."[96] Subsequently, however, the Supreme Court of Mississippi confined the reach of *Planters' Bank* to the immediate parties, asserting that the "nature and extent of the right under the contract depend upon the law of the State, and must be determined by its own tribunals."[97] Not only did this opinion flatly contradict Supreme Court declarations that it was the final arbiter of the existence and scope of contracts but the state court ruling underscored the willingness of some state courts to defy the Supreme Court's contract clause rulings.

Woodruff v. Trapnall (1851) involved regulations governing the affairs of a state-owned bank, the State Bank of Arkansas.[98] Organized in 1836, its charter provided that the notes of the bank should be received in payment of debts owed the state. When the bank subsequently became insolvent, the legislature repealed the section guaranteeing the acceptance of the notes. The Court majority found that the act constituted a contract between the state and the holders of bank notes and that the legislature could not impair this contract by rescinding the guaranty provision with respect to notes in circulation before the time of repeal. Lawmakers, it added, were free to repeal the section, and hence future emissions of bank notes were not covered by the contract. The insolvency of the State Bank of Arkansas set the stage for another contract clause challenge to state legislation in *Curran v. Arkansas* (1853).[99] A series of acts in the 1840s declared the assets of the bank to be vested in the state, and unpaid creditors charged that such actions impaired the obligation of contract. Writing for the Court, Justice Curtis insisted that the assets of the insolvent bank belonged to the creditors rather than the state as sole stockholder. It followed that a law withdrawing assets from the bank impaired "the obligations of the contracts of the bank, and also the obligation of the contract between the State and the creditors, arising from the provisions of the charter devoting these funds to the payment of the debts of the bank."[100] Nor was Curtis impressed with the argument that the laws affected only the remedy and did not touch the underlying cause of action. By withdrawing the property from the bank, he reasoned, the laws provided no remedy for the creditors and thus materially impaired the contract.

Shifting coalitions of justices dissented from the bank regulation decisions, but Catron and Daniel invariably disagreed with their colleagues. They denied that the legislation establishing the banks created any contracts.

TAX EXEMPTIONS

State governments in the Antebellum Era were generous in granting tax exemptions in order to attract private investment capital and stimulate economic development.[101] Such tax immunities became controversial over time. Critics maintained that tax exemptions constituted favoritism and placed an unfair burden on other taxpayers. They further argued that lawmakers could not relinquish the sovereign power of taxation. The Supreme Court, of course, had ruled in *New Jersey v. Wilson* (1812) that legislative grants of tax exemptions were within the purview of the contract clause. State courts were initially left to grapple with the question of whether a particular statute enacted only a general tax policy subject to revision as circumstances changed or amounted to a contract of exemption. Courts were clearly bothered by claims of a permanent tax exemption. In 1835 the Supreme Court of Connecticut expressed doubt about "whether a statute, exempting a particular species of property from taxation, is in the nature of a contract, of perpetual obligation."[102] The court, however, was disinclined to reopen this question apparently settled by prior authority. Likewise, the Supreme Court of New Hampshire declined to decide whether the state could grant away the taxing power but declared that no relinquishment of the taxing power could be assumed. It found no clear legislative intent to grant a permanent exemption from taxes on land held by Dartmouth College.[103] In *Herrick v. Town of Randolph* (1841) the Supreme Court of Vermont differentiated between tax exemption provisions contained in specific charters, which were deemed irrevocable, and general laws exempting certain lands from taxation.[104] The court viewed the latter as ordinary legislation that did not bind subsequent legislatures.

The Supreme Court under Taney considered the application of the contract clause to claims of tax exemption in a number of cases. The Court never questioned the underlying principle established in *Wilson*, but it addressed several related issues: Could a state legislature bargain away the taxing power? If so, had the lawmakers done so in a particular case? What was the scope of any exemption granted? Given the penchant of Taney and his colleagues for a strict reading of public grants, one would anticipate that they would be disinclined to uphold tax exemptions. Indeed, in its first tax exemption case, *Armstrong v. Athens County* (1842), the Court adopted this mode of analysis and upheld a tax in the face of contract clause objections.[105] An 1804 Ohio law vested lands in Ohio University and provided that the lands "shall be forever exempt from all state taxes." Under an 1826 law the university was authorized to sell the land, and thereafter the legislature ordered the lands to be taxed. Writing for the Court, Justice Catron sought to distinguish the decision in *Wilson* on the ground that the purchasers relied for their title on the 1826 law, which contained no tax immunity language. There is room to doubt this rationale, and the outcome likely reflected Catron's hostility to applying the contract clause to public grants of any kind.[106]

In any event, the Supreme Court soon established a pattern of enforcing clearly expressed tax exemptions under the contract clause, often over heated objections from Catron, Daniel, and Justice John A. Campbell. For example, in 1845 the Court invalidated a tax levied by Maryland upon shares of stock held by stockholders in certain banks as an impairment of contract.[107] An 1821 statute extended the charter of several banks on condition that the banks make payments for the construction of turnpikes and contribute to the school fund. In exchange, the act pledged that the state would not "impose any further tax or burden upon them during the continuance of their charters under this act." The Court readily determined that the 1821 pledge amounted to a contract and construed the exemption to apply not merely to a tax upon the franchise but to encompass a tax upon bank stockholders. Justice Wayne, who wrote for the Court, authored several opinions dealing with corporate tax exemptions and tended to view such provisions as constitutionally protected contracts.[108]

More revealing was a series of cases involving an effort by Ohio to abrogate a favorable tax concession granted to banks in order to attract capital to the state. For the first time the Court squarely addressed the question of whether a state legislature could relinquish by contract its taxing power. Because the cases raised similar issues they are best treated as a unit. An 1845 Ohio statute provided that every banking corporation organized under the act should semiannually pay a percentage of its profits, less expenses, to the state "in lieu of all taxes to which the company, or the stockholders therein, would otherwise be subject." Six years later the Ohio legislature mandated that the capital stock and funds of all banks should be taxed to the same extent as other personal property. This resulted in a higher tax levy on the Piqua Branch, and it resisted payment on ground that the act of 1851 impaired the contract in its charter. Reversing a decision of the Ohio Supreme Court, the Supreme Court in *Piqua Branch of the State Bank of Ohio v. Knoop* (1854) agreed with the bank. It determined that a state could, as an aspect of its sovereignty, make a binding contract for a special tax rate, and that such a contract "can no more be disregarded nor set aside by a subsequent legislature, than a grant for land."[109] Taney, briefly concurring, simply declared, "The words used are too plain to admit of any other construction."[110]

The decision regarding the tax on the Piqua Branch aroused bitter criticism in Ohio, and lawmakers renewed their efforts to increase taxes on banks.[111] The state adopted a new constitution in 1851, which required that all property employed in banking should be taxed at the same rate as that imposed on the property of individuals. An 1852 tax measure was enacted to effectuate this provision. When the law was challenged as an impairment of contract, the state argued in essence that the new constitution superseded the 1845 exemption act. Adhering to its decision in the *Piqua Branch* case, the Supreme Court declared, "A change of constitution cannot release a State from contracts made under a constitution which permits them to be made."[112] In short, a state could not escape its contractual obligations by constitutional amendment any more than by enacting a statute. Ohio, however, did not surrender easily. The state courts refused to follow the interpretation of the 1845 act as a contract adopted by the Supreme Court, and litigation dragged on until the Civil War Era. In *Jefferson Branch Bank v. Skelly* (1862) Wayne authored yet another opinion upholding the tax exemption.[113] Showing signs of fatigue with this issue, he stressed that the tax power had been explicitly relinquished with respect to this group of banks and was disinclined to reopen the constitutional question.

Although the Court majority consistently determined that tax immunities explicitly contained in grants should be enforced under the contract clause, individual justices sometimes differed over whether a particular provision in a charter amounted to a contract. Thus, in *Ohio Life Insurance and Trust Company v. Debolt* (1854), Taney, who invariably voted with the majority in the Ohio tax cases, found that a corporation chartered in 1834 could not claim a tax exemption under the 1845 act. Consequently, taxing the institution on the same basis as other property did not impair the obligation of contract.[114] Taney made several gestures to state sovereignty, stressing that states were free, if permitted by their constitutions, to grant binding tax concessions whenever they thought it proper. Noting that "contracts are sometimes incautiously made by States as well as individuals," he pointed out that the states were "the best judges of what is for their own interest."[115] "When a contract is made," he cautioned, "the Constitution of the United States acts upon it, and declares that it shall not be impaired, and makes it the duty of this court to carry it into execution. That duty must be performed."[116] The Supreme Court would not set aside "injurious" agreements made by states. In interpreting the 1834 grant language, Taney invoked the strict construction rule of *Charles River Bridge.* His opinion, however, did not command a majority of the Court. Catron, Campbell, and Daniel concurred on the very different ground that a state could not make a tax concession that would bind future legislatures. Four justices dissented, contending that there was a contract regarding tax rates.

As noted above, Catron, Campbell, and Daniel consistently rejected the position that explicit grants of tax exemption were contracts protected by the Constitution. Their views merit careful consideration. Seeing a threat to states' rights, the three marshaled a variety of arguments to deny that a state legislature could irrevocably bargain away its taxing authority. Daniel assailed the "suicidal doctrine, which confers upon one legislature, the creatures and limited agents of the sovereign people, by a breach of duty and by transcending the commission with which they are clothed, to bind forever and irrevocably their creator."[117] Citing *West River Bridge,* Catron insisted that "the essential attributes of sovereignty[,] the right of eminent domain and the right of taxation[,] are not distinguishable." A legislature, he continued, could not relinquish the power of taxation just as it could not "cede away the sovereign right of eminent domain."[118] The three dissenters painted a dark picture of corporate machinations without effective state control. Catron warned against "the unparalleled increase of corporations throughout the Union within the last few years; the ease with which charters, containing exclusive exemptions and privileges are obtained; the vast amount of property, power, and exclusive benefits, prejudicial to other classes of society that are vested in and held by these numerous bodies of associated wealth."[119] Similarly, Campbell expressed concern about "the sly and stealthy arts to which State legislatures are exposed, and the greedy appetites of adventurers, for monopolies and immunities from the State right of government."[120] He warned that the consequence of upholding the Ohio bank tax exemptions would be "a new element of alienation and discord between the different classes of society, and the introduction of a fresh cause of disturbance in our distracted political and social system." Campbell asserted that corporations "display a love of power, a preference for corporate interests to moral or political principles or public duties, and an antagonism to individual freedom, which have marked them as objects of jealousy in every epoch of their history."[121] As one scholar has cogently observed, these "opinions read as if inspired by an agrarian (or prebourgeois) fear of northern corporate power."[122]

This strident anticorporation rhetoric reflected a deep fear that protection of business corporations under the contract clause was undermining state self-governance. Seeing the modification of *Dartmouth College* by the strict construction doctrine of *Charles River Bridge* as inadequate to safeguard state control over internal affairs, Campbell, Catron, and Daniel contended that corporate charters should not be treated as contracts at all. This was outside the main currents of the Taney Court's contract clause jurisprudence, which never challenged Marshall's seminal rulings that public contracts were within the purview of the contract clause and was content to rely upon the principle of strict construction of charters. It is noteworthy that Campbell (Alabama), Catron (Tennessee), and Daniel (Virginia) were southerners. As the sectional crisis over slavery mounted in the 1850s, the debate over the contract clause and corporations might well have been a surrogate for the more divisive slavery issue.[123] Increasingly any exercise of federal authority was suspect. Decisions that might have looked unremarkable under other circumstances were now seen as dangerous. Whatever their motives, however, Campbell, Catron, and Daniel highlighted a seeming paradox in contract clause jurisprudence: states could enter binding contracts to limit the taxing power but not to cede the power of eminent domain. Yet both were aspects of sovereignty. The dissenters were also harbingers of renewed attacks on the *Dartmouth College* doctrine in the late nineteenth century. Their views would reappear in later cases involving the exercise of the police power.

Notwithstanding the impassioned pleas of the three dissenters and the reservations of scholars, by the end of the Taney era it was well settled that states could relinquish the taxing power by contract and that the federal courts would uphold such arrangements under the contract clause.[124] The Ohio bank cases called into question the notion advanced by some scholars that the Taney Court clearly differentiated between public and private contracts.[125] The upshot of these cases, the Supreme Court of Pennsylvania lamented in 1860, was "to place the taxing power of the state governments at the disposal of contracting parties." The court added that the legislature "holds the taxing power, and therefore may bargain it away, precisely as they hold and may grant the power of corporate franchises."[126]

A number of state courts experienced little difficulty in sustaining tax exemptions and limitations expressly granted to banks, other corporations, or purchasers of land.[127] Nonetheless, the argument that the taxing power was an aspect of sovereignty with which the legislature could not part was also raised at the state level. Some courts found this reasoning persuasive. In 1857 the Supreme Court of Vermont acknowledged the existence of ample precedent to the contrary but expressed doubt that a legislature could "abridge the general power of every sovereign to impose taxes."[128] Yet the reaction of state courts to this contention was somewhat mixed. The Supreme Court of Arkansas flatly rejected it, pointing to a long line of authorities.[129] The Supreme Court of Pennsylvania, in contrast, was more receptive and labored to vindicate state taxing authority in the face of exemption claims. In 1852 it stressed the essential nature of the taxing power and pointed out that, as a practical matter, to exempt some from the payment of taxes increased the burden of others. The court applied the strict construction doctrine to disallow a claimed tax exemption where there was no stipulation for an exemption in the charter.[130] Eight years later the Pennsylvania Supreme Court emphasized "how unsatisfactory" the Ohio cases were "to several state courts." It determined that the Supreme Court tax exemption decisions were inapplicable because the general banking law allowed the legislature to alter charters. Hence, a tax law enacted pursuant to the reserved power passed constitutional muster without questioning Supreme Court rulings.[131]

PRIVATE CONTRACTS

Although the Supreme Court during Taney's tenure somewhat qualified the range of protection afforded certain public grants, it rigorously invoked the contract clause to safeguard the rights of parties under private agreements.

DEBTORS AND CREDITORS

Notwithstanding the prohibition of the contract clause, state legislatures in the Antebellum Era continued to enact a variety of laws to alleviate the burden of debtors. As one scholar explained, "Postponements in the legal process of debt collection tended to multiply during periods of severe deflation. Democratically elected state governments had a penchant for passing debt relief legislation when widespread economic distress followed events like the panic of 1819 or the economic revulsions of the late 1830s."[132] Unsurprisingly, a new round of such laws was enacted during the depressed years following the Panic of 1837. These measures halted judicial sales of mortgaged property unless the bids reached a set percentage of the appraised value, enlarged the redemption rights of mortgagors, permitted the payment of debts in installments, and increased the exemption of personal property from seizure from debts. Purporting to affect the remedy rather than the contract, they were designed to make the collection of debts and foreclosure of mortgages more difficult. Application of such laws to obligations incurred before the measures were enacted set the stage for protracted litigation in both federal and state courts.

At issue in the leading case of *Bronson v. Kinzie* (1843) was the validity of two Illinois debt-relief statutes enacted in the wake of the Panic of 1837.[133] One statute barred foreclosure sales of mortgaged land for less than two-thirds of the appraised price of such land set by disinterested householders. Lawmakers evidently reasoned that householders would fix a value sufficiently high to prevent the sale. The other law gave a mortgagor the right to redeem the foreclosed premises for a year after the sale.[134] Because these laws operated retrospectively, the mortgagee of an instrument executed before the passage of the laws challenged them as an impairment of the obligation of contract.

As discussed above, Taney in *Bronson* agreed that states had some room to modify contractual remedies, but he insisted that there were definite limits to this power. Taney broadly endorsed the purpose of the contract clause. In forceful language reminiscent of Marshall, Taney stressed the importance of the provision:

> It was undoubtedly adopted as a part of the Constitution for a great and useful purpose. It was to maintain the integrity of contracts, and to secure their faithful execution throughout the Union, by placing them under the protection of the Constitution of the United States. And it would but ill become this court, under any circumstances, to depart from the plain meaning of the words used, and to sanction a distinction between the right and the remedy, which would render this provision illusive and nugatory, mere words of form, affording no protection and producing no practical result.[135]

He found that the redemption law went beyond mere alteration of remedies and acted directly on the contract, placing new and onerous conditions on the mortgagee. Likewise the appraisal law was constitutionally infirm. Pointing out that the mortgage instrument contained express language authorizing the mortgagee to foreclose on the property in the event of a payment default, Taney explained that the consequence of the appraisal law was "to deprive the party of his pre-existing right to foreclose the mortgage by a sale of the premises and to impose conditions which would frequently render any sale altogether impossible."[136] He struck down both Illinois laws as unconstitutional impairments of contract.[137]

Throughout his *Bronson* opinion Taney carefully considered the practical implications of the challenged laws on the conduct of business. He correctly perceived that the drastic overhaul of available remedies, in effect, destroyed the substantive rights under the contract. Charles Warren characterized *Bronson* as "a decision which carried Marshall's view of obligation of contract even further than Marshall had himself."[138] Whereas Marshall had sought to separate right and remedy, Taney saw that contractual rights and remedies were intertwined. Indeed, the *Bronson* opinion raised anew the question of whether the distinction between right and remedy was tenable. Such an inquiry focuses on the form of the legislative change rather than the impact on the rights of the parties. In *Bronson* Taney at least partially rejected this approach by concentrating on the practical results of the laws. But it remained unclear how to determine when an alteration of remedy undercut contractual rights.[139] In any event, the *Bronson* opinion guided the subsequent decisions of federal and state courts regarding debt-relief laws until the 1930s.

Dissenting alone, Justice McLean invoked the reasoning of Marshall in *Sturges* and denied that the remedy was part of the contract protected by the Constitution. He pointed out that states could abolish imprisonment for debt as a remedy for the enforcement of contracts entered into before enactment of the ban. "Every contract," he argued, "is entered into with a supposed knowledge by the parties, that the law-making power may modify the remedy. And this it may do, at its discretion, so far as it acts only on the remedy."[140] McLean showed no appreciation for the fact that, under his narrow reading, states could circumvent the contract clause by retroactively changing available remedies and making the collection of debts virtually impossible. Nor did he ponder the adverse impact of his reasoning on credit markets or attempt to reconcile his approach with the evident intent of the framers to secure contractual rights. Still, in a sense he anticipated post–New Deal jurisprudence that weakened the protective function of the contract clause.[141]

A year later the Supreme Court, in another case involving the same 1841 Illinois appraisal law, strongly affirmed *Bronson* and applied its doctrine where there was no contractual provision authorizing a foreclosure sale.[142] The Court made clear that the law in existence when a contract was made formed part of the contract and that it made no difference whether the right to foreclose was conferred by the contract itself or by law. It explained that *Bronson* was decided "on the broad and general principle" that a state could not enact a subsequent law that impaired the right to conduct a sale by superimposing conditions that effectively prevented such a sale. Otherwise, the Court warned, a state could prohibit a sale for less than the entire appraisal value.

Subsequent decisions by the Taney Court adhered to *Bronson* and continued to vindicate the rights of creditors. In an opinion by Catron the justices invalidated the retroactive application of an Indiana appraisal law. Catron ruled that the appraisal law changed the contract and that the new conditions placed on the mortgagee seeking to foreclose affected the substance of the agreement. He observed that the legislature could not alter the contract by "impairing or defeating the obligation under the guise of regulating the remedy."[143] Likewise, late in Taney's tenure the Court relied on *Bronson* to find that a law extending the period of mortgage redemption to two years ran afoul of the contract clause when applied to a mortgage executed before passage of the act.[144]

It is important to bear in mind that most challenges to the validity of debt-relief measures were heard in state courts. Thus, any assessment of the impact of the contract clause in the field of debtor-creditor relations must take account of how state judges handled such claims. One might speculate that state judges were more likely than federal judges to be influenced by local political pressure and sustain relief legislation. The record, although mixed, does not bear out this assumption.

State courts by and large followed the lead of the Supreme Court and invalidated a host of laws that hampered the foreclosure of mortgages or the collection of debts as applied to antecedent contracts.[145] Although such relief laws ostensibly pertained only to the remedy, state courts often found that they in fact impaired the substantive rights of the parties under the contracts. Relying on *Bronson,* several state courts struck down appraisal laws as violations of the contract clause.[146] In the same vein, they looked skeptically at laws creating or enlarging a redemption period for foreclosed property[147] or for land sold for unpaid taxes.[148] Likewise, a law delaying a mortgagee's right to possession under a defaulted mortgage until the redemption period had expired was held to add additional expense and undermine his security in the premises.[149]

Other relief measures were also deemed to run afoul of the contract clause.[150] In the 1850s many farmers in Wisconsin mortgaged their land to purchase railroad stock in an effort to encourage rail development. When the railroads defaulted following the Panic of 1857 the farmers faced foreclosure, and the legislature responded with a series of statutes calculated to make it difficult for the security holders to foreclosure on mortgaged land. The Supreme Court of Wisconsin declared most of these laws void under the contract clause.[151] For example, it invalidated a fraud-defense act providing that a mortgagor could allege that the mortgage was obtained by fraud and that a jury finding of fraud was binding on even an innocent assignee claiming bona fide status. The court declared "that the legislature cannot interfere with, or impair the obligations of past contracts, by declaring, that as against persons not previously affected by them, certain facts, if set up in the pleadings, and established in evidence, shall be a defense and operate to defeat actions brought to enforce them. It seems a hidden way of attempting to accomplish indirectly that which it was felt could not be done directly."[152] It also struck down an act requiring that a foreclosure action could not proceed until all the testimony desired to be used at trial was taken out of court before a named referee. "All of its provisions," the court concluded, "disclose an intention on the part of the legislature, so to interpose obstacles and delays in the way of foreclosing this class of mortgages, as to leave the creditor without any substantial remedy."[153] Speaking in broad terms, the Supreme Court of Iowa expressed concern that "the legislatures of this country are often betrayed into the enactment of laws striking at the remedy in a manner that threatens the inviolability of the obligation of contracts."[154]

Nonetheless, state court decisions on debt-relief laws were far from uniform, and some courts reached conclusions seemingly at odds with *Bronson* and its progeny. In so doing they narrowly construed rulings by the Supreme Court and maintained that the relief laws pertained only to the remedy. The Supreme Court of Pennsylvania, for example, upheld a statute prohibiting execution sales of property for less than two-thirds of the appraised value. The court attempted to distinguish prior Supreme Court decisions by pointing out that the stay in execution was limited to one year. Admitting that the case was "by no means a clear one," the Pennsylvania court felt that the act "appears not to be so unreasonable as to call for judicial interposition."[155] Other stay laws were also held to pass constitutional muster. In 1858 the Wisconsin legislature, as part of its response to the farm-mortgage struggle, enacted a statute providing that a defendant in a mortgage foreclosure action should have six months in which to answer and further that there could be no execution sale of mortgaged premises except upon six months' notice. The effect of the law was to extend every mortgage for one year. The Wisconsin Supreme Court treated this as a reasonable modification of the remedy in view of "the financial situation of the country." The court stressed that the mortgagee retained the same remedy as before the act, the "only difference being that it was less expeditious."[156] As these cases indicate, the test for ascertaining a contract clause violation appeared to be that the change in remedy was deemed reasonable by the courts.

State courts endorsed other relief measures as well. Texas had long had a reputation as a haven for debtors, dating from its period as an independent republic, and the legal climate was sympathetic to their plight. Reflecting that spirit, the Supreme Court of Texas sustained an appraisal law on grounds that the law was enacted before Texas joined the United States and hence was not barred by the contract clause.[157] Even more striking, the Supreme Court of Alabama found no constitutional objection to applying a two-year period of redemption from sales on execution to antecedent contracts.[158] Likewise, the Supreme Court of Minnesota sustained application of a law extending the period of redemption for three years and allowing the mortgagor to remain in possession for that time to prior mortgages. It explained that the legislature might change remedies at its discretion, adding that "the mere fact that the new remedy is less convenient than the old one, or renders the recovery of debts more tardy and difficult, does not by itself render it unconstitutional."[159] These decisions appear to be in direct conflict with the Supreme Court's rulings and suggest that some state courts simply ignored the Supreme Court in the face of public sentiment strongly favoring debt relief. There was enough state court reluctance to adhere to *Bronson* and its progeny to cause the Supreme Court of California in 1854 to admonish its sister states. "Some of the new States," it lectured, "have, however, persisted in times of depression, when pecuniary distress became general, in the endeavor to avoid the obligations of contracts, by delaying the creditor through redemption, exemption, and limitation laws, and the Courts of those states have endeavored to sustain them, but in no case, that I find, by sound reasoning." The California court warned against the "radical spirit infused into the minds of men in hours of trouble, which in years past influenced to some extent legislative power in different States."[160]

In addition to foreclosure actions, state lawmakers turned their attention to postponing the collection of unsecured debts. In 1861, for instance, the Pennsylvania legislature passed a stay law that required courts to halt executions against a debtor's property when creditors representing two-thirds of the entire indebtedness agreed to the stay of execution. Describing this as "a very extraordinary enactment" that allowed for a stay of unlimited duration, the Supreme Court of Pennsylvania struck down this "novel and dangerous legislation" as an impairment of contractual rights under both the federal and state constitutions.[161]

Laws exempting items of personal property, such as clothing, household furniture, farm animals, and trade tools, from debt collection were another source of controversy. In passing these laws state legislators were animated by the desire to protect debtors and their families from total impoverishment. By 1845 personal property exemptions were widespread, even though they curbed the ability of creditors to recover debts. In *Bronson* Taney had observed that a state could direct that necessary articles were not subject to execution, and that a state could shape such relief "according to its own views of policy and humanity." This language did not make clear, however, whether acts exempting personal property could be applied retroactively or were confined to debts incurred subsequent to passage of the laws.

State courts were generally sympathetic to exemption laws, brushing aside contract clause challenges on grounds that the exemptions pertained only to the remedy. In 1838 the Supreme Judicial Court of Massachusetts declared, "It would not be contended (as we suppose) that the legislature may not lawfully exempt a part of the property of a debtor from attachment on mesne process or levy on execution; for example, articles of furniture, beds and bedding, &c. necessary for the debtor and his family. To that extent the remedy to enforce payment is diminished rightfully."[162] The New York Court of Appeals ruled that a statutory exemption of "necessary household furniture and working tools and team owned by any person being a householder or having a family for which he provides" to the value of $150 was valid as applied to antecedent contracts.[163] It stressed that New York had long exempted certain items of personal property from the reach of creditors. Likewise, the Supreme Court of Michigan held that a law exempting a farmer's yoke of cattle did not impair the obligation of contract as applied to the collection of prior debts.[164] Both the New York and Michigan courts assumed that Taney's intimation about exemption laws covered contracts made before as well as after their passage and sought to distinguish *Bronson* and *McCracken* on grounds that those cases concerned only mortgage appraisal laws.[165]

The Panic of 1837 was likely also a catalyst for the adoption by Texas of the first law extending an exemption from creditors to a family homestead. A number of states soon followed suit. Homestead exemption laws, designed to enhance the security of a debtor's family, were complex and varied widely from state to state. Politically attractive, homestead exemptions were rarely controversial and generated little litigation before the Civil War. As we shall see, however, retroactive application of homestead exemptions to antecedent debts during the Reconstruction Era aroused bitter controversy and prompted arguments that such laws impaired the obligation of contracts.

Vigorous enforcement of the contract clause in the face of debtor-protection legislation might well have played an indirect role in strengthening the property rights of married women. At common law the property that a wife brought to her marriage passed to the control of her husband and could be reached by his creditors. In the mid-nineteenth century, however, states began to pass married women's property acts that provided that the real and personal property of a wife should continue as her separate estate. Hence, in a volatile market economy, a wife's property would no longer be liable for her husband's debts. Mississippi enacted the first such law in 1839. After *Bronson* closed the door on other types of relief laws in 1843, a number of states were motivated to enact married women's property acts. These measures had the effect of placing at least some family property beyond the reach of the husband's creditors without running afoul of the contract clause.[166]

BANKRUPTCY LAWS

Congressional power to enact a bankruptcy system remained dormant, except for brief periods, until the end of the nineteenth century. Absent a national law, states continued to adopt insolvency legislation. Not only did such measures vary greatly from state to state but under the Supreme Court decision in *Ogden v. Saunders* (1827) state insolvency laws could not discharge obligations owed to residents of other states. In view of these defects, many, such as Story, argued that state insolvency laws were insufficient. To their mind the obvious solution to inconsistent and piecemeal state relief laws, as well as recurring contract clause litigation, was a national bankruptcy law. The expanding scope of commercial transactions and growing trade across state lines highlighted the need for a bankruptcy law with uniform application throughout the nation.

Spurred by the Panic of 1837, Congress again enacted a bankruptcy measure. But the 1841 law was even more short-lived than its predecessor of 1800–1803. Bitterly assailed by advocates of states' rights, the 1841 law proved a disappointment to creditors and debtors alike. Debtors, for instance, were upset that the bankruptcy measure eliminated state laws exempting certain personal property from attachment. It was repealed after being in operation for barely a year.[167] With its repeal, contracting parties were relegated to the state debt-relief systems as confined by the contract clause, which barred retroactive interference with agreements.

Of course, the contract clause did not pertain to national legislation. Indeed, federal courts acknowledged that Congress could grant more complete relief to debtors than could the states. Pointing out that the states could not apply insolvency laws to past contracts, the Supreme Court observed in 1848, "Congress alone can do this as to prior contracts, by means of an express permission in the Constitution to pass uniform laws on the subject of bankruptcy, and which laws, when not restrained by any constitution or clause like this as to States impairing contracts, may in that way be made to reach past obligations."[168]

ALTERATION OF CONTRACTUAL TERMS

Most state legislation to modify the position of contracting parties was phrased in terms of remedial reform in an effort to avoid negation under the contract clause. As the record demonstrates, this strategy was only partially successful. State lawmakers, however, sometimes operated directly on the subject matter of a contract itself as distinct from altering the existing remedies. Courts had less difficulty in striking down laws that changed the terms and conditions of the contract. The New York Court of Appeals explained, "The most obvious method by which a contract may be impaired by legislation, would be the alteration of some of its terms or provisions, so that, assuming the validity of the law, the parties would be relieved from something which they had contracted to do, or would be obligated to do something which the contract did not originally require."[169]

Nonetheless, a few state laws attempted to, in effect, rewrite agreements. For example, a Georgia law that altered the terms of a prior state land sale and imposed a forfeiture of the land for failure to obtain the grant within a set period ran afoul of the contract clause. Writing for the Georgia Supreme Court, Justice Lumpkin observed, "It is conceded, that the contract cannot be enlarged or abridged, or saddled with conditions not expressed in the contract, except by mutual consent of both parties to the agreement; and that any law having this tendency, is unconstitutional and a nullity."[170]

Similarly, the Supreme Court of California found that an act requiring all persons with existing claims against the treasurer of a county that was being divided to present those claims by a certain date or be forever barred from enforcing payment impaired the obligation of contract. It reasoned that the legislature could not impose new conditions on preexisting creditors.[171]

A legislative move to change interest rates also gave rise to a contract clause challenge. The Supreme Court of Florida ruled that a law reducing the legal rate of interest could not be applied to an antecedent debt. The parties, the court determined, contracted with reference to the law as it existed at the time, and consequently "no statute altering the rate of interest can be made to affect contracts entered into before its passage."[172]

LANDLORD-TENANT RELATIONS

The contract clause also had important implications for the relationship of landlord and tenant. This was vividly demonstrated by the pivotal role played by the provision in the anti-rent war that engulfed New York's Hudson River Valley between 1839 and the Civil War. The origins of the controversy can be traced to the vast patroonships introduced by Dutch settlers in the seventeenth century. Rather than sell land outright, the patrons entered into perpetual leases of farms in exchange for annual rent and periodic services. Tenants were also required to pay fees if they sold their leases outside the family. Dissatisfaction with this arrangement, which had smoldered since the late colonial period, erupted into the anti-rent movement when in 1839 landlords attempted to collect back rent. Anti-rent militants sometimes resorted to violence to enforce a rent strike and to frustrate recovery of rent by officials. On several occasions governors called out the militia to restore order.[173]

Governor William H. Seward was sympathetic to the tenants and urged the legislature to find an appropriate means of extinguishing the perpetual leases, which he saw as a remnant of feudalism. But almost at once the contract clause loomed as a formidable barrier to elimination of the leases, which were clearly contracts within the protection of the Constitution. As one historian has noted, "The principle underlying the Contract Clause had become a cultural norm, not merely a juristic one, during the early nineteenth century."[174] Gulian C. Verplanck, a prominent New York political figure, spoke for many when he observed in 1838 that the contract clause "and the series of wise and salutary decisions under it . . . form the most important safeguard of the rights of industry and labor possessed by the American citizen."[175]

The legislature inconclusively debated proposals to abolish the manorial tenancies, including a suggestion to employ the power of eminent domain, for years. Critics of reform proposals repeatedly cited the contract clause as a hurdle to change. Obviously a legislative move to directly eliminate the manorial leases would go well beyond just a modification of available remedies and would almost certainly violate the Constitution. So legislators considered a variety of indirect attacks on the legal position of the landlords but were careful not to deprive landlords of all remedies for the recovery of back rent.

The common law right of landlords to collect unpaid rent by means of distress was a particular source of controversy. When notified of an arrearage of rent payable to the landlord, the sheriff could enter the leased premises, seize any goods or chattels found there, and conduct a summary sale of the seized property to satisfy the rent obligation. This extraordinary remedy was applicable to no other contracts than those arising from the landlord-tenant relationship. Hoping to improve the bargaining position of the tenants, the legislature in 1846 abolished the right of distress and substituted an action of ejectment to recover possession of the premises for unpaid rent. The New York Court of Appeals sustained this as applied to leases made before the law was enacted, picturing the law as a mere alteration of remedy that did not affect the contractual obligations of the tenant.[176] Yet this reform fell short of addressing the fundamental problem of the perpetual leases.

The complex and tangled story of the anti-rent movement cannot be reviewed in detail here. Ultimately neither the political or legal system was able to provide meaningful relief to the tenants.[177] Eventually economic pressures persuaded the landlords to sell their holdings to raise cash. For our purposes the crucial point is to recognize the extent to which the contract clause, and a legal culture supportive of contracts, limited the options available to the legislature. Without doubt the contract clause had an impact on the formulation of public policy in New York.

MARRIAGE AND DIVORCE

The implications of the contract clause for the grant of divorces were unsettled in the Antebellum Era. The potential application of the provision to marriage and divorce raised two fundamental questions: (1) Was marriage a contract within the meaning of the Constitution? and (2) Should divorce be seen as a remedy for breach of a marriage contract?[178]

In the colonial period divorce was rare and was generally regarded as a matter for the legislature. After the Revolution some states continued the practice of legislative divorce by passing private acts to terminate marriages. Other states began to enact general laws specifying the grounds for divorce and authorizing courts to dissolve marriages based on evidence produced at trial. Over time judicial divorce gradually replaced legislative divorce.

The Supreme Court never considered the impact of the contract clause on the dissolution of marriage. However, as discussed in Chapter 2, there was early authority that the contract clause did not bar the grant of divorces. Recall that in *Dartmouth College* Marshall opined that the provision "never has been understood to embrace other contracts, than those which respect property, or some object of value. . . . It has never been understood to restrict the general right of the legislature to legislate on the subject of divorces. Those acts enable some tribunal, not to impair a marriage contract, but to liberate one of the parties because it has been broken by the other."[179] Here Marshall would seem to suggest that the contract clause did not apply to marriages. He also appears to be speaking in terms of judicial divorce based on a finding of fault. In his concurring opinion Story took a somewhat different tack. Treating marriage as a contract subject to the Constitution, he asserted, "A *general* law regulating divorces from the contract of marriage, like a law regulating remedies in other cases of breaches of contracts, is not necessarily a law *impairing the obligation of such a contract.* It may be the only effectual mode of enforcing the obligations of the contract on both sides."[180] Yet Story expressed doubt that a legislative divorce without breach of the marriage contract would be valid under the contract clause. The observations by both of these jurists, as courts and commentators repeatedly noted, were mere dicta entitled to no precedential weight. Nonetheless, state courts often looked to these comments for guidance.

Moreover, James Kent clearly affirmed the authority of the states to grant divorces, declaring, "It has generally been considered that the state governments have complete control and discretion" over the dissolution of marriages. He felt that "in ordinary cases the constitutionality of the laws of divorce, in the respective states, is not to be questioned."[181] Kent correctly anticipated the developing pattern of cases dealing with marriage and the contract clause.

A number of state courts examined the contractual nature of marriage in cases that considered divorce actions as well as legislative efforts to strengthen the property rights of married women.

A New York court found that the marriage relationship was not a contract "in the full common law sense of the term" but rather a civil institution. It ruled that the relationship of marriage was not within the purview of the contract clause. In reaching this conclusion, the court gave weight to the long-standing practice in many states of legislative grants of divorce.[182] Most state courts took similar positions. They too stressed the long-standing practice of legislative divorce and found that a marriage contract was unlike commercial contracts.[183] In 1857 the Supreme Court of Indiana aptly summed up the dominant view, insisting that "the practice of this country has determined that marriage, as a contract, is not within the protection of the United States constitution."[184] Pointing to Marshall's language, it stressed that marriage was a status and was not primarily about property. In addition, the court stated that both general divorce laws and special legislative acts dissolving marriage had been enacted in most states.

Despite this trend, at least one state followed a different path. The Supreme Court of Florida, invoking the analysis advanced by Story, stated that there was "no reason why the word contract, as used in the constitution, should be restricted to those of a pecuniary nature, and not embrace that of marriage."[185] It concluded that divorce in Florida was a judicial act and that legislation dissolving a marriage unconstitutionally impaired the obligation of contract. But this approach found few adherents. By 1868 Thomas M. Cooley could report that "laws permitting the dissolution of the contract of marriage are not within the intention" of the contract clause "seems to be the prevailing opinion."[186] Indeed, the number of divorces steadily grew throughout the nineteenth century, and the contract clause was largely irrelevant to this trend.

JUDICIAL IMPAIRMENT OF CONTRACTS

The question of a judicial impairment of contracts has perplexed both courts and commentators.[187] Recall that the Supreme Court under Taney insisted that it had the authority to decide both whether a contract existed and whether a state law impaired such contract. State court determinations on these points were not conclusive. A more vexing problem was posed where there was no retroactive legislation but a judicial decision reversing an earlier ruling and in effect destroying a contract. Could such a judicial decision run afoul of the contract clause? Does the term "law" in the clause encompass judicial as well as legislative interference with agreements? In assessing these inquiries one should consider both the language and the purpose of the contract clause.

The clause declares that no state shall "pass any law" impairing the obligation of contract. If emphasis is placed upon the word "pass" the reach of the provision is seemingly restricted to state legislation. Only legislators "pass" laws. On the other hand, if the term "law" is highlighted the clause might readily be construed to cover judicial decisions because courts as well as legislators make "law." In addition to textual analysis, a functional approach indicates that the clause could extend to judicial decisions overruling prior adjudications. The overarching purpose of the contract clause was to protect existing agreements from retroactive abridgment.[188] With respect to the contracting parties, it makes little sense to distinguish between a change in judicial interpretation and a change in legislation. From their perspective the impact is much the same regardless of which branch of state government is involved.[189]

In 1847 counsel arguing before the Supreme Court urged a broad reading of the contract clause. To make this constitutional provision effective, he maintained, "it must operate, not only where its violation is the result of the direct language of the law, but wherever the law is so applied by that branch of the State government—its judiciary—which enforces the law, as to produce this result, to violate this prohibition." He added, "The language of the constitution itself is more comprehensive than if it meant to prohibit an infringement of its provision by mere legislative 'act'; it seems to use the term 'law' in a broader sense, as if it was the complete and sovereign action of a State."[190] The Court unanimously rejected this argument, reasoning that state courts were to construe state statutes and their interpretations, even if mistaken, not subject to review. "The power delegated to us," the Court explained, "is for the restraint of unconstitutional legislation by the States, and not for the correction of alleged errors committed by their judiciary."[191] Yet this case did not involve the destruction of a contract by overruling a prior decision.

Subsequent decisions indicated that the Supreme Court was prepared to uphold the validity of preexisting contracts and, if necessary, to ignore state court decisions. At issue in *Rowan v. Runnels* (1847) was a clause in the Mississippi Constitution barring the introduction of slaves into the state for purposes of sale as of May 1833. In 1841 the Supreme Court held that the clause by its own force did prevent such importation of slaves and that a slave sales contract made before an 1837 state law effectuated the ban was valid and binding.[192] Thereafter the Mississippi Supreme Court ruled that the constitutional provision by itself, without implementing legislation, effectively barred the introduction of slaves for sale. In a diversity of citizenship suit brought by a citizen of Virginia to recover on notes given in connection with an 1836 slave contract, the Supreme Court declined to follow the Mississippi decision and enforced the agreement. Conceding that the Court must respect decisions of state courts regarding their constitution and laws, Taney, writing for the Court, nonetheless maintained, "We ought not to give to them a retroactive effect, and allow them to render invalid contracts entered with citizens of other States, which in the judgment of this court were lawfully made."[193] In his opinion the chief justice never referred to the contract clause and was apparently motivated to preserve the federal forum for citizens of other states in diversity actions who might have relied on the federal judgment. Moreover, the Supreme Court of Mississippi had not reversed a prior decision, only disagreed with the Supreme Court's conclusion. Presumably the state court's opinion would be binding in any future litigation. But Taney's language, although dictum, opened the door for the Supreme Court to decline to follow other judicial rulings that made changes in state law voiding contracts when the Court felt that the agreements were valid.

Taney explored further the matter of judicial impairment of contracts in the *Debolt* decision, one of the Ohio bank tax exemption cases treated above. This case involved an appeal of a state court ruling that rejected a contract clause claim. In his opinion Taney observed:

> The duty imposed upon this court to enforce contracts honestly and legally made, would be vain and nugatory, if we were bound to follow those changes in judicial decisions which the lapse of time, and the change in judicial officers, will often produce. And the sound and true rule is, that if the contract when made was valid by the laws of the State, as then expounded by all the departments of its government, and administered in its courts of justice, its validity and obligation cannot be impaired by any subsequent act of the legislature of the State, or decision of its courts, altering the construction of the law.[194]

This language, equating state legislation and judicial decisions as sources of possible contractual abridgment, is certainly susceptible to a broad application. Although Taney spoke only for himself and Justice Grier, two other justices agreed that a state court could not nullify a contract by overturning a long-accepted construction of the state constitution.[195] So at least four justices were receptive to the notion of judicial impairment.

The Supreme Court took a major step in that direction in *Gelpcke v. City of Dubuque* (1864), a case decided late in Taney's tenure as chief justice.[196] The case grew out of the widespread practice in the Antebellum Era of state and local governments granting financial assistance to railroads. As these governments incurred sizeable debts to encourage railroad construction, some states adopted constitutional provisions to curtail this practice. The Iowa Constitution of 1846, for instance, barred the state from becoming a stockholder and limited state indebtedness. In 1853, however, the Iowa Supreme Court upheld the authority of counties to issue bonds to help finance railroad projects.[197] This ruling was reaffirmed several times, and during the 1850s voters in many Iowa localities endorsed such aid. Railroad bonds usually traded in the eastern credit markets, and most bond purchasers were from eastern states or Europe. Dissatisfaction with the slow pace of construction and allegations of fraud caused public sentiment regarding railroad bonds to gradually shift. Mirroring this attitudinal change, the Iowa Supreme Court in *State v. County of Wapello* (1862) reversed its earlier ruling and held that the legislature had no power under the state constitution to empower localities to issue bonds to subscribe for railroad stock.[198] It reasoned that the constitutional ban was intended to protect the state as well as its political subdivisions from heavy indebtedness. The upshot was to repudiate bonds now in the hands of bona fide investors. Aware that this outcome could seem unjust, the court ended on a defensive note: "We are not insensible that in so doing, at this late day, we are liable to expose ourselves and our people to the charge of insincerity and bad faith, and perhaps that which is still worse, inflict a great wrong upon innocent creditors and bondholders. . . . Yet it is one of those unfortunate misadventures which sometimes will happen in the best governed and best intentioned communities."[199] One scholar has slammed these remarks as "crocodile tears" and a "piece of hypocrisy" because the judges of the Iowa Supreme Court must have known that under their ruling the bonds would not be paid.[200]

A group of foreign investors, not content with expressions of goodwill, brought suit in federal court in Iowa based on diversity jurisdiction to recover interest on the bonds. The lower federal court invoked the Iowa Supreme Court decision invalidating the bonds and dismissed the action. On appeal, the attorney for the bondholders stressed that the Iowa court had disregarded its own precedents and effectively destroyed "millions of property." The Supreme Court, in a short and rather opaque opinion by Justice

Noah Swayne, reversed. Swayne declined to treat the most recent decision by the Iowa Supreme Court as a settled adjudication, declaring, "It cannot be expected that this court will follow every such oscillation, from whatever cause arising, that may possibly occur."[201] He quoted Taney's remarks in *Debolt,* adding that the "same principle applies when there is a change of judicial decision as to the constitutional power of the legislature to enact the law."[202] Swayne never mentioned any constitutional principles but did refer to "universal commercial usage" regarding bonds. Justice Miller, who frequently disagreed with his colleagues in municipal bond cases, authored a lengthy solo dissenting opinion. He maintained that a state court had the right "to decide as a finality upon the construction of State constitutions and State statutes."[203] Like the majority, Miller did not mention the contract clause, but he observed that "it is not pretended" that the decision of the Iowa court was in conflict with the Constitution.[204]

The outcome in *Gelpcke* was of considerable practical significance. It did much to strengthen the national bond market. It is noteworthy that legal commentators, if uncertain about the rationale of the Court, applauded the result in the case. There was widespread concern that bond repudiations had national implications and threatened to destroy public credit. Moreover, the Iowa court had obviously changed the rules governing the authority to issue bonds in the middle of the game, rules on which the nonresident bondholders had relied.[205] Not surprisingly, therefore, *Gelpcke* triggered the appeal of some 300 municipal bond cases to the Supreme Court, most of which resulted in judgments for the out-of-state investors.[206]

Nonetheless, the doctrinal basis of the *Gelpcke* decision was uncertain and a source of continuing controversy. Wright cogently pointed out that "the constitutional justification for the decision has never been clear."[207] Plainly Swayne's opinion was grounded on the notion that contracting parties must be able to rely on the law in force when the contract was made.[208] But the key question remains: Was *Gelpcke* an application of the contract clause? Here, unlike most contract clause cases, there was no subsequent legislation that impaired a contract. Instead, the Supreme Court seemingly endorsed Taney's dictum in *Debolt* and extended the constitutional prohibition to encompass judicial as well as legislative interferences with prior agreements. Some commentators have understood *Gelpcke* to hold that the Iowa Supreme Court's reversal of its prior ruling impaired the contract at issue and thus ran afoul of the contract clause.[209] It is therefore entirely plausible to see *Gelpcke* as the cornerstone of an emerging judicial impairment doctrine. Although never explicitly so stating, the Supreme Court strongly intimated that the contract clause applied to judicial decisions as well as legislation. The full implications of the *Gelpcke* line of decisions and the theory of judicial impairment will be explored more fully in later chapters.

An alternative explanation of *Gelpcke* deserves consideration. Some scholars have argued that *Gelpcke* was not a contract clause case but just an expression of the Court's willingness to fashion a uniform commercial law in diversity cases under *Swift v. Tyson* independent of state law.[210] Adherents of this position point to the fact that the Court refused to hear direct appeals from state courts concerning a claimed judicial impairment. Yet *Gelpcke* does not easily fit under the *Swift* umbrella. In *Gelpcke* the Court was not devising an independent rule but was enforcing the state law existing at the time the contract was formed. Nor did the Court indicate that its decision would apply to contracts made subsequent to the 1862 Iowa decision. Finally the diversity and contract clause rationales are not necessarily inconsistent. Principles derived from contract clause jurisprudence—notably the strong desire for stability and uniformity in commercial relations—could inform the Court's efforts to develop a national commercial law in diversity cases. In any event, the Court's inability to articulate a clear doctrine in the bond cases has caused ongoing confusion.[211]

A STRENGTHENED CONTRACT CLAUSE

By the end of Taney's tenure as chief justice in 1864 the contract clause had achieved a prominent place in constitutional jurisprudence. Regularly litigated at both the national and state levels, the provision became the principal vehicle by which the Supreme Court could oversee state laws. Taney and his colleagues largely built upon the foundational decisions of the Court under Marshall. Certainly the Taney Court did not make a sharp break with the prior reading of the contract clause. On the contrary, the record demonstrates that on the whole Taney and his associates employed the clause forcefully to protect both public and private agreements from state interference. Even with respect to grants of corporate privilege, they repeatedly upheld tax exemptions notwithstanding their professed commitment to a narrow interpretation of such grants. Moreover, they followed Marshall's path by vindicating the sanctity of private bargains. Hovenkamp has pointed out that the Taney Court "continued vigorous, even broadened protection to creditors victimized by states' debtor relief."[212] In addition, the justices tentatively forged a doctrine of judicial impairment.

There was relatively little public opposition to the contract clause rulings of the Taney Court. These decisions harmonized with the widely shared desire to foster economic growth by honoring contractual arrangements. There was common worry that investors would be deterred by state interference with bargains. This progrowth sentiment dovetailed with a general opinion that the settled expectation of contracting parties should not be retroactively upset. Of course, particular contract clause decisions aroused intense local criticism. The Ohio bank tax exemption decisions were bitterly resented in the Buckeye State. The *Gelpcke* ruling aroused hostility in Iowa and some other states in the Midwest. Yet these decisions also had defenders and never triggered a large-scale revolt against a muscular contract clause.

Developments at the state level also reinforced the high standing of contractual rights in the constitutional order. As discussed above, new states commonly inserted a contract clause into their constitutions, a step that suggests both general acceptance of the principle of contractual stability and the absence of any fundamental disagreement with existing contract clause jurisprudence.

None of this is to suggest that arguments grounded on the contract clause invariably prevailed. The cloudy right/remedy distinction remained perplexing and afforded an escape from a literal reading of the provision. Following *Charles River Bridge,* courts uniformly rejected claims of implied monopoly privilege. Beyond the strict construction of corporate grants, they also began to fashion eminent domain and the inalienable police power as vehicles to curtail the reach of the contract clause. During periods of economic distress, moreover, state lawmakers continued to enact debt relief measures designed to hamper the enforcement of contracts. Although the record of state courts on this issue was checkered, some resisted the Taney Court's firm insistence on contractual stability and sustained such laws. They reasoned that the relief laws pertained to the remedy and not the contractual rights, reaching results not easily reconciled with the teachings of the Supreme Court. Bear in mind that state court decisions disapproving claims of contractual impairment were rarely reviewed by the Supreme Court. Moreover, even when federal and state judges invalidated laws under the contract clause, the practical impact of such rulings was often muted. As we saw in Chapter 2 with respect to debt-relief laws, various stay and appraisal laws were typically in effect for several years before they were held unconstitutional. As Warren correctly pointed out, adverse judicial decisions "did not, in fact, cause great hardship to debtors, because, by reason of the intervals of time which elapsed between enactment of these stay-laws and the Courts' decisions as to their invalidity, the laws to a great extent achieved their main purpose of preventing sacrifice of debtor's property."[213]

The fact that the contract clause proved an imperfect mechanism for safeguarding contractual rights from state interference, however, does not denigrate its significance. Contract clause jurisprudence did much to foster a legal climate supportive of agreements both public and private. Moreover, the contract clause had important implications for federalism. Before adoption of the Fourteenth Amendment the contract clause was the primary means by which the Supreme Court could review state legislation. Hence, the provision was central to the antebellum debate over the allocation of power between the national government and the states. The Taney Court's contract clause jurisprudence reflected the need to balance the constitutional protection of contracts with state regulatory authority.

By 1864 the basic principles of contract clause jurisprudence had been established. Yet as novel issues surged to the fore in the wake of the Civil War and Reconstruction, courts were frequently called upon to apply these principles in different and contentious situations.

CHAPTER 4

The Eras of the Civil War and Reconstruction

The Civil War and Reconstruction were pivotal eras in US history. The war and the adoption of the Thirteenth Amendment destroyed slavery as a form of property. Moreover, the Fourteenth Amendment, ratified in 1868, provided in part that no state shall "deprive any person of life, liberty, or property, without due process of law." This guarantee created new possibilities for federal judicial supervision of state laws and in time would partially eclipse the contract clause. Taken together, these developments significantly altered the balance of power between the federal government and the states.

The eras also generated a torrent of contract clause litigation. Many of these disputes grew directly out of the sectional conflict and its impact on the defeated states of the Confederacy. Attempts by southern legislators to deal with postwar conditions, such as emancipation and widespread indebtedness, were a fertile source of laws challenged as violations of the contract clause. At the same time, courts wrestled with contract clause issues similar to those addressed in the antebellum years and considered in Chapters 2 and 3.

During the mid-nineteenth century, leading commentators continued to extol the importance of contracts as the foundation of modern society. The English jurist Henry Sumner Maine articulated this view when he famously observed in 1861, "The movement of the progressive societies has hitherto been a movement *from Status to Contract.*"[1] To Maine, the triumph of the contract constituted a step away from a fixed hierarchical system in which one's place was determined by birth and status and toward a society in which relationships were governed by agreements between individuals. Maine found a receptive audience in the United States because many political thinkers linked voluntary exchange with individual freedom and social progress. In 1867 the influential editor E. L. Godkin, for example, maintained, "The tendency, both of legislation and of usage, in modern times," is "to submit our social relations more and more to the dominion of contract simply."[2] In line with these sentiments, Congress included the right "to make and enforce contracts" among the rights accorded former slaves in the Civil Rights Act of 1866.[3] Amy Dru Stanley has pointed out, "In postbellum America contract was above all a metaphor of freedom."[4] This powerful intellectual current reinforced the high standing of the contract clause and the need for contractual stability.

In addition to this libertarian premise, it was recognized that contracts represented a significant amount of wealth and played a vital role in the economy. "A very large proportion of the property of civilized men," Chief Justice Salmon P. Chase remarked in 1870, "exists in the form of contracts."[5] The Supreme Court of Appeals of Virginia emphasized that the faithful performance of agreements was essential for ensuring prosperity. "The inviolability of contracts, public and private," it maintained, "is the foundation of all social progress, and the corner-stone of all the forms of civilized society, wherever an enlightened jurisprudence prevails."[6]

Both jurists and legislators affirmed the central place of the contract clause in the constitutional order. In 1867, for example, the Supreme Court of South Carolina declared that the contract clauses in both federal and state constitutions "form the ultimate basis on which reposes the confidence that is itself the support of all credit, and the security of the whole fabric of social prosperity."[7] A Mississippi judge stressed the utilitarian importance of the provision in terms of promoting commerce and the national market. He observed that it would be "impossible that the business and commerce, now so extensive and ramified among the people of these states, could be conducted safely and prosperously, except on the basis of a uniform currency . . . and the inviolability of contracts."[8] Similarly, Chase pictured the clause as "that most valuable provision of the Constitution of the United States, ever recognized as an efficient safeguard against injustice."[9] A year later a congressional measure creating a new government for the District of Columbia contained a contract clause.[10] States admitted to the Union during these years, such as Nevada in 1864 and Nebraska in 1867, included a provision safeguarding contracts in their state constitutions. As the Supreme Court of Appeals of Virginia explained in 1873, "So important did the several States regard this barrier against loose and unsound legislation . . . that many of them, not content with the shield of the Federal constitution, have severally adopted the same restriction as part of their state constitutions; thus giving to it an additional sanction."[11]

Given the prevailing mind-set, it was not surprising that the Supreme Court continued to insist that the question of whether a contract existed was one for the Court to determine. "If it were not so," Justice Samuel F. Miller exclaimed, "the constitutional provision could always be evaded by the State courts giving such construction to the contract, or such decisions concerning its validity, as to render the power of this court of no avail in upholding it against unconstitutional State legislation."[12]

Nonetheless, scholars and judges were also aware that the contract clause had given rise to sharp controversies. Discussing the contract clause, Thomas M. Cooley insisted in 1868, "Since its adoption no clause which the Constitution contains has been more prolific of litigation, or given rise to more animated and at times angry controversy."[13] In the same vein, three years later the Supreme Court of Tennessee concluded that "there has not only been great diversity of judicial opinion as to the proper construction of this simple clause of the Constitution as to what it means, but still more as to its precise application."[14] The elusive distinction between contractual rights and the remedy available for the enforcement of contracts remained a source of confusion, and one commentator termed the distinction "arbitrary and unnecessary."[15] Despite frequent praise for the contract clause, there were persistent misgivings about the reach of the provision and its potential to curb state legislative authority.

ISSUES EMANATING FROM THE CIVIL WAR AND RECONSTRUCTION

Confederacy

So widely shared was the conviction that agreements should be honored that the Constitution of the Confederacy, notwithstanding its affirmation of state sovereignty, contained a clause barring the states from abridging contracts.[16] In sync with the US Constitution, the Confederate framers were prepared to curb state authority over contracts. Indeed, in one respect the Confederate Constitution moved beyond the contractual protection in the US Constitution. The Confederates empowered Congress to enact bankruptcy laws but provided that "no law of Congress shall discharge any debt contracted before the passage of the same."[17] Consequently, the Confederate Congress could not retroactively grant bankruptcy relief to debtors.

The Confederacy never established a Supreme Court during its brief existence, but state courts were not hesitant to invalidate laws interfering with the enforcement of debts. In 1861 the Supreme Court of North Carolina struck down a state law forbidding the issuance of executions and the sales of property under existing executions. It reasoned that this measure ran afoul of the contract clause in the Confederate Constitution.[18] Likewise the

Supreme Court of Arkansas voided a statute delaying all lawsuits until after ratification of peace between the Confederacy and the United States.[19] It determined that this indefinite delay in effect destroyed the remedy for enforcing contracts and thus ran afoul of the contract clause in the Arkansas Constitution. Nor was the court impressed with the contention that under wartime circumstances the general welfare of the state would be served by a continuance of lawsuits. It warned, "In the confusion of war, in the excitements produced by sympathy with the wants and distresses of particular classes of the people, the rights of others, and the well-being of the whole society are likely to be endangered and to be sacrificed."[20] After the war the Supreme Court of Texas found a similar 1863 stay law to violate the contract clause of the US Constitution because it withheld a contractual remedy indefinitely.[21]

However, the Confederate attitude toward violation of contracts was decidedly mixed. In 1861 the Confederate Congress enacted a sweeping sequestration law directed at "alien enemies," that is to say, citizens of states loyal to the Union. It purported to confiscate property of such "alien enemies" and to sequester debts owed by a Confederate citizen to a citizen of a loyal state. All Confederate citizens were under a legal duty to inform the government of any property owned by unionists and any debts owed to northerners of which they were aware. Debtors were compelled to pay their debts to a receiver of the Confederate government, with the payment acting as a discharge of the obligation. Confederate officials pursed an aggressive course regarding confiscation. Sequestration posed an especially serious problem for southern business interests, because they had complex credit relationships and commonly owed debts to northerners.[22]

The validity of the Sequestration Act was questioned in *Williams v. Bruffy* (1877).[23] The plaintiffs, residents of Pennsylvania, sold goods to George Bruffy of Virginia in March of 1861. After the war they brought suit against Bruffy's estate to recover the unpaid debt. The defendant estate raised the Sequestration Act as a defense, asserting that the estate was discharged from the debt by virtue of a payment to a Confederate receiver in 1862. Speaking for the Supreme Court, Justice Stephen J. Field ruled that legislation of the Confederate Congress had no validity whatsoever. Treating the sequestration measure as a law given sanction by Virginia, Field declared that the contract clause bars states from passing laws impairing agreements and "equally prohibits a State from *enforcing* as a law an enactment of that character, from whatever source originating." He added, "The debtors cannot claim release from liability to their creditors by reason of coerced payment of equivalent sums to an unlawful combination."[24] It followed that all sequestered debts paid by southerners to the Confederate government were still due to their northern creditors.

Another group of cases addressed the legal status of contracts executed in southern states during the Civil War calling for payment in Confederate currency. Confederate notes were the principal currency within the southern states, and numerous contracts were made with reference to them. In *Thorington v. Smith* (1869) the Supreme Court held that such contracts in the ordinary course of business, and not in aid of the rebellion, could be enforced in federal court "to the extent of their just obligation." It further declared that the party to be paid in Confederate dollars could recover "their actual value at the time and place of the contract, in lawful money of the United States."[25] The Court recognized that Confederate money had some speculative value during the war but insisted that it was not identical in value to US dollars.

A number of southern states in the postwar period took a more categorical position, enacting laws that sought to void contracts payable in Confederate currency. Unlike most state laws challenged as violative of the contract clause that turned upon the question of whether an alteration of the available remedy impaired the obligation of contract, these statutes purported to nullify an entire species of contracts. Not surprisingly, both state and federal courts looked askance at such laws. Pointing out that as a practical matter contracting parties were compelled to use Confederate currency as a medium of exchange, the Supreme Court of Alabama in 1870 declared that a state law giving either party an option to rescind contracts not payable in US currency violated the contract clause.[26] Two years later the Supreme Court of Florida reached the same conclusion, ruling that a provision of the Florida Constitution attempting to invalidate contracts made in consideration of Confederate currency was an unconstitutional impairment of prior contracts.[27] These state court decisions anticipated the ruling of the Supreme Court in *Delmas v. Insurance Company* (1872).[28] At issue was a provision of the Louisiana Constitution that rendered all contracts payable in Confederate notes or money void, a requirement adopted after the contract in dispute was made. Justice Miller, speaking for the Court, declared that the contract was validly executed and thus within the shelter of the contract clause. He stressed that an agreement, valid when made, could not be retroactively impaired, and that "any judgment of a State court resting on such enactment of a State constitution after the date of the contract" must be reversed.[29] Miller distinguished the instant case from situations in which state courts struck down contracts on the ground of a public policy existing when the contract was executed.

Nor would the Supreme Court allow states to alter the rules governing recovery under contracts for payment in Confederate notes. As the Civil War progressed and southern hopes faded, Confederate currency suffered a severe depreciation in value. In the postwar era southern lawmakers were concerned that it was difficult to scale the value of Confederate currency and felt that a more equitable method of determining value of the consideration would be to ascertain the value of the items purchased. An 1866 North Carolina law, for instance, authorized a jury to consider the value of the property purchased and to "determine the value of the said contract in present currency." Warning that legislation allowing a jury to place its own value on contracts "would create an insecurity in business transactions which would be intolerable," the Supreme Court, in an opinion by Justice Field, found the statute to violate the contract clause.[30] The state, he maintained, interfered with the terms of the contract by giving another value to the contract than that stipulated by the parties. In a similar case, the Court invoked the contract clause to strike down an 1867 Virginia statute providing that in disputes growing out of land sales a trial court or jury could look to the "fair value" of the land instead of the contract terms specifying payment in Confederate money. It explained that the statutory rule "was nothing less than substituting for the contract of the parties a new and different one."[31]

Slave Purchase Contracts

The abolition of slavery triggered a bitter controversy over the enforceability of contracts for the purchase of slave property.[32] Many former slave owners were heavily in debt and resisted payment of promissory notes given for slaves prior to emancipation. Pointing to principles of commercial law, they argued that there was a failure of consideration that rendered such contracts unenforceable. This defense was flatly rejected by southern courts. The Supreme Court of Florida, for example, ruled in 1867 that slave purchase agreements were legal when made and that the seller was not responsible for the subsequent change in the legal status of slaves.[33]

However, the controversy over slave purchase agreements soon entered a new phase that raised contract clause issues. During 1867–1868 six southern constitutional conventions (Alabama, Arkansas, Florida, Georgia, Louisiana, and South Carolina) adopted provisions to bar the enforcement of such contracts. The delegates supporting a ban harbored different objectives. Some favored the provision as a form of debt relief for planters who would bear the loss if slave contracts were enforced. In effect, refusal to enforce the promissory notes shifted the loss arising from emancipation to sellers rather than buyers. Other delegates found the enforcement of debts to buy slaves to be morally repugnant. Because in their view slavery never legally existed under natural law, it followed that slave contracts were illegitimate and not entitled to any judicial sanction.[34] Of course, any measure declaring certain prior contracts void would trigger contract clause scrutiny.

The debate over these constitutional provisions posed a number of interrelated questions. Was a slave purchase agreement, lawful when made, rendered unlawful through a change in public policy? Did these state constitutional provisions entail a retrospective judgment about the legitimacy of slave property? Should slave contracts be treated as ordinary commercial transactions and thus fall within the purview of the contract clause?

Four state supreme courts promptly ruled that the constitutional provisions prohibiting enforcement of slave contracts ran afoul of the contract clause. Citing the *Thorington* decision, upholding the validity of contracts for payment in Confederate money, the Supreme Court of Alabama held that slave property was a valid consideration when the contract was made and that the constitutional ordinance destroyed such contracts in contravention of the contract clause.[35] Reaching the same conclusion, the Supreme Court of South Carolina emphatically declared, "Slaves, in South Carolina, when this contract was made, were the legitimate subjects of sale and purchase." It lectured that one cannot "view the events of the past by the reflected light of the present day."[36] The Supreme Court of Arkansas also found the ban on enforcing slave purchase agreements to unconstitutionally impair the obligation of contracts valid when entered and declined to distinguish between "transactions in slave property and those arising upon dealings in ordinary goods and chattels."[37] Following suit, the Supreme Court of Florida concluded that the state constitutional prohibition was "a law operating retrospectively upon the contract and the rights of the parties. In this respect it impairs the obligation of the contract and is void."[38]

Not all courts were on the same page. By sustaining the state constitutional bans they set the stage for review by the Supreme Court. In a problematic opinion the Supreme Court of Georgia upheld a provision in the 1868 Georgia Constitution declaring that no state court could take jurisdiction of a lawsuit to enforce slave contracts and denied that the provision

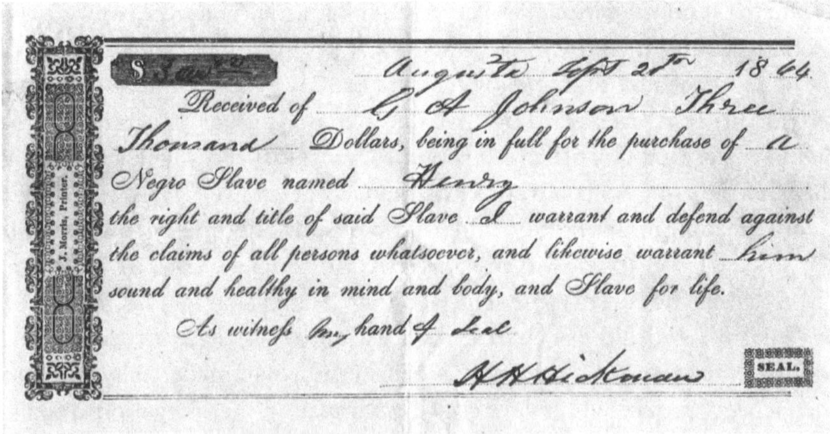

Augusta Sept 21st 1864

Received of G A Johnson Three Thousand Dollars, being in full for the purchase of a Negro Slave named Henry the right and title of said Slave I warrant and defend against the claims of all persons whatsoever, and likewise warrant him sound and healthy in mind and body, and Slave for life.

As witness my hand & Seal

H H Hickman SEAL.

J. Morris, Printer.

Following the Civil War the Supreme Court ruled that contracts for the purchase of slaves were enforceable and that state laws barring the collection of debts owed for the sale of slaves violated the contract clause. (Library of Congress)

violated the contract clause.[39] It asserted that the slave contract provision had been part of a constitution "dictated by Congress, as the representative of the conqueror" and merely "accepted" by the people of the state.[40] Under this analysis, the prohibition was imposed by Congress in the process of restoring Georgia to the Union. Georgia itself had not impaired any contract. Because the contract clause did not pertain to acts of Congress, the contested prohibition was beyond the reach of that clause. Dissenting, Judge Hiram Warner insisted that slaves were recognized as property when the contract was made and that the Georgia constitutional provision was "a *palpable* violation" of the contract clause.[41]

The only federal court to refuse to honor a slave purchase agreement advanced different and more challenging arguments to sustain the state ban on enforcement. The US Circuit Court for Arkansas invoked natural law as a basis to withhold enforcement of a debt for the purchase of slaves. It also upheld the provision of the Arkansas Constitution declaring such arrangements "null and void," contending that the Thirteenth and Fourteenth Amendments necessarily limited the contract clause with respect to contracts that presumed the existence of slavery. The court maintained that the contract clause was never intended to restrict state authority over the institution of slavery. It reasoned that recognizing a right of action on a note for slaves would inhibit the abolition of slavery.[42] The problem with this analysis, however, was that creditors were seeking to collect a debt, not to affirm the continuance of slavery as an institution. Thus, the relevance of the Thirteenth Amendment was unclear.

In a pair of 1872 opinions by Justice Noah Swayne the Supreme Court settled this controversy, ruling that states could not bar the collection of debts for the purchase of slaves. In *White v. Hart* Justice Swayne made short shrift of the arguments advanced by the Georgia court.[43] He insisted that Georgia had never been out of the Union despite attempted secession and remained subject to constitutional restrictions on state authority. Swayne dismissed the notion that the 1868 Georgia Constitution had been dictated by Congress and did not represent an action by the state as "clearly unsound."[44] Treating the contract at issue as valid when made, he found that the Georgia provision on slave contracts impaired the obligation of contract by removing all remedy. "When the contract here in question was entered into," Swayne explained, "ample remedies existed. All were taken away by the proviso in the new constitution. Not a vestige was left. Every means of enforcement was denied, and this denial if valid involved the annihilation of the contract."[45]

In *Osborn v. Nicholson* Swayne similarly concluded that the language in the Arkansas Constitution voiding all agreements for the purchase or sale of slaves constituted an unconstitutional abridgment of contracts lawful when made.[46] Unimpressed with speculation about natural law, he pointed out that slavery had long been recognized in the United States and that the Thirteenth Amendment was adopted after the rights under the purchase contract had become vested. "We cannot regard [the slave purchase contract]," Swayne observed, "as differing in its legal efficacy from any other unexecuted contract to pay money made upon a sufficient consideration at the same time and place." He tellingly added, "Neither the rights nor the interests of those of the colored race lately in bondage are affected by the conclusions we have reached."[47]

Chief Justice Chase, long an antislavery advocate, dissented alone in both *White* and *Osborn.* In declining health, he penned only a brief outline of his views. Chase contended that slave purchase contracts were "against sound morals and natural justice" and that state laws supporting slavery were annulled by the Thirteenth Amendment. He maintained, without explanation, that state laws barring suits on such agreements did not run afoul of the contract clause. Chase's unspoken premise appeared to be that enforcement of debts for slaves implied the legitimacy of slavery.

The federal and state cases requiring the payment of debts for the purchase of slaves after emancipation initially seem dubious to modern eyes.

Two observations are in order. First, it bears emphasis that, as the Supreme Court pointed out, the rights of newly freed slaves were not at issue. Instead, the typical litigation involved a lawsuit by a seller of slaves against a purchaser for recovery of an unpaid debt. The moral distinction between those parties was thin, and therefore courts might have felt that it was inappropriate for state legislators to interfere with how the contracts allocated the risk of loss. Second, the fact that courts would invoke the contract clause in such a sharply contested area as sales of slaves attests to the high standing of the provision in the constitutional order of the mid-nineteenth century.

Legal Tender Cases

Most of the contract clause litigation emanating from the Civil War pertained to the brief existence of the Confederacy. However, steps by Congress to finance the unprecedented expenditures caused by the Civil War gave rise to the *Legal Tender Cases*, treating the contract clause.[48] On the eve of the Civil War legal tender for the satisfaction of debts was gold or silver coin. As a practical matter, commercial activity was largely transacted through state bank notes convertible into coin upon demand. With the outbreak of hostilities, however, gold was generally withdrawn from circulation. In 1862 Congress issued new notes, popularly known as greenbacks because of their color, that were not redeemable in gold or silver coin. Further, the new notes were declared to be "lawful money and a legal tender in payment of all debts, public and private, within the United States." During the debates over the Legal Tender Act questions were raised about the constitutional authority of Congress to compel persons to accept the new currency. Nonetheless, more than $4 million of greenbacks were issued and remained in circulation after the war. Recall that abuse of paper money and legal tender laws by the states in the Post–Revolutionary War years had been a factor in the adoption of the contract clause by the constitutional convention. Chase, as secretary of the Treasury, was a champion of hard money but reluctantly endorsed the issuance of greenbacks as a temporary expedient.[49] Greenback dollars rapidly depreciated in value as compared to gold, reflecting the runaway inflation of the war years. Not surprisingly, creditors resisted payment of contractual debts in greenbacks. This laid the foundation for lawsuits challenging the payment of debts denominated in dollars with greenbacks instead of gold.

The first Supreme Court decision addressing the constitutionality of the legal tender provision was *Hepburn v. Griswold* (1870).[50] At issue was

An 1862 act of Congress authorizing the issuance of greenback currency and making such notes legal tender gave rise to a pair of Supreme Court decisions considering whether the legal tender law could be constitutionally applied to debts contracted before enactment of the provision. (National Numismatic Collection, National Museum of American History)

an action to recover on a promissory note executed before enactment of the 1862 legal tender law. The creditor refused a tender of payment in greenbacks, insisting upon specie. Speaking for four justices,[51] Chase, now chief justice, found that the act altered the terms of the contract by making greenbacks legal payment for debt instead of gold and silver coin, which were the only legal tender when the contract was executed.[52] Holding that the Legal Tender Act was unconstitutional with respect to debts incurred before its enactment, Chase struggled to formulate a persuasive rationale for his ruling. He recognized that the contract clause did not by its terms apply to the federal government, yet nonetheless maintained that the provision impliedly inhibited national power. Chase declared:

> But we think it clear that those who framed and those who adopted the Constitution, intended that the spirit of this prohibition should pervade the entire body of legislation, and that the justice which the Constitution was ordained to establish was not thought by them to be compatible with legislation of an opposite tendency. In other words, we cannot doubt that a law not made in pursuance of an express power, which necessarily and in its direct operation impairs the obligation of contracts, is inconsistent with the spirit of the Constitution.[53]

Reliance on an amorphous "spirit" of the contract clause was problematic and hinted at an extension of the clause to congressional legislation. As a practical matter, *Hepburn* applied only to pre-1862 debts, many of which had already been satisfied, but the ruling increased the burden of discharging any such remaining obligations.

Speaking for the three dissenters, Justice Miller conceded that the Legal Tender Act impaired the obligation of contracts made before its enactment. He stressed that the constitutional bar against such laws did not apply to Congress. Instead, Miller pointed out that the Constitution gave Congress authority to enact a uniform system of bankruptcy, "the essence of which is to discharge debtors from the obligation of their contracts."[54] He found no constitutional infirmity with the Legal Tender Act, a measure he saw as necessary to provide a circulating currency and finance the war effort.[55]

Despite the outcome in *Hepburn*, Miller's views regarding the Legal Tender Act ultimately prevailed. On the very day that the Supreme Court announced its decision in the case, President Ulysses S. Grant nominated two candidates to fill vacant seats on the Court. Both were expected to sustain the validity of the act. Miller pushed to reopen the issue of legal tender before the revamped Court. In *Knox v. Lee* (1871) the justices by a vote of five to four overturned *Hepburn* and upheld the constitutionality of the Legal Tender Act with respect to the payment of past obligations.[56] Under these circumstances the overruling of *Hepburn* triggered a bitter controversy over alleged political influence compromising judicial independence. Our concern, however, is with the Court's assessment of the contract clause. Newly appointed Justice William Strong, writing for the majority, warned against the financial instability that would result if the Legal Tender Act was deemed invalid. Strong denied that the Legal Tender Act impaired prior contracts because the contractual obligation was to pay in whatever currency the law recognized as lawful money at the time of payment. He also asserted that Congress was free to impair contracts, stressing that with bankruptcy laws it could authorize the obliteration of contracts entirely. Strong broadly added that "contracts must be understood as made in reference to the possible exercise of the rightful authority of the government, and no obligation of a contract can extend to the defeat of legitimate governmental authority."[57] Such a capacious reading of governmental power to alter contracts would potentially point toward a weakening of the protection afforded by the contract clause.

The four dissenters authored three opinions. Chase adhered to his earlier position that the Legal Tender Act was "inconsistent with the spirit of the Constitution in that it impairs the obligation of contracts."[58] He insisted that Congress could only discharge the obligation of contracts through its bankruptcy power. There was, Chase argued, no general power in Congress to interfere with agreements. Field agreed with Chase that the Legal Tender Act impaired the obligation of contracts executed before its enactment. He expansively defined the notion of contractual impairment: "A law which changes the terms of the contract, either in time or mode of performance, or imposes new conditions, or dispenses with those expressed, or authorizes for its satisfaction something different from provided, is a law which impairs its obligation, for such a law relieves the parties from the moral duty of performing the original stipulation of the contract, and it prevents their legal enforcement."[59] Field reasoned that, aside from the special exception for a bankruptcy system, Congress possessed no unlimited authority to impair contracts. Emphasizing the bitter post-Revolutionary experience with paper money and tender laws, he expressed doubt that the framers intended to "vest in the new government created by them this dangerous and despotic power, which they were unwilling should remain with the States, and thus widen the possible sphere of its influence."[60]

In a sense the *Legal Tender Cases* did not directly involve the contract clause because the issue pertained to congressional, not state, legislation. Yet the various opinions made reference to the provision, and at least four justices were prepared to apply principles derived from the contract clause to actions of the federal government. Still, the upshot of the *Legal Tender Cases* was to affirm that the prohibition of the clause was confined to the states, leaving Congress free to interfere with contracts as circumstances might dictate. Left uncertain was the extent to which Congress could repudiate its own undertakings, an important question but one beyond the scope of the contract clause.[61]

Military Service

The pressing need for the Union to rapidly raise a large army in 1861 caused lawmakers to encourage volunteering by granting a stay of legal proceedings against soldiers mustered into military service. Lawmakers felt that soldiers should not have to worry about prewar debts. In April of 1861, for example, the Pennsylvania legislature stayed any civil proceedings against soldiers for the term of their service and suspended the statutes of limitations of any claims against such persons. This was challenged as an indefinite postponement of remedies that impaired the obligation of contract in violation of both the US and Pennsylvania Constitutions. Insisting that the legislature had authority to modify remedies, the Supreme Court of Pennsylvania held that the stay was not indefinite but was limited to the three-year period of enlistment. In view of the emergency circumstances, the court found that "there is nothing unreasonable in exempting a soldier's property from execution whilst he is absent from home battling for the supremacy of the constitution and the integrity of the Union."[62] Acknowledging that a three-year stay was long and might not be justified in other situations, the court concluded that the law manifested "no wanton or careless disregard of the obligation of contracts."[63]

Debt Relief in the Post–Civil War South

The states of the former Confederacy were economically devastated by the Civil War. The huge loss of life and widespread physical destruction caused by the conflict, combined with abolition of slave property and the unsettling transformation of the labor market, contributed to the general economic distress. Property values plummeted. "The destruction wrought by the war and the sudden act of emancipation," Morton Keller has aptly observed, "had catastrophic effects on southern property values."[64] The transportation network was near collapse. Individuals from all segments of society found themselves encumbered with mountainous debt. "The whole South is now bankrupt," a planter's wife complained.[65]

In response to these unhappy conditions, southern lawmakers initiated a fresh round of measures to stay the collection of debts, delay foreclosures, and facilitate the redemption of land from tax delinquency sales. Other stay laws remained in effect from the war years. Many states also increased the exemption of personal property from the reach of creditors.[66] In March of

1866, for instance, the Georgia legislature adopted a law suspending the sale of property under execution on any contract made before June of 1865. The act recited a litany of problems affecting the state, including occupation by hostile forces, destruction of crops, repudiation of Confederate and state debt, and the loss of capital invested in slave property.[67] Seeking to justify the stay laws, one Georgia judge explained that "the people demanded time to enable them to recuperate their wasted estates, so as to enable them to meet their liabilities, without being deprived of the little remnant which had escaped the vicissitudes of the war."[68] Three points warrant emphasis. First, there was in part a sectional dimension behind the enactment of stay laws. Some of the impetus was to avoid repaying prewar loans to northern merchants. Second, the stay laws by southern legislatures were reminiscent of similar legislation passed by many states in the wake of the Revolution. Third, although prevailing public opinion clamored for debt-relief laws, there was an undercurrent of opposition. Critics charged that stay laws undermined the availability of credit.

Not surprisingly, these stay laws were attacked as violations of the contract clause. Counsel defending stay laws invoked the economic distress of the region[69] and commonly argued that legislatures retained authority to modify contractual remedies. Although the details of the stay laws varied, southern courts proved receptive to constitutional challenges regarding application of such measures to antecedent agreements. Courts in Alabama,[70] Georgia,[71] Mississippi,[72] North Carolina,[73] South Carolina,[74] Tennessee,[75] Texas,[76] and Virginia[77] struck down stay laws as in effect destroying the remedy and thereby impairing the rights secured by the contract. A number of courts pointed out that the stay laws violated the contract clause in both federal and state constitutions, likely a step to soothe local sensibilities.[78] Several also sought to explain the negative implications of stay laws for reviving the states' economies. An Alabama judge maintained that the stay law "materially affects the credit system, which in our present condition is a serious injury."[79] The Court of Errors of South Carolina warned against "unwise and unjust measures of relief" adopted under urgent pressure and characterized the contract clauses in federal and state constitutions as forming "the ultimate basis on which reposes the confidence that is itself the support of all credit, and the security of the whole fabric of social prosperity."[80] Clearly southern courts were unimpressed with pleas of financial hardship as a justification for stay laws that interfered with the collection of debts or foreclosure of mortgages. The Supreme Court of Appeals of Virginia in 1873 decried the "tendency of State Legislatures, in times of trouble and pecuniary pressure, to fall into the lax and unsound system of legislation," steps that in turn fueled adoption of the contract clause.[81]

Courts also frowned upon other legislative obstacles to the enforcement of contractual obligations. Georgia was especially imaginative in this regard. The Georgia Constitution of 1868 declared all contracts made in support of the Confederacy to be void, a proposition consistent with the Supreme Court's view. It further provided that when the defendant swore that he had reason to believe a contract was used for this purpose, the plaintiff then had to prove that the contract, and any instruments of debt made in connection with the contract, had not been used for such an illegal purpose. The US Circuit Court for Georgia reasoned that this requirement "imposes upon the plaintiff an impossibility, and is tantamount to destroying the contract on the simple oath of the defendant."[82] The court readily concluded that the constitutional provision ran afoul of the contract clause. In the same vein, an 1870 Georgia act mandated that a claimant, before bringing suit in a state court to collect a debt based on a contract executed before June of 1865, must have paid all taxes chargeable for each year upon such contract. Speaking for the Supreme Court, Justice Swayne pointed out that the statute retrospectively imposed a penalty for nonpayment of taxes. "The purpose of the act was plainly not to collect back taxes," he stated, "but to bar the debt and discharge the debtor." Although he acknowledged that states could change remedies, Swayne made clear that the parties must be left with a substantial means of enforcement. "A clearer case of a law impairing the obligation of a contract, within the meaning of the Constitution," he declared, "can hardly occur."[83]

Most debt-relief laws took the form of changing the available remedies, either by postponing the time of payment or hampering access to the judicial system. Legislators less frequently sought to vary the substantive terms of agreements. Still, occasional state laws altered the duties of the parties under an antecedent contract. In 1873 Virginia lawmakers empowered juries and judges in actions to recover money under contracts made before April of 1865 to abate interest for the period of the Civil War. The Supreme Court of Appeals of Virginia determined that interest on a principal sum was a legal incident of the debt and that the legislature could not confer upon juries and judges the authority to remit interest. The mere existence of war, it maintained, neither abrogated debts nor halted the running of interest. Because the law at issue altered the rights of the parties existing at the time the contract was entered, the measure impaired the obligation of contract in violation of both the US and Virginia Constitutions.[84]

Yet not all debt-relief measures were invalidated. An 1870 Virginia law required that an official selling personal property to satisfy a debt contracted prior to April of 1865, upon request by the debtor, to sell such property for credit for twelve months rather than for cash. The Supreme Court of Appeals of Virginia sustained the measure, reasoning that it merely set the terms for execution sales and was thus remedial in nature. It distinguished this act from stay laws, pointing out that the power of a creditor to seize a debtor's property was preserved. The court asserted that a sale for cash "would result in a ruinous sacrifice," whereas a sale on credit "is alike beneficial to creditor and debtor, as a class."[85]

Homestead Exemptions

The enlargement of homestead exemptions in the postbellum southern states was a particularly controversial form of debt relief.[86] Starting with Texas in 1839, most states in the region had by the time of the Civil War enacted homestead laws that exempted family residences from the reach of creditors. Although details of the homestead laws varied widely, such measures typically exempted family residences from execution up to a certain acreage or monetary amount and required the consent of a spouse to sell the property. The purpose was to promote homeownership and shelter families from destitution in a volatile market. Of course, the homestead law necessarily curbed the rights of creditors. There was renewed interest in homestead exemptions after the war as planters and yeoman farmers sought to prevent losing their land to creditors. Accordingly, southern lawmakers took a number of steps to strengthen homestead protection. Most states in the region placed homestead provisions in their constitutions. In addition, lawmakers greatly expanded the extent of the homestead exemption. A Georgia lawyer complained, "In most of the Southern States the homesteads and exemptions are so exorbitant and extravagant, that there are but few cases in which any property of the debtor is left, out of which creditors can procure their money."[87] The most contested move, however, was the application of the homestead exemption to debts contracted before the effective date of these measures. Unhappy that the security on which they had relied was being eliminated, creditors mounted a series of challenges arguing that retroactive application of the enlarged exemptions constituted an unconstitutional impairment of their contracts.

In marked contrast to their treatment of stay laws, southern courts were generally sympathetic to the purpose behind the enlarged homestead exemptions. They tended to brush aside contract clause arguments and to uphold the application of homestead laws to antecedent debts. In so doing, southern judges developed three themes that guided their opinions. First, they gave considerable weight to the depressed economic plight of the region. In 1869 Chief Judge Joseph E. Brown of Georgia emphasized "the general wreck of the fortunes and destruction of rights, caused by the war" and depicted homestead laws "as a means of equalizing losses to some extent, and of retaining and inviting population, by securing to each family a home, free of old liens." He added, "The homestead measure was a necessity, and its adoption was dictated by sound public policy, to save a large class of intelligent, patriotic citizens and their families from despondency."[88]

Second, courts often compared protection of homes to long-standing exemptions of items of personal property. They maintained that both federal and state courts had approved statutes granting immunity from antecedent debts to a debtor's personal property necessary for subsistence or for carrying on a trade. Noting the state's long history of retrospectively exempting farming and mechanical tools, certain farm animals, and household furniture from execution, the North Carolina Supreme Court concluded, "If the Legislature can exempt personal property, it is not pretended that it may not in like manner exempt real estate—a homestead."[89]

Third, courts commonly insisted that the homestead laws simply amounted to a modification of the remedy to enforce contracts and were therefore well within the scope of legislative power. The exemption of real and personal property from levy, it was argued, did not impair the contract but only afforded relief to an impoverished populace. The Supreme Court of Georgia, for example, explained that the state constitutional provision establishing a homestead "is only a regulation of the remedy, and is not an impairing of any right, express or implied, secured to creditors then existing by their ordinary contracts."[90] Judicial opinions upholding the application of homestead exemptions to antecedent debts invariably invoked Chief Justice Roger B. Taney's dictum in *Bronson v. Kinzie* (1843) that a state could modify remedies based on "its own views of policy and humanity."[91] Thus, the Supreme Court of North Carolina declared in 1873 that the state's homestead laws were grounded upon "'policy and humanity'; and they do not impair, but are paramount to debts."[92]

To strengthen the contention that homestead exemptions pertained solely to the remedy, as distinct from rights under the contract itself, a number of southern courts compared homestead laws with the abolition to imprisonment for debt.[93] The movement to end confinement for debt was a major reform of the mid-nineteenth century. Although this change in the law eliminated a potentially efficacious remedy available to creditors, the Supreme Court, as discussed in Chapter 2, had sustained it with respect to contracts made before the abolition was adopted.[94] Southern courts maintained that if states could eliminate imprisonment for debt without running afoul of the contract clause, then surely they could make homestead exemptions apply retroactively to preexisting contracts.

Although the prevailing view among southern jurists was to treat homestead and exemption laws favorably, not all judges spoke with the same voice. Some contended that application of enlarged homestead exemptions to antecedent debts unconstitutionally despoiled the contractual rights of creditors and encouraged fraud. In a dissenting opinion Judge Hiram Walker of Georgia insisted that Taney's remarks about state exemption laws pertained only to future contracts. He declared that the homestead exemption, as applied to agreements made before its adoption, violated the contract clause. Nor was Walker impressed with the emphasis upon economic hardship emanating from the Civil War. Summoning the experience of the framers, he pointedly observed:

> But it has been said that a great necessity existed, growing out of the results of the war, which would justify and sanction the violation of these great fundamental principles of government and constitutional law. Those who make this assertion should always remember that both creditor and debtor were equal sufferers by the calamities of the war. The framers of the Federal Constitution had just emerged from a seven years' war, and well knew the evils which resulted therefrom, and the general demoralization of society, in regard to performing their contracts. If we may believe the contemporary expounders of that Constitution, one of the main objects of those who framed it was to provide against and prevent the very state of things which is now attempted to be carried into effect by a majority of this Court.[95]

In addition to scattered dissents, the Supreme Court of Appeals of Virginia, in the *Homestead Cases* (1872), struck down a homestead measure applicable to prior debts.[96] It was the only southern court to do so in advance of decisions by the Supreme Court, and thus the opinion warrants careful consideration. The Virginia court questioned the distinction between laws that abridged contractual rights and those that purported to operate only on the remedy. "Nothing can be more material to the obligation," it explained, "than the means of enforcement. The ideas of validity and remedy are inseparable, and both are parts of the obligation."[97] The Virginia court took the position that any law that eliminated a remedy a creditor had at

Justice Noah Swayne authored a number of opinions in the mid-nineteenth century invoking the contract clause to strike down retroactive debt relief and to bar municipal bond repudiation, and emphasizing the public interest in the faithful performance of contracts. (Library of Congress)

the time the agreement was made constituted an impairment of contract in direct violation of the Constitution. It brushed aside the dictum of Chief Justice Taney upon which other southern judges had heavily relied. The court maintained that Taney's remarks had been taken out of context and that in fact Taney had ruled that a retrospective alteration of remedy could impair contracts. It pointed out that in the past the Virginia legislature had always adopted exemption laws prospectively. If the legislature had sole discretion over the amount of homestead exemptions, it continued, then lawmakers would be empowered to wipe out every debt by withdrawing property from levy.

Turning to the practical consequences of the Virginia homestead law, the court expressed concern that the measure would exempt the property of 90 percent of debtors in the state from the reach of creditors, in effect cancelling their obligations. Indeed, it speculated that potential homestead exemptions exceeded the value of all the real property in the state. Nor was the Virginia court impressed with arguments of counsel that sought to array creditors against debtors. Rejecting any class distinctions among citizens of the state, it lectured, "But the truth is, there is no such thing as a 'debtor class and a creditor class' among the people of the State. . . . In the great majority of cases, every man is both a creditor and a debtor."[98] The court concluded by acknowledging the financial hardships that many were suffering but insisted that this was no reason to disregard contractual obligations.[99]

Despite frequent litigation at the state level, the validity of the enlarged and retroactive homestead exemptions did not reach the Supreme Court until 1873. In *Gunn v. Barry* Justice Swayne, speaking for a unanimous bench, invalidated Georgia's constitutional provision on homesteads insofar as it applied to antecedent debts. Noting "the greatly increased magnitude" of the exemptions in the state constitution over previous law, Swayne stressed that the measure "does not merely impair, it annihilates the remedy. There is none left."[100] He ruled that remedies for the enforcement of agreements existing at the time the contract was entered were part of the obligation and that a state could alter them only if there was no impairment of a substantive right. It followed that the Georgia homestead provision impaired the obligation of antecedent contracts and infringed the contract clause.

Following *Gunn* most southern courts acquiesced in that decision. The Supreme Court of Mississippi, for example, reversed an earlier decision and determined that an 1865 statute that greatly enlarged the exemption for both personal property and homesteads would be void if applied to prior debts. It pictured the contract clause as "founded on the motive of shielding the people in their persons and property from the effect of legislation arising in passion and impulse, caused by unusual emergencies, to which communities, like individuals, are exposed."[101] The court avoided a condemnation of the 1865 act under the contract clause by finding that the measure was applicable only to after-acquired liabilities. Concluding on an instrumental note reflecting the concerns of the framers, it expressed confidence that the decision would promote the public good. "The principle vindicated," the court reasoned, "will give stability and uniformity to the business and industries of the people."[102]

On the other hand, the Supreme Court of North Carolina sought to distinguish that state's homestead provision from the invalid Georgia measure. It pointed out that the 1868 North Carolina Constitution actually reduced the amount of homestead exemption previously available, apparently thinking that the magnitude of the exemption rather than its retrospective application was the decisive factor in *Gunn.*[103] This set the stage for a second homestead decision by the Supreme Court. In *Edwards v. Kearsey* (1878) the Court, in another opinion by Justice Swayne, held that the North Carolina provision also ran afoul of the contract clause.[104] Emphasizing that the obligation of contract encompassed the means of enforcement, he compared the homestead exemption to clearly unconstitutional stay laws. "No community can have any higher public interest," Swayne intoned, "than in the faithful performance of contracts and the honest administration of justice."[105] He maintained that any subsequent law that so affected the remedy as to lessen the value of a contract was barred by the Constitution. Two justices who concurred in the finding that the North Carolina homestead provision was invalid were nonetheless bothered by the potential sweep of Swayne's opinion. Seeing room for "humane legislation" that exempted necessary items of personal property without violating the contract clause, they claimed that the extent of the challenged homestead exemption was so excessive as to impair the creditor's remedy.[106]

With the second decision by the Supreme Court the question of retroactive application of homestead exemptions by the states to debts contracted before enactment of such laws was put to rest as a matter of constitutional law. Several observations are in order. First, the Supreme Court, unlike the southern state courts, made no mention of the financial hardships in the region, thus implicitly rejecting economic emergency as a justification for abridging contracts. Instead, it stressed the purpose of the contract clause and the significance of contractual stability for society at large. Second, given the Supreme Court's firm attitude, one might ponder what southern legislators and judges achieved by passing and sustaining these homestead laws. In fact, they gained partial success. The homestead laws provided protection to landowners for the limited time between passage and subsequent nullification by the Supreme Court. As Charles Warren aptly concluded, the homestead laws, even if eventually overturned, "largely achieved their purpose of giving temporary protection to the debtor and the conservation of his property from forced sale, during the interval between the enactment of the law and its invalidation by the Court."[107] Even short-term relief gave southern landowners an opportunity to regain their economic footing. Because the laws reflected the dominant public sentiment to preserve existing property relationships for as long as possible, there was no political downside to passing homestead legislation. Creditors, on the other hand, found the experience frustrating. Notwithstanding eventual victory in the Supreme Court, in practice they received belated and inadequate protection for their interests from the contract clause.[108]

NON-WAR-RELATED ISSUES

Although the Supreme Court heard significant contract clause cases arising from the Civil War and Reconstruction, more routine litigation also figured prominently on the Court's docket. As might be expected, many of these disputes had their origins in the Antebellum Era and presented issues similar to those already addressed by the Court. Likewise, the state courts continued to hear a steady stream of contract clause claims.

Corporate Charters

The extent of corporate privileges conferred by their charters remained a much-contested subject. In *Binghamton Bridge* (1866) a majority of the Supreme Court found that the language in a tangled series of corporate charters granted a perpetual exclusive right to operate a toll bridge within a set distance over a river.[109] It ruled that a New York law authorizing the construction of another bridge within the prohibited distance was a violation of the original contract protected by the Constitution. In so doing, the Court affirmed the principle of the *Dartmouth College* case in sweeping terms, declaring, "We have supposed, if anything was settled by an unbroken course of decisions in the Federal and State courts, it was, that an act of incorporation was a contract between the State and the stockholders. All courts at this day are estopped from questioning the doctrine. The security of property rests upon it, and every successful enterprise is undertaken, in the unshaken belief that it will never be forsaken."

The Court warned that any departure from *Dartmouth College* "would involve dangers to society that cannot be foreseen" and would "unhinge its business interests."[110] With its stress upon the importance of encouraging investment in risky ventures, the opinion was reminiscent of Justice Joseph Story's dissent in the *Charles River Bridge* case. The three dissenters persuasively protested that the majority failed to apply the principle of strict construction of ambiguous wording in corporate charters and gave "a construction most favorable to the monopolist, and injurious to the people."[111] Ultimately the dissenters carried the day. Notwithstanding *Binghamton Bridge* both federal and state courts almost universally rejected claims of monopoly privilege.[112]

Legislative changes to corporate charters also ran afoul of the contract clause. In *Hawthorne v. Calef* (1865), for example, an 1836 railroad company charter provided that the individual property of shareholders would be liable to the amount of their stock for all corporate debts.[113] In effect the stockholders became sureties for the debts of the company. After the debt at issue was contracted, the Maine legislature repealed the individual liability clause of the charter. Striking down the repeal as applied to prior debts, the Supreme Court reasoned that the measure violated both an implied contract between the stockholders and creditors and "the principal contract" between the creditors and the corporation. With the company now insolvent, the repeal act was seen as abolishing the security of the creditor. This decision fit neatly within a long pattern of cases invoking the contract clause to protect the rights of creditors.

Another case with roots in the Antebellum Era was *Furman v. Nichol* (1869).[114] At issue was an 1838 Tennessee banking charter that provided that bank notes were receivable in payment for debts due the state. This measure was repealed in 1865. When a county clerk refused to receive bank notes in payment of taxes, two note holders argued that the repeal legislation amounted to an impairment of a contract between the bank and the holders of the bank notes. Adhering to the rule in *Woodruff v. Trapnall* (1850), the Supreme Court had no difficulty in finding that the repeal impaired the obligation of contract with respect to bank notes in circulation at that time.

State regulation of corporate enterprise raised a variety of issues pertaining to alleged privileges contained in charters of incorporation. State courts heard an increasing number of cases challenging such regulatory authority as a violation of the contract clause. Adhering to the rule of strict construction of corporate charters, state judges usually sustained legislative power. They also expressed the view, first articulated in the Antebellum Era, that lawmakers could not abrogate the police power to safeguard the health, safety, and morals of the public. The police power, they insisted, must prevail over any rights conferred by a contract with the state. A crucial question, therefore, was the extent of the police power to impose regulations that curtailed contract rights. Courts often blended the doctrine of strict construction with the sovereign authority of states to enact police regulations in decisions that turned upon provisions in corporate charters.

Fire was a frequent hazard emanating from the operation of railroads. Consequently, in the mid-nineteenth century a number of states enacted laws making railroad companies liable for all damages from fire caused by their activities. The carriers argued that these laws altered their charter by imposing a new burden not specified in the original contract. Brushing aside this contention, the Supreme Court of Iowa stressed that there was no implied contract that the laws governing the corporation would never be changed. It further concluded that the fire liability statute was grounded on the police power and that this power was "very extended in its application."[115]

State courts looked skeptically at claims of monopoly status. The Supreme Court of Mississippi, for example, insisted that any claim of monopoly privilege must rest upon an express provision in the corporate charter. Finding no such language in the charter of a cotton trading company, the court rejected the argument that a subsequent law mandating that all cotton be weighed by a public official before sale impaired the contract between the state and the company. For good measure, the court declared that weight and measure regulations were an aspect of the police power and that a relinquishment of sovereignty to enact such laws could never be implied.[116]

To be sure, not every case was resolved against a right embedded in a corporate charter. An 1871 lease by a state-owned rail line in North Carolina expressly stipulated that the lessee carrier had the right to change the track gauge. When the lessee began to widen the gauge, the state legislature passed a law in 1875 to bar such alteration. Recognizing that the lease amounted to a contract with the state, the Supreme Court of North Carolina agreed that the legislature could impose safety regulations on railroads. But the police power, it emphasized, was not unlimited. "A State," the court declared, "cannot violate its contract under a pretended exercise of its police power. The act must be *bona fide* intended to relieve some evil within the reach of that power, and strictly applicable to that end."[117] Unconvinced that there was a safety justification for the gauge law, the court declared that the measure ran afoul of the contract clause. The dissenting judge urged deference to the legislative determination that the law was within the police power to control railroad operations.

The widespread adoption by state legislatures of reservation clauses in corporate charters and general incorporation statutes, a process well under way before the Civil War, provided another vehicle to dilute the protection conferred upon corporate enterprise by the contract clause. As the Chancery Court of New Jersey explained, under the *Dartmouth College* case experience demonstrated that "great inconveniences resulted, and that provisions incautiously inserted, too much restricted the power of future legislatures." Hence, it bluntly declared, the reservation of legislative power to alter or repeal charters "was to avoid the rule in the *Dartmouth College* case."[118]

State courts tended to give a broad reading to reservation clauses, undercutting claims grounded on alleged impairments of the corporate charter.[119]

The New York Court of Appeals declared that "under the reserved power, the legislature might interfere in many important respects with the powers of corporations, by subjecting them to new restrictions or increased burdens."[120] Adopting such an expansive view of statutory reservation language, the Supreme Judicial Court of Massachusetts in 1870 upheld the authority of the legislature to compel a water power company to construct a fish way in a dam across a river, although there was no such requirement in the corporate charter. Admitting that the extent of the reserved power could be a subject of some dispute, the court nonetheless ruled that "it at least reserves to the legislature the authority to make any alteration or amendment in a charter granted subject to it, that will not defeat or substantially impair the object of the grant, or any rights which have vested under it."[121] In 1874 the Supreme Court of Wisconsin, pointing to the reservation language in the state constitution, sustained a law fixing maximum charges by railroad companies notwithstanding charters authorizing the carriers to set rates. It emphatically observed that the effect of the reservation clause was to circumvent the *Dartmouth College* rule.[122]

Although the Supreme Court had few opportunities during the Reconstruction period to address the impact of reservation clauses, it readily applied them to affirm legislative authority to modify corporate charters. The Court signaled, however, that there were somewhat vague limits to the exercise of legislative power based on reservation clauses. Thus, it explained that such power to legislate "cannot be exercised to take away or destroy rights acquired by virtue of such a charter, and which by the legitimate use of the powers granted have become vested in the corporation."[123]

Of even greater long-term significance was an attitudinal shift with regard to the contract clause that began in the post–Civil War period. Attorneys and state court judges began to increasingly express the view, first articulated in the Antebellum Era, that legislators could not even by express language divest themselves of the authority to utilize the police power to safeguard the health, safety, and morals of the public. "One legislature," the attorney for the Binghamton Bridge argued, "cannot place the sovereignty of the State or any portion of it beyond the reach of all succeeding ones."[124] Similarly, the New York Court of Appeals, upholding the revocation of retail liquor licenses, declared, "The necessary powers of the legislature over all subjects of internal police, being a part of the general grant of legislative power given by the constitution, cannot be sold, given away or relinquished." It continued, "But no one legislature can curtail the power of its successors to make such laws as they deem proper, in matters of police."[125]

Likewise a Mississippi jurist explained that the contract clause "was not designed to limit the authority of the state in dealing with subjects promotive of health, happiness and morals within its limits."[126] A dissenting North Carolina judge boldly insisted, "All contracts and all rights are subject" to the police power.[127]Although the Supreme Court had not yet addressed this issue, the state courts decidedly adopted the view that the police power could not be alienated and in so doing anticipated future developments.[128] As this view gained ascendancy in the late nineteenth century, the consequence was to undercut the protective function of the contract clause, especially with respect to state contracts. Much depended on how the police power was defined and on whether this emerging notion of an alienable power applied to private as well as public contracts. How courts addressed these questions will be treated in later chapters.

The same era also witnessed a sustained assault on the contract clause jurisprudence of John Marshall. Not only did some scholars challenge the application of the contract clause to state contracts but they took special aim at *Dartmouth College.* Consider the evolving views of Thomas M. Cooley. In the original 1868 edition of his landmark volume *A Treatise on the Constitutional Limitations Which Rest upon the Legislative Power of the States of the American Union,* he simply noted the *Dartmouth College* rule, indicating that grants of corporate charters were protected by the contract clause and could not be revoked or have their benefits diminished by subsequent laws. Cooley expressed no qualms about the inclusion of public contracts within the ambit of the clause.[129] By the time of the second edition in 1871, however, Cooley's position had markedly changed. Critical of the use of the contract clause as a shield for corporate charters, he warned:

> It is under the protection of the decision in the Dartmouth College Case that the most enormous and threatening powers in our country have been created; some of the great and wealthy corporations actually having greater influence in the country at large, and upon the legislation of the country, than the States to which they owe their corporate existence. Every privilege granted or right conferred—no matter by what means or on what pretense—being made irrevocable by the Constitution, the government is frequently found stripped of its authority in very important particulars, by unwise, careless, or corrupt legislation.

In addition, Cooley narrowly characterized the contract clause as a provision "whose purpose was to preclude the repudiation of debts and just contracts."[130] At first blush Cooley's change of heart may seem rather curious.

After all, he was instrumental in fashioning the due process clause of the Fourteenth Amendment into a substantive restraint on state power to regulate economic rights. But reflecting his Jacksonian roots, Cooley came to perceive the public branch of contract clause jurisprudence as fostering corporate special privilege. Such a result was anathema to Cooley, who was committed to equal access to business opportunities. He endorsed the notion that states could not contract away the police power.

Others echoed Cooley's concerns. In 1873 James A. Garfield, a member of Congress from Ohio and future president, lamented the application of the contract clause to railroad companies, which he argued had thereby escaped effective state control. Advancing a much-repeated theme, Garfield stressed that when *Dartmouth College* was decided in 1819 Marshall "did not contemplate the class of corporations that have since come into being."[131] He intimated that Marshall's understanding of corporate charters as protected contracts was unsuited to the new age of large-scale enterprise.

In addition to criticism by Cooley and Garfield, a number of articles appeared in the 1870s challenging Marshall's decisions regarding public contracts.[132] Perhaps the most important was by Clement H. Hill, an assistant attorney general under President Ulysses S. Grant. In an 1874 piece Hill sharply questioned the basic premise that the contract clause was intended to curtail the exercise of sovereign powers by the states, such as taxation and control over corporations.[133] His particular target was *Dartmouth College*, the consequences of which he warned were "now beginning to press heavily upon great communities, and the pressure, we believe, will increase rather than diminish." He darkly added, "The truth is, that the *Dartmouth College* case, instead of protecting the weak against the strong, is a decision all on the side of power, making the strong stronger, and the weak weaker, almost to helplessness."[134] Questioning the notion that corporate charters were contracts, he charged that the need to supervise "huge monopolies like railroads" has been "greatly limited and shackled by this decision."[135] Recognizing the deep roots of the *Dartmouth College* doctrine in the polity, Hill tentatively suggested a constitutional amendment to overturn it. As one scholar has cogently observed, it is apparent that the "real concern" of these critics was "not with the substance of the Marshall Court's early contract clause decisions but rather with the consequences of these decisions in terms of later legal, political, and economic developments in the nineteenth century."[136]

It is noteworthy that Hill did not take the position that states could never be bound by their agreements. He contended that the contract clause extended to "all pecuniary and monetary obligations arising out of contracts." Repudiation of public debt by the states, Hill insisted, "was undoubtedly violating the obligation of contracts with the meaning of the Constitution."[137] Moreover, a state selling property was acting as a private person. It followed, therefore, that the Georgia land grant at issue in *Fletcher v. Peck* could properly be seen as a private transaction within the protection of the contract clause. The distinction between public and private contracts, Hill concluded, "must depend upon its subject-matter, and not upon the parties to it."[138]

Despite mounting unhappiness with the protection of corporate charters under the contract clause, there is room to doubt that *Dartmouth College* actually warranted such censure. As discussed above, the case had already been weakened by a cluster of developments—strict construction of charters, availability of eminent domain, adoption by the states of reservation clauses in charters and general corporation laws, and gradual acceptance of state police power as trumping contractual commitments. Contrary to the fears of critics, the contract clause posed no significant obstacle to the spread of state business regulations in the late nineteenth century.

Land Grants

State land grants were rarely the subject of contract clause litigation in the Reconstruction period. Still, the policy in antebellum Texas of making grants of public land to railroad companies to encourage rail construction gave rise to a case reminiscent of *Fletcher v. Peck*. In 1856 Texas granted certain public lands to a railroad conditioned upon the construction of fifty miles of track by 1861 and an additional fifty miles within two years. As might be expected, the intervention of the Civil War caused delays. In response, the Texas legislature in 1866 extended the time for construction for ten years. Three years later, however, a new state constitution provided that all lands granted or reserved for railroad companies were forfeit to the state. The receiver for an insolvent railroad sought an injunction to prevent the governor from issuing patents on land earmarked for the company, charging that the Texas constitutional provision impaired the obligation of contract. Citing *Fletcher*, the Supreme Court agreed in *Davis v. Gray* (1873).[139] It found that the land grant was a contract and that the state should be treated as a private person who was party to such an agreement. The Court demonstrated no disposition to depart from the landmark *Fletcher* ruling.

Tax Exemptions

In contrast to land grants, legislative grants of tax exemptions to a wide variety of enterprises were a fertile source of contract clause disputes. Anxious to encourage both economic growth and charitable activity, states frequently granted either partial or total tax immunity. Subsequently lawmakers often reconsidered this policy and sought to rescind such exemptions. Adhering to Marshall's opinion in *New Jersey v. Wilson* (1812) as well as to the line of antebellum Supreme Court decisions discussed in Chapter 3, both federal and state courts generally sustained tax immunities under the contract clause. Although courts were disinclined to find privileges in corporate charters, they tended to treat tax exemptions as something of an exception to the notion that states could not contract away their essential powers. In 1868 Cooley felt that the question of a tax exemption as a protected contract "can no longer be considered an open one."[140] To be sure, this view was never unanimous. Some Supreme Court justices regularly protested against seeing tax exemptions as protected contracts, and state courts sometimes expressed their unhappiness with the doctrine. Criticism of rulings protecting tax immunities under the contract clause mounted in the 1870s, with commentators maintaining that *Wilson* was incorrectly decided and arguing that the power to levy taxes was more important than the police power and could never be the subject of a binding contract.[141] In 1874, for example, a leading treatise considered the ability of states to make binding stipulations exempting property from taxation as "firmly settled" but expressed concern that this doctrine would result in "building up enormous monopolies" and opined that the Supreme Court might be persuaded to abandon the notion that states could relinquish the taxing power.[142]

In the post–Civil War period the Supreme Court first considered tax exemptions in *McGee v. Mathis* (1866).[143] To encourage the reclamation of swampland, the Arkansas legislature in 1851 offered an inducement to purchasers by exempting such land from taxation for ten years or until reclaimed. Four years later the legislature repealed the tax immunity and taxed swampland as other land. The Court had little difficulty in finding that the 1851 act constituted a contract between the state and purchasers of the land. Having agreed to refrain from imposing a tax for the specified time, Arkansas impaired the contract by changing the terms of the agreement.

In 1869 a pair of companion cases involving tax exemptions for charitable institutions—a home for destitute females and a university—laid bare divisions among the justices regarding permanent tax relief.[144] Some years after the grant of tax exemptions the state sought to levy taxes on the property of these institutions. The Court majority ruled in both cases that the charters containing the tax immunities constituted a contract between the state and the incorporators. The prevailing justices acknowledged that charters should be construed favorably to the state but found that the words conferring an exemption were clear. Rejecting the argument that state legislatures had no authority to contract away the power of taxation, they emphasized that it was well settled that a state, for a consideration, could grant exemptions for either a limited time or permanently. Moreover, they ruled that "the exemption is presumed to be on sufficient consideration, and binds the State if the charter containing it is accepted."[145] In these cases the objects of the charitable institutions were deemed by the lawmakers beneficial to the community.

The dissenting opinion in these cases by Justice Miller, joined by Chief Justice Chase and Justice Field, is revealing because it highlights continuing concerns about grants of tax exemptions. Miller began by agreeing with the Court majority that legislators could, by enacting laws, make contracts that they could not subsequently impair. He further shared the broad judicial conviction about the importance of the contract clause:

> We are also free to admit that one of the most beneficial provisions of the Federal Constitution, intended to secure private rights, is the one which protects contracts from the invasion of State legislation. And that the manner in which this court has sustained the contracts of individuals has done much to restrain the State legislature, when urged by the pressure of popular discontent under the suffering of great financial disturbances, from unwise, as well as unjust legislation.[146]

Nonetheless, Miller, a persistent critic of sheltering tax exemptions under the contract clause, insisted that no legislative body had the authority "to bargain away forever the taxing power of the State." He added, "This is a power which, in modern political societies, is absolutely necessary to the continued existence of every such society." Miller's stance was strengthened by his worry that the wealthy would primarily benefit from the grants of tax exemptions. He fretted that relinquishing the taxing power "for an unlimited time" would benefit "rich corporations, as railroads and express companies, or rich men, making contracts with the legislatures, as best they may." The result of such "special and partial legislation" would be to place the burden of government on those who could not obtain immunity.[147] Miller seems to have harbored a somewhat pessimistic opinion of legislators, who were, after all, the ones who granted the tax exemptions. Moreover, given his frequent expressions of alarm over perpetual exemptions, there is room to question whether Miller would have necessarily felt that a grant of tax immunity for a limited period was unprotected by the contract clause.

Miller's strictures against tax concessions appear overdrawn in two respects. First, he gave no weight to the purpose behind the grant of tax exemptions, which was to encourage the investment of capital in risky ventures. Many jurisdictions adopted this policy of indirect subsidy in the hope of gaining societal benefit.[148] Second, Miller's complaint directed at rich corporations ignored the fact that many railroads and other transportation projects were unprofitable.

During the late Reconstruction Era the Supreme Court heard a number of cases in which antebellum legislatures had granted tax exemptions in the charters of railroad companies. In most of these the justices, often unanimously, ruled that subsequent laws levying a tax on railroad property impaired the obligation of contract. The Court's reasoning was well illustrated in *Wilmington Railroad v. Reid* (1872), in which the railroad charter provided that "the property of said company and the shares therein shall be exempt from any public charge or tax whatsoever."[149] Justice David Davis invoked the strict construction principle, emphasizing that "when a corporation claims an exemption from taxation, it must show that the power to tax has been clearly relinquished by the State, and if there be reasonable doubt about this having been done, that doubt must be solved in favor of the State." He even conceded "that it were better for the interest of the State, that the taxing power, which is one of the highest and most important attributes of sovereignty, should on no occasion be surrendered." Davis noted that the ability of states to raise revenue from every type of property could be vital to meet changing needs. Still, he determined that courts could not provide a remedy for "improvident legislation" where the corporate charter clearly created a contract of exemption.[150] The Supreme Court, relying heavily on *Reid*, adhered to this position in several other decisions involving railroad tax exemptions.[151]

Although the Supreme Court frequently found that a state legislature had contracted to exempt certain property from taxation, it bears emphasis that the Court did not vindicate all claims of tax immunity under the contract clause. Harking back to Marshall's opinion in *Providence Bank*, the Court stressed that a state was never presumed to have surrendered the taxing power. Absent clear and unambiguous contractual language conferring an exemption, the state retained its authority to levy taxes. The Court rejected the notion of implied exemptions and in so doing declined to uphold some exemption claims grounded on the contract clause.[152]

The Court also distinguished a tax exemption embedded in a corporate charter from a general law enacting a particular tax policy. At issue in *Salt Company v. East Saginaw* (1872) was an 1859 Michigan statute providing a tax exemption for all property employed in manufacturing salt.[153] Two years later the legislature limited the exemption to five years, and the salt company argued that the amendment impaired its contract with the state. Writing for a unanimous Court, Justice Joseph Bradley, building upon state court precedent,[154] concluded that the measure was "a bounty law" rather than a contract. It was a determinable arrangement effective only so long as it remained unrepealed. "General encouragements," Bradley observed, "held out to all persons indiscriminately, to engage in a particular trade or manufacture" were under legislative control and could be discontinued at any time.[155]

Moreover, the Supreme Court emphasized that tax exemptions did not necessarily transfer to a successor company. Many such cases involved the consolidation of railroads. Justice Field, speaking for the Court in 1876, determined that a tax exemption privilege was not part of a "franchise" and did not pass to a successor absent express legislative sanction.[156] This opened another avenue to extinguish tax immunities, as would become increasingly apparent in the final decades of the nineteenth century.

State courts likewise wrestled with claims of tax exemption and, following the lead of the Supreme Court, sustained a number of exemptions as protected contracts.[157] However, a number of state judges made plain their reservations about treating perpetual tax exemptions as binding contracts. Although feeling obligated to follow Supreme Court precedent and uphold a tax exemption for a railroad company, a Florida judge asserted that in his view the legislature could not relinquish permanently the sovereign right to levy taxes on any particular property.[158] Sustaining a limitation on taxes contained in an 1848 railroad charter, the Supreme Court of Mississippi expressed a wish that the legislature would be more guarded in making such grants. "If this decision," it intoned, "results in the exemption, practically perpetual, of an enormous moneyed monopoly, we can only express the hope that it may at least serve as a warning to future legislatures."[159]

As with other corporate privileges, a state could readily circumvent any contract clause protection of tax immunity by means of a reservation in the charter itself or with a general law of the authority to alter or repeal charters.[160] Thus, Justice Field, writing for the Court in *Tomlinson v. Jessup*

(1873), acknowledged that tax exemptions had been viewed as having the characteristics of a contract but ruled that under an 1841 South Carolina general statute lawmakers could revoke immunity from taxation in a subsequent charter. "The reservation," he explained, "affects the entire relation between the State and the corporation, and placed under legislative control all rights, privileges, and immunities derived by its charter directly from the State."[161] Other courts followed suit.[162] Given the widespread adoption of reservation provisions, tax exemptions gradually became less significant during the late nineteenth century, notwithstanding the contract clause.

Debt Repudiation

The mirror image of decisions validating tax exemptions under the contract clause was cases requiring government to impose taxes to discharge contractual obligations. Municipal debt mounted rapidly between 1860 and 1875 as cities subsidized transportation projects and improved public services, such as streets and sewers. In the Reconstruction Era state legislatures struggled to deal with debt-laden cities and looked favorably upon repudiationist schemes. The problem was not confined to any region but was especially acute in the impoverished Reconstruction South.[163] Courts confronted a variety of legislative schemes calculated to repudiate or reduce the value of financial obligations incurred by state and local governments.

In the leading case of *Von Hoffman v. City of Quincy* (1867) Justice Swayne, for a unanimous bench, firmly shut the door on legislative attempts to withdraw the power to levy taxes, an indirect means of undercutting debt.[164] In the 1850s the legislature had authorized the city to levy a special tax to pay the interest on railroad bonds. After the bonds were issued in reliance on these measures, the lawmakers repealed this authorization in 1863 and limited municipal taxing power. Bondholders challenged the statute restricting the city's taxing power as an impairment of their contract. Swayne agreed, holding that the 1863 act was a nullity with respect to these bonds. He reiterated several key dimensions of contract clause jurisprudence. First, Swayne affirmed that laws that existed at the time of making a contract formed a part of the agreement. It followed that the provision authorizing municipal taxation was part of the contract between the city and the bondholders. Second, Swayne considered at length the time-honored right/remedy distinction first articulated by Marshall. "Nothing can be more material to the obligation," Swayne observed, "than the means of enforcement. . . . The ideas of validity and remedy are inseparable, and both are parts of the obligation, which is guaranteed by the Constitution against invasion." He pointed out that the Court had made no attempt "to fix definitely the line between alterations of the remedy, which are to be deemed legitimate, and those which, under the form of modifying the remedy, impair substantive rights." Each case, he added, must be decided upon its own facts. Going a step further, and anticipating future developments, Swayne then questioned the "soundness of the reasoning which maintains a distinction between the contract and the remedy."[165] Invoking a comparison with cases in which a state contracted to relinquish the taxing power, he concluded that similarly a state could not withdraw an authorized local tax until the contract was satisfied.

As discussed in Chapter 5, the Supreme Court repeatedly ruled in the late nineteenth century that states could not withdraw from local governments the power to meet their valid financial obligations. Lower federal courts and state courts reached the same conclusion.[166] In 1875, for example, the Supreme Court of Ohio held that a law taking away from a city the authority to satisfy its existing contracts impaired contracts in violation of both the federal and state constitution.[167] After the city of Cincinnati contracted for services to improve streets, a state law deprived the municipality of the power to make property assessments in an amount equal to the price of the work. Striking down the state law with respect to existing contractual obligations, the Ohio court maintained that such a municipal contract was protected by both constitutions to the same extent as contracts between private parties. It lectured that "too often" local governments demonstrated "the absence of that sense of binding obligations which is generally felt by individuals to perform their obligations."[168]

Legislative efforts to impose changes on the terms of public contracts or modify the security pledged for bonded debt also ran afoul of the contract clause. State courts invalidated a variety of schemes designed to reduce public debt at the expense of creditors. An 1865 Nebraska law provided that county warrants, drawing interest at 10 percent, had to be exchanged for bonds payable in 1873 at 7 percent. The Supreme Court of Nebraska reasoned that this amounted to the substitution of a "radically different" contract for the one made between the county and the creditors in violation of the contract clauses in both the federal and state constitutions.[169] The court expressed alarm that if this could be done, there was "no limit to the exercise of arbitrary, despotic power by the legislature over personal contracts."[170]

Likewise, in 1871 a New York court struck down a measure that removed lands pledged as security for bonds and substituted a sinking fund. Finding that creditors relied on a specific lien upon the land, not a city fund, the court held that the "security cannot be taken away without impairing the obligation of that contract."[171] In the same vein, the Supreme Court of Pennsylvania voided a statute that indefinitely postponed payment of interest on bonds unless the creditors were prepared to release a large part of the indebtedness.[172]

The Supreme Court joined the chorus in *Board of Liquidation v. McComb* (1876). In 1874 the Louisiana legislature passed the Funding Act, a move to reduce the state debt.[173] The act provided for the issuance of new consolidated bonds, which were to be exchanged for existing bonds at sixty cents on the dollar. As an inducement for creditors to accept these arrangements, the lawmakers provided security guarantees for payment of the consolidated bonds. In addition, an amendment to the Louisiana Constitution declared the consolidated bonds to constitute contracts between the bondholders and the state. A year later the legislature authorized the issuance of consolidated bonds to the Louisiana Levee Company to satisfy an outstanding debt and provided that the company should receive the full amount of what it was owed. In a diversity action a bondholder sought to enjoin the issue of consolidated bonds to the company on the ground that the new debt depreciated the value of the existing consolidated bonds and impaired the obligation of contract of those creditors who were induced to accept the consolidated bonds at less than face value. Justice Bradley, speaking for a unanimous Court, agreed. He maintained that creditors had a right to rely on the scheme of the Funding Act and that the proposed financing of the levee debt destroyed their anticipated benefits.

Alteration of available remedies also raised contract issues regarding bonded debt. Statutes of limitation were usually seen as pertaining to the remedy, not the contract itself. Consequently, state legislatures enjoyed wide discretion to shorten the period of limitations with respect to both existing and future causes of action. But state authority was not unlimited. States had to allow a reasonable time for the parties to commence suits on contracts existing when the statute was adopted.

For instance, when the city of Watertown in Wisconsin issued bonds in 1853 payable in ten years the statute of limitation was twenty years. In 1872 the state legislature reduced the limitation period to recover money on bonds to six years but allowed one year within which a party could bring suits otherwise barred by the law. The federal circuit court found that the 1872 law fixed an unreasonable time to sue on the existing bonds and thus violated the contract clause. It stressed that the bonds were likely negotiated in money markets outside the state and perhaps even in Europe. The court reasoned the bondholders could not have expected "such great and extraordinary change" and that the 1872 law "tends to the destruction of confidence, and to encourage repudiation in violation of the plain letter and spirit of the federal and state constitution."[174]

Public Morals

As in the Antebellum Era, the regulation of public morals produced a handful of contract clause claims. Courts, however, gave a wide berth to state control of liquor sales and the operation of lotteries. A New York court held that liquor licenses were not contracts between the state and the persons licensed but merely temporary permits issued as an exercise of the police power.[175] It followed that such licenses were revocable without regard to the contract clause. Likewise, in 1873 the Supreme Court of Mississippi determined that a corporate charter provision authorizing the conduct of a lottery for twenty-five years, for which the company had paid a consideration of $5,000, was a license and not a contract and was therefore unprotected from revocation by the Constitution. Decrying the "pernicious" and "demoralizing" effects of lotteries, the court ruled that a state has the right to repeal "any reckless legislation whose certain tendency is to corrupt the fountain of public morals."[176] As discussed in Chapter 5, this decision anticipated a similar analysis of a grant to conduct a lottery by the Supreme Court.

By the post–Civil War period divorces were less frequently challenged as violations of the contract clause. The prevailing view was that marriage was not a contract within the reach of the Constitution. This was illustrated by an 1867 decision by the Supreme Court of Pennsylvania upholding the grant of a legislative divorce and observing that the contract clauses in both federal and state constitutions were inapplicable to divorce proceedings.[177]

JUDICIAL IMPAIRMENT OF CONTRACTS

As discussed in Chapter 3, the Supreme Court during Taney's tenure as chief justice indicated that, under some circumstances, a state court ruling might amount to an impairment of contract in violation of the Constitution.[178] The justices continued to grapple with this issue in the years following the Civil War. It bears emphasis that these cases typically involved attempted bond repudiations, a practice that threatened the national credit market.[179]

Although the pattern of decisions was uneven and the analysis somewhat cloudy, the Supreme Court strongly intimated that the contract clause applied to judicial as well as legislative actions.

In 1866 the Court unanimously reaffirmed the doctrine set forth in *Gelpcke v. City of Dubuque* (1864) that a state court could not invalidate contracts it had previously sustained.[180] It concluded that a change of opinion by the Supreme Court of Wisconsin regarding the validity of a statute authorizing counties to issue bonds to raise funds for the purchase of railroad stock could not be applied to securities issued prior to such a changed opinion. It stressed that a contract valid when made could not be impaired by subsequent legislative or judicial action.

This ruling was soon extended to cover a change in the remedy to enforce contracts. At issue in *Butz v. City of Muscatine* (1869) was a request for a writ of mandamus to compel a municipality in Iowa to levy a sufficient property tax to pay a judgment for interest on certain bonds issued in 1854.[181] Jurisdiction was based on diversity of citizenship because the bondholder was a resident of Pennsylvania. An 1851 state statute required municipal corporations to levy taxes to pay judgments. A year later, however, the legislature passed a law limiting property taxes in the city of Muscatine to 1 percent of assessed value. After the bonds were issued, the Iowa Supreme Court held that the 1852 limitation on taxes applied to judgments on unpaid bonds. The amount of the tax collected under that limitation was entirely consumed by the city's current expenses, leaving the judgment creditor with no prospect of payment.

Justice Swayne, a leader in judicial efforts to enforce municipal bonds who often spoke for the Court in these cases, made clear his sympathy with the bondholder. He insisted that the Court could determine for itself the construction of state statutes concerning the rights of creditors regardless of whether a case arose under diversity jurisdiction or appeal from state supreme courts. "Our duty," Swayne proclaimed, "depends upon the questions involved, and not upon the channel through which the case come before us."[182] Clearly grounding his reasoning on contract clause jurisprudence, he viewed the case as one in which the remedies available to the creditor in 1854 had been eliminated. Swayne revealingly explained:

> Here the remedy is taken away; not by a subsequent repeal, but by subsequent judicial decisions. The effect upon the contract is the same as if the provisions of the code had been repealed. . . . The fact that one of the elements in the case is a statute of the State does affect the legal result. We are of the opinion that under the statutes of Iowa, in force when the contract was made, the realtor is

> entitled to the remedy he asks, and that this right can no more be taken away by subsequent judicial decisions than by subsequent legislation. It is as much within the sphere of power and duties to protect the contract from the former as from the latter, and we are no more concluded by one than the other. We cannot in any other way give effect to the contract of the parties as we understand it.[183]

To the majority it appeared that Iowa courts were altering the rules after the bonds had been sold. Disagreeing with his colleagues, Justice Miller, who regularly dissented in municipal bond cases, argued that the issue before the Court involved the construction of state tax laws, not the validity of the contracts.[184] He failed, however, to address the majority's conclusion that the remedy available to enforce the judgment on the unpaid bonds had been effectively destroyed by the Iowa court rulings.

The Court's emphasis upon the contract clause in municipal bond cases was underscored in *Township of Pine Grove v. Talcott* (1874).[185] There was a fresh wave of bond repudiations in the wake of the depression of 1873. The Supreme Court responded by employing language stressing the constitutional basis for rejecting bond repudiation, notwithstanding state court decisions to the contrary. In *Pine Grove,* for example, the justices heard another suit, based on diversity jurisdiction, to recover the amount of certain municipal bonds issued to aid railroad construction pursuant to an 1869 Michigan statute. After the bonds were sold the Supreme Court of Michigan found the statute invalid under the state constitution. Justice Swayne, writing once more for the Court in a bond case, refused to follow the state court adjudication. He pointed out that similar laws had been sustained in a large number of states. Swayne felt that the dispute, which concerned commercial securities, was a matter of general jurisdiction under the rule of *Swift v. Tyson* (1842), leaving the federal courts free to fashion their own determinations based on federal common law. Rather than rest on this point, however, he emphatically declared, "The National Constitution forbids the States to pass laws impairing the obligation of contracts. In cases properly brought before us that end can be accomplished unwarrantably no more by judicial decisions than by legislation."[186] This decision represented a further extension of *Gelpcke* to situations in which the contracts had not been previously upheld by a state court and subsequently struck down. The Supreme Court appeared to be acting to protect the reasonable expectation of the bondholders and in so doing once more suggested that state judicial decisions could impair contracts.

Yet an assessment of judicial impairments is complicated by the fact that in several cases the Supreme Court refused to hear direct appeals from state courts raising the question of judicial impairment, sending somewhat conflicting signals.[187] This has led some commentators to conclude that *Gelpcke* and its progeny did not rest on the contract clause but reflected rules devised for diversity cases only.[188] They express skepticism about the judicial impairment doctrine.

Such arguments, however, are far from conclusive. The grounds on which the Supreme Court declined to entertain direct appeals were not clearly explained. Indeed, practical considerations help to explain the outcome of these cases. In *Railroad Company v. Rock* (1867), for instance, it does not appear that any constitutional issues were raised in the state court. Justice Miller, writing for the Court, insisted that the state court decision rested solely on the requirements of local law or the question of fraud. He rightly maintained that every case in which a state court set aside a contract for routine causes did not present an issue of impairment for the Supreme Court.[189]

Moreover, most of the bonds were sold not locally but to out-of-state and foreign creditors. Diversity jurisdiction was sufficient to safeguard their interests and thus bolster the national credit market. Pragmatically there was little to be gained by extending the emerging doctrine of judicial impairments to essentially local disputes.[190] Whatever the Court's rationale, it clearly adopted language indicating that retroactive changes in law by state courts regarding existing contracts could run afoul of the contract clause.

CONTRACT CLAUSE AT THE CROSSROADS

By the end of the Reconstruction Era in 1876 the contract clause remained one of the most litigated provisions of the Constitution and had been applied by both federal and state courts in a wide variety of cases. The Supreme Court seemed poised to extend the reach of the provision to state court decisions that impaired prior agreements. The sanctity of contracts was a widely shared societal norm. Nonetheless, conflict mounted between state police power and the constitutional shelter given contracts. Although the contract clause was vigorously invoked by both state and federal judges, cracks began to appear in contract clause jurisprudence as courts sought to deal with novel issues in a complex economy. The strict construction of corporate charters and the embryonic notion of an alienable police power would in time erode the protection afforded agreements by the contract clause. This process was hastened by the emergence of the due process clause of the Fourteenth Amendment as a shield for economic rights in the late nineteenth century. In short, the decade of the 1870s constituted a high-water mark for the importance of the contract clause in constitutional history.

CHAPTER 5

The Gilded Age

US society underwent sweeping changes in the late nineteenth century. Industrialization and urbanization profoundly altered the social landscape as a new urban nation gradually supplanted the older country of rural communities. The emergence of large-scale corporate enterprise fundamentally changed workplace relations and aroused latent fear of monopoly power. In response, state and federal legislators began to intervene more aggressively in the economy, enacting laws to protect public health, safety, and morals and to impose rate regulations on certain industries.[1]

The Supreme Court in the Gilded Age was broadly supportive of property rights and private economic ordering. In so doing the Court developed a robust property-conscious jurisprudence, increasingly turning to the due process clause of the Fourteenth Amendment as a vehicle to invalidate state laws deemed to interfere unreasonably with property and liberty. Still, it is a myth that the jurists sought to impose a strict laissez-faire regime. Not only would such a task exceed judicial capacity but the Court upheld the vast majority of challenged regulations.[2]

Notwithstanding heightened judicial solicitude for the rights of property owners, the contract clause paradoxically declined in importance in the last decades of the nineteenth century. To be sure, both federal and state courts heard a steady stream of contract clause litigation. In 1896 Justice George Shiras accurately remarked, "No provision of the Constitution of the United States has received more frequent consideration by the Court than that which provides that no State shall pass any law impairing the obligation of contracts."[3] Although courts repeatedly invoked the contract clause, they ceased to read the provision in an innovative or expansive manner and began to rely on other constitutional language to safeguard economic rights. This chapter will explore the pattern of contract clause decisions in the Gilded Age and consider why the clause started to fade in significance.

PERSISTENT CONCERN WITH CONTRACTS

Of course, the contract clause did not shrivel away overnight. As Lawrence M. Friedman explained, the nineteenth century was "an age that exalted voluntary agreement."[4] Given the key role of contracts in the growth of market activities throughout the century, it is not surprising that courts continued to stress the importance of contracting. In 1877 the Supreme Court, for example, emphatically declared, "A compact lies at the foundation of all national life. Contracts mark the progress of communities in civilization and prosperity. They guard, as far as possible, against the fluctuations of human affairs. They seek to give stability to the present and certainty to the future. . . . They are the springs of business, trade, and commerce. Without them, society could not go on."[5] Similarly, courts and commentators lavishly celebrated the contract clause. Justice William Strong, speaking for the Court in 1878, proclaimed, "There is no more important provision in the Federal Constitution than the one which prohibits the states from passing laws impairing the obligation of contracts, and it is one of the highest duties of this Court to take care that the prohibition shall neither be evaded nor frittered away."[6] A few years later Henry Sumner Maine, the English political economist, likewise observed, "There is no more important provision in the whole Constitution" than the contract clause, which he pictured as "the bulwark of an American individualism against democratic impatience and Socialist fantasy."[7] The broad impact of the contract clause was widely noted even by those who were skeptical about some applications of the provision. As Justice Samuel F. Miller put it, "The frequency with which this court has been called on to declare State laws void, because they do impair the obligation of contracts, shows how very important and far-reaching that provision is."[8] "From the first," Joel Prentiss Bishop wrote in 1887, "the great importance and wide effect of this provision were recognized." He admitted that the contract clause had been a source of dissent and discord but maintained, "The results are such as, on a review, are found to accord with sound reason and common sense."[9]

SCOPE OF PROTECTION

Long-standing interpretative issues resurfaced to both guide and confound contract clause jurisprudence. The Supreme Court in the Gilded Age repeatedly reaffirmed the principle that it had paramount authority to determine the existence of contracts and whether their obligations had been impaired. It was not necessarily governed by previous decisions of state courts on these points.[10] The Court continued to grapple with whether a particular statute amounted to a legislative contract. As Miller explained,

"The difficulty in this class of cases has always been to distinguish what is intended by the legislature to be an exercise of its ordinary legislative function in making laws, which, like other laws, are subject to its full control by future amendments and appeals, from what is intended to become a contract between the State and other parties when the terms of the statute have been accepted and acted upon by those parties." He stated that this distinction "has always been a very fine point."[11]

Even more troublesome was the persistent uncertainty over the differentiation between the contractual rights and the enforcement remedies. At what point did a change in the available remedy impair the rights under the contract? Both courts and commentators expressed frustration with the supposed distinction. "All of the confusion and conflict which have arisen on this subject," the Supreme Court of Mississippi lamented in 1877, "grew out of the difficulty of distinguishing, in all cases, between the right and the remedy. The one must not be impaired; the other may be modified." It acknowledged that a law might strike "at the right by denying the remedy."[12] Courts increasingly recognized the artificiality of the right/remedy distinction. "The idea[s] of right and remedy," the Supreme Court of Arkansas insisted in 1883, "are so intimately associated as often to be inseparable."[13] Three years later a commentator complained, "Of all the complications which have arisen" under the contract clause, "there is perhaps none which has been productive of greater embarrassment and confusion than the distinction between the obligation of the contract and the remedy for its enforcement." The prevailing rule, he asserted, appeared "to rest on the *extent* to which the change in the law affects the remedy and, through it, the contract." This rule, he pointed out, "opens up a very wide ground of debate."[14]

Despite sustained criticism, courts struggled to ascertain the dividing line between legislative changes affecting only the remedy and those impairing the contractual undertaking as well. The complexity of this task can be highlighted by reconsidering the abolition of imprisonment for debt for contracts made when imprisonment was a remedy available to the creditor. In 1880 the Supreme Court had no hesitation in affirming the well-settled rule that the elimination of this remedy was not such a change as to impair the obligation of contract.[15] This judicial attitude clearly reflected the sentiment of the age, which regarded such imprisonment as cruel and counterproductive. At the same time, a credible argument could be made that abolition destroyed an efficacious remedy. As a Kansas judge aptly pointed out, "That imprisonment is a potent means of enforcing the payment of debts is fully understood by every intelligent citizen, as well as by members of the bar."[16] He questioned why states were free to retroactively abolish this effective remedy but not to modify other remedies to afford some relief to hard-pressed debtors. As the nineteenth century drew to a close, the viability of the distinction between remedies and contractual rights was increasingly drawn into doubt.

In addition, the Supreme Court adhered to its position that the contract clause pertained to agreements respecting property. It followed that the provision had no application to laws regulating public institutions and offices. Legislation establishing a county seat, for instance, was found not to constitute a contract that barred subsequent relocation of the county seat.[17]

PRIVATE CONTRACTS

During the Gilded Age federal and state courts heard relatively few cases involving state abridgment of contracts between private parties. In accord with the previous pattern, most of these involved the application of debt-relief measures and state insolvency laws to antecedent agreements. The bulk of this litigation arose in southern and western states, where farmers and local merchants felt acutely the burden of economic distress. These areas provided much of the support for the Populist movement of the 1890s. Although courts tended to look skeptically at relief legislation, they did not break any new doctrinal ground and adhered to precedent.

The bulk of the challenges to debt-relief legislation was heard at the state level. State courts, for example, invalidated laws that increased the exemption of personal property from the reach of creditors[18] and made it clear that homestead exemptions could not be applied to prior debts.[19] Laws regulating foreclosure sales were a recurring source of controversy. Relying on the contract clause in the state constitution, the Supreme Court of New Jersey in 1881 voided an act delaying a suit on the bond of a mortgage in default until after foreclosure on the property and enlarging the conditions of redemption.[20] Two years later the Supreme Court of Arkansas struck down a measure retroactively declaring that land could not be sold at less than two-thirds of an appraised value and providing that any land sold could be redeemed at the sale price for one year.[21] Nor could a legislature impose a one-year stay on the sale of foreclosed land, then mandate that any sale must produce 80 percent of the appraised value. Rejecting the common argument that these requirements merely affected the remedy, the Supreme Court of Washington decided that the law placed new burdens on mortgagees and lessened the value of preexisting mortgage contracts.[22] The Supreme Court of Minnesota voided a law that in effect abolished foreclosure under power of sale as provided in the mortgage contract. It reasoned that the legislature could not impair the contractual stipulation conferring power of sale as to mortgages entered before the law was enacted.[23]

In the wake of the Depression of 1893, a number of states enacted laws enlarging the period of redemption from mortgage sales. These measures generated a good deal of litigation and set the stage for the only Supreme Court decision dealing with the impairment of a private contract. At issue in *Barintz v. Beverly* (1896) was a Kansas statute authorizing the redemption of foreclosed property when no such right had previously existed.[24] Justice Shiras, speaking for a unanimous bench, cited a line of cases back to *Bronson v. Kinzie* (1843) and concluded that change in the law substantially impaired the rights of the mortgagee under the mortgage contract. Several state courts, following *Barintz,* subsequently determined laws that extended the period of redemption could not constitutionally be applied to sales under mortgages executed before passage of the laws.[25]

An analogous line of cases dealt with laws that sought to extend the redemption period for land sold for delinquent taxes before passage of the statutes. Courts generally ruled that the purchase of land at a tax sale amounted to a contract and was governed by the law in force at the time of the sale. It followed that laws purporting to enlarge the redemption period imposed new terms on antecedent contracts and violated the contract clause.[26]

State laws altering how the proceeds of life insurance should be paid also were found to conflict with the contract clause. Generally life insurance proceeds payable to the estate of the deceased became assets of the estate and were liable for the payment of debts. Anxious to protect a surviving spouse and heirs, several states enacted measures that provided that part of the insurance proceeds should inure to the benefit of such parties and remain exempt from any debts. Treating these laws as in effect exemption statutes, state courts held that the measures impaired the obligation of contract as applied to antecedent policies.[27]

Not all statutes affecting the debtor-creditor relationship were barred by the contract clause. Recall that the provision did not apply prospectively. Justice Miller summarized this rule well: "But the doctrine has long been settled that statutes limiting the rights of the creditor to enforce his claim against the property of the debtor, which are in existence at the time the contracts are made are not void, but are within the legislative power of the States, where the property and the debtor are to be found."[28] State insolvency laws in effect when a debt was incurred were deemed part of the contract. Consequently, application of an insolvency law to the disposition of an insolvent's property raised no contract clause issue.[29] Some retrospective laws also passed muster. The Supreme Court determined that repeal of the Texas usury law did not violate the contract clause with respect to agreements made before such repeal. It held that repeal of the usury law simply eliminated a defense previously available to the enforcement of contracts and was "a privilege that belongs to the remedy, and forms no element in the rights that inhere in the contract."[30] The material rights of the parties under the contract were not impaired.

The record amply demonstrates that courts in the late nineteenth century evidenced a high regard for the sanctity of private contracts and were not reluctant to invoke the contract clause to safeguard such agreements. Courts regularly struck down laws retroactively modifying debtor-creditor relationships. Judicial reliance on the contract clause in this area, however, was overshadowed by the torrent of litigation that implicated the public branch of contract clause jurisprudence. Here the Supreme Court began a slow retreat from the full implications of *Dartmouth College.*

DARTMOUTH COLLEGE DOCTRINE UNDER SIEGE

At a superficial glance the *Dartmouth College* case appeared to enjoy landmark status in constitutional law. The Supreme Court repeatedly affirmed the importance of this decision. In 1880 Chief Justice Morrison R. Waite proclaimed that the *Dartmouth College* doctrines "have become so imbedded in the jurisprudence of the United States as to make them for all intents and purposes a part of the Constitution itself."[31] More than a decade later the Court recognized criticism of the decision but insisted that the case "has been reaffirmed and applied so often as to have become firmly established as a canon of American jurisprudence."[32] The New York Court of Appeals added that the "celebrated" *Dartmouth College* case "has, although sometimes criticized, been universally acquiesced in by the courts of the several states as the law of the land, and may be regarded as too firmly established to admit of question or dispute."[33]

In marked contrast to such judicial praise, commentators directed steady criticism at *Dartmouth College* and the notion that corporate charters were inviolate. Enlarging upon the earlier critique that emerged in the

1870s, critics in the Gilded Age focused on two central themes. First, they charged that *Dartmouth College* was wrongly decided because the framers did not envision the constitutional protection of corporate charters.[34] Second, they maintained that *Dartmouth College* was simply unworkable in an era of large-scale business enterprises and a rapidly growing economy. As a corollary to this point, they expressed the fear that business corporations could escape effective public control by virtue of the *Dartmouth College* ruling. In essence, critics sought to reopen the antebellum debate about the scope of the contract clause.

In 1884 Francis Wharton, for example, noted "a growing tendency to doubt the correctness of the general rule laid down" in *Dartmouth College*. He stressed that in view of technological developments the claim of inviolable corporate charters was "in conflict with the general policy of the country, if not with necessary conditions of social life."[35] Likewise, Bishop asserted that acts of incorporation, rather than being contracts, should be treated as ordinary legislation subject to repeal. He fretted that "any foolish legislature" could "create an artificial monster which no power can ever thereafter slay."[36]

In 1890 Christopher G. Tiedeman, a leading constitutional theorist, argued that the contract clause should be construed narrowly to prevent the "repudiation of public or private debts by State legislation."[37] Decrying the "dangerous consequences" of the doctrine of inviolate corporate charters, Tiedeman noted that "the power of private corporations has increased rapidly, every advance in science and industry tending to develop the proportions and the strength of corporations, until there is a general fear of a usurpation by them of control of the government." Yet he perceptively pointed out that changes in public opinion and consequent alterations in constitutional doctrine greatly diluted *Dartmouth College*, and he concluded that the Supreme Court outwardly affirms the opinion "while the rule is substantially modified, if not abrogated altogether."[38]

Another commentator was more supportive of *Dartmouth College* but acknowledged difficulties in applying the doctrine to modern business conditions. Picturing the decision as security for property and enterprise, the author argued that few would deny that "the numerous decisions setting aside acts of State legislatures avoiding or abrogating contracts, and doing this upon the precedent of the College case, have been a benefit to the country."[39] Recognizing widespread concern about the power of corporations, he doubted that the "existing evils arising from corporate abuses are mainly to be attributed to the decision in the College case."[40] The author emphasized that the Supreme Court had adopted "many qualifications and limitations" that diminished the impact of *Dartmouth College* with respect to corporations and achieved a "progressive modification" of the decision "to suit the altered circumstances of the country."[41] He concluded by praising the contract clause as "simply a statement of an immutable principle of government with regard to good faith in contracts, plainly applying to private and public arrangements alike."[42]

Several observations about this barrage of criticism directed at *Dartmouth College* are in order. It is noteworthy that the commentators concentrated on the supposed evils of that decision and did not question the broader proposition that the contract clause reached public as well as private contracts. Indeed, some commentators specifically took the position that the provision barred state repudiation of public debts as well as legislative infringement upon private agreements. Nevertheless, these complaints about *Dartmouth College* paved the way for a broader assault on contract clause jurisprudence in the early twentieth century as scholars associated with the Progressive movement asserted that the provision applied only to private agreements.

There was a curious shadowboxing nature to the attacks on *Dartmouth College.* Much of the ire was both misdirected and overstated. State legislators, not judges, granted corporate charters and conferred special privileges, such as tax exemptions and monopoly status. Such inducements were seen at the time as serving the public interest by fostering commerce, a point too often ignored by later commentators in their haste to complain about corporate power. Moreover, before the Civil War state lawmakers had largely ceased to grant irrevocable charters, so the problem was confined to the older states and was diminishing in scope. The critics were clearly reacting to perceived economic evils of the Gilded Age and fears of state-conferred monopoly power. They tended to project their concerns about the unwisdom of concessions granted to business corporations before the Civil War onto the Marshall Court and *Dartmouth College.* This adverse outlook clearly colored their views about the contract clause. But it is historical nonsense to blame the problems associated with the rise of the new industrial order on *Dartmouth College.* In fact, the doctrine of inviolate corporate charters had already been drained of much vitality. As discussed below, the combination of strict construction of corporate charters, widespread adoption of reserved legislative power to amend or repeal charters, and the rise of an inalienable police power virtually emasculated *Dartmouth College.* Courts often paid lip service to the decision but rarely invoked it.[43] Herbert

Hovenkamp has cogently observed that during the late nineteenth century "the notion that a corporate charter was a contract according vested privileges to the corporation substantially fell apart."[44]

RAILROAD RATE REGULATIONS

One of the most vexing and protracted controversies of the late nineteenth century concerned efforts by state legislatures to regulate the rates charged by railroads. This complex dispute cannot be reviewed in detail here. Railroads questioned the constitutionality of rate controls on a number of grounds.[45] The most important challenge for the purposes of this study was whether such regulations impaired the obligation of contract by altering provisions in railroad charters. Pointing to language in their charters, some carriers plausibly insisted that they had been expressly given the authority to set their own charges free of legislative control. As the Supreme Court observed, a question commonly presented was whether state authority to regulate charges "had not been, by stipulations of the charter, or other legislation, amounting to a contract, surrendered to the company, or been in some manner qualified."[46] To be sure, the Court acknowledged in 1877, in one of the Granger cases, a contract clause defense to rate regulation was possible, declaring that railroads were "subject to legislative control as to their rates of fare and freight, unless protected by their charters."[47] However, the Court consistently rebuffed railroad arguments grounded on charters and the contract clause. In every case it found that either (1) the charters had not conferred rate-setting privileges,[48] or (2) the charters had been granted under state constitutions reserving the power to alter or amend charters.[49] Chief Justice Waite, who authored most of the rate regulation decisions in the 1870s and 1880s, adhered to the strict construction principle enunciated in *Charles River Bridge* and was sympathetic to laws regulating state-chartered enterprises.[50]

In an especially revealing decision, *Stone v. Farmers' Loan and Trust Company* (1886), the Supreme Court made clear its reluctance to find that any charter provision was sufficiently clear to exempt the railroad from state regulatory authority.[51] In 1848 the Mississippi legislature granted a railroad charter that provided, "It shall be lawful for the company . . . from time to time to fix, regulate, and receive the tolls and charges by them to be received for transportation for persons or property on their railroad." The railroad challenged a subsequent Mississippi statute creating a commission

Railroad charters were a fertile source of contract clause litigation concerning tax exemptions and state attempts to impose rate regulations. (Library of Congress)

empowered to set rates as an infringement of its contractual right to oversee charges on its line. Waite, writing for the Court majority, held that the charter manifested no intention by the state to surrender its authority to set rates. Because the common law required that charges by common carriers must be reasonable, Waite declared that the state was free to determine what amounted to reasonable charges. Dissenting, Justice John Marshall Harlan found a contract clause violation because the state transferred a power conferred by the charter on the carrier to a commission. "In short," Harlan charged, "the companies are placed in the same condition they would occupy if their charter had not conferred upon them the power to fix and regulate rates for transportation."[52] In a separate dissent, Justice Stephen J. Field opined that the act was a "plain impairment of this essential right" and expressed concern that state-imposed rates might hamper the ability of the company "to receive a fair return upon its value."[53]

Harlan, a stalwart champion of contract clause enforcement, made a telling point. If this charter language was not sufficient to establish a railroad's authority to determine rates, would any wording ever be found to achieve that purpose? Did not the majority opinion simply read the rate-setting provision out of the charter? Benjamin F. Wright conceded that this case represented "indeed an extreme instance of interpretation favorable to the state."[54]

This pattern continued throughout the 1880s, with the Supreme Court brushing aside railroad arguments based on the contract clause.[55] The consolidation of railroad companies, a common practice in the late nineteenth century, provided another avenue for the Supreme Court to strictly construe the rate language in rail charters. It ruled that any special privileges, such as the right to fix charges, did not transfer to a merged company absent an express statutory direction to that effect. Consequently, a state-imposed maximum rate for passengers did not infringe any right granted to one of the original carriers.[56]

In fact, the Supreme Court never struck down a state railroad-rate law on contract clause grounds. A commentator accurately wrote in 1896, "The court will not discover a contract in any railroad charter that no interference with rates shall be had by the state legislature."[57] The *Dartmouth College* case clearly had no force in this area of law.

As it became obvious that railroad companies could expect little assistance from the contract clause, they turned to the due process clause of the Fourteenth Amendment for protection against unreasonable rates. At issue in the seminal case of *Chicago, Milwaukee, and St. Paul Railway Company v. Minnesota* (1890) was the validity of an order by the state railroad commission fixing a rate for the shipment of milk.[58] The corporate charter empowered the company directors to make rules regarding "the rates of toll and the manner of collecting the same." Counsel for the railroad argued, among other points, that the legislature, acting through a commission, impaired the obligation of the contract contained in the charter. The Supreme Court gave short shrift to this contention, holding in accord with recent precedent that the charter did not constitute an irrevocable contract that the company was free of state control over rates. Yet the justices then broke new ground, ruling that the question of the reasonableness of transportation rates was a matter for judicial inquiry and that to deprive a company of the authority to charge reasonable rates amounted to a deprivation of property without due process of law.[59] In the ensuing decades railroads relied on the due process clause to secure judicial review of reasonable rates, relegating the contract clause to the sidelines in such cases.[60]

RESERVATION CLAUSES

In addition to the doctrine of strict construction, the near universal adoption of provisions authorizing legislatures to amend or repeal corporate charters did much to weaken any protection afforded such charters under the contract clause. "The general adoption of this reservation in one form or another," Wright maintained, "has, with the possible exception of the rise of due process, been the principal factor in the decline of the contract clause."[61] In 1888 the New York Court of Appeals noted "the adoption by the legislatures of the various states, of the practice of incorporating such reservations in acts of incorporation."[62] Many states placed reservation language in their constitutions, thereby making such provisions part of every subsequent contract.

The Supreme Court addressed a variety of issues pertaining to the meaning and legal effect of reservation clauses. One question related to the extent to which the reservation was applicable in particular cases. Unlike those states that had constitutional provisions, New Jersey put reservation language in a general corporation law. The Court declared that a statutory reservation of such a right was not binding on succeeding legislatures, which were free to enter irrevocable contracts. On the facts presented, it ruled that the legislature had granted an irrevocable tax exemption protected by the contract clause.[63]

Yet the justices repeatedly sustained statutes altering or repealing corporate charters based on reservation clauses. In addition to the railroad rate cases mentioned above, a few examples must suffice. Pointing to the original franchise reserving power in the city of Richmond to govern railroad operations, the Court rejected an argument that an ordinance barring steam engines on certain streets impaired any contractual right in the corporate charter.[64] Likewise, the Court found that the right of a water company to supply water at prices set by a commission was subject to the reserved power of alteration and repeal in the state constitution and that consequently the state was free to create a new mode of determining charges. Speaking for the Court, Chief Justice Waite added, "The power to amend corporate charters is no doubt one that bad men may abuse, but when the amendments are within the scope of the power, the courts cannot interfere with the discretion of the legislatures that have been invested with authority to make them."[65] The Court was also unimpressed with the contention that a franchise to install underground wires in the streets of New York City was infringed when the city changed the public agency responsible for supervising the project. It noted the expressly reserved power of the state or municipality to regulate use of the streets.[66]

State courts similarly invoked the reservation of legislative power to alter or repeal charters in order to defeat corporate claims based on the contract clause. For example, in 1886 the New Jersey Court of Errors and Appeals rejected the contention that a subsequent tax on railroad property violated a special provision in prior charters limiting such a levy. It reasoned that by virtue of the reserved power clause the legislature retained the power to levy future taxes.[67]

Building on earlier cases, courts in the Gilded Age grappled with the extent of the reserved power to alter or repeal charters. Although uniformly upholding the reserved power, judges sought to cabin its reach to protect property and vested rights. As the Supreme Court declared in *Shields v. Ohio* (1877):

> The power of alteration and amendment is not without limits. The alterations must be reasonable; they must be made in good faith, and be consistent with the scope and object of the Act of incorporation. Sheer oppression and wrong cannot be inflicted under the guise of amendment or alteration. Beyond the sphere of the reserved powers, the vested rights of property of corporations, in such cases, are surrounded by the same sanctions and are as inviolate as in other cases.[68]

Thomas Cooley, while on the Supreme Court of Michigan, made clear that a general power to amend charters was not boundless. Cooley's views are particularly revealing because, as discussed in Chapter 4, he was critical of *Dartmouth College* and the notion of corporate charters as irrevocable contracts. Nonetheless, he looked skeptically at a state law requiring road companies to move their tollgates outside the boundaries of any city. The city of Detroit defended this measure by pointing to the reservation language in both the general corporation law and the charter of the defendant company. Cooley would have none of it. "But there is no well-considered case," he proclaimed, "in which it has been held that a legislature, under its power to amend a charter, might take from the corporation any of its substantial property or property rights."[69] Cooley asserted that a statute in effect denying the company the ability to collect tolls on a segment of its road "would not be a statute to amend franchises, but a statute to confiscate property; it would be not be a statute of regulation, but of spoliation."[70] In short, the power to amend did not encompass depriving a corporation of any rightfully acquired property. Citing Cooley's opinion, the New York Court of Appeals concluded that a reservation clause enabled the legislature to terminate the existence of a corporation or enact regulations but did not extend to taking property or valid franchises from the dissolved corporation.[71]

Justice Field, in a dissenting opinion, also echoed Cooley's analysis. Field declared that reservation clauses applied "only to the control of incorporation, to the corporate existence, franchise, and privileges granted by the State."[72] He maintained that the state could not, under its reserved power, appropriate the property of the corporation without paying compensation. The upshot was that states could broadly utilize reserved power to impose changes on corporate charters and even dissolve corporations and thus circumvent *Dartmouth College.* This reserved power, however, was subject to judicial oversight and could not be used to confiscate property.[73]

POLICE POWER

In addition to the doctrine of strict construction of corporate charters and the prevalence of reserved legislative authority, the gradual embrace of the principle of an inalienable police power to protect the public would significantly erode the protection of charters under the contract clause.[74] As we have seen, state courts began to suggest in the Antebellum Era that legislatures could not barter away their power to safeguard the health, safety, and morals of the public. Leading commentators, such as Cooley, endorsed this position in the 1870s. The Supreme Court first intimated acceptance of an alienable police power in an opinion by Justice Field in *Boyd v. Alabama* (1876).[75] The Court ruled that there was no valid contract to conduct a lottery and that therefore repeal of the lottery privilege did not constitute an impairment. Moving beyond the holding, Field added in dicta, "We are not prepared to admit that it is competent for one legislature, by any contract with an individual, to restrain the power of a subsequent legislature to legislate for the public welfare, and to that end to suppress any and all practices tending to corrupt the public morals."[76]

The *Boyd* decision was a harbinger of a cluster of rulings in the next few years in which the Supreme Court put its seal of approval firmly on the doctrine that states could not, even by express contractual language, divest themselves of the authority to exercise the police power to safeguard the health, safety, and morals of the public. In *Beer Company v. Massachusetts* (1878), for instance, the Court dismissed a contract clause challenge to a state prohibition law that rendered worthless a corporate franchise to manufacture liquor.[77] It first pointed out that the company charter was subject to the reserved power of the legislature to regulate the business of corporations or repeal any act of incorporation. It then observed, "All rights are subject to the police power of the State." Consequently, the Court insisted that a state could not by contract bargain away its power to legislate for "the protection of the lives, health, and property of the citizens, and to the preservation of good order and the public morals."[78]

A stronger assertion of the role of the police power came in *Fertilizing Company v. Hyde Park* (1878).[79] An 1867 act incorporated the company for fifty years and authorized it to convert dead animals into fertilizer in a designated area. The works were located in a nearly uninhabited place but were subsequently incorporated into a village. Complaints about the stench of animal matter carried through the streets led the village in 1872 to ban the transportation of any offal through the streets. Arguing that the law made it impracticable to carry out its business, the company claimed that the measure impaired the obligation of contract in its charter. Rejecting this contention, the Supreme Court held that contractual arrangements were subject to the police power to abate a nuisance. The charter, it emphasized, did not guarantee a fifty-year exemption from an exercise of the police power.

The dissenting opinion by Justice William Strong raised two salient points that warrant examination. Picturing the operation of the fertilizing company in a sympathetic light, he noted that the large slaughtering industry in Chicago necessitated the removal of offal from the city and that the company had selected a then-lawful location for its plant. Because the state lawmakers must have been aware of the nature of the fertilizer business, Strong stated that the charter was "therefore, a grant of a right to maintain a local nuisance."[80] Finding that the village ordinance infringed the contractual rights of the company, he called into question the very concept of an inalienable police power. Strong observed:

> The police power of a State is no more sacred than its taxing power. We have held again and again that a State may by contract with one of its corporations bind itself not to tax the property of that corporation. If so why may it not bind itself not to exercise its police power over certain employments [sic]. It would be a monstrous stretch of credulity to conclude that the legislature of Illinois did not intend such a relinquishment of police power when it granted the charter to the plaintiff in error.[81]

Strong highlighted an issue that confounded contract clause jurisprudence throughout the late nineteenth century: Why were courts more receptive to surrender of the taxing power than the police power?

Acknowledging that states could regulate business enterprise under their police power, Strong also raised the crucial question of the scope of that power. "Nothing, I admit," he said, "is more indefinite than the extent or limits of what is called police power." Strong contended that the police power could not be "exerted for the destruction of a chartered right distinctly granted by a contract."[82] As he recognized, the emergence of a police

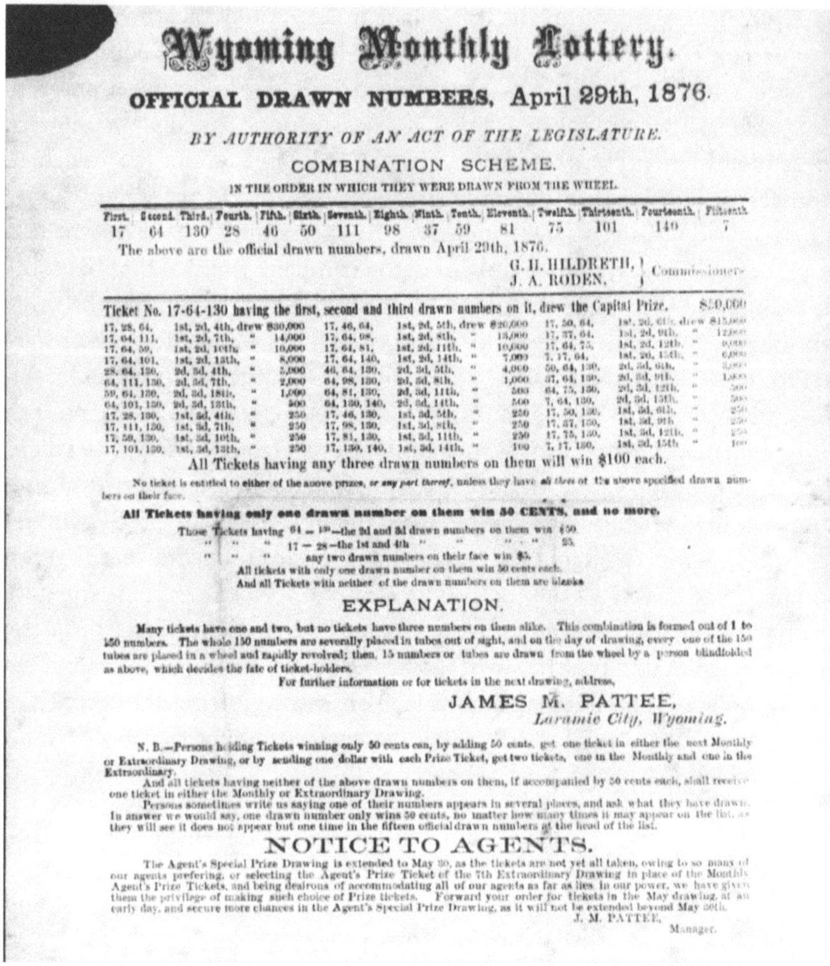

Wyoming Monthly Lottery.

OFFICIAL DRAWN NUMBERS, April 29th, 1876.

BY AUTHORITY OF AN ACT OF THE LEGISLATURE.

COMBINATION SCHEME.

IN THE ORDER IN WHICH THEY WERE DRAWN FROM THE WHEEL.

First.	Second.	Third.	Fourth.	Fifth.	Sixth.	Seventh.	Eighth.	Ninth.	Tenth.	Eleventh.	Twelfth.	Thirteenth.	Fourteenth.	Fifteenth.
17	64	130	28	46	50	111	98	37	59	81	75	101	140	7

The above are the official drawn numbers, drawn April 29th, 1876.

G. H. HILDRETH, } Commissioners
J. A. RODEN, }

Ticket No. 17-64-130 having the first, second and third drawn numbers on it, drew the Capital Prize. $50,000

17, 28, 64,	1st, 2d, 4th, drew	$30,000	17, 46, 64,	1st, 2d, 5th, drew	$20,000	17, 50, 64,	1st, 2d, 6th, drew	$15,000
17, 64, 111,	1st, 2d, 7th, "	14,000	17, 64, 98,	1st, 2d, 8th, "	13,000	17, 37, 64,	1st, 2d, 9th, "	12,000
17, 64, 59,	1st, 2d, 10th, "	10,000	17, 64, 81,	1st, 2d, 11th, "	10,000	17, 64, 75,	1st, 2d, 12th, "	9,000
17, 64, 101,	1st, 2d, 13th, "	8,000	17, 64, 140,	1st, 2d, 14th, "	7,000	7, 17, 64,	1st, 2d, 15th, "	6,000
28, 64, 130,	2d, 3d, 4th, "	5,000	46, 64, 130,	2d, 3d, 5th, "	4,000	50, 64, 130,	2d, 3d, 6th, "	3,000
64, 111, 130,	2d, 3d, 7th, "	2,000	64, 98, 130,	2d, 3d, 8th, "	1,000	37, 64, 130,	2d, 3d, 9th, "	1,500
59, 64, 130,	2d, 3d, 10th, "	1,000	64, 81, 130,	2d, 3d, 11th, "	500	64, 75, 130,	2d, 3d, 12th, "	500
64, 101, 130,	2d, 3d, 13th, "	500	64, 130, 140,	2d, 3d, 14th, "	500	7, 64, 130,	2d, 3d, 15th, "	500
17, 28, 130,	1st, 3d, 4th, "	250	17, 46, 130,	1st, 3d, 5th, "	250	17, 50, 130,	1st, 3d, 6th, "	250
17, 111, 130,	1st, 3d, 7th, "	250	17, 98, 130,	1st, 3d, 8th, "	250	17, 37, 130,	1st, 3d, 9th "	250
17, 59, 130,	1st, 3d, 10th, "	250	17, 81, 130,	1st, 3d, 11th, "	250	17, 75, 130,	1st, 3d, 12th, "	250
17, 101, 130,	1st, 3d, 13th, "	250	17, 130, 140,	1st, 3d, 14th, "	100	7, 17, 130,	1st, 3d, 15th "	100

All Tickets having any three drawn numbers on them will win $100 each.

No ticket is entitled to **either of the above prizes**, *or any part thereof*, unless they have *all three* of the above specified drawn numbers on their face.

All Tickets having only one drawn number on them win 50 CENTS, and no more.

Those Tickets having 64 – 130—the 2d and 3d drawn numbers on them win $50.
" " " 17 – 28—the 1st and 4th " " " " 25.
" " " any two drawn numbers on their face win $5.
All tickets with only one drawn number on them win 50 cents each.
And all Tickets with neither of the drawn numbers on them are blanks

EXPLANATION.

Many tickets have one and two, but no tickets have three numbers on them alike. This combination is formed out of 1 to 150 numbers. The whole 150 numbers are severally placed in tubes out of sight, and on the day of drawing, every one of the 150 tubes are placed in a wheel and rapidly revolved; then, 15 numbers or tubes are drawn from the wheel by a person blindfolded as above, which decides the fate of ticket-holders.

For further information or for tickets in the next drawing, address,

JAMES M. PATTEE,
Laramie City, Wyoming.

N. B.—Persons holding Tickets winning only 50 cents can, by adding 50 cents, get one ticket in either the next Monthly or Extraordinary Drawing, or by sending one dollar with each Prize Ticket, get two tickets, one in the Monthly and one in the Extraordinary.

And all tickets having neither of the above drawn numbers on them, if accompanied by 50 cents each, shall receive one ticket in either the Monthly or Extraordinary Drawing.

Persons sometimes write us saying one of their numbers appears in several places, and ask what they have drawn. In answer we would say, one drawn number only wins 50 cents, no matter how many times it may appear on the list, as they will see it does not appear but one time in the fifteen official drawn numbers at the head of the list.

NOTICE TO AGENTS.

The Agent's Special Prize Drawing is extended to May 30, as the tickets are not yet all taken, owing to so many of our agents prefering, or selecting the Agent's Prize Ticket of the 7th Extraordinary Drawing in place of the Monthly Agent's Prize Tickets, and being desirous of accommodating all of our agents as far as lies in our power, we have given them the privilege of making such choice of Prize tickets. Forward your order for tickets in the May drawing at an early day, and secure more chances in the Agent's Special Prize Drawing, as it will not be extended beyond May 30th.

J. M. PATTEE,
Manager.

Courts were frequently called upon to ascertain whether legislative grants of authority to conduct lotteries constituted contracts protected by the Constitution or merely revocable licenses. (Library of Congress)

power exception to the contract clause raised a number of crucial inquiries. Was the police power virtually boundless?[83] If so, a state could destroy any contract. The police power cases to this point all dealt with grants by the states. Did the exception also apply to private agreements? To what extent should courts defer to legislative judgments about the reach of the police power? If states wished to escape grants that subsequently appeared unwise, should they be expected to resort to eminent domain rather an expansive reading of the police power?

Historians have frequently cited *Stone v. Mississippi* (1880) as the case in which the Supreme Court clearly established a police power exception to the protection afforded corporate charters under the contract clause.[84] At issue was the right of a corporation under an 1867 Mississippi law to conduct a lottery for twenty-five years. States often pursued an inconsistent course with respect to lotteries, first granting charters and then seeking to revoke them as public sentiment shifted. As we have seen, the legal status of lottery charters had sometimes been raised in contract clause litigation since the Antebellum Era. Although there were occasional decisions to the contrary,[85] courts tended to treat lotteries as licenses subject to revocation rather than contracts.[86] In *Stone*, Chief Justice Waite, speaking for a unanimous Court, made clear his distaste for lotteries, terming them "a species of gambling, and wrong in their influences." Stressing state police power, he proclaimed, "No legislature can bargain away the public health or the public morals."[87] Yet Waite's analysis was somewhat ambiguous. He admitted that a threshold inquiry was whether the lottery charter had in fact been a contract. Waite ended his opinion by finding that the charter was "nothing more than a license to enjoy the privilege" until abrogated by the state.[88] He maintained that a lottery charter was received with "the implied understanding" that it could be withdrawn at any time. If the lottery privilege was merely a license, then obviously it would not be protected under the contract clause, and the discussion of the police power was dicta. Despite the vagueness of the *Stone* opinion, however, it came to stand for the proposition that there was an inalienable police power that could trump provisions in corporate charters.[89] More particularly, it definitively settled that a lottery grant was not a contract within the meaning of the contract clause.[90]

Taken together, *Beer Company*, *Fertilizing Company*, and *Stone* enlarged state authority in the face of contract clause challenges to regulations. There was little doubt that a robust police power would likely prevail over claims of corporate privilege contained in charters. At the same time, these decisions diluted the protective function of the contract clause. In 1890 Tiedeman aptly observed that "the court has permitted the practical destruction of corporate property and privileges, guaranteed by legislative grant" and suggested that in effect the justices had abrogated the *Dartmouth College* rule.

To this point the Supreme Court had addressed cases involving public morals and health. A few years later the Court took an important step to apply the same principle to laws designed to enhance public safety by imposing new and expensive duties on railroads. In an opinion rendered by Chief Justice Melville W. Fuller in 1894, the Supreme Court brushed aside a contract clause challenge to a state law directing the removal of a railroad grade crossing annually at the sole expense of the company. The railroad claimed a financial hardship, arguing that compliance with the statute would impair contracts between the company and bondholders. Noting that with an increase in population, grade crossings were a menace to public safety, Fuller reasoned that the contract clause was "not violated by the legitimate exercise of legislative power in securing the public safety, health, and morals." He further stated that the "governmental power of self-protection cannot be contracted away."[91]

The Court reiterated this position in a case involving a contract between the City of Omaha and a railroad. Pursuant to an agreement, the city and the carrier shared the cost of constructing a viaduct. Subsequently the state legislature enacted a law authorizing cities to require railroads to repair and maintain viaducts at their sole expense. When Omaha took steps to enforce this obligation, the railroad alleged that the measure constituted an impairment of its contract with the city.[92] In a revealing opinion Justice Shiras, speaking for a unanimous bench, explicitly differentiated between private and public contracts for purposes of contract clause analysis. With respect to private agreements he commented, "Where a contract, not contrary to public policy, has been entered into between parties competent to contract, it is not within the power of either party to withdraw from its terms without the consent of the other; and the obligation of such a contract is constitutionally protected from hostile legislation." When dealing with "persons or corporations whose rights were created for public purposes, by legislative acts," however, he promulgated a different rule. Contracts of this character, Shiras wrote, "are held to be within the supervising power and control of the legislature when exercised to protect the public safety, health and morals, and that clause of the Federal Constitution which protects contracts from legislative action cannot in every case be successfully invoked."[93] He stressed that it was not competent "for the city and the railroad company, by entering into an agreement between themselves, to withdraw the subject from the reach of the police power, and to substitute their views for that of those of the legislature."[94] It therefore followed that the viaduct repair statute did not run afoul of the contract clause. As we have seen, the Supreme Court had already been treating public and private contracts differently even if both were under the shelter of the Constitution. But this opinion expressly recognized that the two should be viewed separately and that public contracts contained in corporate charters were subject to greater legislative control.

As might be expected, state courts also relied on the police power to vindicate safety legislation notwithstanding language in corporate charters. The Supreme Court of Appeals of Virginia, for example, readily found no violation of the contract clause when the city of Richmond revoked a prior privilege to maintain a gunpowder magazine. It viewed the ordinance as a safety measure well within the scope of the police power.[95] Asserting that the police power was an essential attribute of sovereignty that could not be limited by contract, the Supreme Court of Colorado upheld a statute imposing a duty on canal companies to cover their canals carrying water within cities. The court was unimpressed with the argument that the statute placed a burden on the company not specified in its original charter and this impaired the obligation of contract. It reasoned that the law was a reasonable safety measure that did not interfere with the business of the canal.[96]

Moving beyond the traditional police power concerns with public health, safety, and morals, the Supreme Court gingerly enlarged the police power to encompass economic matters. Two cases illustrate the relationship between state efforts to curb monopolies and the contract clause in the Gilded Age.

The Supreme Court showed its willingness to sustain wide state authority over state-granted monopolies. In 1869 the Louisiana legislature granted the Crescent City Livestock Company an exclusive privilege to conduct the slaughter of livestock within New Orleans for twenty-five years.[97] Ten years later the state adopted a new constitution that abolished the monopoly features in all business corporations except railroads. When New Orleans enacted laws that opened the right to build slaughterhouses to general competition, the Crescent City Livestock Company brought suit arguing that the 1869 act amounted to a contract the state could not impair. The Supreme Court, speaking through Justice Miller, repeated the by-now-familiar theme that states could not by contract limit their powers to safeguard public health and safety and found no contract clause violation.[98]

Yet both the provision of the Louisiana Constitution and Miller's opinion seem driven more by antimonopoly feelings than by health concerns. The Louisiana provision makes no reference to health considerations. Likewise, Miller made no attempt to link repeal of the monopoly privilege to health. It seems most likely that the health rationale was a pretext for the Court to accommodate changed economic policies and uphold the abolition of an exclusive franchise. Fearing that the Court opinion opened the door for wider application of the police power to contracts, E. L. Godkin, writing in the *Nation*, perceptively declared:

> The constitutional amendment, moreover, is distinctly directed at the 'monopoly' feature of the contract; and, as far as we can see, the only effect of this case is to give any State the right to destroy the obligation of the most solemn contracts, provided the judges at Washington can extract from its actions some shadow of a reason growing out of what they regard as the cause of 'health' or 'morals.' This is a wide definition of police power and gives the Supreme Court and the State Legislatures a power of interference with contracts and property such as nobody ever dreamed they possessed.[99]

As discussed in subsequent chapters, Godkin's premonition that an expansive police power would in time overwhelm the protective function of the contract clause proved accurate in the twentieth century.

Hostility to monopolies mounted in the late nineteenth century, as evidenced by passage of the Sherman Anti-Trust Act by Congress in 1890, and influenced contract clause jurisprudence. Antimonopoly sentiment permeated the Supreme Court's decision in *Pearsall v. Great Northern Railway Company* (1896).[100] At issue was the right of Great Northern, as conferred in its charter, to consolidate operations with a competing carrier. A subsequent state law barred railroads from consolidating with or in any way controlling parallel or competing lines, and Great Northern claimed a violation of the contract clause. In a lengthy but cloudy opinion, Justice Henry Billings Brown made reference to the doctrine of strict construction and the reserved power of the legislature but appears to have grounded his ruling on the inalienable police power.[101] The purpose of the act, he maintained, was "to prevent such a combination between the two as would constitute a monopoly." Brown argued that the legislature could revoke an unexercised power in a corporate charter inasmuch as the legislature could decide that the public interest was best served by competition between the carriers, not consolidation. He concluded with a ringing statement that "it was competent for the legislature, out of due regard for the public welfare, to declare that its charter should not be used for the purpose of stifling competition and building up monopolies."[102] *Pearsall* should best be seen as an attempt to harmonize the understanding of the contract clause with the antitrust principles of the Sherman Act. Yet, as discussed below, the Court did not apply the antimonopoly principle of the police power to public utilities.

In addition to express reliance on the police power, the Supreme Court on occasion read an implied condition into a corporate charter as a basis to uphold state regulations. An Illinois act of 1865 incorporated the Chicago Life Insurance Company. Subsequent laws imposed regulations on such companies and provided that the state auditor could seek an injunction to prevent an insolvent insurance company from continuing to do business. Pursuant to the statutes, the auditor determined that the Chicago Life Insurance Company was insolvent. He obtained both an injunction against the conduct of further business and the appointment of a receiver. The defendant company argued that the statute impaired the obligation of contract between the company and the state. Speaking for a unanimous bench, Justice Harlan brushed this contention aside. He reasoned that implied in every grant of incorporation was the condition that the conferred privileges should not be abused and that the corporation was subject to reasonable regulations that did not materially interfere with the purposes of the corporation. Because the challenged statutes were directed only at misconduct, Harlan found no abridgment of any contract.[103] In essence, Harlan treated the subsequent insurance regulations as an exercise of the police power to protect the public from mismanagement and fraud.[104]

TAX EXEMPTIONS

As in the Reconstruction Era, state tax exemptions or limitations, often granted in the Antebellum Era, proved a fertile source of contract clause litigation.[105] Such exemptions took several forms. A common practice was to grant a commutation of taxes by specifying a payment in lieu of all other levies. Exemptions set forth in corporate charters, initially calculated to encourage enterprise and economic growth, were increasingly viewed as a form of special privilege that produced questionable benefits. During the depression of the 1870s the exemptions given railroads stirred particular resentment as critics charged that the cost of government was cast upon the less affluent.[106] "The people of Florida," the attorney for the state collector of revenue argued in 1882, "feeling the great hardship and inequality wrought by the exemption of these railroad corporations from their proper share of the burdens of government," clamored for relief.[107] As states sought to reassert their power of taxation, railroads and other businesses resisted the imposition of higher taxes on the basis of express exemptions in their charters. These cases raised much-debated questions of the construction of charters. Although courts usually took the position that grants of tax exemption must be strictly construed against the corporate grantee,[108] a number of such exemptions passed muster as contracts protected by the Constitution against abridgment. Concomitantly, courts fashioned doctrines that effectively limited the duration of many tax immunities.

To be sure, not all Supreme Court justices were sympathetic to claims of tax exemption. Justices Miller and Field regularly protested that taxation was an element of sovereignty and that states could not relinquish by contract the ability of future legislatures to levy taxes.[109] Moreover, commentators expressed strong doubts about the legitimacy and wisdom of legislative grants of tax immunity. "It has been questioned, with great force of reasoning," Bishop declared, "whether a State legislature has the power thus to surrender its right of taxation, so as to bind future legislatures."[110] Other commentators, echoing Justice Strong's dissent in *Fertilizing Company*, asked why a state could not bargain to relinquish its police power or power of eminent domain but could enter binding contracts to give up the taxing power, either permanently or for a specified term. The police power and eminent domain, one critic pointed out, were "certainly not more important or of higher rank in the scale of sovereign attributes than the right of taxation."[111]

This seeming anomaly warrants exploration. It might be explained in terms of respect for a landmark decision by Chief Justice John Marshall. Justice Joseph Bradley said as much in an 1886 opinion: "We do not feel disposed to question the decision in *New Jersey v. Wilson*. It has been referred to and relied on in so many cases from the day of its rendition down to the present time, that it would cause a shock to our constitutional jurisprudence to disturb it now."[112] But regard for precedent did not prevent courts from fashioning doctrines to undercut *Dartmouth College*, so this is not an entirely compelling explanation. Chief Justice Waite, speaking for the Court in *Stone v. Mississippi* (1880), offered a different rationale for the divergent treatment of police power regulations and the power of taxation for contract clause purposes. He stated:

> While taxation is in general necessary for the support of government, it is not part of the government itself. Government was not organized for the purposes of taxation, but taxation may be necessary for the purposes of government. No government dependent on taxation for support can bargain away its whole power of taxation, for that would be substantially abdication. All that has been determined thus far is, that for a consideration it may, in the exercise of a reasonable discretion, and for the public good, surrender a part of its powers in this particular.[113]

To Waite, taxation was ancillary to the other functions of government but not essential itself. He was therefore more willing to uphold state relinquishment of the taxing power than the police power. Still, Waite signaled that there were limits to grants of tax immunity.

Notwithstanding critics and the misgivings of some justices, the Supreme Court continued to enforce charter provisions that restricted the tax liability of various enterprises. It sustained tax exemptions for railroads,[114] bank capital stock,[115] and universities.[116] These cases typically required a close examination of the terms in charters, making generalization difficult. The Court had to determine both the existence and scope of claimed exemptions. Although the Court articulated a strong presumption against surrender of the power to tax, the legislative language often left little doubt that lawmakers had intended to confer an exemption.

There was, however, ample room to dispute the extent of particular immunities. A good illustration of the difficulties in construing tax exemptions was presented in *Mobile and Ohio Railroad Company v. Tennessee* (1894).[117] At issue was an 1848 legislative grant that exempted railroad property from taxation for twenty-five years from the completion of the road and further provided that "no tax shall ever be laid on said road or its fixtures which will reduce the dividends below eight per cent." The railroad had never declared a dividend. When Tennessee sought to collect back taxes on railroad property for five prior years in 1891, the carrier resisted and argued that the levy impaired the obligation of its contract with the state. Noting that the "manifest object of the clause was to invite and encourage the investment of private capital in the enterprise of building the road," a majority of five concluded that the charter language plainly extended the period of exemption until the company was paying a dividend of 8 percent annually on its cost.[118] Writing for the four dissenters, Chief Justice Fuller maintained that the language was unclear and did not constitute an indefinite exemption from taxation. Agreeing that "a State must be held to the bargains it makes, however improvident," he protested that the majority opinion "practically leaves it to the company to say when it may be taxed and when not."[119]

In other cases the construction of doubtful language was favorable to state taxing authority. In *Vicksburg, Shreveport, and Pacific Railroad Company v. Dennis* (1886) the Supreme Court was called upon to interpret wording in an 1853 charter exempting railroad property "from taxation for ten years after the completion of said road."[120] A sharply divided bench held that the provision conferred no exemption until completion of the line and that consequently the company was liable for taxes until that time. The dissenters protested that the provision should logically be construed to confer a tax immunity lasting until ten years after completion. "This exemption," they maintained, "was designed to aid the road, and was, therefore, much more needed during its construction than when completed."[121] Similarly, the Court determined that a tax exemption conferred on a railroad in 1834 did not by its terms extend to branch lines. Hence, a state tax on branch lines constructed years later did not impair a contract for immunity.[122] The Supreme Court of Colorado handed down a decision based on the same principle, strictly construing the scope of a tax immunity conferred on an educational institution as covering only property used for educational purposes.[123]

In addition to grappling with the construction of claimed exemptions in corporate charters, the Supreme Court, adhering to precedent, continued to differentiate between tax exemptions in particular charters and general schemes of taxation calculated to encourage economic development. It was disinclined to find a contract where the legislature was not making a specific promise of tax immunity but enacting a policy that was subject to change. The Court treated such general laws as a gratuity or bounty that lawmakers were free to withdraw at any time.[124] In contrast, at least one state took the position that the building of rail lines, in reliance on a general tax exemption measure, constituted a binding contract. Stressing the acute need for rapid transportation in the territory, the Supreme Court of New Mexico viewed the exemption law as a bid for railroad construction that became part of a contract upon actual building.[125]

A much-contested issue was the transfer of tax immunities to successor companies. As the pace of mergers quickened in the late nineteenth century, courts were repeatedly called upon to decide whether the consolidated enterprise could take advantage of the exemptions granted in the original charters. Most of these cases involved railroads. The Supreme Court adhered to the settled rule that the privilege of a tax immunity was not transferable except with the consent of the legislature.[126] As Justice Field explained, a tax exemption "must be considered as a personal privilege not extending beyond the immediate grantee, unless otherwise so declared in express terms."[127] Moreover, the Supreme Court took the position that, if a new corporation was formed as the result of a consolidation of two or more companies, the new corporation was a distinct entity subject to any statutory or constitutional limitations then in force. The new corporation, for example, was bound by a reserved power in the legislature to amend or repeal charters imposed since the original corporations were created. It followed that, even if one or more of the original companies had a tax immunity, that immunity was effectively waived, and a state tax on railroad property did not impair the obligation of contract.[128] The Supreme Court of Arkansas likewise found that a consolidation of railroads created a new corporation, and that a tax immunity did not pass to the consolidated enterprise absent express legislative approval.[129]

Infrequently, however, the Supreme Court ruled that a tax exemption did transfer to a successor railroad company. At issue in *Tennessee v. Whitworth* (1886) was wording in the 1866 act of consolidation that the new company was entitled to "all the powers and privileges" of the original companies. Chief Justice Waite held that, because the capital stock of both original companies was exempt from taxes, the capital stock of the united corporation was also exempt.[130] Relying on *Whitworth*, the New Jersey Court of Errors and Appeals (1886) reached the same result, declaring that a lease transferring "immunities" and "privileges" embraced a tax exemption.[131]

Even when courts upheld tax exemptions as part of an irrevocable corporate charter under the contract clause, state legislators could devise strategies to induce the grantees to relinquish their exempt status. New Jersey granted tax concessions to several railroads in the 1830s and 1840s. By the 1870s, however, changed economic circumstances in the state convinced lawmakers to in effect renege on these exemptions and levy a tax on the carriers. Although the highest court in New Jersey upheld the tax immunities under the contract clause, the legislature conditioned extensions of time to complete lines or authority to merge or lease their property upon surrender of their exemptions by the railroad companies. In the end political pressure prevailed over the supposed sanctity of contracts, despite judicial backing.[132]

It is no easy task to reconcile the welter of tax exemption cases. Yet the overall pattern seems clear. Judicial skepticism about claims of tax immunity was reflected in the strict construction doctrine and the pronounced trend to limit the transfer of exemptions. As Warren aptly pointed out, the Supreme Court "displayed a marked tendency to restrict the scope of tax exemptions and to uphold the State's denial of their legal existence."[133] States granted fewer seemingly perpetual tax concessions, and virtually all corporate charters were now subject to reservation clauses. Although *New Jersey v. Wilson* retained some vitality, by the end of the nineteenth century, contract clause protection of tax exemptions was of diminishing significance. Indeed, there appears to have been a disconnection between the criticism heaped by commentators on the treatment of tax exemptions as binding contracts and the reality of weakened constitutional support.

EMINENT DOMAIN

In addition to the police power and the power of taxation, eminent domain was seen as an aspect of state sovereignty. As discussed in Chapter 3, it had been settled since the Antebellum Era that states could employ eminent domain to appropriate a contract for public use upon payment of just compensation. The issue was infrequently litigated in the Gilded Age. In 1897 the Supreme Court affirmed the rule, holding that a state could constitutionally take the tangible property of a water company as well as its franchise and contracts.[134] Appropriation of a contract was not viewed as an impairment. Indeed, the exercise of eminent domain prevailed even when a contract expressly provided that certain property should not be taken. Thus, the Supreme Court of Pennsylvania held that the use of eminent domain to place a road through a cemetery despite a grant declaring that such land was exempt from the opening of a road did not violate the contract cause.[135]

MUNICIPAL FRANCHISES FOR UTILITY SERVICES

Privately owned utility companies dominated the provision of gas, water, and electrical services in most US cities during the late nineteenth century. Such enterprises typically operated under a franchise arrangement for a fixed period of years. Dissatisfaction with existing levels of service led lawmakers to grant similar franchises to rival companies. Even more striking, a shift in public opinion in favor of municipally owned utilities sparked a move to replace existing private companies with municipal facilities.[136] Consequently, courts heard a number of cases that involved efforts to alter the terms of previously granted utility franchises, with the original companies arguing that their franchises were contracts protected from abridgment by the Constitution. As with tax exemptions, the terms of a franchise grant were often determinative.[137]

Writing for the Supreme Court in a cluster of 1885 cases, Justice Harlan treated these franchises as contracts. In the leading case of *New Orleans Gas Company v. Louisiana Light Company* (1885) he construed a franchise grant conferring "the sole and exclusive privilege" of selling gas lights in New Orleans until 1895.[138] Subsequently, however, the legislature incorporated another company and gave it the exclusive right to sell illuminating gas in the city effective in 1875. The original company brought suit to enjoin the newcomer from supplying gas until its exclusive privilege expired. Harlan was unimpressed with the argument that the original grant amounted to a monopoly, contending that the right to operate a gasworks was not a common occupation and could not be carried on without special authority. He noted that grants of exclusive privilege had been sustained as contracts protected against state impairment. With respect to these public utilities there was none of the antimonopoly sentiment expressed in *Pearsall.*

Harlan made two essential points in finding that the change of policy by the state impaired the obligation of the original franchise contract. First, he cabined the reach of the police power. Conceding that a state could not contract to relinquish the police power, Harlan limited that authority to protection of the public health, safety, and morals. But he insisted that the present case did not involve those considerations. The state and city, Harlan pointed out, retained ample power to supervise the manufacture and distribution of gas. To uphold the grant, he continued, did not obstruct the state in the exercise of its police power. Second, Harlan gave weight to the importance of contractual stability as a means of attracting investment capital. He observed that the state could have erected a gasworks at public expense but instead preferred "that some inducement be offered to private capitalists to undertake, at their own cost, this work." Harlan expressed concern for "those who have made large investments upon the assurance by the State that the contract with them will be performed."[139] The state, of course, was free to change policies and bar exclusive privileges for private corporations but not to abridge prior agreements. If the state deemed it necessary to eliminate existing exclusive privileges, Harlan suggested it resort to taking such franchises by eminent domain upon payment of just compensation.[140]

Where contractual language so indicated, the justices were also prepared to protect franchises against competition by the city. In *Walla Walla City v. Walla Walla Water Company* (1898) the city in 1887 gave a water company a franchise to provide water for twenty-five years and agreed not to "erect, maintain or become interested in any water works."[141] Nothing in the grant, however, created a monopoly or prevented the award of franchises to other private companies. Six years after the original franchise, the city took steps to establish a municipal water system. A unanimous Supreme Court held that the city's action constituted an impairment of its agreement with the water company. Justice Brown's opinion advanced several ideas that merit attention. Brown rejected the city's position that it could abrogate the water franchise under its police power. He insisted that the city's police power, even if inalienable, was confined "to contracts prejudicial to the peace, good order, health or morals of its inhabitants." There was no evidence, Brown went on, to suggest that the purity of water furnished was in question. He pointed out that the franchise did not grant an exclusive right but merely prevented the city from entering into direct competition during the life of the contract. Brown stressed the fact that in "establishing a system of water works the company would necessarily incur a large expense" and would have a right to expect that the city would not enter into competition with it. Here again the Court seemingly acted to safeguard reasonable reliance by a private party on a contract with a municipality. Lastly, Brown hinted at a degree of judicial skepticism about urban government. He explained that the company understandably sought a contractual guarantee against competition by the city considering "the sudden changes of public opinion to which all municipalities are more or less subject."[142]

Still, the Supreme Court carefully scrutinized claims that municipalities had relinquished their authority to establish public utility services. In *Lehigh Water Company v. Easton* (1877), for instance, a private water company had an exclusive franchise under an 1874 statute to provide water to the inhabitants of Easton.[143] Pursuant to an 1867 law, however, Easton decided to erect a public system of water supply. Alleging a violation of the contract clause, the water company sued to enjoin the construction of a public system. Harlan, speaking for the Court, pointed out that only statutes enacted after the making of a contract could impair the agreement. Moreover, he rejected the notion that the Supreme Court could review "the judgment of the state court in every case involving the enforcement of contracts."[144] Harlan stressed that only state court judgments giving effect to state constitutional provisions or statutes raised contract clause issues reviewable by the Supreme Court. The justices reached the same result in several other cases, concluding that nothing in contracts with utility companies prevented the state from authorizing municipalities to build water systems or gasworks, and hence there was no constitutional violation.[145]

LAND GRANTS AND PUBLIC TRUST

During the Gilded Age the Supreme Court heard few contract clause cases dealing with state land grants. It had been the governing rule since *Fletcher v. Peck* (1810) that states could not rescind grants of public land. In keeping with that decision, the Court determined that a Texas constitutional provision limiting land grants to "actual settlers" could not be applied to a scheme authorizing railroads to earn lands by construction of lines made

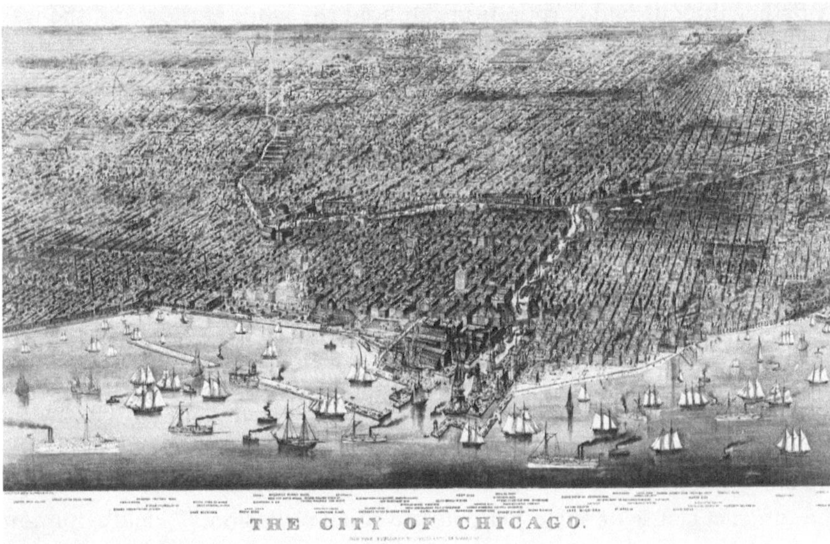

In an 1892 decision dealing with submerged land on the Chicago waterfront, the Supreme Court first articulated the public trust doctrine, thereby curtailing the reach of the contract clause over land deemed subject to the public trust. (Library of Congress)

before adoption of the constitution in 1869.[146] Such an interpretation of the state constitution in effect cut off the right of the carrier to secure additional land and impaired the obligation of the contract between the state and the railroad company.

Strikingly, the most important land grant decision of the era effectively restricted the ambit of the contract clause. This development was in line with the strict construction of corporate charters and the recognition of an inalienable police power. At issue in *Illinois Central Railroad v. Illinois* (1892) was an 1869 grant by the Illinois legislature to the railroad of more than 1,000 acres of submerged land along the Chicago waterfront.[147] The purpose of the act was to facilitate commerce by enabling the carrier to enlarge the harbor and construct docks and depots. In 1873 the legislature repealed the measure and asserted the right to reclaim the land. The railroad objected, arguing that the repeal impaired its contract with the state. Anxious to clarify the matter, Illinois filed suit for a judicial determination of title to the submerged land.

Writing for a plurality of four justices, Field, in a problematic opinion, upheld the state's contention. He misleadingly stated the question to be "whether the railroad corporation can hold the lands and control the waters by the grant, against any future exercise of power over them by the State."[148] In fact, the railroad made no such claim, and even in the late nineteenth century property owners were not immune from regulation. Field declared, without precedential support, that a title to land under navigable waters was different than that for other land. "It is a title held in trust for the people of the State," he declared, "that they may enjoy the navigation of the waters, carry on commerce over them, and have liberty of fishing therein freed from the obstruction or interference of private parties."[149] A state, Field continued, could no more relinquish its title over public trust land than abdicate its police power. It followed that a grant of submerged land subject to the public trust was necessarily revocable and amounted to little more than a license. Field admitted that there was no authority for holding such a land grant invalid. It is also noteworthy that Field never cited the contract clause or any other constitutional provision.[150] Field's opinion may well have reflected his aversion to state-conferred monopoly privilege, given his perception that "the harbor of a great city and its commerce" had passed to the control of a private corporation.[151] Field's views regarding the contract clause are addressed in detail later in this chapter.

The three dissenters, in an opinion by Justice Shiras, pointed out that a state had the same power to convey submerged land as to transfer any other state-owned property.[152] Because the state made a valid grant of the submerged land, and the railroad was complying with the terms of the grant, they maintained that the repeal act impaired the obligation of contract. The dissenters insisted that the state retained its sovereign power to regulate "as obtain in the case of other owners of property."[153] Further, they suggested that if the state wished to escape an undesirable contract, "she can take the rights and property of the railroad company in these lands by a constitutional condemnation of them."[154]

Commentators early recognized that *Illinois Central* marked a departure from the prevailing jurisprudence regarding land grants.[155] Indeed, the Supreme Court appeared to move away from a broad reading of *Illinois Central* in *Shively v. Bowlby* (1894).[156] It held that there was no uniform rule regarding disposition of land under navigable waters and that states were free to deal with such land according to their own policies. As discussed in Chapter 6, the Supreme Court in 1926 further limited the reach of *Illinois Central*. As this indicates, the notion of public trust had little application for decades.

Nonetheless, *Illinois Central* is the fountainhead of the modern public trust doctrine and has generated a large literature as scholars seek to come to grips with the rationale of the decision.[157] In the late twentieth century some commentators and state courts have taken the position that the public trust doctrine could be extended from ownership of submerged land to encompass a host of other resources and to promote environmental goals.[158] The expansive use of the public trust doctrine is beyond the scope of this study, but the contract clause does not afford much protection to the owners of land deemed subject to the public trust.

MUNICIPAL DEBTS

State and local governments, particularly in the South and West, frequently sought to either repudiate or lessen the amount of their indebtedness. Some of these obligations had been incurred to provide financial aid for railroad development. Because some of the promised lines were never built, and others proved unprofitable, public opinion turned against the payment of railroad bonds. Impoverished conditions in the southern states also contributed to the political pressure to scale back financial obligations. Consequently, state and local governments enacted a variety of measures to reduce their debts, alter the rates of interest owed, or limit the remedies of creditors. Such moves raised a welter of contract clause questions.

Some lawmakers turned to the taxing power as a vehicle to affect contracts. In *Murray v. Charleston* (1878), for instance, the city of Charleston had issued bonds carrying interest at 6 percent.[159] In 1870 the city adopted an ordinance directing that a tax of 2 percent be retained out of the interest on the bonds. The effect was to reduce the effective interest rate to 4 percent. Justice Strong, speaking for the Court, found that the city's attempt to use the taxing power to reduce its obligation ran afoul of the contract clause. No municipality, he lectured, can "by its own ordinances, under the guise of taxation, relieve itself from performing to the letter all that it has expressly promised to its creditors."[160]

The federal courts continued to look skeptically at state legislation that purported to withhold from local governments the authority to levy taxes to satisfy their debts. Pointing to the leading case of *Von Hoffman v. City of Quincy* (1876), several federal circuit courts readily concluded that the power of taxation existing when bonds were issued became part of the obligation of the contracts and could not be eliminated as long as the bonds remained outstanding.[161] Mindful of the distressed economic circumstances in some communities and of the public hostility to the payment

State and municipal debt repudiation, particularly in the South, aroused sectional antagonism and generated a wave of lawsuits grounded in the contract clause. This cartoon compares southern debt repudiation to the murder of prospective voters. (*Puck*, February 14, 1883)

of outstanding bonds, one judge nonetheless insisted, "Popular opinion, for the time being, in particular localities, however unanimous it may be, and from whatever cause arising, cannot in a court of justice be allowed to prevail against the constitution and legal rights of the humblest suitor."[162]

Louisiana tested judicial patience with a bizarre scheme to restrict the taxing power of New Orleans. An 1876 act limited the power of taxation upon land in the city and denied payment upon existing bonds unless exchanged for so-called premium bonds. Payment of both interest and principal on these premium bonds was to be determined by chance in a periodic lottery. Payment thus turned upon which bondholders drew the lucky numbers. The process could take years. Under this plan the city had no obligation to pay the bonded debt aside from the lottery scheme. Not surprisingly, the Supreme Court, in two unanimous opinions authored by Field, struck down the 1876 law as an impairment of contract.[163] He maintained that it was well settled that the power of taxation could not be limited to undermine the security of prior contracts made in reliance on such authority. Field was unsparing in his denunciation of the Louisiana scheme, describing it as "little less than open repudiation of the city's faith." He added, "We shall not waste words upon the scheme thus developed to evade the just obligations of the city."[164] Field directed that a mandamus be issued to New Orleans to compel the annual levy of a tax to pay current interest and arrearages on the original bonds.

Yet another stratagem to frustrate the collection of debts was for legislators to eliminate existing municipalities or to alter their boundaries. As early as 1872 John F. Dillon declared, "No repeal of a charter of a municipal corporation can so dissolve it as to impair the obligation of the contract, or, it may probably safely be added, preclude the creditor from recovering his debts."[165] The Supreme Court took the same position in *Mount Pleasant v. Beckwith* (1879).[166] It ruled that under the contract clause municipal debts could not be extinguished by annulling the charter of a municipality. The rights of municipal creditors were constitutionally protected, and it would be assumed that the contractual obligations of the dissolved debtor town passed proportionately to the other towns that received territory from the former town.

STATE BOND REPUDIATION

Although the federal courts generally invoked the contract clause to protect creditors against defaulting municipalities, litigation regarding the repudiation of state bonds worth millions of dollars proved more complicated. In the 1870s and 1880s many southern states sought to disavow their public debt. "The extent of this repudiation," Charles Warren observed, "had become a National scandal."[167] This refusal to pay bonded debt obviously implicated the contract clause, and bondholders brought suit in federal court claiming a violation of the Constitution.

In the leading case of *Louisiana ex rel. Elliott v. Jumel* (1883) Chief Justice Waite, speaking for the Court, denied relief to the bondholders, reasoning that their suit was barred by the Eleventh Amendment.[168] In dissent, Field forcefully protested that Louisiana's bond repudiation was a direct violation of the contract clause. He pictured the provision as "a barrier against the agrarian and despoiling spirit" and argued that when "a state enters into the markets of the world as a borrower, she, for the time, lays aside her sovereignty and becomes responsible as a civil corporation."[169] If a state can repudiate its obligations, Field warned, other property rights will not be respected, and public faith "will be the synonym of public dishonesty."[170] Harlan, dissenting separately, charged that under the majority opinion a state may "destroy rights of contract, the obligation of which the constitution declares shall not be impaired by any state law."[171] Creditors were predictably outraged. There was even an unsuccessful proposal in Congress to repeal the Eleventh Amendment and to empower Congress to provide "by appropriate legislation for the legal enforcement of the obligation of contracts entered into by any of the States of the Union." Nonetheless, the *Jumel* case and its progeny enabled most states of the former Confederacy to repudiate a sizeable portion of their bonded debt.[172]

It remains to consider why the Supreme Court countenanced a seemingly clear violation of the contract clause by finding jurisdictional shelter in the Eleventh Amendment. After all, as we have seen, the justices had no hesitancy to invoke the contract clause with respect to the debts of local governments. Indeed, the Court expressly held that the Eleventh Amendment pertained only to suits against states and did not prevent their political subdivisions from being sued in federal court.[173] Changing political circumstances help to explain the Court's willingness to allow the Eleventh Amendment to trump the contract clause. With the end of Reconstruction public opinion in the North lost interest in coercing the southern states and was anxious to preserve sectional harmony. As the Court in *Jumel* pointed out, any judicial remedy "would require the court to assume all the executive authority of the state, so far as it related to the enforcement of the law, and to supervise the conduct of all persons charged with any official duty in respect to the levy, collection, and disbursement of the tax in question until the bonds, principal and interest, were paid in full."[174] The justices did not relish this task. With uncertain political support and facing unified opposition from southern states, the Court simply did not want to issue an unenforceable order against a state. The same political considerations did not apply so strongly to cities and counties.[175]

If most southern states were able to circumvent the contract clause and repudiate bonded debt, Virginia proved to be a conspicuous exception. Both state and federal courts relied on the contract clause to require the Old Dominion to honor its bonds. This singular tale warrants separate treatment.

On the eve of the Civil War Virginia had accumulated a large public debt. The state suspended payment on this debt during hostilities, and the unpaid interest added to the outstanding obligations. The separation of West Virginia removed one-third of the prewar Old Dominion, complicating the revenue picture. As a result, the state was having problems in raising sufficient revenue to support governmental functions and repaying its debts. Anxious to attract northern capital, the legislature in 1871 passed the Funding Act. The act provided that bondholders could exchange their existing bonds for new consolidated bonds maturing in thirty-four years and paying interest at 6 percent. As a further incentive to bondholders, the interest coupons attached to the bonds were payable to bearer and receivable at maturity for all state taxes. Thus, there would always be a market for these bonds, and indeed the fact that the coupons could be used to pay taxes constituted a major part of the value of the bonds. Many creditors promptly took advantage of the new scheme and exchanged bonds.[176]

Payment of the bonded debt, however, soon proved politically difficult.[177] The public resisted higher taxes to pay off the bonds. Moreover, the coupons received in lieu of taxes reduced the state's revenue and threatened the ability of the state to finance the newly created public school system. A coupon agency even sold coupons from nonresident bondholders to Virginia taxpayers. Alarmed by the declining revenue, the legislature in 1872 halted the issuance of additional consolidated bonds and repealed the tax-receivable feature of the Funding Act. This set the stage for a prolonged conflict over the state's refusal to honor its prior pledge. "A veritable legal war," one commentator observed, "ensued between the State of Virginia and the bondholders, in the course of which the ingenuity of the legislature in obstructing the use of the tax-paying coupons was matched against the authority of the federal courts to which the 'merciless bondholders' applied."[178] The repeal of the provision that coupons for interest should be received in payment of taxes was promptly challenged before the Virginia Supreme Court of Appeals. The court held that the undertaking by the state that the coupons should be so received amounted to a legislative contract. It then readily found that the 1872 act annulled an essential part of the contract and thus ran afoul of the contract clause in both the state and federal constitutions. The court concluded that "temporary relief from pecuniary pressure is too dearly bought, at the price of the violated faith of Virginia."[179]

Because the direct assault on the coupons failed, state legislators turned to a variety of devices, popularly known as "coupon killers," to defeat the use of coupons to pay taxes. The first step involved the power of taxation. In 1873 lawmakers placed a tax on the market value of the bonds, to be deducted from maturing coupons tendered to pay other state taxes. In effect, the coupons would not be accepted at face value. In *Hartman v. Greenhow* (1881), however, the Supreme Court invalidated the tax as applied to coupons separated from the bonds and held by different owners. Writing for the Court, Field asserted that the coupons payable to the bearer constituted distinct contracts and could be transferred. It followed that a tax levied on coupons held by different owners than the bond itself impaired the contract contained in the Funding Act.[180]

Not inclined to give up easily, the legislature in 1882 erected procedural barriers to the receipt of tax-paying coupons. Under the pretense of combatting forgery, they required taxpayers to pay their taxes in money and then bring a lawsuit to establish the validity of the coupons. Only after a judicial determination would the state receive the coupons and refund the money paid. As contemporary observers noted, the transparent purpose of this measure was to delay and vex those taxpayers who presented coupons.[181] In a troublesome opinion by Chief Justice Waite, the Supreme Court in *Antoni v. Greenhow* (1882) sustained the 1882 act. A taxpayer brought suit to compel the Richmond tax collector to receive a coupon in payment of taxes without following the new procedures. Waite treated the central issue as one relating not to the rights of the coupon holder but the remedies available if receipt for taxes was denied. Although acknowledging that "the commercial value of the bonds and coupons has been impaired by the hostile legislation of the State," Waite reached the remarkable conclusion that the change in remedy was "substantially equivalent" to that in force when the coupons were issued, and hence there was no violation of the contract clause.[182] Waite's opinion well illustrates the untenable nature of the right/remedy distinction in contract clause jurisprudence because here the drastic change in remedy virtually destroyed any rights.

Field authored a blistering dissent, insisting that the 1882 measure impaired the obligation of contract in the 1871 Funding Act. "Not only does this act entail prolonged delay and expense in every case," he lamented, "but, in a majority of cases, the expense would exceed the amount of the coupon." Field boldly proclaimed, "This is a most palpable and fragrant impairment of the obligation of contract. No legislation more destructive of all value to the contract is conceivable, unless it should absolutely and in terms repudiate the coupon as a contract at all. It is practical repudiation."[183]

Virginia officials did not have long to savor their victory because the creditors devised a new and successful strategy. A taxpayer would simply tender bond coupons to the tax collector. When the coupons were refused the taxpayer took no further steps and requested no affirmative relief from the courts. When the tax collector levied upon the property of the taxpayer to pay delinquent taxes, the taxpayer sued the collector. In a group of cases known as the *Virginia Coupon Cases* (1885) a divided Supreme Court ruled that the tender of the coupons was equivalent to payment and that subsequent attempts to enforce payment by seizing property was wrongful.[184] The Court declared that the Eleventh Amendment did not exempt states from the operation of the contract clause, pointing out that it had long been settled that agreements between states and individuals were protected by the Constitution. Unlike the *Antoni* case, here the taxpayer did not seek any compulsory process against the state. The Court held that Virginia had bound itself by contract to receive the bond coupons in payment of taxes and that the right to have them so received could not be taken away without running afoul of the contract clause.

Angered by this setback, Virginia lawmakers renewed their efforts to prevent use of the tax-receivable coupons. They required taxpayers tendering coupons to produce in court the bond from which the coupons had been removed. Because most of the bonds were held outside of the state, such a duty was entirely impractical. As the Supreme Court correctly perceived in *McGahey v. Virginia* (1890), "It would have the effect of rendering valueless all coupons which have been separated from the bonds to which they were attached, and have been sold in the open market. It would deprive them of their negotiable character."[185] The Court readily found that the requirement impaired the obligation of contract by materially altering the remedy for enforcing it. In a companion case, the Court also invalidated a prohibitory license fee on those offering the coupons for sale on the ground that such a huge fee interfered with the negotiability of the coupons.[186] Concluding its discussion, the Court expressly urged an arrangement to relieve both the courts and the parties "from all further exhibitions of a controversy that has become a vexation and a regret."[187]

Perhaps exhausted by the protracted struggle, the legislature named a commission to negotiate with a committee of bondholders. An 1892 settlement scaled down the amount of Virginia's public debt and authorized new century bonds, carrying interest at 2 percent for 10 years and 3 percent thereafter, to mature in 100 years. The coupons were not receivable for taxes. Certainly the Supreme Court's resolve to enforce the contract clause in the face of Virginia's dogged attempt to repudiate a large part of its public debt was instrumental in securing a settlement.

JUDICIAL IMPAIRMENTS REVISITED

During the Gilded Age the Supreme Court persisted in sending mixed messages regarding the extent to which judicial decisions could amount to impairment of contracts. Although the Court intimated that decisions in the municipal bond cases were governed by the contract clause, it stopped short of squarely holding that state judicial decisions could impair the obligation of contracts. The issue was complicated because many cases arose under diversity of citizenship jurisdiction rather than direct appeal from a state court. This gave rise to a sharp difference of opinion as to whether the outcome was dictated by the constitutional protection of contracts or the federal doctrines employed in diversity cases.

A number of Supreme Court opinions contain language to the effect that a change in judicial decisions affecting contracts is the same as subsequent legislation. In 1880, for example, Chief Justice Waite stated, "The true rule is to give a change of judicial construction in respect of a statute the same effect in its operation on contracts and existing contract rights that would be given to a legislative amendment; that is to say, make it prospective, but not retroactive." After a statute has received a settled judicial construction, he added, the construction becomes part of the contract, and a change in decision is the same as a legislative enactment.[188] Field echoed this observation a few years later in a case on appeal from the Supreme Court of Louisiana. The validity of a contract, he maintained, "cannot be impaired by any subsequent decision altering the construction. . . . A subsequent change in the interpretation can affect only subsequent contracts."[189]

Yet other cases expressed the view that the Supreme Court could only exercise jurisdiction under the contract clause when a state court had given effect to a statute passed after making the agreement challenged as abridging the obligation of contract. Justice Bradley insisted that the contract clause did not empower Congress to enact laws for the general enforcement of contracts. Federal jurisdiction, he asserted, rested upon passage of a state law because "the constitutional prohibition is against *State laws* impairing the obligation of contracts."[190] In 1887 the Court endorsed this position, holding that it could not examine every judgment of the state courts involving the enforcement of contracts. The Court limited its oversight of state court judgments to situations in which that court applied some state constitutional provision or statute, enacted subsequent to the making of the contract, claimed to impair that agreement.[191] Clearly the justices were disinclined to serve as a tribunal of last resort for resolving questions concerning rules of construction for contracts.

In *Central Land Company v. Laidley* (1895) the Supreme Court sought to summarize its position on judicial impairments.[192] At issue was the validity of a conveyance of land in West Virginia. The outcome turned upon whether the wife had properly relinquished her marital interest in the deed of conveyance. It was alleged that the Supreme Court of West Virginia had changed its prior construction of the state code. Unlike the bond repudiation cases that implicated the national credit market, this case was of only local interest and involved an interpretation of state law. Finding no federal jurisdiction, Justice Horace Gray, writing for the Court, declared that to come within the purview of the contract clause a contract "must have been impaired by some act of the legislative power of the State, and not by a decision of the judicial department only."[193] The Supreme Court, he continued, had jurisdiction only when the state court had upheld a statute alleged to be unconstitutional, not when a valid act was supposedly misconstrued. Gray distinguished the *Gelpcke* line of cases as grounded on principles of general law applicable in diversity cases. *Laidley* could be seen as a prudential move to close the door on hearing appeals involving the routine construction of contracts. Still, as we shall see, it was not the final word on the question of judicial impairments. The muddle continued into the early twentieth century.

Commentators also debated whether and under what circumstances a change of judicial opinion could amount to an impairment of contract. Looking to the purpose of the contract clause, Conrad Reno, a Boston attorney and treatise writer, argued that both legislative and judicial actions divesting contract rights violated the contract clause. He maintained, "The object of this inhibition is to secure the inviolability of property rights in contract against State action. Regarding the spirit and not merely the letter of this clause, and considering that property rights in contract may be as greatly impaired by subsequent overruling decisions as by subsequent statutes, justice seems to require that the two modes of impairment be held equivalent for jurisdictional purposes."[194] Anticipating jurisprudential developments of the early twentieth century, he analogized courts to legislatures and asserted that judges in effect make laws. Reno declared, "Any rule of conduct announced by the duly constituted authorities of a State, which has the force of law within the State, is a 'law' within the meaning of the contract clause of the constitution, whether it be in the form of a constitution, a statute, a municipal ordinance, or a judicial decision."[195] Why, he asked, "should not courts be held to the same responsibility as legislatures upon this point?"[196] Other commentators, however, had doubts about the notion of judicial impairment. A New York attorney agreed that "an extension of the Federal jurisdiction to the protection of contracts from judge-made law as well as from statutes, would be legislation in the interest of justice and fair dealing." Taking a literal rather than a functional view of the contract clause, he nonetheless maintained that the provision was aimed at state legislatures and argued that courts did not "pass" laws.[197] Likewise, James Bradley Thayer maintained that the contract clause was aimed solely at state legislation.[198]

By the end of the nineteenth century the status of the judicial impairment doctrine, despite frequent Supreme Court decisions and scholarly analysis, remained unsettled. The Supreme Court contributed to the confusion by poorly articulating its reasoning concerning judicial abridgment of contracts and applying the doctrine largely in municipal bond cases. This raised the question of whether the doctrine was employed selectively to address the issue of state court bond repudiation.[199] This was a matter of particular concern to the federal courts, which feared the impact of repudiation on national credit markets.[200] Justice Harlan, for example, usually voted to require payment of municipal bonds as a means of encouraging interstate commerce. "A national market for local bonds," one scholar has pointed out, "could only exist if repudiation was controlled."[201]

MARRIAGE

In his *Dartmouth College* opinion John Marshall articulated the view that marriage was not a contract within the scope of the contract clause. This position was generally accepted by courts throughout the nineteenth century. It was definitively settled by the Supreme Court in *Maynard v. Hill* (1888).[202] Field, writing for the Court, declared that marriage was an institution governed by laws and not a mere contract that could be modified by the parties. Accordingly, he ruled that a legislative divorce did not impair any contract.[203]

JUSTICE FIELD AND THE CONTRACT CLAUSE

Justice Field was in many respects the most influential jurist of the Gilded Age. He is best remembered as a champion of a substantive reading of the due process norm and for his adherence to a philosophy based on the right to pursue lawful callings. Field's views toward the contract clause have received less attention from scholars but shed light on shifting attitudes toward that provision.[204] A believer in the sanctity of contract, he urged a liberal construction of the contract clause "to secure from direct attack not only the contract itself, but all the essential incidents which give it value and enable its owner to enforce it."[205] Field invariably supported invoking the provision to safeguard private agreements from state interference. Thus, he looked skeptically upon state laws that altered debtor-creditor arrangements or sought to apply homestead exemptions to prior debts. In addition, Field voted to invalidate state constitutional provisions barring lawsuits to enforce slave purchase contracts and to void the Legal Tender Act as an impairment of contract.

Guided by his commitment that the state should not confer special privileges, Field's attitude toward contracts by states was more nuanced. He shared the prevailing view that charters of incorporation should be strictly construed. Field also adhered to the principle that states could not divest themselves of sovereign powers. For example, he parted with the Court majority and consistently opposed irrevocable grants of tax exemptions because taxation was an inherent power of government. Equally important, Field embraced the principle of an inalienable police power. In his mind, a state could not relinquish by contract its authority to legislate to protect the public health, safety, morals, and welfare. Moreover, he refused to allow grants of monopoly privilege any shelter under the contract clause. This may well explain his reliance on the novel "public trust" doctrine to strip waterfront property from a major railroad company. Thus, Field contributed to the process of diluting the protection accorded corporate charters under *Dartmouth College.*

Still, according to Field, states were not free to disregard the strictures of the contract clause. This was most evident in the bond repudiation cases. Repudiation of debt was anathema to Field, and he consistently favored judicial protection of bondholders. He pictured investment of capital, as represented by bonded debt, as the basis for sustained economic growth. Field was particularly outraged with Virginia's artifices in seeking to evade receipt of the tax-paying bond coupons. "No greater calamity could, in my

The most influential jurist of the Gilded Age, Justice Stephen J. Field urged a broad reading of the contract clause to safeguard private agreements from legislative abridgment and to prevent state repudiation of bonded debt. However, he endorsed the strict construction of corporate charters and was deeply skeptical about claims of irrevocable tax exemptions. (Library of Congress)

judgment," he lectured, "befall the country than the general adoption of the doctrine that it is not a constitutional impairment of contracts, to embarrass their enforcement with onerous and destructive conditions, and thus to evade performance of them."[206]

Field's disinclination to apply the contract clause against the states, aside from barring debt repudiation, contrasted with his vigorous support for protecting economic rights under the due process clause of the Fourteenth Amendment. A glance at Field's role in the protracted controversy over railroad rate regulations illustrates the shifting place of the contract clause in the constitutional order of the Gilded Age. Although Field maintained that police power regulations could override contractual provisions, he drew the line at state regulation of charges for the use of private property. Absent special situations, such as a grant of monopoly status, Field asserted that rate regulations were constitutionally impermissible. In several cases he argued in dissent that the charter of a railroad conferred the right to set rates free from state interference. When this line of argument proved fruitless, Field increasingly contended that rate regulations could deprive an enterprise of property without due process of law in violation of the Fourteenth Amendment. His underlying concern was that rates could be set so low as to deny a company a reasonable return on its invested capital. Such a result amounted to an indirect confiscation of property. By 1890 a majority of the Supreme Court had gravitated to Field's position. As the premise that the due process norm placed substantive restraints on state power over private property gained momentum, the contract clause was simply sidelined.

LIBERTY OF CONTRACT

It is essential to differentiate the contract clause from the emerging liberty of contract doctrine. Courts in the late nineteenth century began to develop the principle that the right to make contracts was constitutionally protected by the due process clause of the Fourteenth Amendment.[207] State courts took the lead in fashioning the liberty of contract doctrine and in striking down laws seen as infringing the right of persons to enter agreements. The Supreme Court endorsed the freedom of contract norm for the first time in *Allgeyer v. Louisiana* (1897). Justice Rufus W. Peckham, writing for a unanimous bench, broadly declared that liberty in the Fourteenth Amendment included "the right of the citizen to be free in the enjoyment of all his faculties; to be free to use them in all lawful ways; to live and work where he will; to earn his livelihood by any lawful calling; to pursue any livelihood or avocation, and for that purpose to enter into all contracts which may be proper, necessary and essential" to this purpose.[208] The line of decisions invoking the liberty of contract doctrine, which extended into the twentieth century, was a source of controversy and spawned a vast literature.[209] That is a discrete topic beyond the scope of this volume.

Rather, for our purposes, it bears emphasis that the contract clause was concerned with the stability of existing agreements and barred retroactive abridgment of contracts. It had no prospective effect and was therefore inapplicable to the making of contracts after a statute was in force.[210] The state was free to ban or regulate contracts entered after a statute was enacted. In contrast, the liberty of contract doctrine was concerned with the right to make future contracts without state oversight. Although application of the doctrine was spotty, it had a potentially wide reach.

FEDERAL IMPAIRMENT

By its terms, of course, the contract clause prohibited only state abridgment of agreements. Indeed, the Constitution expressly granted Congress the power to enact bankruptcy laws, and in 1898 Congress finally enacted an enduring bankruptcy measure. The Supreme Court, in an opinion by Chief Justice Fuller, broadly affirmed congressional authority to retroactively interfere with contracts. "The grant to Congress," he explained, "involved the power to impair the obligation of contracts, and this the States were forbidden to do."[211] The national bankruptcy law superseded state insolvency measures and reduced the flow of debtor-creditor cases before the Supreme Court.

There was also speculation whether Congress might be bound by its contracts without regard to the contract clause. In 1886 Tiedeman argued that "there can be no doubt that similar action by Congress would likewise be unconstitutional, because it would deprive one of his property without due process of law."[212] The implications of this observation will be explored in later chapters.

A WANING PROVISION

The contract clause retained considerable vitality throughout the Gilded Age, and it was frequently the subject of litigation. Courts regularly relied on the provision to uphold private agreements and to prevent municipal bond repudiations. Yet in other respects, by the end of the nineteenth century the contract clause was of diminishing importance in constitutional jurisprudence. The police power exception and the adoption of reservation clauses weakened the extent to which the provision protected corporate charters from state interference. The *Dartmouth College* doctrine no longer had many teeth. Courts ceased to read the contract clause expansively. Starting in the 1890s attorneys relied less frequently on the contract clause as the principal basis to challenge state regulatory legislation. They increasingly joined a contract clause claim with an argument that the contested state law constituted a deprivation of property without due process. Relegated to a secondary place in constitutional law, the contract clause entered the twentieth century in a weakened condition.

CHAPTER 6
The Early Twentieth Century

The contract clause continued to erode in the early decades of the twentieth century. By the 1920s the number of contract clause cases before the Supreme Court dwindled, and the significance of those cases declined. For purposes of discussion it is useful to divide the history of the clause in these decades into segments, with the first covering the period 1900 to 1933, before the advent of the New Deal. The second segment will examine the profound impact on contract clause jurisprudence by the changes in the political and legal culture brought about by the New Deal.

PRE–NEW DEAL ERA

Many contract clause decisions in the first three decades of the twentieth century presented familiar issues—attempts to alter debtor-creditor relationships, tax exemptions, and regulation of public utilities. There were also some novel matters, such as residential rent controls. The bulk of the litigation under the contract clause in this period concerned contracts made by the states, not agreements between private parties. Most of the cases turned upon already established interpretative principles and simply required courts to apply them to new sets of facts. The contract clause was certainly not a dead letter because both federal and state courts wielded the provision to safeguard agreements from state abridgment. Moreover, the Supreme Court continued to insist that, to enforce the constitutional guarantee of the inviolability of contracts, it had paramount authority to determine the existence and meaning of contracts independent of state court judgments.[1]

Nonetheless, the Supreme Court gave less attention to the contract clause and increasingly relied on the due process clause of the Fourteenth Amendment as a basis to review state legislation.[2] The tone of Court opinions regarding the clause began to change. There was noticeably less judicial rhetoric stressing the importance of contracts to society and praising the virtue of the contract clause.[3] As the courts tended to compile a mixed record in handling contract clause claims, it was difficult to make the decisions fit any coherent pattern. Symptomatic of the downward path of the contract clause was the Supreme Court's opinion in *Pennsylvania*

Coal Company v. Mahon (1922).[4] In this landmark case the Court placed its seal of approval on the doctrine that a regulation might be so severe as to constitute an unconstitutional taking of property. But our interest lies elsewhere.

In the anthracite region of Pennsylvania the coal companies conveyed the surface rights in parcels of land to individuals but retained the right in the deeds to remove all the coal beneath the surface without liability for any damage caused by such mining. The risk of loss was clearly placed on the landowners. Concerned about the prospect of a massive subsidence of surface property, the state legislature in 1921 enacted the Kohler Act. This measure prohibited any mining that would cause a residence to cave in or subside. The Pennsylvania Coal Company promptly challenged enforcement of the act.[5] Given the importance of this case in establishing the regulatory takings doctrine, it is largely forgotten today that the company relied heavily on the contract clause in attacking the statute. Although the company raised other issues, it plausibly argued that the law impaired the contract contained in the deed of conveyance. Revealingly, Justice Oliver Wendell Holmes, speaking for the Court, invalidated the Kohler Act as an unconstitutional taking of property but did not even mention the contract clause. Dissenting alone, Justice Louis D. Brandeis abruptly rejected the contract clause argument. "If the public safety is imperiled," he wrote, "surely neither grant, nor contract, can prevail against the exercise of the police power." Stressing the state's authority to guard public safety, Brandeis added, "Nor can existing contracts between private individuals preclude exercise of the police power."[6] With the contract clause ignored or dismissed, *Pennsylvania Coal* highlighted the growing marginalization of the provision in the early twentieth century.

REASONS FOR DECLINE

How does one account for the gradual withering of the contract clause? The Supreme Court, of course, had already recognized several limitations to the reach of the clause involving contracts made by states. Such reasoning was now sometimes applied to the distinct problem of contracts between private parties. Several other factors also coalesced to undercut the protective features of the contract clause. As discussed previously, the clause by its express terms was binding only on the states and afforded no safeguards against congressional interference with agreements. This was not a major problem for most of the nineteenth century when the states were the primary locus of economic regulations. But the contract clause was of little avail as Congress became more active in legislating on economic matters.

In addition, changes in the economy reduced the amount of contract clause litigation. Repudiation of debts by state and local governments, once a major concern, sharply declined in the early decades of the twentieth century. Similarly, there were fewer cases involving state grants of tax exemptions. Although belief in the sanctity of contract persisted well into the new century, it was tempered to some extent with the rise of the consumer economy. Both legislators and judges found it necessary to take a fresh look at contracts in order to protect the interests of parties with less bargaining power. State lawmakers, for example, overhauled the rules dealing with life insurance contracts to protect policyholders.[7]

In addition to these practical considerations, the Progressive movement of the early twentieth century promoted new attitudes toward the place of contracts in society. Progressives launched a sustained intellectual attack on individual rights. Skeptical about constitutional doctrines that curtailed governmental power, they questioned both the voluntary nature of contracts and the market economy.[8] Scholars associated with the Progressive movement directed their principal fire at the liberty of contract doctrine evolved under the due process norm, but their attacks inevitably shaped thinking about the importance of contractual rights generally. Wandering far from the views of the founding generation, Progressives argued that contracts were merely products of society that could be altered or abolished to serve the needs of society.[9] They challenged the individualistic understanding of contracts and in essence argued that contracts were not deserving of special constitutional protection.[10] Reflecting this outlook, Progressives called for an expansive reading of the police power that could trump contractual provisions when utilized by lawmakers for the general welfare.[11] As society came to assign less value to contracts, the contract clause was necessarily viewed in a new and diminished light.

Of course, the traditional understanding of the contract clause continued to have strong defenders during the Progressive Era. In 1905 Elihu Root, a prominent attorney and political figure, argued before the Supreme Court: "The legislature cannot violate the Constitution, and redeem the violation by the claim that it was done 'for the public benefit.' The repudiation of contract obligations is quite usually sought to be justified by the plea of 'the public benefit'; but the Constitution of the United States may not be nullified in so simple and easy a fashion."[12] More than a decade later another commentator expressed concern that "the contract clause of the Constitution is to be swallowed up in the capacious and ever-expanding maw of the police power."[13] Notwithstanding such misgivings, the Progressive critique of contracts left a lasting mark. The Progressive Era laid the intellectual groundwork for a jurisprudence that substantially stripped contractual rights of constitutional protection against state abridgment.

PRIVATE CONTRACTS

Both federal and state courts continued to invoke the contract clause to invalidate state debtor-relief laws that infringed contractual obligations. Yet the Supreme Court heard only two debt-relief cases in this period. In *Bradley v. Lightcap* (1904), for example, Chief Justice Melville W. Fuller, for a unanimous Supreme Court, declared unconstitutional an Illinois law that retroactively forfeited the legal title and right of possession of a foreclosing mortgagee for failure to obtain a deed within a set time.[14] He held that the law existing at the time the mortgage contract was entered controlled the rights of the parties. Yet the justices reached a different conclusion when an independent purchaser bought property at a foreclosure sale. Where the laws governing redemption from the mortgage sale had been altered subsequent to the date of the mortgage but prior to the sale, they found no contractual impairment. The Court reasoned that the transaction involving the independent purchaser was governed by the law existing at the time of the sale because the purchaser had no connection with the original mortgage.[15] The distinction drawn by the Court seems rather formalistic and could be seen as undercutting a mortgagee's rights in the mortgage contract by chilling independent parties from bidding at the foreclosure sale.[16] Clearly the Court did not bar any state legislation regulating the debtor-creditor relationship.

Following a familiar pattern, state courts wielded the contract clause to strike down laws that sought to enlarge the period of redemption for prior mortgages.[17] Similarly, the Supreme Court of North Dakota construed a law altering the right of a mortgagee to rents for occupancy of the property during the period of redemption to apply prospectively only, thereby avoiding a contract clause violation.[18] The Supreme Court of Tennessee likewise ruled that a statute declaring that any authority to confess judgment given before an action was instituted was void could not be applied to prior promissory notes. It found that confession of judgment in case of a default in payment was an efficacious remedy and that to deprive the creditor of the security of this remedy would impair the obligation of contract.[19]

Laws changing the terms of insurance policies were also a fertile source of litigation. The Supreme Court had no difficulty in striking down a Louisiana statute exempting the proceeds of life insurance payable to the deceased's estate from antecedent debts.[20] State courts reached conflicting conclusions as to whether state lawmakers could override an insurance contract provision that suits for loss must be commenced within six months from the time the cause of action arose. The Supreme Court of Iowa took the position that such a law altering contractual rights was void as to prior contracts, whereas the Supreme Court of Appeals of Virginia held that the measures pertained solely to the remedy and passed constitutional muster.[21] None of these cases broke any new ground.

The most interesting insurance case involving the contract clause had its origins in the Russian Revolution of 1917. At issue in *Sliosberg v. New York Life Insurance Company* (1927) was an action by a Russian exile to recover the cash surrender value of a life and endowment policy.[22] The insurance company declined payment, pointing to a New York statute enacted after the making of the contract suspending the performance of contracts payable in rubles until thirty days after the United States recognized the government in Russia. Drawing upon precedent from the Civil War Era, the New York Court of Appeals ruled that laws that suspended proceedings to enforce contracts for an indefinite period ran afoul of the Constitution. It found no public welfare rationale to justify the law. Although the court vindicated the contract clause in the instant case, it also signaled restrictions on the provision's reach by emphasizing that all agreements were subject to state authority. "That the government may be required, in times of public stress," the court observed, "so to legislate as to nullify private contracts, is an implied term in every contract, so that such legislation, if enacted, does not impair the obligation of contract within the meaning of the limitation."[23]

Despite occasional decisions safeguarding private agreements from state abridgment, the protection accorded such arrangements under the contract clause began to erode in the early twentieth century. In *Manigualt v. Springs* (1905) the Supreme Court opened the door to this result by extending the police power exception to contracts between private parties.[24] As discussed earlier, the courts in the late nineteenth century had determined that state legislatures could not bargain away their police power. This doctrine had been developed to deal with public contracts to which a state was a party, such as grants to various corporations. It had been utilized to modify or revoke corporate privileges. In *Manigault*, however, private contracts were subordinated to the inalienable police power as well. The case arose out of a 1898 contract between adjoining riparian owners on a navigable creek that the creek should remain free of obstructions. In 1903 the South Carolina legislature, anxious to promote land drainage, authorized one party to erect a dam across the creek and required that he pay damages for any injury caused by the dam to other landowners. The legislation was challenged as both an impairment of contract and a deprivation of property without due process of law. Speaking for the Court, Justice Henry Billings Brown, without any analysis or explanation, declared that the contract clause "does not prevent the State from exercising such powers as are vested in it for the promotion of the common weal, or are necessary for the general good of the public, though contracts previously entered into between individuals be affected." He added that the police power was "paramount to any rights under contracts between individuals."[25] Brown then pointed out that the legislature had wide discretion to ascertain what was necessary for the public good. In an attempt to bolster the opinion he cited several irrelevant cases involving state grants, a matter not at issue here.

Manigault marked a watershed in the treatment of private agreements under the contract clause. Although the decision might be explained on grounds that it concerned a public waterway, the Court's language went far beyond such a rationale. One scholar persuasively wrote that *Manigault* "was perilously close to saying that states could impair contractual obligations whenever they had a good reason."[26] Of course, if private arrangements could be abridged when a state legislature deemed it necessary, the contract clause provided little protection to private contracts.

Thereafter the Supreme Court repeatedly reaffirmed that private contracts were subject to the state police power. At issue in *Hudson County Water Company v. McCarter* (1908) was a 1905 New Jersey statute making it unlawful to transport water from any river or lake of the state into other jurisdictions. Speaking for the Court, Justice Holmes summarily disposed of a contract clause attack on the measure as applied to both prior and subsequent contracts to convey water to parties in New York. Stressing the dominion of states over natural resources within their boundaries to safeguard the public welfare, he observed, "One whose rights, such as they are, are subject to state restrictions, cannot remove them from the power of the state by making a contract about them." Holmes added that the contract "was illegal when made."[27] More than a decade later he amplified this point: "The operation of reasonable laws for the protection of the public cannot be headed off by making contracts reaching into the future."[28] This line of cases signaled a sharp limitation on the protection afforded private agreements under the Constitution.

RENT CONTROL

The diminished status of private contracts was manifested by litigation growing out of unprecedented rent-control laws enacted to apply in several cities following World War I. Aside from some tenement reform laws directed at health and safety concerns, the relations between residential landlords and tenants had long been governed by bargaining and leases. The outbreak of World War I had the effect of increasing the cost of labor and building supplies. With the entry of the United States into the war in April of 1917, residential construction came to a halt. This exacerbated the already existing housing shortage in many urban areas. Faced with rising expenses, landlords raised rents. This in turn prompted fears about rent profiteering. Tenants who resisted the higher rents faced eviction.[29] Reacting to concern over rental practices, Congress in 1919 passed the Ball Rent Act, which imposed rent controls in the District of Columbia for a period of two years. It established a commission to determine "fair and reasonable" rents for residential units and barred the eviction of tenants who paid the rent fixed by the commission. A year later the New York legislature, driven in part by fear of a radicalized tenantry, enacted similar legislation for New York City, also limited in duration to two years. In addition, a number of other jurisdictions adopted rent-control measures. The legislation amounted to a sweeping overhaul of landlord-tenant relations. By regulating rents and curtailing evictions the laws significantly limited the control of landlords over their property. These laws were predicated upon the existence of a public emergency in housing conditions growing out of the war.

The heavy reliance on emergency conditions as a justification for rent-control laws raised a cluster of interrelated questions. What constituted an emergency? Who determines that an emergency exists? To what extent can courts inquire into the basis for a legislative declaration of emergency? Should an emergency be limited to wartime situations? Can the assertion of an emergency permit legislators to override existing contracts in seeming contravention of the Constitution? The resolution of these issues would add a new dimension to contract clause jurisprudence. It bears emphasis that the Constitution makes no mention of an emergency powers doctrine,

Rent strikes in New York City during 1919 prompted the state legislature to enact unprecedented rent control measures. A divided Supreme Court sustained the law as a response to emergency housing conditions, brushing aside the argument that an emergency did not justify the impairment of existing leases. (*New York Times*, September 1919)

although the concept has frequently been invoked by the executive branch of government.[30]

Unsurprisingly, landlords promptly attacked the rent-control laws. They charged that the laws impaired the obligation of contract, amounted to a taking of property, and deprived the owners of property without due process of law. Our concern is solely with the first of these arguments. Opinion was divided as to the constitutionality of the measures, and the lower courts reached different conclusions.[31] In March of 1921 the New York Court of Appeals brushed aside the various objections and sustained the rent-control laws.[32] Observing that the lawmakers had made "the tenants in possession a preferred class," it ruled that the existence of a public emergency was a question of fact primarily for the legislature. Noting that the field of regulation was constantly expanding, the court opined that the contract clause "puts no limit on any lawful exercise of legitimate governmental power." It added, "The rule alike for state and nation is that private contract rights must yield to the public welfare, when the latter is appropriately declared and defined and the two conflict." Although the court professed to hold private contracts in high regard, by according the legislature wide latitude over contracts it, as a practical matter, moved in the opposite direction.[33]

Judge McLaughlin dissented alone. He found the rent-control laws unconstitutional on several grounds, including a direct violation of the contract clause. "It is the substitution of a new contract which the parties never made," he insisted, "and to the terms of which they never agreed."[34] McLaughlin reasoned that the laws destroyed the existing lease and warned that an exercise of the police power cannot override the Constitution.

A month later in *Block v. Hirsh* (1921) a sharply divided Supreme Court, in an opinion by Holmes, upheld the validity of the Ball Rent Act for the District of Columbia.[35] Treating the law as a temporary measure to meet emergency conditions, he rejected the contention that it deprived landlords of property without due process or amounted to a taking of property. Because the law at issue was an act of Congress, Holmes did not address the contract clause. In a companion case the Supreme Court, in a five-to-four vote, sustained the New York rent-control law as well. Holmes, again writing for the majority, assumed that an emergency existed and largely disposed of the case on the basis of his opinion in *Block*. Dealing in a cursory manner with the contract clause, he simply declared, "Contracts are made subject to this exercise of the power of the State when otherwise justified, as we have held this to be."[36] Holmes evidently did not believe that arguments grounded on the contract clause warranted much attention.

Speaking for the four dissenters in both cases, Justice Joseph McKenna denied that an emergency could justify an impairment of leases in the face of the absolute prohibition of the contract clause. Nor was he impressed by the fact that the Ball Rent Act was limited to two years, presciently noting that it could be made to last longer. In language reminiscent of nineteenth-century jurists, McKenna stressed that contracts were the basis of life and business in the United States. He concluded by asking, If states could invoke the police power to nullify contracts, what other provisions of the Constitution could also be subordinated to that power?[37]

As McKenna feared, both the Ball Rent Act and the New York rent controls were repeatedly extended upon expiration of their original two-year period on the ground that the housing emergency still existed. In *Chastleton Corp. v. Sinclair* (1924), however, the Supreme Court indicated that there were limits to its willingness to accept a legislative declaration of emergency conditions.[38] Holmes, once more speaking for the Court, agreed that respect was due to a legislative finding of an emergency but insisted, "A Court is not at liberty to shut its eyes to an obvious mistake when the validity of the law depends upon the truth of what is declared." He explained, "A law depending upon the existence of an emergency or other certain state of facts to uphold it may cease to operate if the emergency ceases or the facts change, even though valid when passed." According to Holmes, it was "a matter of public knowledge" that the need for housing in the District of Columbia had diminished. He opined that the increased cost of living by itself could not justify the Ball Rent Act. Although observing, "Upon the facts that we judicially know, we should be compelled to say that the law has ceased to operate," Holmes remanded the case to a lower court to ascertain the facts pertaining to local housing.[39] The Court of Appeals for the District of Columbia readily concluded that the housing emergency had ended, and hence there was no constitutional basis for a continuation of rent controls. Highlighting a concern with reliance on supposed emergencies that linger without fixed limits, the Court stated, "If the emergency in question is not at an end, then this legislation may be extended indefinitely, and that which was 'intended to meet a temporary emergency' may become permanent."[40]

Although the judicial inquiry into the continued existence of the housing emergency in *Chastleton* did not directly involve the contract clause, it was relevant to the larger issue of whether a claim of emergency conditions could provide a satisfactory reason for abridging contracts. With the onset of the Great Depression only a few years in the future, lawmakers repeatedly invoked the concept of an emergency to justify interference with existing contracts. *Chastleton* suggested some degree of judicial oversight of declarations of emergency, but the overall legacy of the rent-control cases was to weaken the contract clause. Not only did courts tend, at least initially, to accept at face value the legislative determination of an emergency, but they treated an emergency as enlarging the scope of the police power vis-à-vis private agreements.

PUBLIC CONTRACTS

The largest proportion of contract clause cases in this period involved grants to business corporations, which commonly sought shelter under the provision in the face of state taxation and regulation. As discussed previously, however, courts had already weakened the protection afforded corporate charters under *Dartmouth College*. Indeed, by 1904 Ernst Freund, a noted legal scholar, could tellingly observe that courts had substantially modified the *Dartmouth College* doctrine "with the result of leaving the law very much where it would be if there were no Dartmouth College Case."[41]

Moreover, in a number of cases the Supreme Court, exercising its independent judgment as to the existence of a contract, found that there was no contract between the state and private parties.[42] This reasoning was closely akin to the principle of strict construction of corporate charters. The upshot, of course, was that the state law at issue did not abridge any contractual arrangement in violation of the Constitution.

Tax Exemptions

As we have seen, grants of tax-exempt status to railroads were a fertile source of controversy in the late nineteenth century. State legislatures had ceased to grant such immunities long before 1900, but some were of indefinite duration and remained the subject of contention. There was only a handful of contract clause cases relating to claims of tax exemption in the early twentieth century, and the pattern of decisions followed that of the prior century.

In a few cases the Supreme Court sustained partial tax exemptions. At issue in *Stearns v. Minnesota* (1900), for example, was an 1865 Minnesota statute that authorized a railroad to pay a tax on gross earnings in lieu of any other taxes.[43] When thirty years later the state sought to impose a tax on railroad land, the company charged that the levy impaired its contract with the state. The Supreme Court found that there was a valid contract to commute the payment of taxes and that the attempted property tax ran afoul of the contract clause. Exemptions in charters also posed questions of interpretation. In *Wright v. Georgia Railroad and Banking Company* (1910) the Court was called upon to construe an 1833 charter limiting the tax liability on company stock to "one-half of one per cent per annum on the net proceeds of their investment."[44] Considering the public policy at the time the charter was granted, the Court held that the immunity covered the property of the railroad and not just the shares of stock. It followed that a state law levying a tax on the property or franchise of the railroad impaired the obligation of contract.[45]

In the main, however, the Supreme Court tended to either reject or narrowly construe claims of tax-exempt status. The justices repeatedly stressed that only a clear expression of intent to surrender the sovereign power of taxation would bind a state.[46] In a number of cases the Court invoked the long-standing distinction between a tax exemption contained in a corporate charter and a general law seeking to encourage certain enterprises. A scheme of tax benefits, it reasoned, did not amount to a promise and was simply a legislative policy subject to change.[47] Hence there was no contract to impair. As discussed above, cases involving tax exemptions often grew out of corporate mergers. It was well settled that a tax immunity did not automatically transfer to a new enterprise but required express legislative authorization.[48] The Court also stressed that a tax immunity or exemption from a regulatory burden did not pass to a purchasing company by virtue of a statute authorizing the transfer of corporate "privileges."[49] Following the principle of strict construction, any doubt was to be resolved in favor of the state's taxing authority. Consequently, the question of constitutionally protected tax exemptions, contested since the time of John Marshall, was of slight significance in contract clause jurisprudence after 1930.

Rate Regulation

As pointed out in Chapter 5, the Supreme Court consistently declined to rely on the contract clause as a basis to invalidate state-imposed regulations on the rates charged by railroads. The Court's record in the early twentieth century regarding rate regulations for other utilities, however, was mixed. In *Los Angeles v. Los Angeles City Water Company* (1900) the Court showed its willingness to uphold utility contracts in the face of state regulation.[50] The City of Los Angeles entered a thirty-year contract in 1868 leasing the municipal water works to private parties. The city retained the right to regulate water rates but agreed not to reduce the water rates below "those now charged." Finding an impairment of contract, the Court struck down an 1897 ordinance that reduced the water rates below what was charged in 1868.

Moreover, in a line of cases decided in the first two decades of the twentieth century the Supreme Court wielded the contract clause to curb municipal efforts to reduce the standard five-cent streetcar fare. In the lead case of *Detroit v. Detroit Citizens' Street Railway Company* (1902) Justice Rufus W. Peckham, writing for a unanimous Court, found that a five-cent fare ordinance embodied a contract between the city and the street railway company and that the reservation of a right for the city to prescribe rules and regulations did not encompass the power to alter the rate structure.[51] He ruled that an ordinance reducing the fare for passengers ran afoul of the contract clause. Peckham declared, "The fixing of rates is . . . among the most vital provisions of the agreement between the parties contained in the ordinance."[52] A number of cases followed this decision in the ensuing years.[53] The Supreme Court decisions with respect to the street railway fares appear somewhat anomalous. There has been some speculation as to why the Court was more receptive to contract clause arguments in this context than to similar contentions grounded in railroad charters.[54]

States increasingly regulated the charges of street railways by means of a commission, giving rise to new questions. Where the Public Service Commission was empowered to increase maximum rates to provide a fair return to companies, the New York Court of Appeals determined that a subsequent street railway franchise was subject to the commission's authority. Because statutes existing when contracts were made formed part of the agreement, the court concluded that no obligation of a prior contract was abrogated if the commission increased the five-cent fare.[55] The emergence of commission governance, coupled with the expiration of the original nineteenth-century grants setting such maximum fare, helps to explain the gradual disappearance of contract clause cases concerning street railways from judicial dockets in the 1920s.

As a general proposition, moreover, the Supreme Court looked skeptically at arguments that state control over utility or street railway rates was limited by private contracts. In *Knoxville Water Company v. Knoxville* (1903), for example, a municipal ordinance reduced the rates charged by the company for supplying water to customers.[56] Justice Holmes, for the Court, readily found that there was no contract between the city and the company setting water rates. He went on to assert that any contract between the company and its customers was subject to the city's regulatory authority, which the company could not undercut by private contracts. More than a decade later the Court was even more emphatic on this point. Brushing aside the contention that a contract between a utility and a customer providing a set rate for electricity was impaired by a subsequent commission order fixing a higher rate, the Court rejected the argument that the commission order violated the contract clause as almost frivolous. It proclaimed, "The right of private contract must yield to the exigencies of the public welfare" when determined by the state in the exercise of the police power.[57]

State courts also upheld broad regulatory authority over public utilities. The Supreme Court of Indiana sustained legislative power to approve sale of a telephone company and to withdraw power previously vested in the city of Indianapolis to consent to the sale. It broadly observed that "all contracts made for services to be furnished by public utilities must be regarded as made in contemplation of the regulatory power of the state, and that, when the state exercises such power by changing rates or conditions of services, such change does not impair the obligations of existing contracts, although such contracts must yield to the changes so made."[58]

Thus, the Supreme Court increasingly withdrew from policing public utility rates under the contract clause. The development paralleled the earlier move to reject review of railroad charges under the same provision and to hear any disputes over the reasonableness of state-imposed rates under the rubric of due process.

Municipal Franchises Revisited

In the early years of the twentieth century the impetus to establish public ownership of utilities gained ground.[59] Consequently, the Supreme Court continued to hear cases growing out of municipal attempts to alter existing arrangements for providing water or other services to their inhabitants. In *Skaneateles Water Works Company v. Skaneateles* (1902) a private water company brought suit to enjoin the village of Skaneateles from constructing a water system of its own.[60] It alleged that such a step would impair a contract between the company and the village and deprive the plaintiff of property without due process of law. Although the company had been granted a franchise in 1887 to operate and maintain a water system for the village, a prior contract to supply water had expired before the village commenced to build its own waterworks. Justice Peckham, speaking for a unanimous Court, found no implied contract in the grant of a franchise for an exclusive privilege in the company, declaring that such a limitation on the powers of a municipality was too important to be left to implication. He ruled that because there was no contract there was, of course, no impairment. The Court reached a similar result in a number of cases, often relying on the principle that grants of franchise should be strictly construed in favor of the public.[61] Even where a city agreed not to grant the same privilege to another corporation for a time, courts held that such an arrangement did not preclude the municipality from creating its own system.[62] The fact that a competing municipal enterprise would inevitably inflict economic hardship on the franchisee was deemed immaterial.

To be sure, where the provisions of a franchise were explicit, the Supreme Court was prepared to invoke the contract clause to protect an exclusive franchise against competition by a municipality.[63] But generally the Court was disinclined to find a violation of contract when a municipality desired to establish a utility plant of its own. "No legal obstacle," Morton Keller aptly observed, "impeded municipal ownership and operation."[64] As with tax exemptions and rate regulations, claims of an exclusive franchise gradually disappeared as matters of contract clause concern.

Railroad and Highway Regulations

The Supreme Court heard a number of cases involving duties and regulations imposed on transportation companies. This litigation reflected the changing urban landscape, with increased traffic density and technological advances. The Court upheld a number of statutes requiring railroads to build, repair, and remove structures. For example, the Court agreed that a railroad could be required to lower a tunnel under the Chicago River at its expense in order to accommodate navigation by larger vessels. Brushing aside a contract clause argument, the Court held that the city ordinance authorizing construction of the tunnel contained no provision curtailing the power of the city to protect river navigation or stipulating that the city would meet the expenses of a tunnel alteration.[65] Relying on the inalienable police power, it reached a similar result in other cases. Thus, the Court sustained laws mandating that railroads repair viaducts[66] and construct openings and ditches to carry off surface water.[67] On the other hand, where a contract expressly provided that a city would bear the cost for a street crossing, a subsequent order that the railroad pay part of the expense was held to violate the contract clause.[68]

Following its previous pattern, the Court continued to look favorably on laws regulating the operations of railroads. In *Atlantic Coast Line Railroad Company v. City of Goldsboro* (1914) the city imposed several restriction on rail activities within the municipality.[69] Among other things, it set limits on train speed, required the posting of flagmen to warn of approaching trains, and restricted the length of time cars could stand on certain streets. Finding that the regulations were designed to protect the public health and safety from the dangers of rail operations, the Court had no difficulty in rejecting a contract clause challenge. Indeed, it emphasized that the contract clause did not override the police power and that "all contracts and property rights are held subject to its fair exercise."[70] The justices took the same position four years later, ruling that a contract authorizing a railroad to construct tracks on streets in Denver was subject to the exercise of the police power. Accordingly, there was no violation of the contract clause when the city directed the railroad to remove its track from a busy intersection of two streets.[71]

Nor could a railroad avoid liability for the death of an employee caused by its negligence by asserting an exemption from such liability contained in its charter. Subsequent legislation repealing this provision was assailed on contract clause grounds. Invoking the police power to guard health and safety, the Supreme Court stressed that the civil liability of railroads for the death of employees was a matter of public concern. It followed that any exculpatory language in the charter was subject to state regulatory authority and could not be the subject of a binding contract.[72]

Yet on occasion the Supreme Court relied on the contract clause to prevent a municipality from halting railroad construction on a city street. An 1868 ordinance authorized a railroad to construct its line through the city of South Bend and to build a double track on one street. In 1901 the city repealed the ordinance insofar as it conferred a right to a second track. Treating the 1868 ordinance as a contract between the city and the carrier, the Court declared that the contract was subject to repeal or alteration by the city in the exercise of the police power. It agreed that the city retained broad authority to regulate railroad operations to secure public safety. Nonetheless, on the fact presented, the Court concluded that the repeal was not a reasonable exercise of the police power, and thus the repeal impaired the 1868 contract. Making an independent assessment of the circumstances, it lectured that the mere inconvenience of running trains through a city did not justify nullification of part of the railroad's franchise.[73]

States were also accorded broad latitude to control the use of roadways notwithstanding the contract clause. At issue in *Sproles v. Binford* (1932) was a Texas statute imposing weight and length restrictions on trucks using the state highways.[74] The state defended the regulation by pointing to the fact that heavy loads damaged the highways and proved costly to the state. The truckers maintained that the regulations interfered with their ability to carry out prior contracts with customers. Writing for the Supreme Court, Chief Justice Charles Evans Hughes abruptly dismissed this argument and proclaimed, "Contracts which relate to the use of the highways must be deemed to have been made in contemplation of the regulatory authority of the State."[75]

By 1930 it was settled that, absent special circumstances, courts would not invoke the contract clause to bar regulation of transportation facilities. As in other areas of dispute, an expansive reading of the police power was deemed to prevail over claims grounded on the contract clause. In a 1915 case the Supreme Court defined the police power to encompass not only public health and safety but also "regulations designed to promote the public convenience or the general welfare and prosperity."[76] As the understanding of the police power grew, there would be correspondingly less room for agreements to find shelter under the contract clause.

Public Trust Doctrine Curtailed

In a pair of cases the Supreme Court relied on the contract clause to vindicate the rights of landowners and limit the reach of the public trust doctrine. At issue in *Appleby v. City of New York* (1926) were deeds executed in the 1850s conveying lots below the tidewater on the east side of the North River in New York City to private parties in fee simple with rights of wharfage.[77] Pursuant to subsequent statutes, the city constructed piers and commenced dredging operations on the premises. The landowners brought suit to enjoin the city from dredging the lots and from using the water over their land as mooring places for vessels. They charged that the activities of the city amounted to an impairment of the contractual obligations contained in the deeds.

Speaking for the Court, Chief Justice William Howard Taft applied New York law and affirmed the right of the state to convey property under navigable waters to private parties in fee simple whenever the legislature deemed such grants to be in the public interest. Such a conveyance, he continued, limited the power of the city to impose regulations that would interfere with the ownership and enjoyment of the submerged lots. It followed that the challenged statutes abridged the contracts between the city and the grantees. Taft rejected a public trust argument based on *Illinois Central Railroad v. Illinois.* First, he distinguished the case before him from *Illinois Central* by stressing that a vast harbor area was at issue in *Illinois Central* instead of a few lots. Second, Taft pointed out that the conclusion in that case "was necessarily a statement of Illinois law."[78] In effect he underscored the role of state law in determining the reach of the public trust doctrine. Taft concluded by complaining that the application of the New York statutes "would reduce the rights which were intended to be conveyed to practically nothing, and would leave the grantees only the privilege of paying taxes for something quite unsubstantial."[79] Under Taft's analysis, where state law permitted the grant of lots under water with all privileges, a subsequent law limiting such rights impaired the contract.[80]

EMINENT DOMAIN

It had been settled since the Antebellum Era that the contract clause did not bar the states from utilizing the power of eminent domain to appropriate existing contracts upon payment of just compensation. This point was reiterated in the early twentieth century.[81] In 1917 the Supreme Court went a step further, holding for the first time that even a contract that expressly attempted to prevent the exercise of eminent domain could not divest the state of such power. Eminent domain was so much an aspect of governmental authority, it reasoned, that it could not be restrained by the contract clause.[82]

CHANGES IN REMEDY

The right/remedy distinction, which loomed so large in early contract clause jurisprudence, received less judicial attention in the first decades of the twentieth century. Generally the Supreme Court sustained the power of state legislatures to make reasonable alterations in the remedies available to enforce prior contracts as long as an efficacious remedy remained. For example, Justice John Marshall Harlan, speaking for the Court, upheld Wisconsin legislation requiring that claims against the city of Oshkosh be presented to the city council before bringing any suit against the city and setting a time limit for an appeal to the courts. He concluded that this requirement did not unreasonably delay a creditor's recovery against the city and was "a reasonable regulation for the protection of the city against the cost of unnecessary litigation."[83]

Remedial changes in the corporate arena similarly passed constitutional muster. Many cases raised alterations of remedies in the context of means to enforce stockholder liability. In *Pittsburg Steel Company v. Baltimore Equitable Society* (1913) Justice Holmes found no contract clause violation when a statute made a bill in equity on behalf of all creditors the sole remedy and abated pending suits brought by individual creditors.[84] He reasoned that in practice the original remedy was less effective than the substituted remedy.

In 1935 Justice Benjamin Cardozo noted the long pedigree of judicial ruminations on the distinction between changes in the substance of contracts and alterations of the remedy. "The dividing line," he pithily explained, "is at times obscure."[85] Cardozo implicitly suggested that this elusive distinction had outlived its usefulness.

ALTERING PUBLIC CONTRACTS RELATING TO DEBT

The Supreme Court continued to look skeptically at laws that changed financial obligations involving states or municipalities. At issue in *Houston and Texas Central Railroad Company v. Texas* (1900) was an action to collect from a railroad the amount due on bonds issued to the state by the company as security for loans.[86] Laws of 1863 and 1864, treated as implied contracts by the Court, provided that railroad companies could discharge their obligation on such bonds by tendering state treasury warrants. The state received them in payment without objection for years. In 1870, however, the legislature enacted another law governing railroad repayment of the loans. The Texas Court of Civil Appeals construed this measure as striking out the prior payment in treasury warrants. Pursuant to this new statute, the state refused to credit the earlier payment in warrants and insisted upon a second payment in money. The Supreme Court treated this as an attempt by the state to repudiate the payments in warrants, which amounted to a material impairment of the contract between the parties.

Other schemes of repudiation also ran afoul of the contract clause. It had seemingly been established since the Gilded Age that municipalities could not escape their financial obligations by pointing to state laws that withheld from local government the authority to levy taxes. Louisiana was particularly slow in learning this lesson. In *Louisiana v. City of New Orleans* (1909) a receiver brought suit to compel the city by writ of mandamus to assess taxes to pay a judgment pertaining to the Metropolitan Police District.[87] The city argued that its authority to levy taxation for that purpose was ended by legislation enacted subsequent to incurring the obligation. Adhering to precedent, the Supreme Court rejected this contention, reiterating its view that where a city is empowered to contract and to exercise taxing authority to meet its contractual obligations, this power cannot thereafter be eliminated until the contracts are satisfied.

State courts also demonstrated hostility to legislation that hampered recovery of public debt. This was sometimes accomplished by altering the boundaries of local government units in ways that diluted the tax base pledged to pay the principal and interest on bonds. In 1928, for example, the Supreme Court of Arkansas struck down a state statute that removed a large part of the territory of a school district and transferred such land to a new district. The court found that the legislation weakened the security of the previously issued school bonds by reducing the tax base upon which the bondholders had relied. Consequently, the legislation ran afoul of the contract clause in both the state and federal constitutions.[88] Likewise, the Supreme Court of Florida ruled that the division of a town into two jurisdictions could not be invoked to defeat the rights of bondholders in view of the federal contract clause.[89] Legislation that reduced the tax rate was found to diminish the means of discharging bonded debt and thus impair the obligation of contract.[90]

EXCLUSIVE PRIVILEGES

There was little contract clause litigation in this period relating to the issue of exclusive rights in transportation facilities. In *Larson v. South Dakota* (1929) the Supreme Court was called upon to consider a claim by the holder of an "exclusive" ferry franchise on the Missouri River that the subsequent construction of a bridge impaired the obligation of his contract with the state.[91] The operator maintained that the bridge would destroy the value of the ferry franchise. Speaking for the Court, Chief Justice Taft invoked the line of cases emanating from *Charles River Bridge,* which established that grants of franchises should be strictly construed in favor of the state. He held that an "exclusive" ferry franchise did not exclude the erection of a competing bridge absent explicit language to that effect. State courts were divided on this subject. The Supreme Court of Appeals of Virginia reached the same conclusion as the Supreme Court,[92] but the Supreme Court of Arkansas distinguished *Charles River Bridge* and ruled that the state could not impair the rights granted in an exclusive turnpike charter by opening a parallel public road.[93]

APPROPRIATION OF CORPORATE PROPERTY

In two cases, both involving canal companies, the contract clause provided a barrier to state attempts to seize corporate property without compensation. An 1858 Louisiana corporate charter provided that at the expiration of the period of corporate existence, set at fifty years, the canal company would revert to the state upon payment of compensation. In 1906 the legislature created a board of control for the canal, which was authorized to take possession of the company's property without compensation. Justice McKenna, speaking for the Supreme Court, determined that the 1858 act granting the charter amounted to a contract and that the 1906 act impaired the obligation of contract by in effect altering the terms providing for compensation.[94]

Nearly a decade later South Carolina brought suit under a 1917 statute to recover possession of the Columbia Canal, alleging that the company had forfeited the property by failure to fulfill certain conditions upon which continued title depended. The key question was whether a provision in the contract requiring completion of the canal within a specified time was a condition subsequent, the breach of which triggered a forfeiture, or a covenant, which was enforced by less drastic means. The Supreme Court in *Columbia Railway, Gas, and Electric Company v. South Carolina* (1923) ruled that the provision was in the nature of a covenant.[95] Justice George Sutherland, writing for the Court, declared that the 1917 act sought to convert a covenant into a condition subsequent and that such a change in the penalty for violation constituted an impairment of contract. "The impairment of a contract," he insisted, "may consist in increasing its burden, as well as in diminishing its efficacy."[96]

CONTINUED DEBATE REGARDING JUDICIAL IMPAIRMENTS

By the start of the twentieth century there were two seemingly different lines of authority with respect to whether state judicial decisions could amount to an impairment of contracts.[97] One line of cases articulated the view that only subsequent legislation could run afoul of the contract clause. The Supreme Court explained in 1909 that in order to review a state court judgment claimed to violate the contract clause, "the impairment must be by some subsequent legislation of the State which has been upheld or given effect" by that court.[98] This position was repeatedly affirmed in the early decades of the century.

Yet the justices again flirted with the notion that retroactive judicial changes undercutting contractual understandings might violate the contract clause. This fresh interest in judicial impairment arose from the prolonged litigation over the construction of elevated railroads in New York City as authorized by an 1892 statute.[99] Property owners sought compensation when such railroads were built in front of their premises, pointing to a depreciation in property values and a reduction in rental income. New York courts initially ruled that the abutting owners had easements of light, air,

The construction of elevated railroads in New York City during the late nineteenth century triggered renewed litigation over whether retroactive changes in state judicial opinions affecting the rights of parties could amount to an unconstitutional impairment of contract. (Library of Congress)

and access to public streets and must be compensated for the loss of these interests. In a subsequent suit by adjacent owners seeking compensation, however, the New York Court of Appeals distinguished its prior decision and determined that the owners had no property interests abridged by the construction of an elevated structure in place of a street-level railroad.

Elihu Root argued the appeal on behalf of the property owners in the Supreme Court in *Muhlker v. New York and Harlem Railroad Company* (1905).[100] He maintained that the building of the elevated railroad was both a violation of the contracts in deeds from predecessors-in-interest and amounted to a taking of property in violation of the Fourteenth Amendment. Giving particular stress to the contract clause, Root broadly assailed the police power justification for overriding contractual obligations. He insisted that the contract clause "is to be liberally construed."[101] As would be expected, the defendant railroad countered that contracts were subject to the state's police power and that regulation did not amount to an impairment of agreements within the meaning of the Constitution.

Root's argument proved persuasive to a plurality of the Supreme Court.[102] In a murky opinion, Justice McKenna ruled that the easements previously recognized by the New York courts were in the nature of implied contractual rights as expressed in those cases and that such rights could not be extinguished without the payment of compensation.[103] Relying heavily on contract clause analysis, he maintained that states were not free to diminish property rights by overturning precedent. In telling language, McKenna insisted that the power of state courts to modify their decisions "cannot be exercised to take away rights which have been acquired by contract and have come under the protection of the Constitution of the United States. And we determine for ourselves the existence and extent of such contract." He added that "when there is a diversity of state opinions the first in time may constitute the obligation of contract and the measure of rights under it."[104] Although McKenna made reference to the 1892 statute, this measure was not dispositive of the case and seems to have been invoked solely to justify application of the contract clause.[105] The outcome in *Muhlker* blended contract clause reasoning with the just compensation requirement. In a similar case the Supreme Court again invalidated a state court decision on the ground that the contract clause barred judicial impairments, but that would mark the last application of the judicial impairment doctrine to strike down a state court opinion on this ground.[106] In 1907 the Court affirmed the judicial impairment doctrine but distinguished *Muhlker* on the facts from the present case. "The theory upon which the *Muhlker* case stands and upon which it was put in the opinion of the court," it declared, "is that in deciding against Muhlker the state court had overruled its own decisions, and changed the interpretation of the contract upon which he had the right to rely."[107]

Speaking for the four dissenters, Justice Holmes took the position that the owners' claimed rights were "a construction of the courts" and were never the subject of an express grant. He asserted that the owners were in actuality claiming a property right and that their claimed right was "called contract merely to bring it within the contract clause of the Constitution."[108] Holmes worried that the effect of *Muhlker* would be to freeze state court decision pertaining to property rights and prevent change or modification.

As an understanding that courts make law gained currency in the early twentieth century, contemporary commentators were receptive to the concept of a judicial impairment of contracts. For example, W. E. Dodd, a University of Chicago political scientist, asserted in 1909, "Although technically a judicial decision may not be considered a law, there are strong arguments for treating it as such. A decision declaring a statute unconstitutional may have the same effect as a law repealing the statute and declaring void all contract rights acquired under it."[109] Given the similar impact on the contracting parties, he queried, why should court decisions be treated differently for contract clause purposes? Dodd further pointed out that the Supreme Court on occasion had reviewed "state decisions impairing contracts, when a statute impairing contract rights was very remotely if at all involved."[110] James E. Babb, an Idaho attorney with a commercial law practice, echoed these views, maintaining that the overturning of a state judicial decision and a subsequent legislative enactment had the same consequence for the contracting parties and should be treated alike. He observed, "Having provided in the Federal constitution that no state legislature could pass an act impairing the obligation of a contract, it would necessarily educate the conscience, in the course of time, to believe that a contract made in reliance upon a decision of court of last resort ought to secure some rights and should not be subject to be stricken down by an overruling decision."[111]

He argued that the Supreme Court had long extended the contract clause to state court decisions overruling prior precedent notwithstanding later attempts to explain the outcome of some cases in terms of general law applicable in diversity cases rather than constitutional law.

After decades of vacillation and unclear rulings, the Supreme Court in *Tidal Oil Company v. Flanagan* (1924) closed the door on the judicial impairment doctrine.[112] At issue was a quiet title action to tracts of land in Oklahoma. The decision turned upon the validity of a 1913 oil lease executed by a guardian on behalf of a minor. Subsequent to the lease the Oklahoma Supreme Court changed the rules governing the validity of leases by guardians. In a cursory opinion by Chief Justice Taft, a unanimous Court stressed that the contract clause was directed only against abridgment of agreements by legislation, not the judgments of courts. He treated *Gelpcke* and its progeny as cases not grounded on the contract clause but rather application of general law under diversity of citizenship jurisdiction. He sought to distinguish *Muhlker* on the dubious basis that a statute subsequent to the contract had been passed and was deemed to impair it. As discussed above, this is a questionable reading of the facts in *Muhlker*. Taft admitted that “certain unguarded language” in *Gelpcke* and other opinions “caused confusion, although those cases did not really involve the contract impairment clause of the Constitution.”[113] This decision might have been driven in part by the unspoken concern that every state court ruling involving interpretation of an agreement might give rise to a contract clause challenge, in effect making the Supreme Court a tribunal of last resort in such cases.

Taft’s opinion left much to be desired. His efforts to explain away a large number of cases on diversity grounds are problematic. As Benjamin Wright correctly noted, “In many of these cases the Court did not attempt to determine the state law excepting to rule that a contract valid when made, according to state court decisions, could not be impaired by a subsequent change of interpretation by the state courts.”[114] Moreover, Taft never considered the fundamental purpose of the contract clause to safeguard the stability of contractual arrangements. He also failed to address the functional argument that a state court decision altering prior law could have the same negative impact on the contractual rights of the parties as a subsequent statute. Instead, he took a rather mechanical and narrow view of the protection afforded agreements by the Constitution.

Whatever the shortcomings of Taft’s analysis, courts have made no move to reactivate the notion that reversal of a state court judicial decision might violate the contract clause. Some scholars, however, have called for such a result, pointing out that courts today often act in a manner that resembles a legislative role.[115]

THE GREAT DEPRESSION AND THE NEW DEAL

The Great Depression of the 1930s ushered in a decade of economic and political upheaval. A full treatment of the impact of the Great Depression is beyond the scope of this volume. Suffice it to say that business failures and widespread unemployment prompted demands for governmental intervention in the economy. The election of Franklin D. Roosevelt as president in 1932 constituted a watershed in US political history. Roosevelt’s New Deal program was grounded on the view that government had an affirmative duty to advance the public welfare. Thus, New Deal liberals sought to alleviate economic distress, manage the national economy, and champion the economic interests of the disadvantaged. To accomplish these goals, Congress and the states enacted an extraordinary array of measures that greatly increased governmental supervision of the economy and attempted to redistribute wealth and economic power. The New Deal approach was sharply at odds with adherence to limited government and respect for private property, which were the hallmarks of traditional constitutionalism. A conspicuous casualty of this fundamental shift in constitutional outlook was a robust understanding of the contract clause.

Mortgage Moratorium Laws

Among the problems caused by the Great Depression was the threatened loss of homes and farms from the foreclosure of delinquent mortgages. Unemployed borrowers struggled to stay current with mortgage debt. Housing prices declined, further depressing the market. By 1933 the system of home mortgage financing had largely collapsed. As the rate of foreclosures spiked sharply, state legislatures reacted by experimenting with a variety of relief measures. Taking a page from nineteenth-century relief laws that sought to delay foreclosure sales, lawmakers in at least twenty-seven states enacted laws imposing a moratorium on foreclosure proceedings.[116] Details varied widely, but generally the laws suspended foreclosure for a specific or a court-determined period. Mortgage debtors were usually obligated to pay a rental value set by a state court, from which taxes were deducted before the mortgage holder received any payment. In addition, some states sought to curtail the practice of obtaining deficiency judgments when a foreclosed property sold for less than the outstanding balance on the mortgage. During the Great Depression the only bidder at a judicial sale of a mortgaged property was likely to be the mortgagee, who might bid only a nominal amount. This meant that the debtor might remain liable for a sizeable deficit. Deficiency claims became a major source of controversy. Yet state antideficiency measures applied to existing mortgage contracts and thus were vulnerable to attack under state and federal contract clauses.

State courts initially cast a doubtful eye on moratory laws. At issue in *State ex rel. Cleveringa v. Klein* (1933) was a North Dakota law imposing a two-year extension of the period of redemption from mortgage foreclosure sales.[117] The legislature justified the law by stressing the existence of "a public emergency and crisis" because of the decline in agricultural prices and collapse of farmland values. The North Dakota Supreme Court discussed at length the notion of an emergency as a rationale for overriding the terms of contracts. Although it insisted that a legislative declaration alone did not establish the existence of an emergency, it nonetheless

In the wake of the Great Depression, farmers in Nebraska as well as other states demonstrated in favor of state laws imposing a moratorium on the foreclosure of mortgages. (Nebraska State Historical Society)

found that the legislature had a sound factual basis for such a declaration. The court distinguished numerous cases in which states relied on the police power to vary the terms of contracts, pointing out that in most of those cases the states were parties to the contracts. Invalidating the application of the enlarged redemption period to mortgages in effect at the time of its passage, it emphasized that the Constitution was not suspended during an emergency. The court concluded, "It must not be forgotten that the right of private contracts is no small part of the liberty of the citizen, and that the usual and most important function of courts of justice is to maintain and enforce contracts, unless it expressly appears they contravene public policy or express law."[118]

Likewise, a Texas court determined that a law providing that a mortgagor, upon satisfying certain conditions, had a right to secure a temporary postponement of a foreclosure sale violated both the state and federal contract clauses.[119] The state sought to defend the statute by pointing to a legislative finding of "an extraordinary financial emergency and depression." The court viewed the measure as altering the remedy available when the mortgage contract was made and which did not operate upon any substantive contractual right. It adhered to the rule that "any change in the laws relative to the remedy which essentially affects the rights secured by the contract, or which diminishes the value of the contract" is constitutionally infirm.[120] Brushing aside an argument that the act was within the police power, the court maintained that the police power was subject to constitutional limitations. In the same vein, the Supreme Court of Oklahoma found that a mortgage moratorium infringed the obligation of contract.[121]

State laws that limited or barred deficiency judgments in foreclosure proceedings were also voided under both state and federal contract clauses. Normally a foreclosing party could recover the mortgaged land at the foreclosure sale and receive a deficiency judgment for the difference between the proceeds of the sale and the amount of the outstanding debt. With the sharp decline in land values as a consequence of the Great Depression, however, mortgagors faced not only losing their property but a ruinous judgment they were simply unable to pay for the balance of the underlying debt. State lawmakers responded with a variety of antideficiency judgment laws.

The New Jersey Court of Errors and Appeals struck down a measure changing the manner of determining the amount of any deficiency judgment by requiring a trial court to substitute the fair market value of the land in place of the proceeds of the foreclosure sale.[122] As the court recognized, the effect of the statute might well be to prevent any deficit recovery. It asserted that the measure curtailed the mortgagee's right of recovery under the existing contract and dismissed the contention that the statute merely related to the remedy. Nor was the court impressed with an argument grounded on the police power to address a financial emergency. Revealingly, it added, "Nor do we subscribe to the intimation that an emergency automatically lifts all constitutional restraints."[123] In the same vein, the Supreme Court of Arkansas ruled that a law prohibiting all deficiency judgments in mortgage foreclose proceedings impaired the obligation of contract with respect to existing agreements.[124]

At one level this cluster of state court opinions was not surprising. Courts had been generally upholding the rights of creditors under the contract clause since before John Marshall became chief justice, and thus these decisions fit harmoniously within a well-established pattern. As we have seen, periods of economic distress during the nineteenth century tended to produce a host of stay and mortgage relief measures, and courts had long invalidated such laws.[125] Yet it is striking that state courts in the early 1930s adhered to this traditional position even in the face of widespread hardship caused by the Great Depression. Also noteworthy was the repeated invocation of state contract clauses as well as the federal provision. This might have represented an attempt to bolster support for outcomes that would have been disappointing to a large number of people by stressing two sources of authority. Equally significant was that, without much discussion, the state courts appear to have treated the guarantees of their state contract clauses as equivalent to that of the US Constitution. The scope of state clauses would emerge as an issue later in the decade.

Blaisdell *and the Eclipse of the Contract Clause*

The validity of state moratorium laws reached the Supreme Court in the landmark, if controversial, case of *Home Building and Loan Association v. Blaisdell* (1934).[126] This case involved a 1933 Minnesota law that, among other provisions, sought to limit deficiency judgments. It also authorized the county courts to extend the period of redemption from foreclosure sales. The legislature grounded the statute on an express declaration of an economic emergency. Under the act a mortgagor could apply to the county court for an extension until May of 1935 upon condition that the debtor pay to the creditor a reasonable amount "as to the court shall, under all of the circumstances, appear just and equitable, toward the payment of taxes, insurance, interest, and principal mortgage indebtedness." Moreover, the debtor was able to remain on the property during the period of redemption. Relatively few individual mortgage debtors actually sought protection under the act. Not all debtors could qualify for relief. Some had no hope of redemption, and others could not even pay the amount set by the county court. Still others did not seek relief because they had reached a voluntary arrangement with their mortgagee. Although mortgage foreclosures were commonly pictured as a crisis for family farms, the *Blaisdell* litigation involved a boardinghouse in Minneapolis. Facing loss of their property, the owners petitioned for an extension of the redemption period. As might be expected, the trial judge in Minnesota found that the moratorium ran afoul of the contract clause in state and federal constitutions. The Minnesota Supreme Court reversed this judgment, and an appeal was taken to the Supreme Court.

Writing for a majority of five, Chief Justice Hughes sustained the Minnesota law, rejecting a contract clause challenge. Because his opinion became the basis for the modern reading of the contract clause, it warrants careful

Chief Justice Charles Evans Hughes wrote the majority opinion in *Home Building and Loan Association v. Blaisdell* (1934), upholding a state mortgage moratorium, and in so doing delivered a near-fatal blow to the efficacy of the contract clause. (Library of Congress)

analysis. Hughes championed an open-ended construction of the provision. The existence of the Great Depression clearly influenced his opinion. Hughes put great emphasis on the existence of emergency conditions, but what he said about the relationship between emergency and governmental authority was ambiguous. "While emergency does not create power," he observed in often-quoted language, "emergency may furnish the occasion for the exercise of power."[127] Hughes intimated that constitutional provisions should be viewed in the light of particular conditions. Because economic conditions might call for novel exercise of the police power, he came close to suggesting that an emergency could justify overriding the guarantees of the contract clause. Moving away from the text of the Constitution, Hughes insisted that the prohibition of the contract clause "is not an absolute one and is not to be read with literal exactness like a mathematical formula."[128] He added, "The economic interests of the State may justify the exercise of its continuing and dominant protective power notwithstanding interference with contracts."[129] Moreover, he specifically rejected an originalist understanding of the contract clause, asserting that the provisions of the Constitution could not "be confined to the interpretation which the framers, with the conditions and outlook of their time, would have placed upon them."[130] Citing the rent-control cases, Hughes concluded by proclaiming, "The reservation of the reasonable exercise of the protective power of the State is read into all contracts."[131] Hughes in effect cut the contract clause loose from the constitutional text as well as the views of the framers.[132] In time his broad language would open the door to virtually reading the contract clause out of the Constitution.

Yet the Hughes opinion adopted a Janus-faced approach to the contract clause. Hughes maintained that a legislative declaration of an emergency was not conclusive and that whether there was actually an emergency was open to judicial inquiry. In addition, he set forth five "criteria" to buttress his finding that the Minnesota mortgage moratorium was not unconstitutional: (1) There was an adequate basis to establish the existence of an emergency, (2) the law protected "a basic interest of society," not the advantage of particular individuals, (3) the relief granted was appropriate to the emergency and was granted upon reasonable terms, (4) the moratorium protected the security interest of the mortgagee and did not impair the integrity of the mortgage, and (5) the law was "temporary in operation" and would expire in May of 1935. These factors suggest that Hughes was seeking to cabin the reach of his opinion and did not intend to undercut the future efficacy of the contract clause. A number of scholars have contended that the chief justice likely hoped to allow the states room to address the unusual circumstances of the Great Depression while retaining the contract clause as a meaningful restraint on the states. For example, Samuel R. Olken has written that *Blaisdell* "was actually quite narrow" because it was limited to emergency conditions, and that Hughes "did not intend to eviscerate the constitutional protection of vested contract rights."[133] As we shall

Dissenting in *Blaisdell*, Justice George Sutherland denied that economic hardship furnished a reason for weakening the reach of the contract clause and charged that the Court majority opened the door to future encroachments on both public and private contracts. (Library of Congress)

see, however, the *Blaisdell* Court's reliance on the existence of an emergency and the temporary nature of the relief proved a fleeting limitation on state power over contracts.

In a lengthy and forceful dissent, Justice George Sutherland warned that the majority opinion carried the potential of "future gradual but ever-advancing encroachments upon the sanctity of private and public contracts."[134] Appealing to history, he accurately pointed out that the contract clause was framed during a period of economic hardship and was designed to prevent states from relieving debtors from their obligations. Reviewing the record of judicial enforcement of the contract clause, Sutherland insisted that the present economic distress was not novel but was part of a recurring pattern throughout US history. He found mystifying the Hughes comments about whether emergency creates power, declaring that they have "the effect of affirming that which has been denied."[135] He emphatically denied that an emergency furnished an occasion for relaxing the restrictions of the contract clause. Sutherland ringingly concluded, "If the provisions of the Constitution be not upheld when they pinch as well as when they comfort, they may as well be abandoned."[136]

Despite Sutherland's concerns, the *Blaisdell* opinion did not sound the immediate death knell for the contract clause. On the contrary, in the mid-1930s the Supreme Court distinguished *Blaisdell* in several cases and struck down state relief laws that severely curtailed the contractual rights of creditors for long periods. In *W. B. Worthen Co. v. Thomas* (1934) Hughes invalidated a 1933 Arkansas law exempting life insurance proceeds from levy for payment of the debts of the deceased. He reasoned that the measure was neither limited to a temporary emergency nor conditioned as to amount and circumstances.[137] Likewise, a unanimous Court voided another Arkansas statute that greatly delayed the right of mortgagees to foreclose on the land of delinquent owners for nonpayment of municipal improvement bonds. It pointed out that the law did not impose a requirement that the debtors make any payment toward taxes or interest and disregarded the interests of the mortgagees.[138] On two other occasions, involving the right of withdrawing members to receive payment for their shares in a building and loan association[139] and the rights of purchasers at tax delinquency sales,[140] the Supreme Court held that the state laws abridged the obligation of existing contracts. These cases raised a false hope that the scope of *Blaisdell* would be carefully confined.[141]

Broader change was in the air. In a 1941 dissenting opinion, Justice Hugo Black, the first of the New Deal justices appointed by President Roosevelt, took a generous view of legislative authority. He explained, "For, so nearly universal are contractual relationships that it is difficult if not impossible to conceive of laws which do not have either direct or indirect bearing upon contractual relationships." To his mind, *Blaisdell* "represented a realistic appreciation of the fact that ours is an evolving society and that the general words of the contract clause were not intended to reduce the legislative branch of government to helpless impotency."[142] Black's dissent anticipated a sharply diminished role for the contract clause. In fact, after 1941 the Supreme Court would not apply the provision to void a state law for more than thirty-five years.

That the *Blaisdell* decision had teeth was made evident in a pair of Supreme Court cases sustaining efforts to curb deficiency judgments in foreclosure proceedings.[143] Recall that pre-*Blaisdell* state courts had struck down statutes curtailing deficiency judgments applied to antecedent mortgage contracts. At issue in *Richmond Mortgage and Loan Association v. Wachovia Bank and Trust* (1937) was a North Carolina statute providing that, when a mortgagee purchased property at a deed of trust sale for less than the amount of the unpaid debt, a jury could determine the fair market value of such property.[144] It further declared that any deficiency judgment was to be the difference between the fair market value and the debt. As a practical matter this requirement would limit or eliminate any deficiency. Brushing aside a contract clause challenge, the Court recognized that the act eliminated one previously existing remedy but unanimously reasoned that the measure merely restricted "the mortgagee to that for which he contracted, namely, payment in full."[145]

Whatever Hughes's private thoughts concerning the continued efficacy of the contract clause, his *Blaisdell* opinion did much to eliminate the provision as a meaningful check on state legislative authority to abridge private agreements. To be sure, the clause had already been weakened as courts recognized a growing number of exemptions from its coverage. But Hughes dealt a near-fatal blow, certainly at the national level, from which the contract clause has never recovered. Underscoring the moribund status of this provision, standard constitutional histories typically make no mention of the clause after 1934. *Blaisdell* has generated a vast literature that cannot be reviewed in detail here. Scholars associated with the New Deal and their progeny have hailed the ruling as an adjustment to economic reality and as a rejection of the authority of the framers as a means of constitutional interpretation.[146] In recent years, however, revisionist scholars have turned a more critical eye on *Blaisdell.* Richard A. Epstein, for instance, has declared, "*Blaisdell* trumpeted a false liberation from the constitutional text that has paved the way for massive government intervention that undermines the security of private transactions. Today the police power exception has come to eviscerate the contract clause."[147]

If *Blaisdell* had a profound impact on contract clause jurisprudence, the economic effect of state mortgage-moratorium laws on the position of debtors was decidedly mixed. The laws proved no panacea and did not deal with underlying problems. Indeed, they have been seen as largely ineffective. Relatively few owners secured relief under these state laws, and foreclosures continued throughout the period the moratoria were in force. Further, economic studies point out that moratorium laws had some negative consequences, reflected in higher interest rates and tightened eligibility requirements for prospective borrowers.[148] Still, the measures had some palliative effect. Hard-pressed debtors gained breathing space in which to hopefully recapture their footing, and policy makers bought time in which to formulate a governmental refinancing program.[149] It should also be noted that a number of institutional mortgage holders suspended foreclosures as a matter of business policy.

Blaisdell *in the State Courts*

In the wake of *Blaisdell* state courts continued to hear a torrent of mortgage moratorium challenges based on state constitutional grounds. This litigation squarely raised the issue of whether and to what extent the contract clause language in state constitutions afforded a more fulsome degree of support to contractual arrangements than the federal provision.

The divided opinion by the Supreme Court of Iowa in *Des Moines Joint Stock Land Bank v. Nordholm* (1934) well illustrated the sharp differences among state court jurists.[150] By a five-to-four vote the court sustained a state law extending the period of redemption from a foreclosure sale for two years provided the debtor made court-approved payments. Citing *Blaisdell* and stressing the continued existence of emergency conditions in Iowa, the majority found that the measure passed muster under both federal and state constitutions. Although recognizing that a state court could construe the state constitution more expansively, it concluded that the Iowa contract clause should be interpreted in the same manner as the federal provision. The majority declared, "Good policy and a desired consistency between the two Constitutions rather dictate that the interpretation of the two clauses be similar. Such consistency in interpretation will accomplish consistency in operation. Uniformity in the construction of these contract clauses is most desirable, if not absolutely necessary."[151] Two vigorous dissenting opinions tracked Justice Sutherland and argued that supposed emergencies do not justify legislation that transgresses the Constitution. Pointing to language in the Iowa Constitution that no laws impairing the obligation of contract "shall ever be passed," the dissenting judges asserted that the moratorium ran afoul of the broader guarantee of the Iowa Constitution.

Speaking of the Iowa Constitution, one judge stated, "No personal liberty or right is more specifically guarded by the Constitution than is the obligation of contracts against impairment."[152]

In upholding moratory laws a number of state courts followed the Iowa approach and expressly treated the state contract clauses as essentially the same as the federal provision. Speaking of *Blaisdell* the Supreme Court of Michigan declared in 1934, "Because the constitutional provision is identical in both Constitutions, we are constrained to adopt the ruling as the construction of the clause in our state Constitution upon the situation at bar."[153] Other state courts implicitly treated the state and federal guarantees as functionally equivalent.[154]

In marked contrast, the Supreme Court of Texas gave a more muscular reading to the contract clause in its state constitution. In *Travelers' Insurance Company v. Marshall* (1934) it emphasized that *Blaisdell* had no application to the interpretation of the Texas Constitution.[155] Reviewing at length the circumstances under which the federal contract clause was drafted and the long history of state court decisions striking down various types of stay laws, the court explained that the state constitution "prohibits the enactment of moratory legislation which impairs the obligation of contracts, even though enacted during an industrial depression."[156] It added, "The right to enter into lawful contracts is one of the guaranties of the Texas Constitution. This guaranty is one of the essential liberties of the citizen, and cannot be nullified by legislative enactment empowering courts to substantially rewrite his agreements."[157] The court then voided a moratorium act under the Texas contract clause.

The Texas Supreme Court was the most forceful in rejecting *Blaisdell* and making an independent assessment of a state contract clause, but other courts took a similar step when faced with extensions of moratorium laws. Most of the original moratoria were for two years. Chief Justice Hughes had stressed the temporary nature of the relief as a reason for sustaining the Minnesota moratorium. Such time limitations, however, would soon be superseded by events.[158] It can be difficult to get rid of supposedly temporary laws. Contemporary commentators accurately predicted that there would be pressure to continue the moratoria when they expired. In 1935 many states extended their laws for another two years. The Minnesota law at issue in *Blaisdell* lasted until 1942.

Two state courts determined that the renewal of moratorium laws violated state contract clauses. In 1938 the Supreme Court of Nebraska struck down a 1937 act extending the state moratorium for two additional years.[159]

It pictured *Blaisdell* as grounded on the view that relief was validated by an emergency and was temporary in nature. More telling, the court pointed out that Supreme Court opinions did not control the construction of similar provisions in state constitutions and that the police power was not "a divinely mysterious governmental attribute of superior rank to the Constitution itself."[160] A concurring judge took direct aim at the notion that emergency conditions furnished a basis for abridging agreements. "If a declaration and proof of an emergency can break the restraining chains of the Constitution," he asked, "why have a Constitution?"[161] A year later the Iowa Supreme Court followed suit, finding a continuation of prior mortgage acts invalid under both state and federal constitutions. It reasoned that an emergency must by definition be temporary, because otherwise "it is no longer an emergency but a status and can furnish no basis or authority for legislative action in contravention of" state and federal constitutions.[162] The continued existence of an emergency was deemed a question of fact, and the court ruled that the depressed conditions of 1933 no longer prevailed and hence the moratorium law ceased to operate. In harmony with these decisions, starting in 1937 several state legislatures gradually either restricted the scope of moratorium laws or allowed them to expire. Yet others were repeatedly revived and lasted into the 1940s.[163]

Closely allied to the issue of mortgage foreclosure was the question of deficiency judgments. State courts were divided as to the validity of antideficiency judgment laws. As discussed above, these measures typically set off the fair market value of a property sold at foreclosure against any deficit resulting from the sale. This had the effect of altering the obligations of the parties under preexisting contracts. Relying on *Blaisdell*, the New York Court of Appeals readily sustained that state's antideficiency law as a reasonable and temporary response to the troubled economic circumstances in which the real estate market had collapsed.[164]

At least three state courts, however, declared antideficiency statutes unconstitutional with respect to mortgage contracts made before passage of the law, although it was sometimes unclear if they were relying on the state or federal contract clause. The Supreme Court of California distinguished *Blaisdell* and maintained that economic difficulties did not place legislation "beyond the reach of the constitutional guaranties concerning the obligations of contract."[165] The Supreme Court of Texas reached a like result and expressed impatience with the time-honored right/remedy distinction that bulked large in nineteenth-century contract clause cases. "We are not much concerned," it asserted, "with the superfine distinction sometimes drawn in discussing the impairment of the obligation of contracts, between the 'obligation' and the 'remedies' for their enforcement."[166] The court held that the statute nullified a portion of the contract that entitled the mortgagee to deficiency judgments and thus ran afoul of the Texas Constitution. The Supreme Court of Pennsylvania endorsed the same position. Finding a deficiency act violative of both state and federal constitutions, it invoked the rationale behind the contract clause: "It must be remembered that the chief purpose of the constitutional prohibition was to protect the integrity of contracts especially in those times when the temptation to yield to a policy or repudiation might be intensified by an era of financial depression."[167]

Other Depression-Related Contract Issues

Other legislative efforts to ameliorate financial hardships were challenged as violations of the contract clause. For example, a 1934 amendment to the Florida Constitution granted a tax exemption to homestead property up to a valuation of $5,000. To avoid a conflict with the federal contract clause, the Florida Supreme Court construed the provision to be inapplicable to taxes levied for the payment of preexisting bonds.[168] In addition, state legislation to enlarge property exemptions from the claims of creditors raised issues reminiscent of the nineteenth century. The Supreme Court of Montana held that a statute materially increasing exemptions was invalid under both state and federal contract clauses with respect to antecedent debts. It followed that an exemption of an automobile could not be applied to an execution to satisfy a prior obligation.[169]

Another cluster of cases involved teacher contracts. During the 1930s school boards were sorely pressed to curtail expenditures by reducing salaries for teachers and benefits for retirees. Unsurprisingly they resisted, contending that such actions impaired their employment contracts. The Supreme Court heard a number of cases that addressed the right of teachers and retirees to various benefits. The outcome turned upon whether the legislation governing teacher compensation amounted to a contract that neither the legislature nor school boards could alter.[170] Rejecting claims that reductions in teacher salaries or annuity payments to retirees violated the contract clause, the Court found that no contractual right to benefits was created by state statutes. It reasoned that a statute merely fixing salaries or settling the terms of public employment did not amount to a legislative contract but simply declared a policy that lawmakers could change at their will. The Court invoked the presumption that laws were not intended to create private contractual rights.[171] It followed that state and localities largely retained a free hand to modify compensation arrangements.[172]

The Supreme Court took a different tack with respect to the rights conferred by a state teacher-tenure law. At issue was a 1927 Indiana measure providing that a public school teacher who taught for five successive years should become a permanent teacher with an indefinite contract. Although the law was repealed in 1933 with respect to township schools, the Court concluded that the tenured status of a teacher was part of the contract of employment pursuant to the tenure law and that its repeal ran afoul of the contract clause.[173] Distinguishing the earlier cases dealing with benefits, it maintained that this tenure provision amounted to a contract for continued employment. Brushing aside an argument that the contract was subject to modification under the police power, the Court simply declared that the repeal measure was not a proper exercise of the police power to serve the public good. Dissenting, Justice Hugo Black insisted that the tenure law did not create a contract regarding teacher tenure but reflected a policy that lawmakers were free to change. Black expressed concern that the contract clause should not be read to deprive a state of the ability to experiment and to alter educational policy.[174] His views were a harbinger of the narrow construction of the contract clause favored by the New Deal justices after 1940 and their reluctance to find that legislation amounted to a contract binding on the states.

Decided at a time when few public school teachers were covered by collective bargaining agreements, this now obscure group of cases anticipated subsequent developments. The early twenty-first century saw a wave of litigation over whether public employee benefits for current workers as well as retirees were protected by the contract clause against moves to curtail such benefits by state and localities facing grave fiscal crises. These issues will be explored in a later chapter.[175]

During the Great Depression legislators were also concerned with insolvent financial institutions. State laws authorized officials to take possession of, administer, and seek to rehabilitate such troubled enterprises. Neither the Supreme Court nor state courts saw any contract clause objection to this legislation despite the fact that the contract rights of certain interest holders or nonconsenting creditors were infringed by the proposed scheme.[176] Citing *Blaisdell*, the New York Court of Appeals declared that the economic welfare of the community justified laws that trumped strict enforcement of contracts.[177]

STATE REGULATORY AUTHORITY AFFIRMED

By the late 1930s both federal and state courts broadly sustained state regulatory power in the face of arguments grounded on the contract clause. For example, courts vigorously upheld the authority of the states to regulate prices and override rates set by private contracts. In *Midland Realty Company v. Kansas City Power and Light* (1937) the Supreme Court considered the effect of an order by a state commission requiring higher utility rates upon a steam-heating contract setting a lower rate. The justices cursorily dismissed a contract clause challenge, declaring, "But the State has power to annul and supersede rates previously established by contract between utilities and their customers."[178] Similarly, the Supreme Court of Pennsylvania found that an order of the milk board, ostensibly based on an exercise of the police power to safeguard the public health, requiring higher minimum prices for milk prevailed over those set in an agreement to provide milk.[179] The court stressed that the constitutional protection of contracts was subject to the state police power and that private parties could not limit state regulatory authority by making contracts.

State regulation of natural resources was also held to prevail over private agreements notwithstanding the contract clause. In 1935 Texas lawmakers, as a conservation measure to halt wasteful use of natural gas, banned the use of "sweet" gas for making carbon black. The Supreme Court addressed the validity of this law in *Henderson Company v. Thompson* (1937).[180] The Henderson Company argued that the statute interfered with its ability to fulfill contractual obligations in violation of the Constitution. Finding no merit in this contention, the Court ruled that the "statute challenged is not directed against any term of the contract. It deals merely with the use of an article of commerce; and its effect upon contracts is incidental."[181]

NEW DEAL ASCENDANCY

As the record makes clear, the contract clause had been drained of much vitality even before President Roosevelt's appointees gained control of the Supreme Court, ushering in an era of New Deal jurisprudence. Although the clause retained some vigor at the state level, the Supreme Court had recognized so many exceptions as to greatly dilute the protection of contracts. During the 1940s the New Deal Court substantially altered constitutional doctrines to accommodate more far-reaching uses of governmental power to regulate the economy.[182] The principle of governmental noninterference with contracts, a norm expressed in the contract clause, was sharply at odds with New Deal constitutionalism. Consequently the Supreme Court, often echoed by state courts, effectively destroyed the clause as a meaningful guarantee of agreements.

In short order, the revamped Court jettisoned limitations on state authority over contracts. Recall that Chief Justice Hughes, upholding the mortgage moratorium in *Blaisdell*, had stressed the temporary nature of the law as a response to an economic emergency. In *Veix v. Sixth Ward Building and Loan Association* (1940) the Supreme Court rejected a contract clause challenge to a New Jersey law restricting the preexisting contractual rights of certificate holders to withdraw their funds from a building and loan association.[183] It reasoned that the legislature could protect the economic viability of such associations from excessive withdrawal under the police power. For our purposes, the Court additionally restricted the reach of the contract clause in two important respects. First, it stressed that New Jersey had long regulated building and loan associations. "When [the certificate holder] purchased into an enterprise already regulated in the particular to which he now objects," the Court continued, "he purchased subject to further legislation upon the same topic."[184] Under this bootstrap analysis, a contracting party in a regulated field was deemed to accept the potential for new regulation. Given pervasive regulation, this would prove a major stumbling block to contract clause claims. Second, the Court abandoned any notion that legislative power to abridge contracts was grounded in the existence of an emergency or need take the form of a temporary law.[185]

A year later the Supreme Court, sustaining application of a New York antideficiency law to a prior mortgage, emphasized that a legislative declaration of an emergency was irrelevant for contract clause analysis.[186] Brushing aside a group of nineteenth-century decisions including *Bronson v. Kinzie* (1843), the Court revealingly commented, "We cannot permit the broad language which those early decisions employed to force legislatures to be blind to the lessons which another century has taught."[187] Henceforth history and precedent would play little role in the Supreme Court's determination of contract clause cases.

Justice Felix Frankfurter's opinion for the Court in *East New York Bank v. Hahn* (1945) underscored the dismissive attitude of the New Deal justices toward the contract clause.[188] Upholding the tenth extension of New York's mortgage moratorium law, Frankfurter opined, "When a widely diffused public interest has become enmeshed in a network of multitudinous private arrangements," the regulatory authority of the state could not be confined "by abstracting one such arrangement from its public context and treating it as though it were an isolated private contract constitutionally immune from impairment." He added that the state police power "may be treated as an implied condition of every contract and, as such, part of the contract as though it were written into it, whereby the State's exercise of its power enforces, and does not impair, a contract."[189] Frankfurter further emphasized that courts must respect wide discretion on the part of the legislature to decide what is necessary to protect the public. Of course, if the police power is implied in every contract, and the courts simply defer to legislative judgments about the exercise of that power, the contract clause affords virtually no protection for agreements. In his opinion Frankfurter makes no reference to the purpose of the clause to protect the sanctity of contracts from abridgment.

The New Deal Court employed similar reasoning in the context of municipal debt defaults. In *Faitoute Iron and Steel Company v. City of Asbury Park* (1942) it ruled that a statute, enacted during the Depression, could restructure municipal debts without violating the contract clause even if some creditors suffered a loss.[190] Again writing for the Court, Frankfurter upheld the validity of a New Jersey law establishing a plan to adjust the claims of creditors of insolvent municipalities. Insisting that the plan could be made binding on dissenting bondholders, he observed, "Impairment of an obligation means refusal to pay an honest debt; it does not mean contriving ways and means for paying it. The necessity compelled by unexpected financial conditions to modify an original arrangement for discharging a city's debt is implied in every such obligation for the very reason that thereby the obligation is discharged, not impaired."[191] Frankfurter maintained that the contract clause did not bar the state from an exercise of its "essential reserve power" to protect public credit to assure payment of outstanding claims against municipalities. Practical considerations bulked large in Frankfurter's thinking. He asserted that the remedy to enforce the original bonds was worthless but that with the refinanced bonds creditors could expect partial payment of the contractual obligation. Frankfurter concluded by lecturing that the contract clause should not be read "to make of the Constitution a code of lifeless forms instead of an enduring framework of a government for a dynamic society."[192]

Frankfurter also relied on the principle of strict construction of corporate charters to reject a contract clause attack on a Georgia corporate income tax. Speaking for the Court, he construed a tax exemption in an 1833 railroad charter as pertaining to railroad property, not to an income tax. Frankfurter pointed out that a modern income tax did not exist in 1833 and hence could not have been contemplated by the legislature. Stressing the need to respect legislative authority over tax policy, he proclaimed, "A legislature is not to be presumed to have relinquished its power of taxation beyond the narrowest rational reading of an exemption."[193] Unlike the other New Deal contract clause cases, this decision rested, as we have seen, upon a long line of cases strictly reading grants of tax immunity. With respect to the Supreme Court, this decision effectively marked the end of the trail for attempts to use the contract clause as a shield against state taxation of railroads.

The New Deal Supreme Court was inclined to favor a balancing test in assessing violations of the contract clause. Despite the provision's absolute prohibition of state abridgment of contracts, the Court examined the reasonableness of statutes impairing agreements. Indeed, in 1944 Robert L. Hale cogently noted, "There is at least a tendency for the contract clause and the due process clause to coalesce." He even speculated, "The result might be the same if the contract clause were dropped out of the Constitution" and challenges were heard under the due process norm.[194] But this observation only underscored the lowly status of the contract clause in New Deal jurisprudence. After 1937 the Supreme Court never invalidated any economic legislation on due process grounds, and the review of such laws became perfunctory.

CONTRACTUAL IMPAIRMENT BY THE FEDERAL GOVERNMENT

By its terms the contract clause was binding only on the states, a point repeatedly emphasized by courts.[195] Nonetheless, it was settled that contracts were a form of property within the scope of the takings clause of the Fifth Amendment. Consequently, the government was required to pay just compensation if it acquired a contract for public use.[196]

Yet governmental seizure of the subject matter of a private contract was deemed to end the agreement, not to appropriate it. In *Omnia Commercial Company, Inc. v. United States* (1923), for example, the federal government requisitioned the entire production of a steel manufacturer in 1917 and directed the steel company not to comply with a prior contract to deliver steel plate to a private property. The Supreme Court treated this as a consequential loss to the contracting party resulting from lawful governmental action and found no taking of the contract.[197]

On the other hand, there was authority that vested rights in contracts between private parties and the federal government constituted property protected by the due process clause of the Fifth Amendment. In *Lynch v. United States* (1934) Justice Brandeis affirmed that valid contracts were property and that "the due process clause prohibits the United States from annulling them, unless the action falls within the federal police power or some other paramount power."[198] Noting the economic utility of honoring contracts, he pointed out, "Punctilious fulfillment of contractual obligations is essential to the maintenance of the credit of public as well as private debtors."[199] Brandeis declared that the United States was bound by its contracts and was not free to reduce expenditures by repudiating its obligations.

The principle that the federal government was bound by its agreements would be sorely tested a year later in a cluster of cases known as the *Gold Clause Cases.* Crafted to provide a definite measure of value as a safeguard against depreciation of the currency, clauses requiring payment in gold or in an amount of money measured by gold were common in contracts. In reality, such provisions were treated as "gold value" clauses.[200] As part of the New Deal plan to preserve gold reserves and stabilize the value of the dollar, Congress in 1933 abrogated the gold clauses in both public and private contracts and barred paying an increased number of depreciated dollars to make up the equivalent payment in gold. In fact, under executive direction gold coins had been withdrawn from circulation by this point, and payment in such coinage was impossible.[201] Pursuant to the congressional resolution, contractual obligations that called for payment in gold could be discharged with the existing devalued currency, inflicting a loss on bondholders, who were denied the benefit of their contractual bargain. They challenged this measure, arguing that the gold clauses required the payment of the equivalent value of gold coins in legal tender if payment in gold was not feasible. They contended that the congressional action amounted to a deprivation of property without due process and a taking of property without just compensation in violation of the Fifth Amendment.

Chief Justice Hughes, speaking for a five-member majority of the Supreme Court, sustained the power of Congress to invalidate provisions in existing private contracts that interfered with congressional authority to establish monetary policy.[202] He pictured the gold clauses not as contracts for payment in gold coin but for payment in money. Hughes stressed that private contracts could not fetter the power of Congress or bar the execution of congressional policy in relation to the currency. The ruling was somewhat reminiscent of the Legal Tender Cases of the Civil War Era discussed in Chapter 4, but there was a difference. Those cases did not invalidate express language in contracts calling for payments in specie. Here Hughes went a step further, emphasizing that Congress had made clear its intention to override even express stipulations for payment in gold.

The question of congressional repudiation of the gold clauses in contracts of the United States proved more nettlesome but ultimately yielded a similar result. At issue in *Perry v. United States* (1935) was a government bond providing for payment of principal and interest in "United States gold coin of the present value."[203] A bondholder sued the government for breach of contract, seeking a recovery of $16,900 on a bond with a face amount of $10,000. Writing for a sharply divided Court, Hughes distinguished between the power of Congress to control the contracts of private parties that interfered with an exercise of its authority and the power of Congress to repudiate its own engagements. Citing *Lynch*, he insisted that Congress could not constitutionally disregard its own agreements. Yet the seeming victory for the bondholder was illusory. Hughes reached the problematic conclusion that the bondholder had not demonstrated any actual damages because there was no domestic market for gold. Hence he was not entitled to any recovery beyond the face amount of the obligation. In effect, the chief justice proclaimed the sanctity of governmental contracts and then robbed that premise of any meaning.[204] His Janus-faced opinion facilitated a partial repudiation of the government's bonded debt.

Highly controversial in their time, the *Gold Clause Cases* have failed to attract sustained attention from scholars. They have generally viewed these cases as influenced by the perceived fiscal emergency of the early 1930s.[205] Although the *Gold Clause Cases* did not directly involve the contract clause, the government's argument before the Court relied heavily on decisions that state police power could not be contracted away, and thus similar action by Congress affecting contracts was justified. The upshot was that Congress could apparently nullify provisions in private and public contracts in pursuance of a legitimate legislative policy.

The four dissenters, in a biting opinion by Justice James C. McReynolds, warned that the invalidation of the gold clauses "will bring about confiscation of property rights and repudiation of national obligations."[206] They pointed out that the gold clauses in both private and public contracts were valid when executed. The dissenters were especially caustic in addressing the repudiation of the government's own obligations. In their view, the majority opinion amounted "to a declaration that the Government may give with one hand and take away with the other. Default is thus made both easy and safe!"[207] They proclaimed, "In matters of contractual obligation the government cannot legislate so as to excuse itself."[208] Flatly contradicting Hughes, they asserted that there was no serious difficulty in ascertaining the value of gold and thus paying the creditor the value in currency of the amount promised.

SWAN SONG FOR THE CONTRACT CLAUSE?

As we have seen, the protective reach of the contract clause was steadily diluted throughout the early decades of the twentieth century. By the 1940s the political triumph of the New Deal and the accompanying growth of the regulatory state relegated the contract clause to the periphery of constitutional law. The emergence of an all-encompassing police power, coupled with a judicial policy of heavy deference to legislative determinations, left the clause without any meaningful role. Generally ignored and rarely invoked for decades, the contract clause ceased to be of interest to judges and scholars. Yet the provision proved a hardy plant with deep roots. Like a character in a novel by Charles Dickens, it was recalled to life in the late twentieth century.

CHAPTER 7

The Contract Clause in the Age of Regulation

In the decades following World War II the regulatory regime established by the New Deal was firmly in place. Although sharp differences remained concerning the precise role of government in managing the economy, there were few calls for a return to the largely unregulated market before the New Deal. The dominant political ideology supported the regulatory state and looked for governmental solutions to economic and social ills.[1] The modern welfare state frequently encroached on the freedom of contracting parties. Indeed, in 1974 one leading scholar rather prematurely proclaimed the death of contracts.[2] Not surprisingly, then, issues pertaining to the protection of contractual rights from state abridgment did not figure prominently in the nation's political consciousness.

EBB TIDE FOR THE CONTRACT CLAUSE

During the 1950s, 1960s, and early 1970s the Supreme Court reflected this statist attitude and sanctioned the growing welfare state. Broadly deferring to legislative bodies with respect to economic issues, the Court accepted at face value ostensible legislative objectives to uphold regulatory measures. In this passive climate the security of contractual rights, together with protection of property rights and economic liberty, received scant attention from judges or scholars.[3] The Supreme Court was not much troubled by contract clause litigation for decades. In fact, the contract clause virtually disappeared from the Court's docket for years. The situation at the state level was only marginally more promising. Commentators were generally dismissive of the clause, likening it to the toothless due process clause and wondering if it served any continuing purpose.[4] One could easily have concluded that the last rites were in order for the contract clause.

The unsympathetic treatment of the contract clause was evident in *City of El Paso v. Simmons* (1965),[5] one of the Supreme Court's infrequent decisions dealing with the provision. At issue was the validity of a 1941 Texas statute providing that the right to reinstate forfeited contracts to purchase public lands must be exercised within five years from the time of such forfeiture. Under the prior law an original purchaser had a perpetual right to redeem the contract until the land was sold to a third party. A predecessor in title of the claimant executed an installment purchase contract in 1910, which agreement was forfeited for nonpayment in 1947. When his application for reinstatement was denied as not having been made within the five-year period, the claimant argued that the five-year limit in the 1941 law constituted an impairment of the original contract. Texas countered that the law was necessary to maintain confidence in the stability of land titles and that unlimited reinstatement gave rise to a spate of litigation and land speculation.

Writing for the Court, Justice Byron White upheld the Texas forfeiture statute and brushed aside the contract clause objection. He characterized the *Blaisdell* opinion as "a comprehensive restatement of the principles underlying the application of the Contract Clause."[6] White emphatically rejected the long-standing if problematic right/remedy distinction, which had vexed contract clause jurisprudence since the time of John Marshall. Instead, he insisted that they should both be treated as part of the "obligation" protected by the Constitution. There was certainly some merit in this position. As we have seen, the dividing line between right and remedy had long been a source of confusion to courts and commentators.[7] However, the rest of the White opinion minimized the protection afforded by the contract clause. White stressed that the prohibition of the provision was not absolute and that the states retained sovereign power to modify contracts to serve the public welfare. Consistent with New Deal ideology, he pointed to the need for wide discretion on the part of legislators to determine what was necessary to serve the public interest.[8]

Dissenting alone, Justice Hugo Black accused the majority of employing a balancing test that undermined the guarantee of the contract clause and allowed Texas to dishonor its contractual obligations. Viewing the contract clause as an "unequivocal constitutional command against impairing the obligation of contracts," he sharply criticized the majority for permitting the state to evade the provision because it deemed the state's actions to be reasonable and in good faith.[9] "Thus this Court's judgment as to 'reasonableness' of a law impairing or even repudiating a valid contract," Black asserted, "becomes the measure of the Contract Clause protection."[10] He emphatically insisted that constitutional law could not be reduced to what members of the Supreme Court thought was reasonable. Reviewing the history of the clause in detail, Black declared that the framers believed "that men should not have to act at their peril, fearing always that the State might change its mind and alter the legal consequences of their past acts so as to take away their lives, their liberty or their property."[11] Pointing out that Texas stood to reap a considerable financial gain by repudiating its own contracts, he concluded by arguing that the state should exercise the power of eminent domain and acquire the contractual rights at issue upon payment of just compensation.

Black's forceful dissent in *City of El Paso* is noteworthy in two respects. First, his opinion has ironic dimensions. In the late 1930s Black protested reliance on the contract clause to invalidate state laws and expressed concern that courts were employing the provision to confine legislative authority. During the 1940s he joined in a number of decisions that drained the contract clause of much meaning. Black now appeared distressed at the consequences of a process he once championed. Second, he was the first member of the Supreme Court after 1941 to seriously suggest that the contract clause retained vitality as a check on state legislative authority. Black foreshadowed a modest revival of interest in the clause in the late 1970s.

During this period of desuetude by the federal courts the contract clause retained some efficacy at the state level. To be sure, contract clause challenges were commonly rejected. The New York Court of Appeals, for instance, upheld a state law that sought to eliminate dangerous conditions in multiple dwellings by subordinating the mortgagee's lien on rents to payment of the costs incurred in making repairs.[12] Even when state courts invoked the clause, its application was often hedged with numerous qualifications. A few examples illustrate the range of cases in which state courts found contract clause violations.

State legislative attempts to overhaul franchise agreements were a recurring source of controversy. In 1971 the Supreme Court of Delaware struck down a law retroactively barring the termination of an existing franchise without "just cause." Declaring that the "prohibition of the contract clause is no longer absolute," the court nonetheless added, "The States may not use their police power to alter or strike away the substantive rights and obligations of contracting parties without paying compensation. Only minor impairment or infringement of contractual rights is permissible."[13] It found that the law made a substantial change in the rights of the parties by extending the franchise agreement indefinitely and thus ran afoul of the federal contract clause.

State courts also looked skeptically at laws that altered the terms of leases or mortgages. The Supreme Court of Wisconsin invalidated a law requiring that property tax relief on rental properties be applied to reduce the rent charged to tenants under their leases. Stressing the broad parameters of state police power to impinge on the rights secured by contracts, it stated, "An unequivocal legislative declaration of public policy" that served a "vital public interest" became a part of both antecedent and subsequent contracts. Nonetheless, the court ruled that the law did not protect a vital interest of the public and reduced "the substantive value of a previously negotiated contract."[14] Hence, it held that the measure violated both federal and state contract clauses. In the same vein, the Supreme Judicial Court of Maine voided a law retroactively reducing the period of redemption available to a defaulting mortgagor as an impairment of contract under the federal and state constitutions.[15]

State courts rarely discussed the degree of protection afforded agreements by the state contract clauses. They often cited federal cases in explicating the state provisions and implicitly indicated that the federal and state contract clauses were interchangeable. At least one state, however, strongly suggested that its provision was more protective than the federal clause. In 1975 the Supreme Court of Florida declared that a retrospective application of a law requiring a ninety-day notice to terminate a motor vehicle franchise agreement was unconstitutional. It proclaimed, "To justify retroactive application it is not enough to show that this legislation is a valid exercise of the state's police power because that power, however broad in other contexts, here collides with the constitutional ban on laws impairing contracts. Virtually no degree of contract impairment has been tolerated in this state." The court went on to remark that the state's interest was not so compelling "as to override the sanctity of contract."[16] Significantly, the court did not treat the police power as an all-purpose trump card sweeping away constitutional limitations.

AN UNCERTAIN RENAISSANCE

After decades of neglect the Supreme Court opened a new chapter in the history of the contract clause in the late 1970s by relying on the provision to overturn state laws for the first time since 1941. These decisions represented a modest revival of contract clause jurisprudence but simultaneously confused constitutional analysis by setting forth a jumbled, if not incoherent, standard of review.

At issue in *United States Trust Company v. New Jersey* (1977) was a 1974 state law abrogating a covenant in a 1962 bond agreement limiting the power of the Port Authority, an interstate compact agency, to subsidize passenger transportation from revenues pledged as security for Port Authority bondholders.[17] The covenant was designed to promote investor confidence in the Port Authority by curtailing its exposure to mass transit deficits. The purpose of the repeal was to increase the amount of revenue available for mass transit projects. Justice Harry Blackmun, speaking for a four-member plurality of the Supreme Court, began his rambling opinion by denying that "the Contract Clause was without meaning in our modern constitutional jurisprudence, or that its limitation on state power was illusory." He continued, "Whether or not the protection of contract rights comports with current views of wise public policy, the Contract Clause remains a part of our written Constitution."[18] Blackmun then proceeded to shift gears and to cabin the reach of the provision. He dismissed the right/remedy distinction as "now largely an outdated formalism" and emphasized that the existence of an emergency was not a prerequisite to upholding state abridgment of agreements.[19] Moreover, Blackmun maintained that states "must possess broad powers to adopt general regulatory measures without being concerned that private contracts will be impaired or even destroyed, as a result."[20] He asserted that a law impairing private or public contracts would pass constitutional muster "if it is reasonable and necessary to serve an important public purpose."[21] Blackmun envisioned a relaxed standard of judicial review. "As is customary in reviewing economic and social regulation," he wrote, "courts properly defer to the legislative judgment as to the necessity and reasonableness of a particular measure."[22]

Blackmun's formulation is fraught with problems. Ignoring the language of the contract clause itself, he seemingly adopted a balancing approach heavily weighted in favor of state authority over contracts. His test is little different than rational basis review of economic legislation under the due process norm. Indeed, Blackmun appeared to be of two minds. He groped for a review standard that would achieve a meaningful role for the contract clause while at the same time preserving the post–New Deal preference for minimal judicial oversight of economic regulations. Not surprisingly, Blackmun ultimately failed to reconcile these inconsistent goals.

The justice compounded the already muddled understanding of the contract clause by setting forth a higher standard of review when a state impaired its own obligations. In this context Blackmun observed, "Complete deference to a legislative assessment of reasonableness and necessity is not appropriate because the State's self-interest is at stake." He explained that if "a State could reduce its financial obligation whenever it wanted to spend the money for what it regarded as an important public purpose, the Contract Clause would provide no protection at all."[23] In ascertaining the need for a state to abrogate its own financial commitments, Blackmun insisted, "A State is not completely free to consider impairing the obligation of its own contracts on a par with other policy alternatives."[24] He then ruled that the repeal of the bond covenant was neither necessary nor reasonable in light of alternative means of achieving the state's goals.[25]

Historically the Supreme Court treated public and private contracts on a more or less level playing field and certainly did not accord contracts by states a special degree of solicitude. The abandonment of a unitary standard of judicial review in *United States Trust* was a sharp departure from long-standing contract clause jurisprudence. There are significant problems with this newly minted dual standard. First, there is no textual or historical basis for differentiating between the scrutiny accorded to private and public contracts, nor was that the practice throughout the nineteenth century. In fact, courts historically were more vigilant to police infringements of private agreements and were more deferential to state power over public contracts.[26] *United States Trust* has in effect inverted the contract clause. In the past courts allowed state lawmakers greater latitude to make alterations in public contracts. Second, the Blackmun opinion failed to offer a convincing explanation for this dual standard of review. Cursory references to a state's self-interest are not compelling. The self-interest of legislators could also be at issue when they interfere with contracts between private parties. "All legislative decisions," one scholar has pointed out, "presumably involve the state's self-interest."[27] Third, and equally troublesome, the Supreme Court has never explained what level of deference is applicable to state actions concerning public contracts, and lower federal courts and state courts have been left to grapple with this issue without guidance.[28] "What does giving less deference to the legislature actually mean?" the Second Circuit Court of Appeals asked in 2006. It added, "We hasten to point out that less deference does not imply no deference."[29] As this comment indicates, the notion of less deference has done more to obscure than enlighten.

A year later the Supreme Court, in another closely divided opinion, made clear that the contract clause continued to provide some shelter to private agreements as well. *Allied Structural Steel Company v. Spannaus* (1978) involved a Minnesota law retroactively imposing a significant financial burden on companies that provided a pension plan for employees and then closed their office in the state.[30] The law required pension funding for all employees who had worked for ten years or more, although under the company's original plan employees only qualified for a pension at age sixty-five and by satisfying certain conditions. The effect of the statute was to require the company to pay pension benefits to employees whose benefits had not vested under the company's voluntary plan.

Justice Potter Stewart, writing for the Court majority, found that the act substantially altered the company's contractual relationship with its employees by imposing pension obligations beyond those the company agreed to undertake. He made clear that the contract clause applied to state laws that increased the duties of contracting parties. Still, Stewart appeared to have harbored opposing views concerning the place of the contract clause in modern constitutional law. On the one hand, he declared that the clause "remains part of the Constitution. It is not a dead letter."[31] Stressing the purpose of the provision, Stewart noted the "high value the Framers placed on the protection of private contracts." Echoing sentiments frequently expressed during the nineteenth century, he added, "Contracts enable individuals to order their personal and business affairs according to their particular needs and interests. Once arranged, those rights and obligations are binding under the law, and the parties are entitled to rely on them."[32] On the other hand, Stewart backed away from the full implication of these observations. He pointed out that the contract clause "does not operate to obliterate the police power of the States."[33]

Drawing upon *Blaisdell*, Stewart endeavored to formulate a test to ascertain when a particular interference with a contract ran afoul of the Constitution. The threshold inquiry was whether there was a "substantial impairment of a contractual relationship." He suggested that a minimal alteration of contracts would not trigger contract clause scrutiny.[34] Stewart then set forth a cluster of factors to be considered in resolving a contract clause challenge to state legislation. He concluded that the state law under review did not protect "a broad societal interest" but rather served "a narrow class." Moreover, in his view the pension act did not deal with an economic emergency like the conditions of the 1930s, and it sought to regulate contractual relationships in a field not previously subject to regulation. Nor was the measure temporary in nature. In essence, Stewart balanced the state's concern for pension security with the company's interest in maintaining the integrity of its contract.[35]

The resulting test was highly ambiguous.[36] Much depended on the weight assigned by courts to the various factors to be balanced. How severe is a contractual impairment? What constitutes a broad societal interest? Is the number of people affected relevant to the inquiry? Recall that adoption of the contract clause was motivated by state debt-relief law that reached large numbers of people. Hence, the size of a benefited group alone cannot be a determinative factor. The various criteria in *Allied Structural Steel* are so malleable that a court could justify almost any decision and certainly would have room to uphold even substantial legislative abridgment of contractual terms.[37]

Justice William Brennan, in dissent, launched a veritable broadside against the meaningful enforcement of the property-related provisions in the Constitution, including the contract clause. He lectured that the majority opinion "threatens to undermine the jurisprudence of property rights developed over the last 40 years."[38] In his mind, the relevant history of the contract clause only started with *Blaisdell* and the cases of the New Deal era. Advocating a narrow reading of the contract clause, Brennan advanced the novel and problematic argument that the clause was inapplicable to laws that increased the burdens of a contracting party. But the legislative imposition of new and potentially onerous terms would destroy the stability of agreements, a concern at the very heart of the contract clause.

This pair of Supreme Court decisions in the late 1970s appeared to breathe new life into the moribund contract cause. It sparked renewed interest by scholars, who pondered whether these rulings were forerunners of a more robust property rights jurisprudence.[39] Indeed, *United States Trust* and *Allied Structural Steel* rescued the contract clause from decades of banishment by the Supreme Court. Nonetheless, these decisions stopped well short of establishing a muscular reading of the provision. The Court's hesitant and crabbed opinions, rendered over the strong dissent by three justices dismissive of the contract clause, could not provide a principled basis on which to fashion a vigorous contract clause doctrine.[40] Indeed, the Court soon retreated to a more permissive standard in reviewing claims under the clause.

The Supreme Court's interest in the contract clause proved fleeting. In *Energy Reserves Group v. Kansas Power and Light Company* (1983) the Court denied a contract clause challenge to a Kansas law regulating the price of natural gas in the intrastate market and abrogating price escalator clauses in prior contracts between suppliers and utilities.[41] The case turned upon the alleged impairment of the escalator provisions, common in gas supply contracts as a hedge against rising prices over the course of long-term arrangements. Justice Blackmun, for a unanimous Court, made yet another attempt to devise a formula that balanced the language of the contract clause with the exercise of state police power. The result was an amorphous multipronged test for determining contract clause violations:

1. Has a change in state law operated as a substantial impairment of a contractual relationship? (This inquiry in turn has been subdivided into three components—Is there a contract? Has a change in law impaired that contract? Is the impairment substantial?)
2. If the impairment is substantial, does the law serve a legitimate public purpose, such as remedying a broad social or economic problem?
3. Are the means selected to accomplish this purpose reasonable and appropriate to the public purpose?[42]

Each of these prongs warrant comment in the context of *Energy Reserves Group*. In considering whether the Kansas law substantially impaired the supplier's contractual rights, Blackmun stressed that the parties were operating in a highly regulated industry. The issue of substantiality often turned on the expectation of the contracting parties in a regulated field. Blackmun conceded that the state had not previously controlled natural gas prices, a fact that might have been seen as raising a question about whether price regulations could reasonably have been expected. Blackmun's unspoken premise, however, was that parties in regulated industries must be deemed to enter contracts with the understanding that further regulations might affect their contractual terms.[43] He also minimized the importance of the escalator provision, asserting that Energy Reserves could not have anticipated such a rapid rise in gas prices. Blackmun ruled that the supplier's "reasonable expectations" were not abridged by the Kansas price control scheme.[44]

Despite having resolved the case on the basis that there was no substantial impairment, he nonetheless proceeded to consider the other factors in the multipronged test. Blackmun readily found that Kansas had a legitimate interest in protecting consumers from increasing natural gas prices caused by federal deregulation of the industry. Stressing that the public purpose need not be addressed to emergency conditions, he observed, "The State reasonably could find that higher gas prices have caused and will cause hardship among those who use gas heat but must exist on limited fixed incomes."[45] Lastly, deferring to legislative judgment about the reasonableness of the measure, Blackmun simply declared that the means chosen by the legislature were not "deficient."[46] Reasonableness was somehow equated with lack of deficiency.

The outcome in *Energy Reserves Group* set the stage for much of what followed in contract clause jurisprudence. Its opaque approach necessitates an ad hoc inquiry into finding a contract clause violation. Moreover, the various factors can easily be manipulated to achieve a desired result in particular cases and in practice tilt heavily toward an affirmation of regulatory authority over agreements between private parties. The multifactor test also falls well short of vindication of one of the primary goals of the contract clause—to safeguard the stability of contracts in the face of retroactive legislative interference. It fails to provide consistent or predictable protection for contractual arrangements.[47] Notwithstanding its evident shortcomings, however, the multipronged formula remains in widespread use by both federal and state courts.

The handful of subsequent Supreme Court decisions demonstrates a return to the pattern of not taking the contract clause seriously. For example, the Court upheld an Alabama statute that increased the severance tax on oil and gas extracted from wells in the state and prohibited producers from passing along the tax increase to their purchasers. The pass-through prohibition nullified express contractual provisions permitting the producers to include tax increases in the calculation of prices. Treating the law as a rate-setting scheme, the Court pictured the measure as a rule designed to advance the public interest in protecting consumers from excessive prices.[48] Here again the Court, based on uncertain criteria, rendered a judgment as to whether this statute served a broad public purpose. It adopted an understanding of the police power so broad as to seemingly uphold any type of state economic legislation affecting contracts. Moreover, the Court's reasoning is far from obvious. The authority of government to set utility rates does not necessarily translate into power to override contractual terms dealing with the allocation of severance taxes between contracting parties. The producers would not have had any reason to anticipate such a drastic change in the law effectively destroying its contractual expectations.

Likewise, in *Keystone Bituminous Coal Association v. DeBenedictis* (1987) a five-member majority of the Court rejected a contract clause challenge to a Pennsylvania law preventing the enforcement of contractual waivers of liability for surface damage caused by mining.[49] In a cursory opinion, Justice John Paul Stevens held that the state's interest in preventing environmental harm justified the admittedly substantial impairment of a private contract. His opinion highlighted the confusion inherent in prevailing contract clause analysis. Stevens asserted that a court must be satisfied that the legislation is reasonable and appropriate to the public purpose and then in the next sentence insisted that courts must defer to the legislative judgment as to reasonableness of particular measures.[50] Rhetoric aside, any judicial inquiry on this point is evidently to be purely nominal.

General Motors Corporation v. Romein (1992), now more than twenty years old, was the last occasion to date in which the Supreme Court considered the contract clause.[51] At issue was a change in Michigan law requiring employers to refund certain workers' compensation benefits previously withheld under a 1981 statute. The company challenged the statute mandating these retroactive payments on contract clause grounds, even though the collective bargaining agreement contained no mention of compensation benefits. It argued that the workers' compensation law was an implied term of the agreement and that a subsequent law imposing a duty to pay benefits withheld in reliance on the earlier statute amounted to an impairment of the obligation of contract.[52] Justice Sandra Day O'Connor, speaking for a unanimous bench, affirmed the long-standing principle that the existence of a contract was a question for the independent judgment of federal courts and was not determined by state law. She proceeded, however, to find that there was no implied contractual arrangement regarding workers' compensation benefits and hence no violation of the contract clause. Existing state laws are implied in private contracts, O'Connor explained, only when those laws affect the validity and enforcement of contracts. Thus, changes in state law governing available remedies may impair a contract's binding force and trigger contract clause scrutiny. But she cautioned that reading "every workplace regulation into the private contractual arrangements of employers and employees would expand the definition of contract so far that the constitutional provision would lose its anchoring purpose." The contract clause, O'Connor continued, could not bar all changes in legislation until existing agreements expired because such a construction "would severely limit the ability of state legislators to amend their regulatory legislation."[53] Consequently, legislators were free to alter workers' compensation laws without risking a federal contract clause violation.

THE CONTRACT CLAUSE IN THE LOWER FEDERAL COURTS

The lower federal courts tended to routinely recite the analytical framework established by the Supreme Court for resolving contract clause claims. On the whole, they demonstrate more concern with upholding state regulatory authority than with protecting the rights of contracting parties from state interference. Judge Richard Posner, for instance, correctly noted, "It has been a long time . . . since the contracts clause was interpreted literally." He sought to explain the decline of the clause in functional terms: "The concern that appears to have animated the progressive relaxation of the clause is that a literal interpretation . . . might disable government from dealing with emergencies." Posner conceded that worry "about the paralyzing effect of the literal interpretation may be misplaced, or at least exaggerated." Nonetheless, he expressed unease that "the literal interpretation would impede governmental efforts to regulate for the future, by grandfathering economic rights that would give holders a competitive advantage over new firms."[54] Similarly, the Sixth Circuit Court of Appeals, after paying lip service to the value attached to contracts by the framers, tellingly observed, "Contracts Clause jurisprudence evidences a concern for ensuring that the regulatory power of the State is not eviscerated by a per se ban on legislation impairing private contracts."[55]

Given the Supreme Court's marked neglect and the pronounced tendency of the lower federal courts to defend state regulatory power, it is noteworthy that a number of such courts invalidated state laws on contract clause grounds. A survey of the types of cases voiding state laws under the clause is instructive. Several cases involved laws that modified the rights of parties under existing franchise agreements with respect to termination and transfer of franchises. For example, a statute barring agricultural equipment manufacturers from terminating dealerships for a variety of specified causes substantially curtailed the existing contractual right of manufacturers to end franchise relationships. The Eighth Circuit Court of Appeals found a substantial impairment of contract that could not be sustained by pointing to an asserted public interest. Unimpressed with the state's argument about a legitimate public purpose, the court emphatically declared, "It is clear that the only real beneficiaries under the Act are the narrow class of dealers of agricultural machinery."[56] In contrast, other courts upheld similar laws, reasoning that franchises had long been heavily regulated, and the parties should have foreseen new regulation.[57]

Other federal decisions invoking the contract clause dealt with varied subjects, and did not fall into a pattern. A few examples will illustrate the range of contract clause issues. A state law retroactively altering the contract terms governing the distribution of the surplus accumulated in the workers' compensation reinsurance pool was held unconstitutional. It was found to violate the contractual arrangements between insurance companies and the state reinsurance association. Finding a substantial impairment, the Eighth Circuit Court of Appeals explained, "Heavy regulation of an industry may reduce reasonable expectation. However, regulation does not automatically foreclose the possibility of contract impairment."[58] The court determined that the impairment benefited just a small number of employers, and thus the state failed to demonstrate a significant public purpose for mandating a redistribution of the pool surplus. The contract clause also figured in assessing changes in contractual terms covering landlord-tenant relationships. A Hawaii statute imposing new criteria as part of the rent renegotiation process in long-term commercial leases was held to run afoul of the clause.[59]

Several cases involved states impairing their own contracts or other situations in which a state's financial interest was at stake. Under *United States Trust*, such a circumstance triggers a higher level of judicial scrutiny. A municipal trench cut ordinance, for instance, that required an advance payment by those desiring to perform excavations imposed an additional burden on a utility in disregard of the contractual terms in its franchise agreement with the city.[60] Likewise, a Louisiana law that altered the types of health insurance coverage available to state employees and reopened the enrollment period was seen as an unexpected and substantial abridgment of the existing health-care contracts between providers and the state. The court brushed aside the state's contention that economic protection of a narrow group of in-state companies was sufficient rationale to uphold the law.[61] Further, a New Jersey law reducing the presumptive abandonment period for gift certificates from fifteen to two years and requiring issuers to turn over the remaining value on the unused gift cards to the state was seen as an unconstitutional impairment of contract. Because the reasonable expectation of issuers for realizing a profit on the gift cards by virtue of their contract with the purchasers was frustrated by this measure, the appeals court held that there was a likely violation of the contract clause and enjoined enforcement of the law.[62]

As would be expected, however, federal courts frequently rejected contract clause challenges to state legislation. They read the provision restrictively, stressing the foreseeability of additional regulation in already well-regulated fields as bearing on the substantiality of an alleged impairment, deferring to legislative decisions as to reasonableness, and declaring that the contract clause should be construed narrowly to preserve a wide scope for the exercise of state police power. Again, a few examples demonstrate the range of cases. Changes in landlord-tenant law, invariably to strengthen the legal position of residential tenants, raised contract clause issues. Thus, the Third Circuit Court of Appeals upheld, as applied to current leases, a New Jersey law granting certain senior citizens the right to remain as tenants for up to forty years after the conversion of a unit from rental housing to condominiums.[63] Debt-relief measures also continued to claim judicial attention. An appeals court sustained a Michigan law enacted in the wake of the 2008 recession that retroactively barred personal liability on nonrecourse mortgage-backed loans on the ground that there was no reasonable expectation of a deficiency judgment under the contract.[64]

In several cases the courts determined that there was no impairment of a contractual term and hence no constitutional violation. For example, a municipal ordinance required employers operating on land leased from the city in a particular zone to pay a "living wage." Although the measure was applied retroactively and targeted only a very small number of employers, the Ninth Circuit Court of Appeals reached the dubious conclusion that there was no contractual language relative to employee benefits and hence no abridgment of a contract. Yet in effect the city was unilaterally imposing a new term on an existing long-term lease.[65] Likewise, there was no contractual impairment when Honolulu repealed its leasehold conversion ordinance under which the city might have acquired certain condominium units by eminent domain for resale to the sitting tenants. Because the contract between the city and the tenants specifically contemplated that the city might choose not to condemn the properties, the repeal of the ordinance and the failure to exercise eminent domain did not abridge any contractual obligation.[66] In a case harking back to the nineteenth century, an appeals court, adhering to precedent, held that an agreement between Iowa and a lottery gaming company was a license and not a contract within the protection of the contract clause.[67]

THE CONTRACT CLAUSE IN THE STATE COURTS

A great deal of contract clause litigation over the past thirty years has taken place at the state level, affording state courts the opportunity to explore the protection extended to contracts under state constitutions in a wide variety of situations. A critical threshold inquiry is the standard employed to ascertain violations of state contract clauses. To what extent do state courts construe their state provisions to provide greater protection than the US Constitution? This question is not susceptible to a facile answer. The state judicial opinions are not always clear if the courts are relying on the federal constitution, the state constitution, or both. More than twenty states have treated the state contract clauses as equivalent to the federal provision.[68]

Indeed, a number of state courts explicitly adopted the three-part federal test that as a practical matter gives little safeguard to agreements.[69] Although, as discussed in Chapter 3, the New Jersey Constitution of 1844 adopted broader language than the federal Constitution with respect to the protection of contracts, the New Jersey courts have construed this provision in a manner simply coextensive with the federal guarantee.[70] To complicate matters, some state courts appear to apply the federal framework in a more protective way than the federal courts.

In contrast, state courts in a number of jurisdictions have intimated that their constitutions provide enhanced protection for contracts.[71] A few examples suggest the potential for fashioning a more robust reading of contract clauses at the state level. The Supreme Judicial Court of Virginia observed, "The Contract Clause of the Constitution of Virginia does impose some limits upon the State's power to abridge existing contracts in the exercise of its otherwise legitimate police power."[72] The Court of Appeals of Arizona, quoting John Marshall in *Ogden v. Saunders*, declared, "We cannot ignore or render the prohibition [against legislative impairment of contracts] completely ineffective based upon a currently popular program, even if it is rational." It added, "We can say that, at least, the condition that would allow legislation to impair contracts constitutionally must be of such magnitude as to bring to the general consciousness of the public a feeling of urgency and need. Anything less would undermine the constitutional limitation against impairment of contracts."[73] A Texas court, treating the ban on retroactive laws and impairment of contracts, stated, "The Texas Constitution, we think, is more protective against governmental action and intrusion than is the United States Constitution."[74] Interpreting the state constitution, the Supreme Court of Indiana cut to the heart of the central difficulty of contemporary contract clause jurisprudence: the marked tendency of an expansive police power to swallow up the guarantee of contracts from legislative abridgment. The court observed, "We cannot ignore the clear mandate of our state constitution limiting the power of legislation to impair the obligation of contracts. If the police power exception were construed too broadly, it would operate to eviscerate the constitutional protection. Virtually every legislative enactment could arguably be related to order, safety, health or welfare as a justification for legislative interference with pre-existing contractual rights and duties."[75]

Attempts to reconcile the more relaxed federal standard of review with heightened review by state courts have been a source of confusion. As noted above, the Florida Supreme Court had signaled its willingness to protect contracts more fully than the federal courts. In 1979 the court correctly pointed out that, in construing the Florida contract clause, it was not bound to accept as binding the Supreme Court's interpretation of the parallel federal provision.[76] Nonetheless, it declared, "We now choose to adopt an approach to contract clause analysis similar to that of the United States Supreme Court" on the ground that "such an approach is the one most likely to yield results consonant with the basic purpose of the constitutional provision." The court also endorsed a balancing approach to determine whether an impairment was constitutionally tolerable. It then seemingly shifted gears, ruling, "Some impairment is tolerable, although perhaps not so much as would be acceptable under traditional federal contract clause analysis."[77] Despite its cloudy language, the Florida Supreme Court stopped short of embracing the federal norm. Clarifying its position, the court proclaimed in 1987, "Rights existing under a valid contract enjoy protection under the Florida Constitution. . . . Any legislative action which diminishes the value of a contract is repugnant to and inhibited by the Constitution."[78] Again invoking the contract clause in the state constitution, the court emphatically stated in 1993, "The right to contract is one of the most sacrosanct rights guaranteed by our fundamental law."[79] Revealingly, the Eleventh Circuit Court of Appeals decided that Florida courts construed the state contract clause in a more protective manner than the federal courts.[80]

Given the volume of contract clause litigation at the state level, it is not remarkable that state courts have compiled a mixed record. It is therefore instructive to canvass the range of cases in which claimed violations of the clause have been raised. Of course, where the courts found no contract[81] or merely a trivial interference with no adverse impact,[82] claims of contractual impairment were easily dismissed. Nor have courts shown any inclination to question the long-standing principle that the exercise of eminent domain was not subject to constraint by the contract clause.[83]

As in the federal courts, laws retroactively curtailing the power of franchisors to terminate or limit the transfer of franchise agreements proved a frequent source of controversy. A number of state courts held that such laws did not serve a broad public interest and ran afoul of the state contract clause.[84] In the same vein, several decisions took the position that laws altering the terms of existing insurance agency agreements to limit the termination of such contractual arrangements were unlawful under both the federal and state constitutions.[85]

Debt-relief measures had long been a staple of contract clause jurisprudence. Although the period under review was generally prosperous, periodic downturns in the economy sparked the enactment of laws calculated to delay the foreclosure of antecedent mortgages and allow the redemption of property on terms favorable to the mortgagor. During the 1980s courts in several states invalidated retroactive application of such laws. The Oklahoma Supreme Court, for example, distinguished *Blaisdell* and struck down an act imposing a foreclosure moratorium for one year on any Federal Land Bank as a violation of both the federal and state contract clauses. It was unimpressed with the claimed existence of a farm economic emergency as a justification for the legislature's action.[86] Courts in Kansas and Iowa looked unfavorably on state laws that lengthened the period of redemption and authorized redemption free of the mortgage lien at the fair market value as determined by the court rather than the amount realized at the judicial foreclosure sale. The market value would likely be substantially less than the judicial sale amount. These laws, Kansas and Iowa courts concluded, significantly impaired the right of the mortgagee under the mortgage contract in breach of the federal Constitution.[87] But not all modification of prior mortgages was deemed invalid. The Supreme Judicial Court of Maine sustained the application of a notice of the right to cure a default requirement to the foreclosure proceedings for private residential mortgages, reasoning that the statute was not a substantial impairment of contractual rights and noting that mortgage foreclosures had been regulated since the nineteenth century.[88]

It is noteworthy that during the recession starting in 2008 no state adopted a mortgage moratorium of the type common in the 1930s. Some state legislatures considered such measures but failed to put them into practice. The primary explanation for this behavior is most likely economic. Experience demonstrated that moratoria were not especially effective and negatively affected credit markets.[89] Constitutional objections were probably not the foremost concern. Yet it bears emphasis that in 2008 the governor of Minnesota vetoed a bill that would have permitted a foreclosed borrower to defer a foreclosure sale and remain on the premises upon meeting certain conditions. Among other objections, the governor stated, "The bill also raises significant legal and philosophical concerns. The contract clause of the U.S. Constitution forbids states from enacting legislation that impairs existing contracts. This bill impacts existing mortgage contracts by statutorily changing monthly payment obligations and altering the contracts in other ways."[90] It is rare for political figures to acknowledge that constitutions, federal or state, restrict legislative power over agreements.

As discussed in Chapter 4, the application of enlarged homestead exemptions to antecedent debts had been bitterly contested in the aftermath of the Civil War. This issue occasionally surfaced in the late twentieth century, dividing state courts. Adhering to precedent, the Supreme Court of Mississippi insisted, "It is firmly settled that any law which materially increases the amount of exempt property withdrawn from liability for the debts of the owner of the property impairs the obligation of existing contracts and is, as to existing creditors, unconstitutional because an exemption may not be applied retroactively."[91] On the other hand, the Supreme Court of Montana sidestepped earlier precedent, including one of its own decisions, and determined that the application of an increased homestead exemption to prior debts was constitutional. It found no substantial impairment of a contract, pointing out that the parties should have been aware that the homestead exemption had been regularly increased.[92]

Resort to the contract clause as a shelter against legislative revision of leases was generally unavailing. New Jersey courts upheld a law retroactively mandating a rollback of rents previously permitted under a municipal rent-control ordinance,[93] a statute protecting the continued occupancy of residential tenants against the prior lien of a foreclosing mortgagee,[94] and a measure safeguarding the tenancy of senior citizens in the event their rental units were converted to condominiums.[95] A California appeals court ruled that a statute requiring landlords to reduce rent in proportion to property tax savings passed constitutional muster.[96] In contrast, the Supreme Court of Hawaii readily voided a law requiring landlords, upon expiration of a residential lease, to pay the tenant the value of any leasehold improvements made by the tenant if the tenant decided not to remove them. Characterizing the statute as having "a substantial, material, and, as illustrated by the facts of the present case, even a drastic, and confiscatory effect, on existing contractual obligations, and property rights," it worried that if this measure was sustained then the legislature could change "other material terms of existing leases." The court apparently restricted such sweeping legislative power to emergency situations.[97]

Laws altering the terms of existing insurance policies continued to generate contract clause claims. As before, state courts disagreed as to whether legislators could enlarge the contractual time limit within which policyholders must bring suit or file claims for a loss. The Supreme Court of Tennessee held that application of a law extending the period for filing such suits to insurance contracts executed before its effective date was invalid under the Tennessee contract clause.[98] Taking a different tack, the Supreme Court of Louisiana upheld, under both federal and state contract clauses, a one-year legislative extension of the period for filing insurance claims for losses caused by Hurricanes Katrina and Rita. Although agreeing that the law amounted to a substantial impairment of the insurers' contractual obligation, it reasoned that the legislation was a reasonable means of effectuating a legitimate public purpose to protect the welfare of citizens affected by the hurricanes.[99]

Other legislative changes in insurance policies ran afoul of the contract clause in the federal or state constitutions. Thus, a Tennessee law denying recovery of punitive damages under an uninsured motorist policy could not, consistent with the state constitution, be validly applied retroactively to impair accrued contractual rights.[100] Conversely, a divided Court of Appeals of Maryland ruled that a statute that abrogated parent-child tort immunity could be applied retroactively without impairing existing insurance contracts. It reasoned that there was no substantial impairment in light of the regulated nature of insurance.[101] Emphasizing the high level of state regulation of environmental issues and insurance policies, the Supreme Court of South Carolina saw no substantial abridgment of a pollution liability policy by a subsequent statute providing that private insurance had to be exhausted before resort to public cleanup funds. The court insisted that the carrier had no reasonable expectation that the state would continue its previous policy of distributing funds without regard to private insurance.[102] Although treated by the court as a contract between private parties, the state's self-interest would seem to be clearly implicated and thus dictate heightened scrutiny.

A number of states enacted laws providing that, in the event of divorce, the prior designation of a now-divorced spouse as beneficiary of a life insurance policy was automatically nullified. The purpose of the legislation was to protect divorced owners of life insurance policies who neglected to revoke predivorce designations of their spouses. Here, too, state courts were split on the validity of such measures with respect to contracts entered before the effective date of the statute. Several determined that retroactive application would violate their state's contract clause, finding neither emergency conditions nor a broad public interest to justify invocation of the police power to override private contracts.[103] Yet other courts determined that these laws passed constitutional muster, stressing that the insurance industry was heavily regulated and that there was a public interest in motivating parties to reconsider the disposition of insurance assets in the event of marital dissolution.[104]

Business regulations gave rise to a variety of contract clause cases. An Arizona appeals court held that a law requiring contractors to be licensed could not constitutionally be applied to work performed under a contract entered before the effective date of the law.[105] A Texas court invalidated a municipal ordinance, adopted after a construction contract was made, mandating that a percentage of workers on city projects must intend to live permanently in the city as an impairment of contract.[106] A Florida electric utility successfully argued that a county ordinance materially altering the criteria for the location of transmission lines abridged its contractual rights under a prior franchise agreement.[107] Likewise, a county ordinance limiting the amount of waste that could be received at privately owned landfills violated both the federal and state constitutions with respect to an antecedent contract between the county and the operator.[108]

Yet many regulations survived a contract clause challenge. The Supreme Court of Oklahoma upheld a state law that superseded the royalty clauses in many natural gas leases by imposing a new scheme for allocating revenue derived from gas wells. Pointing to the extensive regulation of the natural gas industry, it insisted, "The parties could not have reasonably expected that their contractual rights were immune from alteration by subsequent State regulation."[109] In the same vein, there was no abridgment of contracts between the state and utility cooperatives caused by regulations implementing a policy of competition in the electricity market when such contracts did not confer any exclusive right to sell electricity.[110] Likewise, a Virginia law prohibiting the use of hydraulic dredges to harvest clams did not impair a lessee's contractual right to take clams because the leases did not grant unlimited discretion in selecting the method of harvesting clams, and the restriction served the public interest in preserving shellfish resources.[111] Laws aimed at health hazards survived contract clause objections even if they affected prior contracts.[112]

A related problem is presented by laws dealing with the terms of employment in the private sector. For example, the Alaska legislature passed an act in 2005 exempting airplane pilots from the state's overtime compensation law and making the change retroactive to 2000. Finding that under state law the overtime provision was included in all contracts of employment, the Alaska Supreme Court determined that the 2005 measure substantially impaired the contractual obligation to pay overtime compensation and did not serve an important public purpose. Consequently, it ruled that the law violated the contract clause of the Alaska Constitution.[113]

On the other hand, a Wisconsin appeals court rejected a contract clause challenge to a municipal ordinance, adopted by public referendum, requiring paid sick leave for employees in the city of Milwaukee. Employers charged that the ordinance violated both the federal and state constitutions by imposing additional and costly benefits on collective bargaining agreements. Stressing deference to legislative judgement, the court ruled that the ordinance was a reasonable and necessary means of achieving a legitimate public purpose.[114]

State courts generally looked with disfavor on a state's attempted abrogation of its own contractual arrangements. Indeed, some states followed the lead of the Supreme Court and assessed legislative interference with state contracts more strictly than in the case of private contracts. Some extended heightened review to situations in which the financial interests of the state were involved even if there was no specific state contract clause. As the Supreme Court of New Hampshire explained in 2010, "For the Contract Clause to retain any vitality, we must be able to consider the reasonableness and necessity of the legislature's chosen action, particularly where the action's substantial impairment of contract rights inures to the State's financial benefit."[115] Several courts invoked the provision to block a state's steps to reduce its bonded obligations. For example, legislatures violated the contract clause by enacting statutes that repealed tax revenue pledged as security for bondholders.[116] Likewise, repeal of a statute granting tax reductions designed to encourage local power production impaired existing agreements between utilities and municipalities that incorporated the tax reduction scheme. Brushing aside a plea of financial necessity, the Supreme Court of New Hampshire strikingly observed, "The legislature has policy alternatives for raising revenue other than breaching of its contractual responsibilities."[117] The distribution of surplus funds in a state-sponsored account to provide medical liability insurance produced contract clause litigation. A state court held that a statute requiring transfer of the surplus funds to the state substantially abridged the contractual rights of the insurance policyholders and did not address a broad societal need.[118]

One must be wary of generalizations based on this uneven pattern of state court decisions dealing with the state and federal contract clauses. Nonetheless, some observations seem in order. First, few of the cases raised the type of broad contractual issues addressed by courts in the nineteenth century. None posed a serious threat to the prevalent regulation of the economy.

Indeed, state courts, like their federal counterparts, often seemed more concerned to affirm state police power than to vindicate contractual arrangements. This tendency was especially evident in the frequent assertion that an existing high level of regulation should lead parties to expect additional legislative changes that could affect their contractual rights. Hence, state courts sustained statutes that arguably abridged contracts in breach of the federal or state constitutions. Second, state courts, with some exceptions, adopted fact-specific balancing tests to ascertain contract clause violations. Although they sometimes recognized the historical importance of the contract clause as a vehicle to safeguard the dependability of agreements, state courts did not consistently act with this in mind.[119] Much turned upon how courts assessed the cluster of criteria in the commonly adopted three-part test. This left ample room for judicial discretion and policy making.

This review of state contract clause decisions speaks to the larger issue of state constitutionalism as a source of protection for individual rights. To this end Justice Brennan in 1977 called for a revival of interest in state constitutional law.[120] The ensuing debate probed the extent to which state courts, in interpreting parallel constitutional texts, should develop their own constitutional doctrines or simply adhere to federal doctrines. Proponents of this view pictured the federal constitution as setting a baseline but urged state courts to read rights guarantees more expansively.

Advocates of an independent state constitutionalism certainly did not have the sanctity of contracts, or indeed any economic rights, in mind. Yet in the area of taking jurisprudence the Supreme Court has explicitly recognized that states are free to adopt stricter standards than those that prevail in the federal courts. In the controversial decision of *Kelo v. City of New London* (2005), sustaining the exercise of eminent domain for purposes of economic development by private parties, Justice Stevens pointed out that "nothing in our opinion precludes any State from placing further restrictions on its exercise of the taking power."[121] In the wake of *Kelo* a number of state courts enlarged the protection accorded property owners by ruling that the "public use" clauses in their state constitutions prevented resort to eminent domain to acquire private property for economic development purposes.[122]

No similar move to beef up the constitutional safeguard of contractual arrangements appears to be on the horizon. Despite occasional suggestions that state courts should fashion criteria to afford greater protection to contracting parties from legislative abridgment,[123] there has been little movement in this direction.[124] Most state courts seem content to work within the federal framework in analyzing contract clause claims. Unlike the outcome in *Kelo*, no contract clause decision in recent decades has touched the public nerve. Few people pay much attention to contract clause cases. Legislative tinkering with the contractual rights of creditors and landlords might even be popular with benefited groups, whereas taking the property of individuals against their will is bound to arouse opposition. To be sure, some states appear more likely than their federal counterparts to look skeptically at contractual impairments. But there is little evidence that state courts are systematically developing an independent reading of state contract clauses.

PUBLIC-SECTOR EMPLOYEE BENEFITS

The most frequently litigated contract clause issue at the time of this writing stems from the on-going financial crisis experienced by many states and localities. Various causes have contributed to this difficulty, but most commentators agree that the large and growing shortfall in funding for public employee retirement and health benefits is a primary source of financial distress. State and local governments too often failed to set aside adequate money to fund promised benefits and compounded this neglect by projecting unrealistic rates of return on pension and health investments. Thus, these governmental units confront declining revenue and increasing benefit claims.[125] The most dramatic illustration of local government financial woes was the 2013 bankruptcy of the city of Detroit. The implications of municipal bankruptcy for contract clause claims will be addressed below.

In this climate of austerity many state and local governments have taken steps to trim benefits for both current and retired public-sector employees. Such measures have taken various forms: reducing pensions for current workers as well as retirees, tightening eligibility requirements, raising the retirement age, suspending cost-of-living adjustments (COLA), imposing wage freezes and mandatory unpaid furloughs, increasing worker contributions to pension and health plans, and modifying both COLA and caps on earnings for retirees. These moves have triggered a wave of litigation alleging a violation of the contract clause in both the federal and state constitutions.[126] Of course, the provision only guards against retroactive impairment of existing agreements. Hence, states and localities have a largely free hand to revamp benefit schemes for new employees.[127] Such changes, however, do little to alleviate present liabilities.

Any contract clause analysis must begin with a determination of whether a binding obligation has been created. Thus, a threshold inquiry is to ascertain if public employee benefits are contractual in nature. Historically such benefits were treated as gratuitous allowances or expectancies rather than vested rights and could be revoked at will, but matters are more complicated today.[128] Some contract clause claims by public employees fail because courts either find no contract or conclude that the contract does not cover a particular benefit. It has been held, for instance, that statements outlining current benefit plans in employee handbooks or similar publications do not evidence a contract that such benefits will continue indefinitely.[129] Likewise, a preexisting statutory reservation of a power to modify agreements was found to form part of the contract with public employees. Hence, there was no contract clause violation when a county, pursuant to such a provision, implemented an employee furlough plan.[130] Nor does the contract clause offer shelter to asserted benefits under invalid legislation or void agreements.[131] Moreover, state and federal courts generally adhere to the long-standing principle that legislation is presumed not to create contractual rights unless there is a clear indication that the legislature intended to be bound. This unmistakability doctrine rested on the premise that the primary purpose of legislation was to enact policies subject to revision as circumstances change, not make contracts. In other words, courts are reluctant to infer binding commitments from a statute absent express language to that effect. Stressing that the unmistakability doctrine limits contractual incursions on state authority, the Supreme Court of Wisconsin determined that pension benefits were protected contracts but that the allocation of contribution rates was not a contractual right within the shelter of the state contract clause. Consequently, municipal employees could be required to contribute more in order to participate in a pension program.[132] Consistent with this presumption that legislation does not establish contractual rights, a number of federal[133] and state courts[134] ruled that legislative repeal or modification of annual COLA set in earlier statutes did not impinge any contractual right. Similarly, the Supreme Court of Florida brushed aside a contract clause attack on a state law eliminating a COLA for services performed after a certain date, declaring that the legislature could "amend a retirement plan prospectively, so long as any benefits tied to service performed prior to the amendment date are not lost or impaired."[135]

Most contract clause claims pressed by public-sector employees, however, cannot be so readily resolved. Today salaries, pensions, and health benefits are often covered by collective bargaining agreements. Moreover, starting with New York in 1938, a number of states enacted constitutional or statutory provisions declaring that state or local pension plans constitute contracts.[136] In addition, despite the presumption against construing statutes as contracts, some state courts take the position that employee participation in a governmental retirement system creates an agreement between the state or locality and its employees.[137] Therefore, public-sector employees can often plausibly assert that their retirement and health benefits are covered by contractual arrangements.

Given the pliable nature of the usual three-prong test and the uncertainty over the standard of review for alleged impairment of public contracts, one cannot be surprised that federal and state courts have reached conflicting decisions regarding state legislation that curtailed the contractual rights of public employees for salaries and benefits. One line of cases found no contract clause violations and upheld the moves by state and local governments to unilaterally alter employment contracts. Although acknowledging that more stringent oversight is required when a state impairs its own contract, these courts insist that some deference to legislative policy decisions is nonetheless warranted.[138] They also typically give great weight to the severity of budgetary problems confronting lawmakers. For instance, in 2011 the First Circuit Court of Appeals opined, "In today's fiscal climate . . . many states face daunting budget deficits that may necessitate decisive and dramatic action."[139]

Agreeing that the pressing need to address a budgetary crisis served an important public purpose, this group of courts turned to the third prong of the test for determining contract clause violation—were the means selected by lawmakers reasonable and necessary? These courts pointedly declined to function, in the words of the Fourth Circuit Court of Appeals, "as super-legislatures" and to second-guess policy alternatives. "Not only are we ill-equipped even to consider the evidence that would be relevant to such conflicting policy alternatives," it explained, "we have no objective standards against which to assess the multitude of alternatives."[140] In the same vein, the Second Circuit Court of Appeals, sustaining a city of Buffalo temporary wage freeze, conjured up the scarecrow of a return to *Lochner* if courts could evaluate whether other policies might have been better to resolve the city's bleak financial picture.[141]

Other courts have looked more skeptically at state legislation that reduced public employee benefits, reasoning that such actions run afoul of the contract clause.[142] These courts gave less weight to the existence of a financial crisis, with some stressing that fiscal problems were foreseeable when collective bargaining agreements were made.[143] They expressed doubt that abridgment of labor contracts served a public interest. For example, the Eighth Circuit of Appeals determined that a city's unilateral action to terminate the payment of retiree health insurance premiums amounted to a substantial impairment of a collective bargaining agreement. The court then turned to consider the city's plea of budgetary concerns as a justification for its plans. "Although economic concerns can give rise to the City's legitimate use of the police power," it explained, "such concerns must be related to 'unprecedented emergencies,' such as mass foreclosures caused by the Great Depression." Because the city failed to demonstrate such a severe emergency, the court ruled that its plan did not advance a significant public purpose and was void under the contract clause.[144] This problematic analysis puts courts in the uncomfortable position of ascertaining when a financial crisis is sufficiently serious to justify a financial impairment. What criteria should be employed in making such a determination? How much weight should be accorded a legislative declaration of an economic emergency?

Even when courts acknowledged the existence of a financial crisis, they sometimes took the position that unilateral reduction of employee benefits was neither reasonable nor necessary in view of other available options. They suggested seeking additional federal aid, reduction of other governmental services, or a tax increase, rather than contract impairment, as a solution to fiscal problems.[145] Such judicial review of legislative decisions places courts in a highly ironic circumstance. Having lectured for decades that courts should not interfere with social and economic policies, some courts and commentators have reversed gears and maintain that there is a duty to examine the reasonableness of legislative policy with regard to public-employee contracts. A recent observation by the Sixth Circuit Court of Appeals in an employee benefits case highlighted this conundrum: "Though the wisdom of policy decisions is beyond the realm of the courts, assessing the *reasonableness* of Defendant's actions is required under the contract clause."[146] There is no escaping the fact that this level of judicial scrutiny would entail complex policy considerations. On what principled basis does a court decide whether a proposed alternative to benefit cuts is feasible or preferable? Would a tax increase negatively affect the business climate and thus further exacerbate the underlying budgetary crisis? Is a wage freeze more reasonable than layoffs,[147] or a reduction in school days or employee work hours? Is the notion of a federal bailout realistic? Should pension plans be funded if other creditors must go unpaid or bondholders face repudiation? There is no obvious answer to these questions.

Underlying judicial attitudes toward the legal status of public employment might also shape the treatment of benefit reform legislation. Recognizing that public-sector employees might feel unfairly dealt with by legislative changes in health-care and retirement plans, the Supreme Court of Michigan pointed out that the terms of public-sector employment were subject to changing circumstances. Comparing public and private employees, the court commented:

> We also note at the outset that all public employees must contend with a variety of future uncertainties, of which they are, or should be aware at the time that they pursue and accept public employment. The terms, conditions, and even continued existence of public employment positions may be influenced by the changing fiscal conditions of the state, the evolving policy priorities of governmental bodies, constitutional modifications and other initiatives of the people, and the ebb and flow of state, national, and global economies. The future is not easily predictable, and public employees, along with individuals working in the private sector, must contend with these realities.[148]

Indeed, the Supreme Court of South Carolina voiced the view that "government should have more flexibility than business with respect to the employer/employee relationship."[149]

In sharp contrast, some courts and commentators have insisted that public-sector employees deserve special solicitude and should not be singled out to bear the brunt of budgetary problems.[150] They intimate that lawmakers are pursuing a politically expedient course in seeking to trim public-employee benefits. Yet it is difficult to see, in view of the general current of contract clause jurisprudence recognizing a broad latitude for states to override agreements in order to effectuate economic policy, that public employees should be categorically shielded from any alterations in benefit schemes. Such an approach by courts looks like an anomaly calculated to serve the economic interests of one particular group.

Controversy over legislative steps to reduce employee and retiree benefits shows at this time no sign of abating. In fact, studies indicate that the funding gap for pension plans is growing worse in many states and localities despite half-hearted efforts to address the problem. It is striking that this issue, so far afield from the concerns of the framers, should become a fertile source of contract clause disputes. As with other areas of current contract clause jurisprudence, it is difficult to detect any consistent pattern in the handling of public-sector cases. If nothing else, these cases underscore the extent to which contract clause analysis has become a jumble. As discussed above, the prevailing three-prong test is an invitation to ad hoc and contradictory decisions. That result is fully on display here.

Three other considerations bear on the extent to which the contract clause affords protection to public-sector agreements. First, recall that a number of states have specific constitutional provisions that seemingly grant such contracts special status. The Illinois Constitution, for instance, not only declares that membership in a public retirement system amounts to a contract but broadly states that "the accrued benefits of members of any state or statewide public retirement system shall not be diminished or impaired."[151] This pension protection clause appears to pose a more formidable obstacle to benefit reform than the contract clause itself. In rapid succession the Supreme Court of Illinois in 2014 and 2015 put sharp teeth into this provision, in effect foreclosing any legislative effort to address the state's dire financial picture by curtailing employee benefits. The court ruled that the clause, although seemingly limited by it terms to retirement benefits, encompassed subsidized health insurance premiums available to members of a retirement system. It stressed that the constitutional clause should be construed liberally in favor of the pensioner.[152] A year later the Illinois court invalidated a law reducing retirement benefits under the same provision in the state constitution. Especially revealing was the court's discussion of the relationship between the state constitution's contract clause and the pension protection clause. It pointed out that delegates to the 1970 state constitutional convention decided not to rely on the contract clause to safeguard employee retirement benefits and instead adopted a new and more specific provision. In so doing, the court observed that the delegates realized that any protection of agreements under the contract clause could be modified through an exercise of the state's police power. Given this history, the court had no difficulty in rejecting the state's contention that contracts pertaining to the public retirement system were subject to modification under the police power in order to meet financial challenges. Although it proclaimed that "there simply is no police power to disregard the express provisions of the constitution," the court never explained why in other cases the police power prevailed over the apparently absolute language of the contract clause.[153] In other words, the court would not read the porous exceptions that have weakened the contract clause into the pension guarantee clause.

Underscoring this conclusion, in 2016 the Supreme Court of Illinois invalidated a state law that modified pension benefits for employees of the city of Chicago. It found that the reduction in annuity benefits for current and future retirees ran afoul of the pension protection clause in the state constitution. The court did not question the existence of a fiscal crisis for the city but again insisted that such economic circumstances did not justify the impairment of contractual pension benefits.[154]

The Supreme Court of Arizona construed the pension clause of its constitution to reach a similar result. It rejected the argument that the pension clause should be analyzed in the same manner as the federal contract clause, permitting contractual impairment in certain situations. Instead, the court declared, "The Pension Clause confers additional, independent protection for public retirement benefits separate and distinct from the protection afforded by the Contract Clause."[155] The decisions in Illinois and Arizona complicate the task of closing yawning budget deficits by giving public-employee pension arrangements more protection than is generally conferred on other agreements.

Second, municipal bankruptcy might provide an avenue whereby local governments could escape the contract clause and gain the flexibility to cancel or alter employee contracts that could not otherwise be changed. The clause, of course, only applies to the states and does not prevent Congress from abridging agreements. It has long been settled that Congress through the bankruptcy power can authorize the impairment of contracts. In 1902 Chief Justice Melville W. Fuller observed, "The subject of 'bankruptcies' includes the power to discharge the debtor from his contracts and liabilities, as well as to distribute his property. The grant to Congress involves the power to impair the obligation of contracts, and this the States were forbidden to do."[156] Recent decisions by bankruptcy courts have underscored this point, ruling that employee pension plans were subject to modification in bankruptcy proceedings.[157] In so doing they made clear that constitutional provisions barring the infringement of contracts imposed no constraints in bankruptcy. As a bankruptcy judge explained in 2015, "Neither the Contracts Clause of the California Constitution nor the Contracts Clause of the Federal Constitution prevents Congress from enacting a law impairing the obligation of contract."[158] These decisions break no new ground, but they dispel any notion that the public-employee contracts were privileged and somehow immune from the reach of bankruptcy power.

Given the ongoing financial crisis in many municipalities and states, it is certainly possible that other jurisdictions will seek relief in bankruptcy. If this comes to pass, it will trigger additional interplay between the bankruptcy code and the contract clause.

Third, the drive to curtail public-employee and retiree benefits has reopened the question of what constitutes the passing of a law for contract clause purposes. A number of state legislatures delegated board powers over municipal finances to emergency managers or local governments. The pivotal issue is whether decisions made pursuant to such delegated authority amount to the enactment of a law. Federal courts have been divided on this matter,[159] and Supreme Court precedent is both old and confusing.[160] This problem recalls the decisions, treated in earlier chapters, as to whether changes in judicial decisions that affected agreements could run afoul of the contract clause. It would appear that the character of the action, not its form, should be determinative. Such an analysis would militate in favor of viewing the exercise of a delegated power as having the nature of a legislative enactment. Otherwise, lawmakers could easily circumvent the protection of the contract clause by the simple expedient of delegating the power to make painful decisions.[161]

IMPAIRMENT OF CONTRACTS WITH FEDERAL GOVERNMENT REVISITED

In *United States v. Winstar Corporation* (1996) the Supreme Court reaffirmed the principle that the federal government could enter contracts binding upon future Congresses. The case arose from the savings and loan crisis of the 1980s. In response, federal regulators sought to stabilize the thrift industry by encouraging solvent savings and loans to take over failing institutions. As an inducement to undertake such risky mergers, regulators promised that the acquiring institutions would be given particular accounting treatment concerning reserve capital requirements. Congress thereafter enacted a new regulatory regime that tightened the capital requirements. The new standards had a severe impact on several saving and loans that had acquired failing thrifts in reliance on the prior arrangements. They brought suit against the United States for breach of contract, seeking monetary damages.

The Supreme Court determined that the federal government had made an express agreement to permit the claimants to take advantage of special accounting rules as part of the merger process. Otherwise, it suggested, the parties would not have entered into the mergers. The government argued that contracts could limit the regulatory authority of Congress only when such consequence was set forth in unmistakable terms. Dismissing this contention, a plurality of the Court explained, "Although the contract clause has no application to acts of the United States, it is clear that the

National Government has some capacity to make agreements binding future Congresses by creating vested rights. The extent of that capacity, to be sure remains somewhat obscure."[162] Drawing heavily upon decisions construing the contract clause, it concluded that the unmistakability doctrine applied when a contract purported to curtail the governmental exercise of a sovereign power, such as taxation or regulation. Here, the Court plurality pointed out, the claimants sought to recover monetary damages and not to bar changes in bank regulations. It acknowledged that awarding damages for subsequent regulatory change might "indirectly deter needed governmental regulation by raising its costs" but insisted that this consideration could not prevail over an express contract and the government's need to be seen as a reliable contracting partner. The plurality emphatically rejected "the suggestion that the Government may simply shift the costs of legislation onto its contractual partners who are adversely affected by the change in the law, when the Government has assumed the risk of such change."[163]

A MODEST REBIRTH

No one could seriously contend that the contract clause today is among the most important and litigated provisions in the Constitution or its state counterparts. Yet the clause has regained some efficacy following its near eclipse in the post–New Deal decades. Despite their shortcomings, the Supreme Court decisions in the 1970s and 1980s opened the door, at least slightly, for a reconsideration of the once-prominent provision. Predicting the future is a hazardous enterprise, but there is potential for more robust protection of contractual arrangements as the New Deal orthodoxy continues to erode.

Epilogue

In August of 1829 Justice Joseph Story delivered an address at Harvard University to mark his inauguration as Dane Professor of Law. Focusing on the importance of studying law as a means of safeguarding individual rights, Story observed, "There can be no freedom, where there is no safety to property, or personal rights. Whenever legislation renders the possession or enjoyment of property precarious; whenever it cuts down the obligation and security of contracts . . . it is still in its essence tyranny."[1] These comments attest to the high standing of contractual rights in the nineteenth century, and at the same time they provide a benchmark from which to gauge how far constitutional jurisprudence has wandered from Story's premise. It is unlikely that many constitutional scholars today would place such an emphasis on the link between contractual reliability and individual freedom. For better or worse, the value assigned to contracting in society has changed since the contract clause was written in 1787. The framers saw contractual stability as essential for the preservation of credit and the encouragement of economic growth. Throughout much of the nineteenth century, enforcement of the contract clause harmonized with the prevailing individualist ethic, which pictured contracts, grounded on voluntary consent, as vehicles for individuals to pursue their own goals. Hence, it was appropriate for both states and individuals to be held to the terms of their bargains. In contrast, the twentieth century witnessed a diminished faith in voluntary contracts. Modern governments impinge upon contractual arrangements in numerous ways to facilitate regulatory objectives. Consequently, a study of the contract clause provides a window into changing assumptions about contracts and the authority of government.

Adopted as part of the Constitution at the end of the convention's deliberations and without extensive discussion, the contract clause came to play a remarkable role throughout much of constitutional history. Chief Justices John Marshall and Roger B. Taney fashioned the clause into a formidable check on state actions impinging agreements. Federal and state courts frequently invoked the provision in a wide variety of settings. During the nineteenth century, therefore, the contract clause was both extravagantly praised as a bulwark of contractual stability and prosperity and sharply condemned as a straitjacket on the states and a shield for special corporate privilege. This study of the clause suggests that both of these assessments were exaggerated. Despite its absolute wording, the contract clause was never understood to bar any legislative interference with agreements. Indeed, the protection afforded contracts steadily eroded in the late nineteenth century. By the middle of the twentieth century the contract clause fell into a period of eclipse and was largely ignored by courts and scholars for decades. Although it never faded entirely from constitutional dialogue, the provision was a pale reflection of its former self.

Several themes stand out in the history of the contract clause. First, the broad reading of the contract clause to encompass state contracts brought land grants, corporate charters, tax exemptions, and municipal bonds within the shelter of the contract clause. Yet these developments triggered a growing reaction that by the late nineteenth century led to the formulation of doctrines that diluted the clause as a guarantee of state-conferred privileges. The contract clause was riddled with exceptions by 1900. Second, before the Great Depression of the 1930s both federal and state courts were in the main alert to uphold private contracts in the face of state legislative interference. Most of this litigation involved debtor-creditor relations in some form. Even in this area, however, the penchant of legislators to pass relief laws during periods of economic distress, and the inevitable time lag between legislative enactment and eventual judicial invalidation reduced the efficacy of the contract clause as safeguard of private rights. Third, contract clause jurisprudence was characterized by continuous interplay between federal and state courts. During the nineteenth and early twentieth centuries the Supreme Court occasionally cited state court decisions construing the contract clause, but these were never treated as dispositive. For the most part state courts followed, reluctantly at times, Supreme Court rulings interpreting the clause. Yet on occasion state courts construed parallel contract clause language in state constitutions to confer greater protection to contracts than did the federal provision. Conversely, at times some state courts resisted or sought to evade Supreme Court decisions applying the contract clause. At the end of the day much of the enforcement of the contract clause rested in the hands of state judges. Fourth, the erosion of the contract clause can be traced in part to the changing relationship of the federal and state governments. By its terms the clause bound only the states and had no application to the national government. Consequently, the provision raised no barrier to congressional legislation infringing agreements. As Congress became more active in regulating the economy, the function of the clause was necessarily reduced. Moreover, the enactment of a permanent bankruptcy law in 1898 established a vehicle by which bankruptcy courts could modify or abrogate the contracts of insolvent debtors. This law had the effect of reducing the necessity for state debt-relief measures, thus cutting back a fertile source of contract clause litigation.

The future of the contract clause is difficult to predict, but one might doubt that it will regain its once prominent place in constitutional jurisprudence without a sea change in judicial attitudes. Periodic calls for revitalization of the contract clause have fallen largely on deaf ears. The Supreme Court has demonstrated no interest in the provision for decades. In marked contrast to its neglect of the contract clause, the Court since the 1980s has gradually strengthened the protection afforded property owners under the takings clause of the Fifth Amendment.[2] The prevailing multifactor test for ascertaining contract clause violations is so plagued with ambiguities as to be virtually worthless. Courts can utilize the opaque factors to reach almost any result, an unpredictable outcome at odds with the very purpose of the clause to protect contractual stability. For all practical purposes, the guarantee of the contract clause has been subordinated to state regulatory authority. Little wonder, then, that many commentators dismiss the contract clause as being of little consequence in modern constitutional law.

Although relegated to a secondary status in the constitutional order, the contract clause has proven a hardy plant. It is not about to disappear. As the application of the provision to state attempts to tighten public employee benefit schemes demonstrates, it continues to feature in vital litigation. The contract clause thus retains a degree of vitality even in contexts far removed from those that animated the framers in 1787.

Notes

INTRODUCTION

1. Murray v. Charleston, 96 U.S. 432, 448 (1878).

2. Home Building and Loan Association v. Blaisdell, 209 U.S. 398 (1934).

3. Michael S. Greve, *The Upside-Down Constitution* (Cambridge, MA: Harvard University Press, 2012), 143.

4. Charles River Bridge v. Warren Bridge, 36 U.S. 420 (1837).

5. James W. Ely, Jr., "Public Employees and the Curious Mini-Revival of Contract Clause Jurisprudence," *Brigham-Kanner Property Rights Conference Journal* 2 (2013): 37–60.

CHAPTER 1. ORIGINS AND EARLY DEVELOPMENT

1. Forrest McDonald, *Novus Ordo Seclorum: The Intellectual Origins of the Constitution* (Lawrence: University Press of Kansas, 1985), 271.

2. James W. Ely, Jr., "Economic Liberties and the Original Meaning of the Constitution," *San Diego Law Review* 45 (2008): 677–687.

3. Lawrence M. Friedman, *A History of American Law*, 3rd ed. (New York: Touchstone, 2005), 27; Gordon S. Wood, *The Radicalism of the American Revolution* (New York: Knopf, 1992), 128; Claire Priest, "Creating an American Property Law: Alienability and Its Limits," *Harvard Law Review* 120 (2006): 408–458.

4. Wood, *Radicalism of the American Revolution*, 162–164.

5. William E. Nelson, "Authority and the Rule of Law in Early Virginia," *Ohio Northern University Law Review* 29 (2003): 357–360. See also William E. Nelson, *The Common Law in Colonial America*, vol. 1: *The Chesapeake and New England, 1607–1660* (New York: Oxford University Press, 2008), 35–36.

6. Allan Nevins, *The American States during and after the Revolution, 1775–1789* (New York: Macmillan, 1924), 404–405, 537, 571; Jerome J. Nadelhaft, *The Disorders of War: The Revolution in South Carolina* (Orono: University of Maine Press, 1981), 155–172; Stuart Bruchey, "The Impact of Concern for the Security of Property Rights on the Legal System of the Early American Republic," *Wisconsin Law Review* (1980): 1138–1140.

7. James W. Ely, Jr, "American Independence and the Law: A Study of Post-Revolutionary South Carolina Legislation," *Vanderbilt Law Review* 26 (1973): 942–943.

8. Noah Webster, "The DEVIL Is in You" (1786), in *A Collection of Essays and Fugitiv Writings on Moral, Historical, Political, and Literary Subjects* (Boston: I. Thomas and E. T. Andrews, 1790), 130.

9. Alexander Hamilton to George Washington, May 28, 1790, in *The Papers of Alexander Hamilton,* vol. 6, ed. Harold C. Syrett (New York: Columbia University Press, 1962), 436.

10. Ogden v. Saunders, 27 U.S. 213, 354–355 (1827) (Marshall, C.J., dissenting).

11. Joseph Stancliffe Davis, *Essays in the Earlier History of American Corporations: Eighteenth-Century Business Corporations in the United States* (Cambridge, MA: Harvard University Press, 1917; reprint, New York: Russell and Russell, 1965), vol. 2, 310–313; F. Cyril James, "The Bank of North America and the Financial History of Philadelphia," *Pennsylvania Magazine of History and Biography* 64 (1940): 62–66; Janet Wilson, "The Bank of North America and Pennsylvania Politics, 1781–1787," *Pennsylvania Magazine of History and Biography* 66 (1942): 3–13.

12. James Wilson, "Considerations on the Bank of North America" (1785), in *Collected Works of James Wilson,* vol. 1, ed. Kermit L. Hall and Mark David Hall (Indianapolis: Liberty Fund, 2007), 71, 72.

13. Jennifer Nedelsky, *Private Property and the Limits of American Constitutionalism: The Madisonian Framework and Its Legacy* (Chicago: University of Chicago Press, 1990), 299n.141.

14. As quoted in Joseph Stancliffe Davis, *Essays in the Earlier History of American Corporations,* vol. 2, 313.

15. Ibid., 312–315, finding that state legislatures at the end of the eighteenth century asserted the power to alter or repeal corporate charters but rarely exercised such power.

16. William Ewald, "James Wilson and the Drafting of the Constitution," *University of Pennsylvania Journal of Constitutional Law* 10 (2008): 910.

17. Pelatiah Webster, *An Essay on Credit in Which the Doctrine of Banks Is Considered* (Philadelphia, PA: Eleazer Oswald, 1786), 37–38. Noah Webster advanced a similar argument in 1788. He maintained that when a legislature "makes *grants* or *contracts* it act[s] as a party, and cannot take back its grant or change the nature of its contracts, without the consent of the other party. A state has no more right to neglect or refuse to fulfil its engagements than an individual." Noah Webster, "Principles of Government and Commerce" in *A Collection of Essays and Fugitiv Writings on Moral, Historical, Political, and Literary Subjects* (Boston: I. Thomas and E. T. Andrews, 1790), 40–41.

18. Bruchey, "Concern for the Security of Property Rights," 1136. See also David Crump, "The Economic Purpose of the Contract Clause," *Southern Methodist University Law Review* 66 (2013): 687, 690–692, noting problems caused by state abrogation of contracts.

19. Max Farrand, ed., *The Records of the Federal Convention of 1787,* rev. ed., vol. 1 (New Haven, CT: Yale University Press, 1937), 147.

20. See Denis P. Duffey, "The Northwest Ordinance as a Constitutional Document," *Columbia Law Review* 95 (1995): 929–968.

21. An Ordinance for the Government of the Territory of the United States North-West of the River Ohio, July 13, 1787, *Journals of the Continental Congress, 1774–1789,* vol. 32, 340. The Northwest Ordinance was reenacted in 1789 by the First Congress under the Constitution. 1 Stat. 50 (August 7, 1789).

22. Matthew J. Festa, "Property and Republicanism in the Northwest Ordinance," *Arizona State Law Journal* 45 (2013): 409, 448–452; John M. Morrison, "The Legislative History of the Ordinance of 1787," *Proceedings of the American Antiquarian Society*, New Series, 5 (1889): 331–332; Andrew R. L. Cayton, "The Northwest Ordinance from the Perspective of the Frontier," in *The Northwest Ordinance 1787: A Bicentennial Handbook*, ed. Robert M. Taylor, Jr. (Indianapolis: Indiana Historical Society, 1987), 21; Duffey, "Northwest Ordinance as a Constitutional Document," 938, 960.

23. Farrand, *Records*, vol. 2, 439.

24. Ibid., 439.

25. Ibid., 440.

26. Ibid.

27. Ibid.

28. Ibid. Connecticut, Massachusetts, and Virginia voted against the motion.

29. Ibid., 448–449.

30. Ibid., 619.

31. As adopted, Article I, section 10, provides in part: "No State shall enter into any Treaty, Alliance, or Confederation; grant Letters of Marque and Reprisal; emit Bills of Credit; make any Thing but gold and silver Coin a Tender in Payment of Debts; pass any Bills of Attainder, ex post facto Law, or Law impairing the Obligation of Contracts, or any Title of Nobility."

32. But see Robert Ernst, *Rufus King: American Federalist* (Chapel Hill: University of North Carolina Press, 1968), 111–112, discussing King's role in the adoption of the contract clause and concluding that King was "persistent and persuasive" and might have convinced other members of the Committee of Style to include the provision.

33. McDonald, *Novus Ordo Seclorum*, 272–273. See also Richard B. Morris, *Witnesses at the Creation: Hamilton, Madison, Jay, and the Constitution* (New York: Holt, Rinehart, and Winston, 1985), 221–222, asserting, "It is most probable that Hamilton persuaded his colleagues on the Committee of Style to add" the contract clause.

34. Warren B. Hunting, *The Obligation of Contracts Clause of the United States Constitution* (Baltimore, MD: Johns Hopkins University Press, 1919), 115–116; Max M. Mintz, *Gouverneur Morris and the American Revolution* (Norman: University of Oklahoma Press, 1970), 201. See also Page Smith, *James Wilson: Founding Father, 1742–1798* (Chapel Hill: University of North Carolina Press, 1956), 247–248, noting that Wilson has been credited with authorship of the contract clause, but concluding, "While there is no evidence definitely disproving Wilson's authorship, certainly no evidence exists to prove it"; Mark David Hall, *The Political and Legal Philosophy of James Wilson, 1724–1798* (Columbia: University of Missouri Press, 1997), 137, finding "little solid evidence" that Wilson was the author, but stressing that Wilson "believed that legislatures should not violate the sanctity of contracts."

35. Nedelsky, *Private Property*, 299n.141.

36. Farrand, *Records*, vol. 2, 619.

37. For an exploration of why the contract clause was applied only to state governments, see Michael W. McConnell, "Contract Rights and Property Rights:

A Case Study in the Relationship between Individual Liberties and Constitutional Structure," *California Law Review* 76 (1988): 267–295.

38. Bruce Ackerman, "Constitutional Politics/Constitutional Law," *Yale Law Journal* 99 (1989): 453, 537. "This was the Federalist effort to link the eighteenth century's affirmation of individual liberty with the rhetoric of contract and private property. Thus, the Federalists valued market 'freedom' so highly that they forbade the states from 'impairing the obligation of Contract' in the original 1787 Constitution, at a time when they believed an elaborate Bill of Rights unnecessary."

39. Kermit L. Hall and Peter Karsten, *The Magic Mirror: Law in American Society*, 2nd ed. (New York: Oxford University Press, 2009), 72.

40. Jonathan Elliot, *The Debates in the Several State Conventions on the Adoption of the Federal Constitution*, vol. 1 (Philadelphia: Published under the Sanction of Congress, 1836–1859; reprint Salem, NH: Ayer, 1987), 492–493.

41. Friedman, *History of American Law*, 203.

42. Charles A. Beard, *An Economic Interpretation of the Constitution of the United States* (New York: Macmillan, 1913), 179. See also Crump, "The Economic Purpose of the Contract Clause," 692–695, arguing that adoption of the contract clause was animated by economic concerns; Paul G. Kauper, "What Is a 'Contract' under the Contracts Clause of the Federal Constitution?," *Michigan Law Review* 31 (1932): 187, 193: "The framers of the Constitution were practical-minded men, most of them of the creditor class; one of their chief objects in establishing a federal government and placing limitations on state action was to insure stability in commercial and mercantile transactions by providing against legislative interference dictated by whim, caprice, or class prejudice."

43. *New Hampshire Spy*, November 3, 1787.

44. *Federalist* No. 7 (Hamilton).

45. Elliot, *Debates*, vol. 4, 333–336.

46. Elliot, *Debates*, vol. 2, 486.

47. David Ramsay, *An Address to the Freeman of South Carolina on the Federal Constitution* (Charleston, SC: 1788), in Paul Leicester Ford, ed., *Pamphlets on the Constitution of the United States* (Brooklyn, NY: 1888; reprint, New York: DaCapo Press, 1968), 379–380.

48. Elliot, *Debates*, vol. 4, 157.

49. *Federalist* No. 44 (Madison).

50. Steven R. Boyd, "The Contract Clause and the Evolution of American Federalism, 1789–1815," *William and Mary Quarterly* 44 (1987): 531.

51. James Madison to Thomas Jefferson, October 17, 1788, in *The Papers of James Madison*, vol. 11, ed. Robert A. Rutland and Charles F. Hobson (Charlottesville: University Press of Virginia, 1977), 297, attributing much of the opposition to the proposed Constitution to the articles on paper money and contracts.

52. Agrippa Letter 16, February 5, 1788 (James Winthrop), in *The Essential Antifederalist*, 2nd ed., ed. W. B. Allen and Gordon Lloyd (Lanham, MD: Rowman and Littlefield, 2002), 56.

53. Brutus, Letter 14, March 6, 1788, in *The Debate on the Constitution*, pt. 2: *Debates in the Press and in Private Correspondence*, ed. Bernard Bailyn (New York: Library of America Press, 1993), 265.

54. Luther Martin, "Genuine Information," November 29, 1787, in *Records of the Federal Convention of 1787*, rev. ed., vol. 3, ed. Max Farrand (New Haven, CT: Yale University Press, 1937), 214–215.

55. Edward S. Corwin, *John Marshall and the Constitution: A Chronicle of the Supreme Court* (New Haven, CT: Yale University Press, 1919), 167–168.

56. Douglas W. Kmiec and John O. McGinnis, "The Contract Clause: A Return to the Original Understanding," *Hastings Constitutional Law Quarterly* 14 (1987): 533–534. The Supreme Court has repeatedly rejected the argument that the contract clause was aimed solely at debt-relief laws. See Sturges v. Crowninshield, 17 U.S. 122, 205–206 (1819) (Marshall, C.J.): "The Convention appears to have intended to establish a great principle, that contracts should be inviolable"; Allied Structural Steel Co. v. Spannaus, 438 U.S. 234, 245n.16 (1978) (Stewart, J.): "The even narrower view that the clause is limited in its application to state laws relieving debtors of obligations to their creditors is . . . completely at odds with this Court's decisions."

57. See, for example, Clement H. Hill, "The *Dartmouth College* Case," *American Law Review* 8 (1874): 189, 196. For the shift in scholarly interpretation of the contract clause during the 1870s and 1880s as well as increased criticism of Marshall's view that public agreements were covered, see Robert L. Clinton, "The Obligation Clause of the United States Constitution: Public and/or Private Contracts," *University of Arkansas at Little Rock Journal* 11 (1988): 353–357.

58. Hunting, *Obligation of Contracts Clause*, 120.

59. Benjamin F. Wright, *The Contract Clause of the Constitution* (Cambridge, MA: Harvard University Press, 1938), 15, 16.

60. Wallace Mendelson, "B. F. Wright on the Contract Clause: A Progressive Misreading of the Marshall-Taney Era," *Western Political Quarterly* 38 (1985): 263.

61. See, for example, Thomas W. Merrill, "Public Contracts, Private Contracts, and the Transformation of the Constitutional Order," *Case Western Reserve Law Review* 37 (1987): 600: "A fairly strong case can be made that . . . the clause was *not* thought to impose a general duty on state governments to honor their own obligations"; Bruchey, "Concern for the Security of Property Rights," 1144. See also Charles F. Hobson, *The Great Chief Justice: John Marshall and the Rule of Law* (Lawrence: University Press of Kansas, 1996), 73: "The prevailing view of Marshall's contract clause jurisprudence is that he substantially enlarged the meaning of the clause beyond the intention of the framers."

62. Mendelson, "B. F. Wright on the Contract Clause," 265.

63. Clinton, "Obligation Clause," 345.

64. Elliot, *Debates*, vol. 4, 191.

65. Ibid., 334.

66. Elliot, *Debates*, vol. 3, 474.

67. Ibid., 478.

68. Hunting, *Obligation of Contracts Clause*, 113: "It will be noticed that Randolph nowhere denies Henry's contention that the 'contracts clause' refers to the contracts of States as well as to those between individuals."

69. *Federalist* No. 44 (Madison).

70. Boyd, "Contract Clause," 535. For the legislative debates, see *City Gazette*,

or the Daily Advertiser (Charleston, SC), October 24, 1788, October 27, 1788, and October 28, 1788.

71. Owings v. Speed, 18 U.S. 420 (1820) (Marshall, C.J.), holding that the Constitution did not take effect until March 1789 and that the contract clause did not apply to state law enacted before that date.

72. Patrick T. Conley, Jr., "The First Judicial Review of State Legislation: An Analysis of the Rhode Island Case of *Champion and Dickason v. Casey* (1792)," in *Liberty and Justice: A History of Law and Lawyers in Rhode Island, 1636–1998,* ed. Patrick T. Conley, Jr. (Providence: Rhode Island Publication Society, 1998), 218–223; D. Kurt Graham, *To Bring Law Home: The Federal Judiciary in Early National Rhode Island* (DeKalb: Northern Illinois University Press, 2010), 128–129.

73. US *Chronicle,* June 14, 1792. See also Providence, RI, *Gazette,* June 16, 1792. Curiously, it appears that no judgment was entered at the June term of the circuit court. At the November term Justice James Wilson, Justice James Iredell, and District Judge Henry Marchant adopted the conclusions of the previous panel and entered final judgment. Conley, *Liberty and Justice,* 222.

74. Chisholm v. Georgia, 2 U.S. 419 (1793).

75. For the controversy aroused by the *Chisholm* decision, see Alfred H. Kelly, Winfred A. Harbison, and Herman Belz, *The American Constitution: Its Origins and Development,* 7th ed. (New York: Norton, 1991); Melvin I. Urofsky and Paul Finkelman, *A March of Liberty: A Constitutional History of the United States,* 3rd ed. (New York: Oxford University Press, 2011).

76. *Chisholm,* at 465. Justice William Cushing, concurring, mentioned that the contract clause and other constitutional provisions designed "to establish some fundamental uniform principles of justice" curtailed state sovereignty. Ibid., at 468.

77. Vanhorne's Lessee v. Dorrance, 2 U.S. 304 (Cir. Ct. Penn. 1795).

78. See generally Christopher Collier, "Article III, Section 2, and the Bloody Background of *Van Horne's Lessee v. Dorrance,*" in *Constitution Day,* ed. Patrick T. Conley, Jr. (Providence: Rhode Island Publications Society, 2010), 157–181; Julian P. Boyd, "Connecticut's Experiment in Expansion: The Susquehanna Company, 1753–1803," *Journal of Economic and Business History* 4 (1931–1932): 38.

79. See Daniel A. Degnan, "William Paterson: Small States' Nationalist," in *Seriatim: The Supreme Court before John Marshall,* ed. Scott Douglas Gerber (New York: New York University Press, 1998); Julian P. Boyd, "William Paterson: Forerunner of John Marshall," in *The Lives of Eighteen from Princeton,* ed. Willard Thorp (Princeton, NJ: Princeton University Press, 1946), 1–23; Leonard Boyne Rosenberg, "The Political Thought of William Paterson," PhD diss., New York, New School for Social Research, 1967.

80. *Vanhorne's Lessee,* at 320.

81. The Paterson jury charge was printed in pamphlet form and widely circulated in 1796, two years before its publication by Alexander Dallas in volume 2 of the US *Reports.* See *The Charge of Judge Paterson to the Jury in the Case of* Vanhorne's Lessee against Dorrance (Philadelphia, 1796).

82. For the background of the Georgia land controversy and the persistent efforts of the Yazoo claimants to secure compensation, see C. Peter Magrath, *Yazoo:*

Law and Politics in the New Republic—The Case of Fletcher v. Peck (Providence, RI: Brown University Press, 1966), 1–49.

83. Julius Gobel, Jr., and Joseph H. Smith, eds., *The Law Practice of Alexander Hamilton*, vol. 4 (New York: Columbia University Press, 1980), 382–384.

84. Ibid., 430–431.

85. Ibid., 384.

86. Robert Goodloe Harper, "The Yazoo Question" (August 3, 1796), *American Law Journal* 5 (1814): 395.

87. Calder v. Bull, 3 U.S. 386, 388 (1798).

88. Derby v. Blake (1799); reprint 226 Mass. 618–625.

89. Peter J. Coleman, *Debtors and Creditors in America: Insolvency, Imprisonment for Debt, and Bankruptcy, 1607–1900* (Madison: State Historical Society of Wisconsin, 1974), 286: "By the end of the eighteenth century, imprisonment for debt commonly lasted only until the defaulter qualified for relief."

90. Joseph Jones to James Madison, December 18, 1787, in *The Papers of James Madison*, vol. 10, ed. Robert A. Rutland and Charles F. Hobson (1977), 329–330.

91. Boyd, "Contract Clause," 548.

92. James Willard Hurst, *Law and Markets in United States History: Different Modes of Bargaining among Interests* (Madison: University of Wisconsin Press, 1982), 12.

93. James W. Ely, Jr., *The Guardian of Every Other Right: A Constitutional History of Property Rights*, 3rd ed. (New York: Oxford University Press, 2008), 63–67.

CHAPTER 2. THE ERA OF JOHN MARSHALL, 1801–1835

1. Steven R. Boyd, "The Contract Clause and the Evolution of American Federalism, 1789–1815," *William and Mary Quarterly* 44 (1987): 540–548.

2. Ex parte Grimball, Cases in the Superior Courts in the State of Georgia 153, 154–158 (1808).

3. An Act to Alleviate the Condition of Debtors and to Afford Them Temporary Relief, Laws of Georgia, May 23, 1808. The Georgia legislature passed another stay law in December of 1808, An Act to Alleviate the Condition of Debtors, Laws of Georgia, December 21, 1808.

4. Grimball v. Ross, Cases in Superior Court, 175, 181 (1808).

5. Gordon S. Wood, "The Origins of Vested Rights in the Early Republic," *Virginia Law Review* 85 (1999): 1421, 1440–1443.

6. Wales v. Stetson, 2 Mass. 143, 146 (1806).

7. The New York Council of Revision was a legal body created by the New York Constitution of 1777 to review all new laws passed by the legislature. Composed of the governor and members of the judiciary, the council could object to proposed legislation and return it to the legislature. The lawmakers could reenact the law by a two-thirds vote in each house. The council was abolished by the New York Constitution of 1821.

8. Alfred B. Street, *The Council of Revision of the State of New York* (Albany, NY: William Gould, 1859), 344–345. See John Theodore Horton, *James Kent: A Study in Conservatism, 1763–1847* (New York: D. Appleton-Century, 1939; reprint DaCapo Press, 1969), 236–237, observing that Kent "regarded a charter as a contract the obligation of which the federal constitution prohibited the state from impairing."

9. As quoted in John W. Cadman, Jr., *The Corporation in New Jersey: Business and Politics, 1791–1875* (Cambridge, MA: Harvard University Press, 1949), 376.

10. Ibid., 379.

11. Fletcher v. Peck, 10 U.S. 87 (1810). For a helpful treatment of this case, see C. Peter Magrath, *Yazoo: Law and Politics in the New Republic—the Case of* Fletcher v. Peck (Providence, RI: Brown University Press, 1966).

12. *Fletcher,* at 136–139.

13. Ibid., at 137.

14. Huidekoper's Lessees v. Douglass, 7 U.S. 1, 70 (1805) (Marshall, C.J.).

15. *Fletcher,* at 138.

16. Benjamin F. Wright, *The Contract Clause of the Constitution* (Cambridge, MA: Harvard University Press, 1938), 31.

17. Suzanna Sherry, "The Founders' Unwritten Constitution," *University of Chicago Law Review* 54 (1987): 1127, 1171.

18. See Warren B. Hunting, *The Obligation of Contracts Clause of the United States* (Baltimore, MD: Johns Hopkins University Press, 1919), 24–25, asserting that Marshall's reading of the contract clause was grounded in natural law theory.

19. For Johnson's opinion in *Fletcher,* see Donald G. Morgan, *Justice William Johnson: The First Dissenter* (Columbia: University of South Carolina Press, 1954), 210–214.

20. *Fletcher,* at 143.

21. Ibid., at 144.

22. Ibid., at 145.

23. Morgan, *Justice William Johnson,* 211.

24. Magrath, *Yazoo,* 114. Based on a survey of leading newspapers, Magrath concluded that *Fletcher* actually aroused "little excitement." Ibid., 225n.13.

25. William E. Nelson, "The Eighteenth-Century Background of John Marshall's Constitutional Jurisprudence," *Michigan Law Review* 76 (1978): 943.

26. New Jersey v. Wilson, 11 U.S. 164 (1812).

27. Ibid., at 167.

28. For criticism of Marshall's reasoning in *Wilson,* see R. Kent Newmyer, *John Marshall and the Heroic Age of the Supreme Court* (Baton Rouge: Louisiana State University Press, 2001), 236–238.

29. Dartmouth College v. Woodward, 17 U.S. 518 (1819).

30. There is a vast literature dealing with the *Dartmouth College* case. See, for example, Francis N. Stites, *Private Interest and Public Gain: The* Dartmouth College *Case, 1819* (Amherst: University of Massachusetts Press, 1972); Charles F. Hobson, *The Great Chief Justice: John Marshall and the Rule of Law* (Lawrence: University Press of Kansas, 1996), 88–95; Newmyer, *John Marshall,* 244–253; Hunting, *Obligation of Contracts Clause,* 58–110; Bruce A. Campbell, "*Dartmouth College* as a Civil Liberties Case: The Formation of Constitutional Policy," *Kentucky Law Review* 70 (1982): 643–706.

31. Trustees of Dartmouth College v. Woodward, 1 N.H. 111, 132 (1816).

32. Ibid., at 120, expressing doubt that the legislature possessed power "to interfere in the concerns of private corporations."

33. *Dartmouth College*, at 628.

34. Ibid., at 631–640. In contrast, the Supreme Court of Alabama found that the University of Alabama was a governmental agency supported by public funds and that the *Dartmouth College* doctrine was inapplicable. *Trustees of the University of Alabama v. Winston*, 5 Stewart and Porter's Reports 17, 24–25 (Ala. 1833).

35. *Dartmouth College*, at 642–650.

36. Stephen A. Siegel, "Understanding the Nineteenth-Century Contract Clause: The Role of the Property-Privilege Distinction and 'Takings' Clause Jurisprudence," *Southern California Law Review* 60 (1986): 1, 31.

37. See Newmyer, *John Marshall*, 248: "Whether Marshall planned it this way is unknown."

38. Bruce A. Campbell, "John Marshall, the Virginia Political Economy, and the *Dartmouth College* Decision," *American Journal of Legal History* 19 (1975): 40–41.

39. *Dartmouth College*, at 669.

40. Ibid., at 699.

41. See R. Kent Newmyer, *Supreme Court Justice Joseph Story: Statesman of the Old Republic* (Chapel Hill: University of North Carolina Press, 1985), 131–135, discussing the relationship between Story's concurring opinion and growth of business corporations.

42. Charles Warren, *The Supreme Court in United States History*, rev. ed., vol. 1 (Boston: Little, Brown, 1926), 487. See also Newmyer, *John Marshall*, 247: "For the remainder of the nineteenth century, the college decision was a potent legal and ideological weapon for corporations who sought to defeat regulation and establish ideological primacy of laissez-faire capitalism."

43. Herbert A. Johnson, *The Chief Justiceship of John Marshall, 1801–1835* (Columbia: University of South Carolina Press, 1997), 176.

44. Longwood v. President, Directors of Planter's and Merchant's Bank, Minor's Repts.

45. *Dartmouth College*, at 675, 712.

46. Argus of Western America, February 26, 1819, as quoted in Warren, *Supreme Court in United States History*, vol. 1, 490.

47. Wright, *Contract Clause of the Constitution*, 58–60; Lawrence M. Friedman, *A History of American Law*, 3rd ed. (New York: Touchstone, 2005), 137; Cadman, *Corporation in New Jersey*, 380–381, noting that by the mid-1830s the New Jersey legislature established a policy of making corporate charters subject to amendment; Hunting, *Obligation of Contracts Clause*, 103: "The effect of the ruling in the *College* case is now and has for some time been very largely nullified by the reservation, in the grants of corporate franchises, of the right to alter, amend, or repeal them, to which the vast majority of existing charters are, without doubt, subject." See also Newmyer, *Justice Joseph Story*, 149–150, noting that Story never questioned the authority of states to regulate corporations.

48. Michael J. Klarman, "How Great Were the 'Great' Marshall Court Decisions?," *Virginia Law Review* 87 (2001): 1147.

49. An Act Concerning the Erection of the District of Kentucky into an Independent State, December 18, 1789, Code of Virginia 27–29 (2010).

50. Paul W. Gates, "Tenants of the Log Cabin," *Mississippi Valley Historical Review* 49 (1962): 3–14.

51. Green v. Biddle, 21 U.S. 1 (1821, 1823). Regarding *Green*, see Johnson, *Chief Justiceship of John Marshall*, 78–79, 187–189.

52. *Green*, at 15–16. For Story's thinking about the controversy over land titles in Kentucky and the contract clause, see Newmyer, *Justice Joseph Story*, 208.

53. *Green*, at 92.

54. James R. Stoner, Jr., "Heir Apparent: Bushrod Washington and Federal Justice in the Early Republic," in *Seriatim: The Supreme Court before John Marshall*, ed. Scott Douglas Gerber (New York: New York University Press, 1998), 337.

55. Warren, *Supreme Court in United States History*, 640–641.

56. *Green*, at 94–108. See Morgan, *Justice William Johnson*, 217–219.

57. Gates, "Tenants of the Log Cabins," 24–31; Klarman, "How Great Were the 'Great' Marshall Court Opinions?," 1152.

58. Hawkins v. Barney's Lessee, 30 U.S. 457 (1831) (Johnson, J.).

59. Johnson, *Chief Justiceship of John Marshall*, 189. But see Wright, *Contract Clause of the Constitution*, 47, describing *Green* as "perhaps the most far-fetched application, if, as it turned out, the least important, extension of the contract clause."

60. Allen v. McKeen, 1 Fed. Cases 489 (C.C.D. Me. 1833).

61. Osborne v. Humphrey, 7 Conn. 335 (1829).

62. Derby Turnpike Company v. Parks, 10 Conn. 521 (1835).

63. Proprietors of the Piscataqua Bridge v. New Hampshire Bridge, 7 N.H. 35, 68 (1834).

64. Dyer v. Tuscaloosa Bridge Company, 2 Port. (Ala.) 296 (1835).

65. Charles Warren, *Bankruptcy in United States History* (Cambridge, MA: Harvard University Press, 1935), 19–21.

66. Boyd, "Contract Clause," 538–541.

67. Jones v. Crittenden, 4 N.C. 55 (1814).

68. Ibid., at 58–59.

69. Peter J. Coleman, *Debtors and Creditors in American History: Insolvency, Imprisonment for Debt, and Bankruptcy, 1607–1900* (Madison: State Historical Society of Wisconsin, 1974), 225.

70. Samuel E. Sewall, "On a National Bankruptcy Law," *American Jurist* 1 (1829): 35, 39–40.

71. *Ogden*, at 302 (Story, J., dissenting): "Whether this is technically a bankrupt or an insolvent law, is of little importance."

72. Golden v. Prince, 10 Fed. Cases 542, 544 (Cir. Ct. Pa. 1814).

73. Adams v. Storey, 1 Fed. Cases 141, 144 (Cir. Ct. New York 1817).

74. Ibid., at 144–148.

75. Sturges v. Crowninshield, 17 U.S. 122 (1819). The court reporter misspelled the party's name, Josiah Sturgis, as "Sturges" on the official record. Regarding *Sturges*, see Hobson, *Great Chief Justice*, 95–100; Coleman, *Debtors and Creditors*, 32–33.

76. *Sturges*, at 197.

77. Ibid., at 206.

78. Ibid., at 200.

79. James Kent, *Commentaries on American Law*, 5th ed., vol. 1 (New York: Printed for the Author, 1844), 455. See also Theodore Sedgwick, *A Treatise on the Rules Which Govern Statutory and Constitutional Law* (New York: John Voorhies, 1857), 643–644, noting that Marshall's language in *Sturges* "has been repeatedly regretted and often criticized."

80. McMillan v. McNeill, 17 U.S. 209, 211 (1819).

81. Townsend v. Townsend, 7 Tenn. 1 (1821).

82. Ibid., at 13–14.

83. Blair v. Williams, 14 Ky. 34, 36–46 (1823).

84. Bank of United States v. Frederickson, 2 Fed. Cases 744 (Cir. Ct. Pa. 1821).

85. Baily v. Gentry, 1 Mo. 165 (1822).

86. Ibid., at 171.

87. Blanchard v. Russell, 13 Mass. 1, 16 (1816).

88. Smith v. Parsons, 1 Ohio 236, 241–242 (1822): state insolvency law could not interfere with contracts then in existence but could regulate future contracts.

89. Ogden v. Saunders, 25 U.S. 213 (1827).

90. Ibid., at 257.

91. Ibid., at 323.

92. Ibid., at 327.

93. Ibid., at 284.

94. See also *Green*, at 84 (Washington, J.): "The objection to a law, on the ground of its impairing the obligation of a contract, can never depend upon the extent of the change which the law effects upon it. Any deviation from its terms, by postponing, or accelerating, the period of performance which it prescribes, imposing conditions not expressed in the contract, or dispensing with the performance of those which are, however minute, or apparently immaterial, in their effect upon the contract of the parties, impairs its obligation."

95. Ibid., at 327.

96. See Lee v. Gamble, 15 Fed. Cases 157 (Cir. Ct. D.C. 1828) (quoting Trimble statement); Sedgwick, *Treatise on the Rules Which Govern Statutory and Constitutional Law*, 644 (quoting Trimble).

97. *Ogden*, at 301–302 (Thompson, J.): "The law in question is nothing more than taking away all remedy, and it be the whole, or some material part thereof, would seem to differ in degree only, and not in principle; and if to have a retrospective operation, might well be considered as falling within the spirit and policy of the prohibition."

98. Joseph Story, *Commentaries on the Constitution of the United States* (Boston: Hilliard, Gray, 1833; reprint Durham, NC: Carolina Academic Press, 1987), Sec. 703.

99. *Ogden*, at 345.

100. Ibid., at 346.

101. Ibid., at 351.

102. Ibid., at 343. Regarding Marshall's dissenting opinion in *Ogden*, see Hobson, *Great Chief Justice*, 100–107; Johnson, *Chief Justiceship of John Marshall*, 184–187;

Wright, *Contract Clause,* 50–52; Siegel, "Understanding the Nineteenth-Century Contract Clause," 14–20.

103. Marshall's concerns were misplaced. State reserve clauses were confined to corporate charters, and no state ever adopted such a provision pertaining to other types of agreements. Siegel, "Understanding the Nineteenth Century Contract Clause," 19.

104. *Ogden,* at 357. Richard A. Epstein has argued that Marshall was correct and that the contract clause should be construed to prevent future interference with contractual arrangements. "Toward a Revitalization of the Contract Clause," *University of Chicago Law Review* 51 (1984): 703, 723–730. I concur, however, with most scholars, that the provision was intended to shield existing contracts from retrospective legislation. See, for example, Douglas W. Kmiec and John O. McGinnis, "The Contract Clause: A Return to the Original Understanding," *Hastings Constitutional Law Quarterly* 14 (1987): 525, 538, 557–559, maintaining that the majority justices in *Ogden* were correct.

105. Johnson, *Chief Justiceship of John Marshall,* 187.

106. Klarman, "How Great Were the 'Great' Marshall Court Decisions?," 1149–1150.

107. Bumgardner v. Circuit Court of Howard County, 4 Mo. 50 (1835).

108. *Dartmouth College,* at 629.

109. James Kent, *Commentaries on American Law,* vol. 2 (New York: O. Halsted, 1827–1828), 89.

110. Starr v. Pease, 8 Conn. 541, 545–546 (1831)

111. *Sturges,* at 207. Marshall made clear, however, that a retroactive application of a law setting the legal rate of interest to contracts already made would impair the obligation of contract.

112. Coleman, *Debtors and Creditors,* 249–268.

113. Holmes v. Lansing, 3 Johns Cases 73, 75 (N.Y. 1802).

114. *Sturges,* at 201.

115. Mason v. Haile, 25 U.S. 370, 378 (1827).

116. Beers v. Haughton, 34 U.S. 329, 359 (1835).

117. See Call v. Hagger, 8 Mass. 423 (1812), distinguishing statutes of limitations from a law preventing any legal remedy upon a contract.

118. *Sturges,* at 207.

119. Barker v. Jackson, 2 F. Cases 811 (Cir. Ct. D.N.Y. 1826); Sedgwick, *Treatise on the Rules Which Govern Statutory and Constitutional Law,* 690–691. During the nineteenth century courts continued to strike down changes in statutes of limitations that failed to afford claimants a reasonable time within which to bring an action. Berry and Johnson v. Ransdall, 61 Ky. 292 (1863).

120. Goszler v. Corporation of Georgetown, 19 U.S. 593 (1821).

121. Ibid., at 597–598.

122. Jackson v. Lamphire, 28 U.S. 280, 290 (1830) (Baldwin, J.). Subsequently the Supreme Court of California relied on *Jackson* and rejected a contract clause challenge to a conveyance recording act. Stafford v. Lick, 7 Cal. 479, 487–488 (1857).

123. Satterlee v. Matthewson, 27 U.S. 380 (1829); Watson v. Mercer, 33 U.S. 88 (1834).

124. Providence Bank v. Billings, 29 U.S. 514 (1830).

125. Ibid., at 561.

126. Ibid., at 563.

127. Coates v. Mayor, Alderman, and Commonalty of the City of New York, 7 Cow. 585 (N.Y. Sup. Ct. 1827).

128. Ibid., at 606.

129. Proprietors of Piscataqua Bridge v. New Hampshire Bridge, 7 N.H. 35, 68–70.

130. West River Bridge Company v. Dix, 47 U.S. 507 (1848). See Chapter 3 for a discussion of eminent domain and the contract clause.

131. John Phillip Reid, *Constitutional History of the American Revolution: The Authority of Rights* (Madison: University of Wisconsin Press, 1986), 90–91: "Natural law was equated with British constitutional law and with English common law."

132. Suzanna Sherry, "The Ninth Amendment: Righting an Unwritten Constitution," *Chicago-Kent Law Review* 64 (1988): 1001, 1006–1007.

133. Suzanna Sherry, "Natural Law in the States," *University of Cincinnati Law Review* 61 (1992): 171; J. A. C. Grant, "The 'Higher Law' Background of the Law of Eminent Domain," *Wisconsin Law Review* 6 (1930–1931): 7, 71–81; James W. Ely, Jr., "'To Pursue Any Lawful Trade or Avocation': The Evolution of Unenumerated Economic Rights in the Nineteenth Century," *University of Pennsylvania Journal of Constitutional Law* 8 (2006): 917, 921–926. See also Kent, *Commentaries on American Law*, vol. 2, 1: "The absolute rights of individuals may be resolved into the right of personal security, the right of personal liberty, and the right to acquire and enjoy property. These rights have been justly considered and frequently declared, by the people of this country, to be natural, inherent, and inalienable."

134. Nelson, "Eighteenth-Century Background," 932.

135. Morgan, *Justice William Johnson*, 221–224, 226–228.

136. See Stephen A. Siegel, "*Lochner*-Era Jurisprudence and the American Constitutional Tradition," *North Carolina Law Review* 70 (1991): 2, 44–50, concluding that Marshall's opinion in *Fletcher* ultimately rested on the contract clause rather than natural law.

137. Enfield Bridge Company v. Connecticut River Company, 7 Conn. 28, 37–38 (1828). See also Jones v. Crittenden, 4 N.C. 55, 57 (1814), insisting that "first principles of justice" dictate that the legislature cannot cancel a contract without consent of parties, and then invoking the contract clause.

138. Terrett v. Taylor, 13 U.S. 43 (1815).

139. For the background of this litigation, see Sarah Barringer Gordon, "The Landscape of Faith: Religious Property and Confiscation in the Early Republic," in *Making Legal History: Essays in Honor of William E. Nelson*, ed. Daniel J. Hulsebosch and R. B. Bernstein (New York: New York University Press, 2013), 23–27.

140. Ibid., 50.

141. Ibid., 52.

142. Johnson, *Chief Justiceship of John Marshall*, 174; Newmyer, *John Marshall*, 239–240; Warren, *Supreme Court in United States History*, 476n.1; Siegel, "*Lochner*-Era Jurisprudence," 47n.256.

143. G. Edward White, *History of the Supreme Court of the United States: The Marshall Court and Cultural Change, 1815–1835* (New York: Macmillan, 1988), 608.

144. Wright, *Contract Clause*, 38.

145. Consequently, Story's opinion had little significance outside the District of Columbia. Gordon, "Landscape of Faith," 27.

146. Sherry, "Founders' Unwritten Constitution," 1175. Well after his opinion in *Terrett*, Story continued to express the view that, independent of the Constitution, "the nature of republican and free governments" imposed some restraint on legislative power. Story, *Commentaries on the Constitution*, sec. 712.

147. Sherry, "Founders' Unwritten Constitution," 1167–1177.

148. Newmyer, *John Marshall*, 240.

CHAPTER 3. THE TANEY ERA

1. Alfred H. Kelly, Winfred A. Harbison, and Herman Belz, *The American Constitution: Its Origins and Development*, 7th ed., vol. 1 (New York: Norton, 1991), 200–221.

2. Daniel Walker Howe, *What God Hath Wrought: The Transformation of America, 1815–1848* (New York: Oxford University Press, 2007), 440–441.

3. R. Kent Newmyer, *Supreme Court Justice Joseph Story: Statesman of the Old Republic* (Chapel Hill: University of North Carolina Press, 1985), 220–221.

4. Howe, *What God Hath Wrought*, 443. See also Timothy S. Huebner, *The Taney Court: Justices, Rulings, and Legacy* (Santa Barbara, CA: ABC-CLIO, 2003), 37–38, asserting that Taney demonstrated a "pragmatic commitment to property rights and economic progress" and that his "view of the Contract Clause proved no threat to commercial interests."

5. Benjamin F. Wright, *The Contract Clause of the Constitution* (Cambridge, MA: Harvard University Press, 1938), 62.

6. See generally Morton J. Horwitz, *The Transformation of American Law, 1780–1860* (Cambridge, MA: Harvard University Press, 1977), 173–210.

7. Timothy Walker, *Introduction to American Law* (Philadelphia: Nicklin and Johnson, 1837; reprint New York: DaCapo Press, 1972), 391.

8. Theophilus Parsons, *The Law of Contracts*, 3rd ed., vol. 1 (Boston: Little, Brown, 1857), 3.

9. James Willard Hurst, *Law and the Conditions of Freedom in the Nineteenth-Century United States* (Madison: University of Wisconsin Press, 1956), 18.

10. Bronson v. Kinzie, 42 U.S. 311, 318 (1843).

11. Cochran v. Van Surlay, 20 Wend. 365, 384 (Court of Errors 1820) (Senator Verplanck).

12. State v. County Court of Crittenden County, 19 Ark. 360, 364 (1858). See also Heyward v. Judd, 4 Minn. 483, 498–499 (1860) (Flandran, J., concurring): "There is no constitutional guaranty that is more valuable to the citizen than that which secures to him the inviolability of his contract rights. There is none more liable to legislative encroachment consequent upon financial fluctuations and popular excitements."

13. Martin v. Somerville Water Power Co., 15 F. Cases 903, 906 (Cir. Ct. D. N.J. 1856).

14. Curran v. State of Arkansas, 56 U.S. 304, 319 (1853) (Curtis, J.).

15. Western Savings Fund Society v. City of Philadelphia, 31 Pa. 175, 181–182 (1858). The Kentucky Court of Appeals also equated the obligation of a contract with the remedy. See Berry and Johnson v. Randall, 61 Ky. 292, 294 (1863): "It is settled that the legal obligation of a contract consists in the remedy given by law to enforce its performance, or to make compensation for the failure to perform it."

16. Theodore Sedgwick, *A Treatise on the Rules Which Govern Statutory and Constitutional Law* (New York: John Voorhies, 1857), 652.

17. *Bronson,* at 315–316.

18. Ibid., at 317.

19. Planters' Bank of Mississippi v. Sharp, 47 U.S. 301, 327 (1848). See also Sedgwick, *Treatise on the Rules Which Govern Statutory and Constitutional Law,* 652–653: "Take away the whole remedy, and it is admitted the contract is gone."

20. *Curran*, at 319.

21. Von Baumbach v. Bade, 9 Wis. 510, 530 (1859).

22. *Western Savings Fund Society*, at 182.

23. New Jersey Constitution, Article IV, sec. vii, para. 3.

24. *Proceedings of the New Jersey State Constitutional Convention of 1844* (New Jersey Writers Project of the Works Progress Administration, 1942), 336.

25. Sedgwick, *Treatise on the Rules Which Govern Statutory and Constitutional Law*, 696–697. See also James Kent, *Commentaries on American Law*, 6th ed., vol. 1 (New York: William Kent, 1848), 419, asserting that the New Jersey clause "is a wise provision, giving additional and material securities to the sanctity and efficacy of contracts."

26. Martin v. Somerville Water Power Co., 16 Fed. Cases 903 (Cir. Ct. N.J. 1856) (Grier, J.).

27. Rader v. Southeasterly Road District, 36 N.J.L. 273, 278 (1873).

28. Woodruff v. Trapnall, 51 U.S. 190, 207 (1851).

29. Winter v. Jones, 10 Ga. 190, 196 (1851). See also Trustees of Bishop's Fund v. Rider, 18 Conn. 87 (1839) (same result); O'Donnell v. Bailey, 21 Miss. 386, 388 (1852) (same result).

30. Butler v. Pennsylvania, 51 U.S. 402, 416–417 (1851) (Daniel, J.).

31. Sedgwick, *Treatise on the Rules Which Govern Statutory and Constitutional Law*, 619, 633.

32. *Butler*, at 416.

33. Ohio Life Insurance and Trust Co. v. Debolt, 57 U.S. 416, 433 (1854).

34. Jefferson Branch Bank v. Skelly, 66 U.S. 436, 443 (1862). See also Bridge Proprietors v. Hoboken Company, 68 U.S. 116, 145 (1864) (Miller, J.), affirming the authority of the Supreme Court to decide independently of state courts whether the legislative act amounted to a contract and finding that the act authorizing construction of a bridge was a contract.

35. Charles River Bridge v. Warren Bridge, 36 U.S. 420 (1837).

36. Stanley I. Kutler, *Privilege and Creative Destruction: The* Charles River Bridge *Case* (Philadelphia, PA: J. B. Lippincott, 1971), 18–53.

37. *Charles River Bridge*, at 548.

38. Ibid., at 549.

39. Ibid., at 552–553.

40. Kutler, *Privilege and Creative Destruction*, 93.

41. *Charles River Bridge*, at 608.

42. Ibid., at 614.

43. Ibid., at 638. For Story's opinion in *Charles River Bridge*, see Newmyer, *Supreme Court Justice Joseph Story*, 224–235. At least one state court seemingly adopted Story's position. At issue in Red River Bridge Company v. Mayor and Alderman of Clarksville, 33 Tenn. 176 (1853) was legislation authorizing the town to erect a free bridge near an existing toll bridge. The Supreme Court of Tennessee, assuming that the original charter granted an exclusive privilege to the toll bridge company, held that the construction of a free bridge would destroy the value of the toll bridge franchise and insisted that this could only be done upon the payment of just compensation.

44. Herbert Hovenkamp, *Enterprise and American Law, 1836–1937* (Cambridge, MA: Harvard University Press, 1991), 112.

45. Sedgwick, *Treatise on . . . Statutory and Constitutional Law*, 627. James Kent, on the other hand, was intensely critical of *Charles River Bridge* and accused the Court of destroying "the sanctity of contracts." James Kent to Joseph Story, June 23, 1837, as quoted in John T. Horton, *James Kent: A Study in Conservatism, 1763–1847* (New York: D. Appleton-Century, 1939; reprint New York: DaCapo Press, 1969), 294.

46. *Debolt*, at 416, 435–436.

47. Ibid., at 442.

48. John P. Frank, *Justice Daniel Dissenting: A Biography of Peter V. Daniel, 1784–1860* (Cambridge, MA: Harvard University Press, 1964), 201.

49. Mills v. St. Clair County, 49 U.S. 569 (1850); Fanning v. Gregoire, 57 U.S. 524 (1854).

50. Richmond, Fredericksburg and Potomac Railroad Company v. Louisa Railroad Company, 54 U.S. 71 (1852).

51. Ibid., at 87 (Curtis, J., dissenting).

52. Bridge Proprietors v. Hoboken Company, 68 U.S. 116 (1864).

53. Ibid., at 146–147.

54. Hartford Bridge Company v. Union Ferry Company, 29 Conn. 210, 223 (1860).

55. Shorter v. Smith, 9 Ga. 517, 524 (1851).

56. Ibid., at 528. See Timothy S. Huebner, *The Southern Judicial Tradition: State Judges and Sectional Distinctiveness, 1790–1890* (Athens: University of Georgia Press, 1999), 83–85, stressing Lumpkin's commitment to economic competition and aversion to implied monopoly privilege.

57. For example, see Illinois and Michigan Canal v. Chicago and Rock Island Railroad Co., 14 Ill. 315 (1853), holding that the canal charter conferred no exclusive right in line of travel; Thompson v. New York and Harlem Rail Road Co., 3 Sand. Ch. 625 (N.Y. 1846), holding that the charter of the toll bridge conferred no exclusive rights and that the charter was not impaired by subsequent law authorizing construction of a railroad bridge near the toll bridge; Mohawk Bridge Co. v. Utica and Schenectady Railroad Co., 6 Paige Ch. 554 (N.Y. 1837), holding that the bridge

company grant did not create a bar to the railroad bridge, which was not a toll bridge and thus not within the meaning of the first grant; Washington and Baltimore Turnpike Road v. Baltimore and Ohio Railroad, 10 G. and J. 392 (Md. 1839), holding that the railroad did not impair the contractual rights of the turnpike by diverting traffic.

58. Tuckahoe Canal Company v. Tuckahoe and James River Rail Road Company, 38 Va. 42, 70–75 (1840).

59. Shorter v. Smith, 9 Ga. 517 (1851), holding that the ferry grant did not prevent another bridge or ferry; Collins v. Sherman, 31 Miss. 679 (1856), holding that the ferry grant gave no exclusive privilege.

60. Hartford Bridge Company v. Union Ferry Company, 29 Conn. 210 (1860).

61. Fort Plain Bridge Company v. Smith, 30 N.Y. 44 (1864).

62. Thorpe v. Rutland and Burlington Railroad Company, 27 Vt. 140 (1855).

63. Ohio and Mississippi Railroad Company v. McClelland, 25 Ill. 140 (1860); Indianapolis and Cincinnati Railroad Company v. Kercheval, 16 Ind. 84 (1861).

64. Boston and Lowell Railroad Corporation v. Salem and Lowell Railroad Company, 68 Mass. 1 (1854). For Shaw's opinion in *Boston and Lowell*, see Leonard W. Levy, *The Law of the Commonwealth and Chief Justice Shaw* (Cambridge, MA: Harvard University Press, 1957), 124–126, 270–273, arguing that Shaw sought to balance the contract clause with public interest and legislative power.

65. Delaware and Raritan Canal and Camden and Amboy Railroad v. Camden and Atlantic Railroad Company, 16 N.J. Eq. 321 (1863).

66. Ibid., at 377–381.

67. *Hartford*, at 149.

68. See Washington Bridge Company v. State, 18 Conn. 52 (1846), reasoning that the act imposed an additional burden on the bridge company. See also Commonwealth v. Proprietors of New Bedford Bridge, 68 Mass. 339 (1854), holding that the amendment of the act of incorporation mandating larger draws in the bridge was an unconstitutional impairment of contract because it imposed additional duties.

69. Enfield Toll Bridge Company v. Hartford and New Haven Rail-Road Company, 17 Conn. 40 (1845). See Wesley W. Horton, "The Pre–Civil War Connecticut Supreme Court," *Connecticut Law Review* 34 (2002): 1209, 1216–1219, contending that Connecticut courts were slow to adopt the *Charles River Bridge* analysis.

70. State v. Noyes, 47 Me. 189 (1859).

71. Dart v. Houston, 22 Ga. 506, 536 (1857).

72. Erie and North-East Railroad Company v. Casey, 26 Pa. 287 (1856).

73. See Edwin Merrick Dodd, *American Business Corporations until 1860* (Cambridge, MA: Harvard University Press, 1954), 141–142, noting that New York enacted the first such reservation provision in a general law in 1827.

74. For example, see Crease v. Babcock, 40 Mass. 334 (1839); Miners' Bank of Dubuque v. United States, 1 Greene 553 (Iowa 1848); Story v. Jersey City and Bergen Point Plank Road Company, 16 N.J. Eq. 13 (1863).

75. Boston Water Power Company v. Boston and Worcester Rail Road, 40 Mass. 360 (1839).

76. Armington v. Towns of Barnet, Reygate, and Newbury, 15 Vt. 742, 748 (1843). See also Brewster v. Hough, 10 N.H. 145, 147 (1839), questioning whether the

legislature has the authority "to grant away the essential attributes of sovereignty, or rights of eminent domain"; *Enfield Toll Bridge*, at 58–61, arguing that if public exigencies require that an existing franchise be impaired to make room for improvements, this should be achieved by exercise of eminent domain, and maintaining that eminent domain is an implied reservation in any contract with the state.

77. West River Bridge Company v. Dix, 47 U.S. 507 (1848).

78. Ibid., at 517.

79. Ibid., at 532.

80. Ibid., at 533.

81. Ibid., at 534. For Daniel's opinion in *West River Bridge*, see Dodd, *American Business Corporations until 1860*, 128–129; Frank, *Justice Daniel Dissenting*, 207–212, contending that Daniel did not confine his opinion solely to eminent domain but broadly endorsed a police power limitation on the contract clause; David P. Currie, "The Constitution in the Supreme Court: Contracts and Commerce," *Duke Law Journal* 1983 (1983): 471, 486–487, questioning broad reading of Daniel's opinion. See also Alfred L. Brophy, "'Necessity Knows No Law': Vested Rights and the Styles of Reasoning in the Confederate Conscription Cases," *Mississippi Law Journal* 69 (2000): 1123, 1145: "But *West River Bridge* came to stand for a much more radical proposition; it was cited to show that certain sovereign powers could not be contracted away."

82. Parsons, *Law of Contracts*, vol. 2, 692–693.

83. See Brophy, "'Necessity Knows No Law,'" 1139–1146, arguing that the Taney Court's contract clause jurisprudence reflected Jacksonian hostility toward business corporations but not dealing with cases involving tax exemptions or private contracts.

84. Dart v. Houston, 22 Ga. 506, 535–536 (1857).

85. Robinson v. Howe, 13 Wis. 380, 384 (1861).

86. Indianapolis and Cincinnati Railroad Company v. Kercheval, 16 Ind. 84, 85 (1861).

87. See, for example, *Thorpe*, at 149–150; *Ohio and Mississippi Railroad Company*, at 140, holding that corporations accept charters on the implied condition they are subject to regulatory power of the state.

88. Gorman v. Pacific Railroad, 26 Mo. 441, 450 (1858).

89. People v. Hawley, 3 Mich. 330 (1854).

90. Calder v. Kurby, 5 Gray (Mass.) 597, 598 (1856).

91. Phalen v. Virginia, 49 U.S. 163 (1850).

92. Ibid., at 168. Two state courts held that the grant of a lottery did not amount to a contract between the state and the lottery grantees but found that a contract by the original grantees transferring the privilege of conducting a lottery to others was protected by the contract clause. State v. Phalen and Paine, 3 Harr. 441 (Del. 1842); Gregory's Executrix v. Trustees of Shelby College, 2 Metcalfe 589 (Ky. 1859).

93. Planters' Bank of Mississippi v. Sharp, 47 U.S. 301 (1848). For a study of the contract clause claims growing out of Mississippi's assault on banks in the 1840s, see Meredith Lang, *Defender of the Faith: The High Court of Mississippi, 1817–1875* (Jackson: University of Mississippi Press, 1977), 31–47.

94. Charles Warren, *The Supreme Court in United States History*, rev. ed., vol. 2

(Boston: Little, Brown, 1926), 162. See also Clifford Thies, "Repudiation in Antebellum Mississippi," *Independent Review* 19 (2014): 191, 200–205.

95. Payne v. Baldwin, 11 Miss. 661 (1844).

96. *Planters' Bank*, at 327. See also Baldwin v. Payne, 47 U.S. 332 (1848) (same result).

97. McIntyre v. Ingraham, 35 Miss. 25, 60–61 (1858).

98. *Woodruff*, at 190, 203–209.

99. *Curran*, at 304.

100. Ibid., at 316.

101. See James W. Ely, Jr., *Railroads and American Law* (Lawrence: University Press of Kansas, 2001), 32–33, noting that states commonly granted tax concessions to railroad companies to promote private investment.

102. Parker v. Redfield, 10 Conn. 490 (1835).

103. Brewster v. Hough, 10 N.H. 138 (1839).

104. Herrick v. Town of Randolph, 13 Vt. 525 (1841).

105. Armstrong v. Athens County, 41 U.S. 281 (1842).

106. See Wright, *Contract Clause*, 71–72, suggesting that in light of *Wilson* the Court should have invalidated the tax.

107. Gordon v. Appeal Tax Court, 44 U.S. 133 (1845).

108. Alexander A. Lawrence, *James Moore Wayne: Southern Unionist* (Chapel Hill: University of North Carolina Press, 1943), 105–109.

109. Piqua Branch of the State Bank of Ohio v. Knoop, 57 U.S. 369, 389 (1854).

110. Ibid., at 393.

111. Warren, *Supreme Court in United States History*, 254–256.

112. Dodge v. Woosley, 59 US. 331, 360 (1856) (Wayne, J.). See also Mechanics' and Traders' Bank v. Debolt, 59 U.S. 380 (1856) (same result).

113. Jefferson Branch Bank v. Skelly, 66 U.S. 436 (1862). See also Franklin Branch Bank v. Ohio, 66 U.S. 474 (1862); Wright v. Sill, 67 U.S. 544 (1863) (Swayne, J.): "The argument upon both sides was exhausted in the earlier cases. It could serve no useful purpose again to examine the subject."

114. *Debolt*, at 416.

115. Ibid., at 428–429.

116. Ibid., at 429.

117. Ibid., at 443.

118. *Piqua Branch*, at 369, 400.

119. *Debolt*, at 442.

120. *Piqua Branch*, at 412.

121. *Dodge*, at 373–375.

122. Austin Allen, *Origins of the* Dred Scott *Case: Jacksonian Jurisprudence and the Supreme Court, 1837–1857* (Athens: University of Georgia Press, 2006), 114. See also Robert Saunders, Jr., *John Archibald Campbell: Southern Moderate, 1811–1889* (Tuscaloosa: University of Alabama Press, 1997), 117–118, discussing Campbell's opinions in the bank tax cases, noting that Campbell's language "revealed a strong anticorporation bias," and concluding Campbell felt that corporations "presented a clear danger to state sovereignty."

123. Allen, Origins of the *Dred Scott* Case, 114–115.

124. For the lower federal courts, see Thompson v. Holton, 23 Fed. Cases. 1049 (Cir. Ct. Ind. 1855) (McLean, J.), holding that the state law exempting land from taxation for five years from the date of purchase amounted to a contract and that later law imposing a tax on a parcel of such land impaired the obligation of contract.

125. Hovenkamp, *Enterprise and American Law*, 19, 25–27.

126. Iron City Bank v. City of Pittsburgh, 37 Penn. St. 340, 347 (1860).

127. President and Directors of the Bank of Cape Fear v. Edwards, 27 N.C. 516 (1845); Bank of Cape Fear v. Deming, 27 N.C. 55 (1846); O'Donnell v. Bailey, 24 Miss. 386 (1852).

128. *Thorpe*, at 146.

129. *Crittenden County*, at 360.

130. Bank of Pennsylvania v. Commonwealth, 19 Pa. St. 144, 151–156 (1852).

131. *Iron City Bank*, at 346–350. See also Mott v. Pennsylvania Railroad Company, 30 Pa. 9 (1858), contending that the state legislature had no constitutional authority to abridge its power to levy taxes.

132. Edward J. Balleisen, *Navigating Failure: Bankruptcy and Commercial Society in Antebellum America* (Chapel Hill: University of North Carolina Press, 2001), 86.

133. *Bronson*, at 311.

134. For the background of Illinois relief laws, see George L. Priest, "Law and Economic Distress: Sangamon County, Illinois, 1837–1844," *Journal of Legal Studies* 2 (1973): 469.

135. *Bronson*, at 318.

136. Ibid., at 320.

137. Although Story did not participate in *Bronson*, he warmly applauded the ruling. Story wrote to Taney, "I read the opinion of the Court in the Illinois case, respecting the stay laws of that State, with the highest satisfaction, and entirely concur in it." He added, "There are times in which the Court is called upon to support every sound constitutional doctrine in support of the rights of property and of creditors." Story to Taney, March 25, 1843, in Samuel Tyler, *Memoir of Roger Brooke Taney* (Baltimore, MD: J. Murphy, 1872), 289.

138. Warren, *Supreme Court in United States History*, 103.

139. See Wright, *Contract Clause*, 69–70, discussing *Bronson* and stating, "This opinion does little more than say that the change in the remedy must, in the opinion of the Court, be a reasonable one"; A. H. Feller, "Moratory Legislation: A Comparative Study," *Harvard Law Review* 46 (1933): 1061, 1070, finding the *Bronson* opinion unclear and declaring, "We have again the familiar line of escape from the rigidity of a constitutional prohibition. A state may legislate so long as it legislates 'reasonably.'"

140. *Bronson*, at 330.

141. Paul Finkelman, "John McLean: Moderate Abolitionist and Supreme Court Politician," *Vanderbilt Law Review* 62 (2009): 519, 535–536.

142. McCracken v. Hayward, 43 U.S. 608 (1844) (Baldwin, J.).

143. Gantly's Lessee v. Ewing, 44 U.S. 707, 717 (1845).

144. Howard v. Bugbee, 65 U.S. 461 (1861) (Nelson, J.).

145. In contrast, there was no contract clause violation when lawmakers reduced

the time for advertising a mortgage foreclosure sale, thereby rendering the remedy more efficacious. James v. Stull and Andrews, 9 Barb. 482 (N.Y. Sup. Ct. 1850).

146. Sheets v. Peabody, 7 Ind. 613 (1845); Rosier v. Hale, 10 Iowa 470 (1860).

147. Thorne v. San Francisco, 4 Ca1.127 (1854); Malony v. Fortune, 14 Iowa 417 (1862).

148. Robinson v. Howe, 13 Wis. 380 (1861).

149. Mundy v. Monroe, 1 Mich. 68 (1843).

150. See, for example, Swift v. Fletcher, 6 Minn. 550 (1861), holding that the statute directing forfeiture of security for debt as a penalty when the creditor first brought suit against the debtor personally impaired the contract.

151. Robert S. Hunt, *Law and Locomotives: The Impact of the Railroad on Wisconsin Law in the Nineteenth Century* (Madison: State Historical Society of Wisconsin, 1958), 44–65.

152. Cornell v. Hichens, 11 Wis. 353, 370 (1860).

153. Oatman v. Bond, 15 Wis. 23, 31 (1862).

154. *Rosier*, at 485.

155. Chadwick v. Moore, 8 Watts and Serg. 49, 52 (Pa. 1844).

156. *Von Baumbach*, at 534. In 1859 the Wisconsin legislature reduced the two periods of six months to ninety days each. Hunt, *Law and Locomotives*, 49. See also Holloway v. Sherman, 12 Iowa 282 (1861), upholding as applied to prior contracts a statute giving defendants in foreclosure action nine months in which to answer.

157. Catlin v. Munger, 1 Tex. 598 (1846).

158. Iverson v. Shorter, 9 Ala. 713 (1846).

159. Heyward v. Judd, 4 Minn. 483, 491 (1860).

160. *Thorne*, at 141.

161. Bunn, Raiguel, and Co. v. Gorgas, 41 Penn. St. 441 (1862).

162. Bigelow v. Pritchard, 38 Mass. 169, 174 (1838).

163. Morse v. Goold, 11 N.Y. 281 (1854).

164. Rockwell v. Hubbell's Administrators, 2 Doug. 197 (1846).

165. See Sedgwick, *Treatise on the Rules Which Govern Statutory and Constitutional Law*, 658, contending the Supreme Court had not settled in *Bronson* whether exemption laws applied to debts under antecedent contracts.

166. Woody Holton, "Equality as Unintended Consequence: The Contracts Clause and the Married Women's Property Acts," *Journal of Southern History* 81 (2015): 313–340.

167. Peter J. Coleman, *Debtors and Creditors in American History: Insolvency, Imprisonment for Debt, and Bankruptcy, 1607–1900* (Madison: State Historical Society of Wisconsin, 1974), 22–24; Charles Warren, *Bankruptcy in United States History* (Cambridge, MA: Harvard University Press, 1935), 79–86.

168. *Planters' Bank*, at 328 (Woodbury, J.). See also In re Irwine, 13 Fed. Cases 125, 130 (Cir. Ct. E.D. Penn. 1842), construing the 1841 bankruptcy law to mean that Congress "may give to the discharge what effect they please, and in consequence may not only impair, but extinguish the obligations and contracts of a bankrupt."

169. *Morse*, at 286.

170. Winter v. Jones, 10 Ga. 190, 198 (1851).

171. Robinson v. Magee, 9 Cal. 81, 84–85 (1858).

172. Myrick v. Battle, 5 Fla. 345, 349–350 (1853).

173. Howe, *What God Hath Wrought*, 552–553. See also David Maldwyn Ellis, *Landlords and Farmers in the Hudson-Mohawk Region* (Ithaca, NY: Cornell University Press, 1946); Reeve Huston, *Land and Freedom: Rural Society, Popular Protest, and Party Politics in Antebellum New York* (New York: Oxford University Press, 2000).

174. Charles W. McCurdy, *The Anti-Rent Era in New York Law and Politics, 1839–1865* (Chapel Hill: University of North Carolina Press, 2001), 30.

175. Cochran v. Van Surlay, 20 Wend. 365, 384 (Court of Errors 1838) (Verplanck, Senator, dissenting).

176. Van Rensselaer v. Snyder, 13 N.Y. 299 (1855). See also Stocking v. Hunt, 3 Denio 274 (N.Y. Sup. Ct. 1846); Van Rensselaer v. Smith, 27 Barb. 104 (N.Y. Sup. Ct. 1858).

177. For a perceptive treatment of complicated legal issues, see McCurdy, *Anti-Rent Era in New York Law and Politics.*

178. See generally Parsons, *Law of Contracts*, 697–699; Sedgwick, *Treatise on the Rules Which Govern Statutory and Constitutional Law*, 635–637.

179. Dartmouth College v. Woodard, 17 U.S. 518, 629 (1819).

180. Ibid., at 695–696.

181. James Kent, *Commentaries on American Law,* vol. 2 (New York: O. Halsted, 1827), 89–90.

182. White v. White, 5 Barb. 474 (N.Y. 1849).

183. Maguire v. Maguire, 37 Ky. 181 (1838); Clark v. Clark, 10 N.H. 380 (1839); In re Opinion of the Justices, 16 Me. 479 (1840).

184. Noel v. Ewing, 9 Ind. 37, 51 (1857).

185. Ponder v. Graham, 4 Fla. 23, 45 (1851).

186. Thomas M. Cooley, *A Treatise on the Constitutional Limitations Which Rest upon the Legislative Power of the States of American Union* (Boston: Little, Brown, 1868), 284.

187. For a thoughtful study of the concept of judicial impairment, see Barton H. Thompson, Jr., "The History of the Judicial Impairment 'Doctrine' and Its Lessons for the Contract Clause," *Stanford Law Review* 44 (1992): 1373. Without much analysis, the Supreme Court of Connecticut stated in 1839 that the prohibition of the contract clause rests on "the legislative department of the state." *Trustees of Bishop's Fund*, at 95.

188. See Conrad Reno, "Impairment of Contracts by Change of Judicial Opinion," *American Law Review* 23 (1889): 190, 199: "The object of the prohibition is to secure the inviolability of property rights in contract against State action. Regarding the spirit and not merely the letter of this clause, and considering that property rights in contract may be as greatly impaired by subsequent overruling decisions as by subsequent statutes, justice seems to require that the two modes of impairment be held equivalent for jurisdictional purposes."

189. See Richard A. Epstein, "Toward a Revitalization of the Contract Clause," *University of Chicago Law Review* 51 (1984): 703, 747–750, stressing the function rather than the text of the contract clause and contending that the provision should

reach state judiciaries as well as legislatures because the modern judiciary often acts in a legislative manner and nullifies contracts.

190. Commercial Bank of Cincinnati v. Buckingham's Executors, 46 U.S. 317, 337, 340 (1847).

191. Ibid., at 343 (Grier, J.).

192. Groves v. Slaughter, 40 U.S. 449 (1841).

193. Rowan v. Runnels, 46 U.S. 134 (1847).

194. *Debolt*, at 432.

195. Ibid., at 450–451 (Curtis and Nelson, JJ, dissenting in part).

196. Gelpcke v. City of Dubuque, 68 U.S. 175 (1864). Taney did not participate in the decision. For the background of this case, see Charles Fairman, *Reconstruction and Reunion, 1864–1888* (New York: Macmillan, 1971), 918–944; Charles A. Heckman, "Establishing the Basis for Local Financing of American Railroad Construction in the Nineteenth Century: From *City of Bridgeport v. the Housatonic Railroad Company* to *Gelpcke v. City of Dubuque*," *American Journal of Legal History* 32 (1988): 236, 248–259.

197. Dubuque County v. Dubuque and Pacific Railroad Company, 4 Greene 1 (Iowa 1853).

198. State v. County of Wapello, 13 Iowa 388 (1862).

199. Ibid., at 423–424.

200. Heckman, "Establishing the Basis for Local Financing of American Railroad Construction in the Nineteenth Century," 254.

201. *Gelpcke*, at 205.

202. Ibid., at 206.

203. Ibid., at 220. Scholars have widely divergent views about Miller's dissent in *Gelpcke*. Compare Michael A. Ross, *Justice of Shattered Dreams: Samuel Freeman Miller and the Supreme Court during the Civil War Era* (Baton Rouge: Louisiana State University Press, 2003), 89–91, 174, concluding that Miller's opinion in *Gelpcke* reflected his sense that "the needs of an indebted community took precedence over those of bondholders," with Heckman, "Establishing the Basis for Local Financing of American Railroad Construction in the Nineteenth Century," 256–257, finding Miller's dissent "a seriously deficient opinion."

204. *Gelpcke*, at 209.

205. See William B. Hornblower, "Conflict between Federal and State Decisions," *American Law Review* 14 (1880): 211, 216, expressing doubt about the majority opinion in *Gelpcke* but declaring that the case before the Supreme Court "was one of extreme injustice on the part of the State judiciary"; L. A. Powe, Jr., "Rehearsal for Substantive Due Process: The Municipal Bond Cases," *Texas Law Review* 53 (1975): 738, 742, asserting that "the Supreme Court's holding in *Gelpcke*, protecting bona fide purchasers who could not have foreseen judicial repudiation, had a decided equitable basis."

206. Warren, *Supreme Court*, 531–532.

207. Wright, *Contract Clause*, 81.

208. Hovenkamp, *Enterprise and American Law*, 90; Warren B. Hunting, *The Obligation of Contracts Clause of the United States Constitution* (Baltimore, MD: Johns Hopkins University Press, 1919), 51.

209. See Warren, *Supreme Court*, 530, rejecting the argument that *Gelpcke* was based on general commercial law principles and reading the Swayne opinion as holding that where a contract was valid when made "it could not be impaired, either subsequent action of a Legislature or a decision of a State Court"; Reno, "Impairment of Contracts by Change of Judicial Opinions," 192, concluding that *Gelpcke* was decided "on the ground chiefly that the latest decision of the State court impaired the obligation of the contract in suit and was therefore void as applied to it."

210. See Fairman, *Reconstruction and Reunion*, 937–938, concluding that *Gelpcke* was grounded on diversity jurisdiction rather than the contract clause; James Bradley Thayer, "The Case of *Gelpcke v. Dubuque*," *Harvard Law Review* 4 (1891): 311, 319–320, stating that *Gelpcke* was not an application of the contract clause but grounded upon special rules for diversity cases. See also Currie, "Constitution in the Supreme Court," 494, finding the basis of the *Gelpcke* decision ambiguous but declaring that it "may well have been an extension of *Swift v. Tyson* rather than an expansive reading of the contract clause"; Powe, "Rehearsal for Substantive Due Process," 741–742, treating *Gelpcke* as an application of the Court's power to create a national commercial law under *Swift* but noting an "unarticulated analogy to the concept of impairment in the contracts clause."

211. For example, Hovenkamp has offered conflicting assessments of *Gelpcke* in *Enterprise and American Law*. At one point he characterized the decision as an application of the contract clause. Ibid., 25. Later Hovenkamp depicted *Gelpcke* as a ruling based on general commercial law under *Swift*. Ibid., 90–91.

212. Ibid., 20.

213. Warren, *Bankruptcy in United States History*, 90.

CHAPTER 4. THE ERAS OF THE CIVIL WAR AND RECONSTRUCTION

1. Henry Sumner Maine, *Ancient Law* (New York: Charles Scribner, 1864), 165. He added, "The society of our day is mainly distinguished from that of preceding generations by the largeness of the sphere which is occupied in it by Contract."

2. E. L. Godkin, "The Labor Crisis," *North American Review* 105 (1867): 177, 183.

3. Civil Rights Act of 1866, ch. 31, sec. 1, 14 Stat. 27.

4. Amy Dru Stanley, *From Bondage to Contract: Wage Labor, Marriage, and the Market in the Age of Slave Emancipation* (Cambridge, UK: Cambridge University Press, 1998), 2.

5. Hepburn v. Griswold, 75 U.S. 603, 624 (1870).

6. Homestead Cases, 63 Va. 266, 301 (1872).

7. Wood v. Wood, 48 S.C.L. 148, 150 (1867).

8. Moore v. State, 48 Miss. 147, 167 (1873) (Simrall, J., concurring).

9. *Hepburn*, at 623.

10. An Act to Provide a Government for the District of Columbia, February 21, 1871, sec. 20, 16 Stat. 419.

11. Garland v. Brown's Administrator, 64 Va. 173, 176 (1873).

12. Delmas v. Insurance Company, 81 U.S. 661, 668 (1872).

13. Thomas M. Cooley, *A Treatise on the Constitutional Limitations Which Rest upon the Legislative Power of the States of the American Union* (Boston: Little, Brown, 1868; reprint, New York: DaCapo Press, 1972), 273.

14. Webster and Mann v. Rose, 53 Tenn. 93 (1871).

15. See R. Hutchinson, "Laws Impairing the Obligation of Contracts," *Southern Law Review* 1 (1875): 401, 424: "The obligation of a contract can certainly be as effectively impaired or destroyed by interference with the remedy as by the most direct legislation to that end."

16. Confederate Constitution of 1861, art. I, sec. 10, cl. 1.

17. Ibid., art. I, sec. 8, cl. 4.

18. See Barnes v. Barnes, 53 N.C. 366, 369–371 (1861), noting that the Confederate Constitution "in this respect" was "the same" as the US Constitution.

19. Burt v. Williams, 24 Ark. 91 (1863).

20. Ibid., at 95.

21. Sequestration Cases, 30 Tex. 688, 695–700 (1868).

22. See Daniel W. Hamilton, *The Limits of Sovereignty: Property Confiscation in the Union and the Confederacy during the Civil War* (Chicago: University of Chicago Press, 2007); Brian R. Dirck, "Prosperity's Blush: Civil Liberties, Property Rights, and Property Confiscation in the Confederacy," *Civil War History* 48 (2002): 237.

23. Williams v. Bruffy, 96 U.S. 176 (1877).

24. Ibid., at 184, 187.

25. Thorington v. Smith, 75 U.S. 1, 11–12, 14 (1869).

26. Roach, Administrator v. Gunter, 44 Ala. 209 (1870).

27. Forcheimer v. Holly, 14 Fla. 239 (1872).

28. *Delmas*, at 661.

29. Ibid., at 667–669.

30. Wilmington and Weston Railroad Company v. King, Executor, 91 U.S. 3, 5 (1875).

31. Effinger v. Kenny, 115 U.S. 566, 574–575 (1885).

32. For a fine discussion of this issue, see Andrew Kull, "The Enforceability after Emancipation of Debts Contracted for the Purchase of Slaves," *Chicago-Kent Law Review* 70 (1994): 493.

33. Walker v. Gatlin, 12 Fla. 9, 16–17 (1867). See also Hand v. Armstrong, 34 Ga. 232 (1866), affirming enforceability of slave purchase agreements.

34. Kull, "Enforceability after Emancipation of Debts Contracted for the Purchase of Slaves," 522–524.

35. McElvain v. Mudd, 44 Ala. 48, 60–63 (1870).

36. Calhoun v. Calhoun, 2 S.C. 283, 307 (1871).

37. Jacoway v. Denton, 25 Ark. 625, 633–647 (1869) (error dismissed), 154 U.S. 583 (1872). See also Sevier v. Haskell, 26 Ark. 133 (1870) (same result).

38. McNealy v. Gregory, 13 Fla. 417, 450 (1870).

39. Shorter v. Cobb, 39 Ga. 285 (1869). See also White v. Hart, 39 Ga. 306 (1869) (same result).

40. *Shorter*, at 304.

41. *White,* at 308 (1869) (Warner, J., dissenting).

42. *Osborn v. Nicholson,* 18 Fed. Cases 846, 854–855 (C.C.E.D. Ark. 1870). Judge Henry C. Caldwell amplified his thinking in Buckner v. Street, 4 Fed. Cases 578, 583 (C.C.E.D. Ark. 1871), arguing that a contract to purchase a slave was not entitled to more protection than property in a slave and depicting slave purchase agreements as by their nature "inherently vicious and contrary to sound morals and natural justice and right, and to the fundamental policy of the government."

43. White v. Hart, 80 U.S. 646 (1872).

44. Ibid., at 649.

45. Ibid., at 654.

46. Osborn v. Nicholson, 80 U.S. 654 (1872).

47. Ibid., at 663.

48. For the background of the dispute over the *Legal Tender Cases,* see Kenneth W. Dam, "The *Legal Tender Cases,*" Supreme Court Review (1981): 367; Charles Fairman, *Reconstruction and Reunion, 1864–1888* (New York: Macmillan, 1971), 677–775; Paul D. Moreno, "'The Legitimate Object of Government': Constitutional Problems of Civil War–Era Republican Policy," in *Constitutionalism in the Approach and Aftermath of the Civil War,* ed. Paul D. Moreno and Johnathan O'Neill (New York: Fordham University Press, 2013), 168–173. See also Irwin Unger, *The Greenback Era: A Social and Political History of American Finance, 1865–1879* (Princeton, NJ: Princeton University Press, 1964), 172–178.

49. See John Niven, *Salmon P. Chase: A Biography* (New York: Oxford University Press, 1995), 439, noting that Chase "had always opposed in principle any governmental reliance on paper currency that had no specie basis."

50. Hepburn v. Griswold, 75 U.S. 603 (1870). The Supreme Court had previously determined that the Legal Tender Act did not apply to contracts that stipulated by their express terms for payment in gold coin. Bronson v. Rodes, 74 U.S. 229 (1868) (Chase, C.J.). See also Trebilcock v. Wilson, 79 U.S. 687 (1871) (Field, J.).

51. Justice Robert C. Grier concurred in the result, making a majority of five. Grier resigned before the opinion was announced.

52. For Chase's role in the *Legal Tender Cases,* see Niven, *Salmon P. Chase,* 438–440.

53. *Hepburn,* at 623. Chase also concluded that the Legal Tender Act constituted a deprivation of property without due process in contravention of the Fifth Amendment, raising issues beyond the scope of this volume.

54. Ibid., at 637.

55. For Miller's opinion in *Hepburn,* see Michael A. Ross, *Justice of Shattered Dreams: Samuel Freeman Miller and the Supreme Court during the Civil War Era* (Baton Rouge: Louisiana State University Press, 2003), 177–183.

56. Knox v. Lee, 79 U.S. 457 (1871).

57. Ibid., at 551. For sharp criticism of Strong's opinion in *Knox,* see Richard H. Timberlake, *Constitutional Money: A Review of the Supreme Court's Monetary Decisions* (Cambridge, UK: Cambridge University Press, 2013), 98–105.

58. Ibid., at 580.

59. Ibid., at 661.

60. Ibid., at 668.

61. In his dissent in *Knox* Field charged that the majority opinion opened the door for Congress to repudiate its own promise to repay borrowed money in gold. Ibid., at 674.

62. Breitenbach v. Bush, 44 Pa. St. 313, 319 (1863).

63. Ibid., at 320.

64. Morton Keller, *Affairs of State: Public Life in Late Nineteenth-Century America* (Cambridge, MA: Harvard University Press, 1977), 199.

65. As quoted in Eric Foner, *Reconstruction: America's Unfinished Revolution, 1863–1877* (New York: Harper and Row, 1988), 326. See also R. H. Woody, "Some Aspects of the Economic Condition of South Carolina after the Civil War," *North Carolina Historical Review* 7 (1930): 346.

66. See Elizabeth Lee Thompson, *Reconstruction of Southern Debtors: Bankruptcy after the Civil War* (Athens: University of Georgia Press, 2004), 26: "A vast array of personal property was also exempt, particularly types of property that would benefit farmers or professionals." See also Mark Wahlgren Summers, *The Ordeal of the Reunion: A New History of Reconstruction* (Chapel Hill: University of North Carolina Press, 2014), 131–132.

67. An Act for the Relief of the People of Georgia . . . , Title XXXII No. 255, Public Laws of Georgia, March 6, 1866.

68. Aycock v. Martin, 37 Ga. 124, 171 (1867) (Walker, J., dissenting).

69. For example, see Jones v. McMahan, 30 Tex. 719, 735 (1868): "We have been apprized by the defendant's counsel of the pecuniary situation of the people of this state, and that there is a real necessity for the stay law."

70. Ex parte Pollard, 40 Ala. 77 (1866); Ashurst v. Phillips' Executors, 43 Ala. 158 (1869).

71. *Aycock*, at 124.

72. Coffman v. Bank of Kentucky, 40 Miss. 29 (1866). But see Hill v. Boyland, 40 Miss. 618 (1866) (upholding 1862 stay law).

73. Jacobs v. Smallwood, 63 N.C. 112 (1869); Johnson v. Winslow, 64 N.C. 27 (1870).

74. State v. Carew, 47 S.C.L. 498 (1866); Wood v. Wood, 48 S.C.L. 148 (1867).

75. *Webster and Mann*, at 93.

76. Sequestration Cases, 30 Tex. 688 (1868); Jones v. McMahan and Gilbert, 30 Tex. 719 (1868).

77. Taylor v. Stearns, 59 Va. 244 (1868).

78. *Aycock*, at 124–138; Coffman v. Bank of Mississippi, 40 Miss. 29, 36 (1866); *Wood*, at 148, 150, 162; *Webster and Mann*, at 93; *Jones*, at 737.

79. *Ex parte Pollard*, at 97 (Byrd, J.).

80. *Wood*, at 150.

81. *Garland*, at 176.

82. Marsh v. Burroughs, 16 Fed. Cases 800, 804 (Cir. Ct. S.D. Ga. 1871).

83. Walker v. Whitehead, 83 U.S. 314, 317–318 (1873). Justice Joseph P. Bradley anticipated this result in an earlier circuit court opinion. See Lathrop v. Brown, 14 Fed. Cases 1178 (Cir. Ct. S.D. Ga. 1871), asserting that the Georgia law imposed "onerous" conditions and declaring, "Restrictions on the remedy which

materially affect a contract tend as much to impair its validity as laws passed to abrogate it."

84. Roberts v. Cocke, 69 Va. 207 (1877). See also Goggans v. Turnipseed, 1 S.C. 80, 83: "The imposition of any condition . . . or any deviation from its terms, in addition to, or diminution of, those which by law existed, when it was made, impairs the obligation"; Bank of the Old Dominion v. McVeigh, 61 Va. 457, 463–468 (1871), an 1864 law authorized payment of debts to a different branch bank than mentioned in the contract and allowed payment in Confederate currency rather than gold, altering the terms of the contract in violation of the contract clause.

85. *Garland*, at 182.

86. For the background on homestead laws and the post–Civil War contract clause challenges, see James W. Ely, Jr., "Homestead Exemption and Southern Legal Culture," in *Signposts: New Directions in Southern Legal History*, ed. Sally E. Hadden and Patricia Hagler Minter (Athens: University of Georgia Press, 2013), 289–314.

87. J. H. Thomas, "Homestead and Exemption Laws of the Southern States, II," *American Law Register* 19 (1871): 149.

88. Hardeman v. Downer, 39 Ga. 425, 440 (1869) (Brown, C.J., concurring).

89. Hill v. Kessler, 63 N.C. 437, 445 (1869).

90. *Hardeman*, at 440. See also Chambliss v. Phelps, 39 Ga. 386 (1869); Pulliam v. Sewell, 40 Ga. 73 (1869).

91. Bronson v. Kinzie, 42 U.S. 311, 315 (1843). See pp. 87–88 infra, discussing *Bronson*. For state court opinions citing the Taney dictum, see Stephenson v. Osborne, 41 Miss. 119, 128 (1866); In re Kennedy, 2 S.C. 216, 221, 224 (1869); *Hill*, at 443; Sneider v. Heidelberger, 45 Ala. 126, 134 (1871). The prominent constitutional scholar Thomas M. Cooley also took the position that increased state exemption laws could be made applicable to prior contracts. Cooley, *Treatise on the Constitutional Limitations*, 287.

92. Garrett v. Cheshire, 69 N.C. 396, 405 (1873).

93. *Stephenson*, at 130; *Hardeman*, at 429.

94. Mason v. Haile, 25 U.S. 370 (1827).

95. *Hardeman*, at 464–465 (Walker, J., dissenting). See also *Hill*, at 448–451 (Pearson, C.J., dissenting), claiming that homestead law had the effect of exempting all property of debtors in nine of ten cases, thus depriving the creditor of any means of enforcing contracts.

96. Homestead Cases, 63 Va. 266 (1872). See also Russell v. Randolph, 67 Va. 705 (1875) (same result).

97. Ibid., at 288.

98. Ibid., at 299.

99. Subsequently the Supreme Court of Tennessee reached a similar result, construing the homestead provision in the 1870 state constitution as operating only prospectively and thereby avoiding any contract clause objection. Hannum v. McInturf, 65 Tenn. 225 (1873). Although decided in September of 1872, the opinion itself was not printed until the following year.

100. Gunn v. Barry, 82 U.S. 610, 622 (1872).

101. Lessley v. Phipps, 49 Miss. 790, 799 (1874). See also Wilson v. Brown, 58 Ala. 63 (1877).

102. *Lessley*, at 805.

103. Garrett v. Cheshire, 69 N.C. 247 (1873); Edwards v. Kearsey, 75 N.C. 294 (1876).

104. Edwards v. Kearsey, 96 U.S. 595 (1878).

105. Ibid., at 603.

106. Ibid., at 608–611. Justice John Marshall Harlan dissented without opinion.

107. Charles Warren, *Bankruptcy in United States History* (Cambridge, MA: Harvard University Press, 1935), 150.

108. Not surprisingly, creditors, especially in the northern states, pushed for a bankruptcy system that would establish national norms for the recovery of debts. In 1867 Congress enacted another short-lived bankruptcy law. This measure, however, not only recognized state homestead laws but was amended to permit retroactive application of such laws to prior debts. Congress, of course, was not bound by the contract clause and under its bankruptcy power could impair antecedent contracts. Dismayed, creditors saw the 1867 bankruptcy law as a failure and called for its repeal. Congress repealed the act in 1878, once again leaving the state debt-relief systems in force. See Peter J. Coleman, *Debtors and Creditors in America: Insolvency, Imprisonment for Debt, and Bankruptcy, 1607–1900* (Madison: State Historical Society of Wisconsin, 1974), 25–26; Warren, *Bankruptcy in United States History*, 105–127.

109. Binghamton Bridge, 70 U.S. 51 (1866).

110. Ibid., at 73.

111. Ibid., at 83.

112. For example, the Supreme Court continued to hear cases involving competing modes of transportation. It readily dismissed the argument of a Maryland turnpike company that the subsequent authorization by the legislature of a railroad whose line ran close to the turnpike impaired the charter of the turnpike company. The Court pointed out that nothing in the turnpike company charter conferred any exclusive privilege. Turnpike Company v. State, 70 U.S. 210 (1866).

113. Hawthorne v. Calef, 69 U.S. 10 (1865) (Nelson, J.).

114. Furman v. Nichol, 75 U.S. 44 (1869).

115. Rodemacher v. Milwaukee and St. Paul Railway, 41 Iowa 297, 306 (1875).

116. Gaines v. Coates, 51 Miss. 335 (1875).

117. State v. Richmond and Danville Rail Road Company, 73 N.C. 527, 533 (1875).

118. Zabriskie v. Hackensack and New York Railroad Company, 18 N.J. Ch. 178, 185–186 (1867).

119. See Parker v. Metropolitan Railroad Company, 109 Mass. 506, 508 (1872), declaring that the "reservation of power is broad and comprehensive" and upholding power of the legislature to regulate ferry tolls.

120. Albany Northern Railroad Company v. Brownell, 24 N.Y. 345, 350 (1862).

121. Commissioners on Inland Fisheries v. Holyoke Water Power Company, 104 Mass. 446, 451 (1870). Dismissing a contract clause argument, the same court in Keene v. Eastern Railroad Company, 103 Mass. 254 (1869), also upheld a legislative mandate that a railroad company erect a station and stop certain trains at a town, pointing to the reservation clause in an 1831 general corporation law. It added, "Whether a reasonable ground for interference is presented in any particular case

is for the legislature to determine; and their determination on this point must be conclusive."

122. Attorney General v. Chicago and Northwestern Railway Company, 35 Wis. 425, 563–575 (1874).

123. Miller v. State, 82 U.S. 478, 498 (1873). See also Holyoke Company v. Lyman, 82 U.S. 500, 522 (1873).

124. *Binghamton Bridge,* at 59.

125. Metropolitan Board of Exercise v. Barrie, 34 N.Y. 657, 667 (1866).

126. Moore v. State, 48 Miss. 147, 167 (1873) (Simrall, J., concurring).

127. *Richmond and Danville Rail Road,* at 540.

128. Theodore Sedgwick, *A Treatise on the Rules Which Govern Statutory and Constitutional Law,* 2nd ed. (New York: Baker, Voorhies, 1874), 588.

129. Cooley, *Treatise on the Constitutional Limitations,* 275–279.

130. Thomas Cooley, *A Treatise on the Constitutional Limitations Which Rest upon the Legislative Power of the States of the American Union,* 2nd ed. (Boston: Little, Brown, 1871), 280n.2.

131. James A. Garfield, *The Future of the Republic: Its Dangers and Its Hopes* (New York: George F. Nesbitt, 1880), 11. See also *Chicago and Northwestern Railway,* at 467–468: "It is not to be overlooked that the decision was made long before the era of great corporations in this country, long before what were then private corporations had become of more public significance than municipal corporations were then."

132. For a fine analysis of the shifting attitude toward Marshall's contract clause jurisprudence and *Dartmouth College,* see Robert L. Clinton, "The Obligation Clause of the United States Constitution: Public and/or Private Contracts?," *University of Arkansas at Little Rock Law Journal* 11 (1988): 343, 353–357.

133. Clement H. Hill, "The *Dartmouth College* Case," *American Law Review* 8 (1874): 189.

134. Ibid., at 191, 192.

135. Ibid., at 235. See also John M. Shirley, *The* Dartmouth College *Case and the Supreme Court of the United States* (St. Louis, MO: G. I. Jones, 1879), arguing that the *Dartmouth College* case was wrongly decided and had a pernicious impact on the law-making authority of the states.

136. Clinton, "Obligation Clause of the Constitution," 357.

137. Hill, "*Dartmouth College* Case," 198.

138. Ibid., at 201.

139. Davis v. Gray, 83 U.S. 203, 232 (1873).

140. Cooley, *Treatise on the Constitutional Limitations,* 1st ed., 281.

141. Hill, "*Dartmouth College* Case," 204–208; Hutchinson, "Laws Impairing the Obligation of Contracts," 429–432.

142. Sedgwick, *Treatise on the Rules Which Govern Statutory and Constitutional Law,* 586–587, 596–599.

143. McGee v. Mathis, 71 U.S. 143 (1866).

144. Home of the Friendless v. Rouse, 75 U.S. 430 (1869); Washington University v. Rouse, 75 U.S. 439 (1869).

145. *Home of the Friendless*, at 438.

146. *Washington University*, at 442.

147. Ibid., at 443–444.

148. For tax concessions to railroads, see James W. Ely, Jr., *Railroads and American Law* (Lawrence: University Press of Kansas, 2001), 32–34, 206–207. Courts sometimes explicitly recognized the policy basis for grants of tax exemption. See City of Richmond v. Richmond and Danville Railroad Company, 62 Va. 604, 614 (1872): "This policy of exemption has been and is continually exercised for wise and beneficent purposes by State Legislatures. . . . An enlightened policy, appreciating these advantages, invites the investment of capital in such enterprises by granting liberal exemptions from taxation."

149. Wilmington Railroad v. Reid, 80 U.S. 264 (1872).

150. Ibid., at 266–267. In the companion tax exemption case of Raleigh and Gaston Railroad Company v. Reid, 80 U.S. 269, 270 (1872), the Court similarly pointed out, "The impolicy of this legislation is apparent, but there is no relief to the State, for the rights secured by the contract are protected from invasion by the Constitution of the United States."

151. Humphrey v. Pegues, 83 U.S. 244 (1873) (Hunt, J.); Pacific Railroad Company v. Maguire, 87 U.S. 36 (1874).

152. North Missouri Railroad Company v. Maguire, 87 U.S. 46 (1874) (Clifford, J.); Tucker v. Ferguson, 89 U.S. 527 (1875) (Swayne, J.).

153. Salt Company v. East Saginaw, 80 U.S. 373 (1872).

154. East Saginaw Manufacturing Company v. City of East Saginaw, 19 Mich. 259 (1869) (Cooley, J.), affirmed 80 U.S. 383 (1872), remarking that taxation was an essential power of sovereignty and anticipating the decision of the Supreme Court by ruling that a general inducement was not a contract of exemption. See also People v. Roper, 35 N.Y. 629 (1866), holding that a general law relieving certain classes of persons from tax burdens was not a contract.

155. *Salt Company*, at 379.

156. Morgan v. Louisiana, 93 U.S. 217 (1876).

157. For example, Oliver v. Memphis and Little Rock Railroad Co., 30 Ark. 128 (1875); Grand Gulf and Port Gibson Railroad Co. v. Buck, 53 Miss. 246 (1876).

158. Atlantic and Gulf Railroad Company v. Allen, 15 Fla. 638, 663 (1876).

159. Mobile and Ohio Railroad Company v. Moseley, 52 Miss. 129, 132 (1876).

160. See Commonwealth v. Fayette County Railroad Company, 55 Penn. St. 452 (1867).

161. Tomlinson v. Jessup, 82 U.S. 454, 459 (1873).

162. Hewitt v. New York and Oswego Midland Railroad Company, 12 F. Cases 75 (Cir. Ct. S.D.N.Y. 1875); Central Railroad and Banking Company v. State, 54 Ga. 401 (1875).

163. Keller, *Affairs of State*, 115–116, 231–232.

164. Von Hoffman v. City of Quincy, 71 U.S. 535 (1867).

165. Ibid., at 552–554.

166. See Maenhaut v. New Orleans, 16 F. Cases 377 (Cir. Ct. D. La. 1875). See also

Milner v. Pensacola, 17 F. Cases 497 (Cir. Ct. N.D. Fla. 1875), declaring that the dissolution of a municipal corporation, which had the effect of terminating its power of taxation, would impair the contractual rights of creditors and could not preclude recovery of any debt.

167. Goodale v. Fennell, 27 Ohio St. 426 (1875).

168. Ibid., at 435.

169. Brewer v. Otoe County, 1 Neb. 373 (1871).

170. Ibid., at 381.

171. Brooklyn Park Commissioners v. Armstrong, 45 N.Y. 234, 247 (1871).

172. William's Appeal, 72 Penn. St. 214 (1872).

173. Board of Liquidation v. McComb, 92 U.S. 531 (1876). For a discussion of *McComb*, see Benjamin F. Wright, Jr., *The Contract Clause of the Constitution* (Cambridge, MA: Harvard University Press, 1938), 224–225.

174. Pereles v. Watertown, 19 F. Cases 227, 229–230 (Cir. Ct. W.D. Wis. 1874).

175. Metropolitan Board of Excise v. Barrier, 34 N.Y. 657 (1866).

176. Moore v. State, 48 Miss. 147, 161 (1873).

177. Cronise v. Cronise, 54 Penn. St. 255 (1867). For decisions reaching the same result, see Starr v. Hamilton, 22 Fed. Cases 1107, 1111 (Cir. Ct. D. Ore., 1867), declaring marriage to be a civil institution, not a contract; Magee and Wife v. Young, 40 Miss. 164 (1866); Carson v. Carson, 40 Miss. 349 (1866).

178. See pp. 98–103 supra.

179. Barton H. Thompson, Jr., "The History of the Judicial Impairment 'Doctrine' and Its Lessons for the Contract Clause," *Stanford Law Review* 44 (1992): 1373, 1410–1412. See also Mary Cornelia Porter, "That Commerce Shall Be Free: A New Look at the Old Laissez-Faire Court," *Supreme Court Review* (1976): 135, 145–146, observing that state and municipal bond repudiation cases "raised, in the mind of the Court, questions of national and foreign commerce."

180. Havemeyer v. Iowa County, 70 U.S. 294 (1866) (Swayne, J.). See also Olcott v. Supervisors, 83 U.S. 678, 690 (1873) (Strong, J.): "This Court has always ruled that if a contract when made was valid under the constitution and laws of a state, as they had been previously expounded by its judicial tribunals, and as they were understood at the time, no subsequent action by the legislature or the judiciary will be regarded by the Court as establishing its invalidity."

181. Butz v. City of Muscatine, 75 U.S. 575 (1869).

182. Ibid., at 583.

183. Ibid., at 584.

184. For Miller's opinion in *Butz*, see Ross, *Justice of Shattered Dreams*, 170–174, noting that "Miller dissented more frequently in municipal bond cases than in any other type" and that he believed "the needs of an indebted community took precedence over those of bondholders."

185. Township of Pine Grove v. Talcott, 86 U.S. 666 (1874).

186. Ibid., at 678.

187. See Railroad Company v. Rock, 71 U.S. 177 (1867); Railroad Company v. McClure, 77 U.S. 511 (1870).

188. Fairman, *Reconstruction and Reunion*, 937–938n.69.

189. *Rock*, at 180–181.

190. Thompson, "History of the Judicial Impairment 'Doctrine,'" 1415–1417.

CHAPTER 5. THE GILDED AGE

1. Morton Keller, *Affairs of State: Public Life in Late Nineteenth-Century America* (Cambridge, MA: Harvard University Press, 1977), 285–342, 371–438.

2. James W. Ely, Jr., "Property Rights and the Supreme Court in the Gilded Age," *Journal of Supreme Court History* 38 (2013): 330.

3. Barnitz v. Beverly, 163 U.S. 118, 121 (1896).

4. Lawrence M. Friedman, *American Law in the 20th Century* (New Haven, CT: Yale University Press, 2002), 381.

5. Farrington v. Tennessee, 95 U.S. 679, 682 (1877) (Swayne, J.).

6. Murray v. Charleston, 96 U.S. 432, 448 (1878).

7. Henry Sumner Maine, *Popular Government* (New York: Henry Holt, 1886), 247.

8. New Jersey v. Yard, 95 U.S. 104, 113 (1877).

9. Joel Prentiss Bishop, *Commentaries on the Law of Contracts* (Chicago: T. H. Flood, 1887), 215.

10. See, for example, Louisville and Nashville Railroad Company v. Palmes, 109 U.S. 244, 256 (1883); Mobile and Ohio Railroad Company v. Tennessee, 153 U.S. 486, 492–493 (1894); Douglas v. Kentucky, 168 U.S. 488, 502 (1897).

11. *Yard*, at 114.

12. Johnson v. Fletcher, 54 Miss. 628, 631 (1877).

13. Robards v. Brown, 40 Ark. 423, 427 (1883).

14. H. Campbell Black, "Legislation Impairing the Obligation of Contracts," *American Law Register* 34 (1886): 81, 92–94.

15. Penniman's Case, 103 U.S. 714 (1880).

16. Watkins v. Glenn, 55 Kan. 417, 40 P. 316, 321 (1895) (Allen, J., dissenting).

17. See Newton v. Commissioners, 100 U.S. 548, 559 (1880) (Swayne, J.), observing that "there can be no contract and no irrepealable law" concerning public offices.

18. Johnson v. Fletcher, 54 Miss. 628 (1877).

19. See Squire v. Mudgett, 61 N.H. 149 (1881), construing the homestead statute to apply prospectively to avoid violation of the contract clause.

20. Baldwin v. Flagg, 43 N.J.L. 495, 502–504 (1881).

21. *Robards*, at 423.

22. Swinburne v. Mills, 17 Wash. 611, 50 P. 489 (1897).

23. O'Brien v. Kreuz, 36 Minn. 136, 30 N.W. 458 (1886). See also Hallibert v. Porter, 28 Minn. 496, 11 N.W. 84 (1881), holding that a statute changing the rate of interest to be paid on redemption of foreclosed land impaired obligation of prior mortgage contracts and was void.

24. Barintz v. Beverly, 163 U.S. 118 (1896).

25. State ex rel. Thomas Cruse Savings Bank v. Gilliam, 18 Mont. 94, 45 P. 661 (1896); Hollister v. Donahoe, Sheriff, 11 S.D. 497, 78 N.W. 959 (1899); Savings Bank of San Diego County v. Barrett, 126 Cal. 413, 58 P. 914 (1899).

26. State v. McDonald, 26 Minn. 145, 1 N.W. 832 (1879); Hull v. State, 29 Fla. 79, 11 So. 97 (1892); State v. Fylpaa, 3 S.D. 586, 54 N.W. 599 (1893). See also Thomas M. Cooley, *A Treatise on the Constitutional Limitations Which Rest upon the Legislative Powers of the States of the American Union*, 4th ed. (Boston: Little, Brown, 1878), 356–357.

27. Rice v. Smith, 72 Miss. 42 (1894); Skinner v. Holt, 9 S.D. 427 (1896). See also In re Heilbron's Estate, 14 Wash. 536, 45 P. 153 (1896), holding that a statute exempting the proceeds of a life insurance policy from liability for the debts of the deceased construed to apply prospectively only so as not to impair existing contractual rights.

28. Denny v. Bennett, 128 U.S. 489 (1888).

29. Brown v. Smart, 145 U.S. 454 (1892).

30. Ewell v. Daggs, 108 U.S. 143 (1883).

31. Stone v. Mississippi, 101 U.S. 814, 816 (1880). See also Samuel Freeman Miller, "The Supreme Court of the United States," address at the University of Michigan, June 29, 1887, in Miller, *Lectures on the Constitution of the United States* (New York: Banks and Brothers, 1891), 393–394, noting that *Dartmouth College* "has been of late years much criticized" but stressing continued influence of the decision to protect the rights of creditors.

32. Pearsall v. Great Northern Railway Company, 161 U.S. 646, 660 (1896) (Brown, J.).

33. People v. O'Brien, 111 N.Y. 1, 49 (1888).

34. John M. Shirley, *The* Dartmouth College *Case and the Supreme Court of the United States* (St. Louis, MO: G. I. Jones, 1879); Charles Doe, "A New View of the *Dartmouth College* Case," *Harvard Law Review* 6 (1892): 161.

35. Francis Wharton, *Commentaries on Law* (Philadelphia, PA: Kay and Brothers, 1884), 554–557.

36. Bishop, *Commentaries on the Law of Contracts*, 218–219.

37. Christopher G. Tiedeman, *The Unwritten Constitution of the United States* (New York: G. P. Putnam's Sons, 1890), 54.

38. Ibid., 57–66.

39. Alfred Russell, "Status and Tendencies of the *Dartmouth College* Case," *American Law Review* 30 (1896): 321, 323.

40. Ibid., 349.

41. Ibid., 353–356.

42. Ibid., 355.

43. For an example of the infrequent reliance on *Dartmouth College* in this period, see Downing v. Indiana State Board of Agriculture, 129 Ind. 443, 28 N.E. 123 (1891), holding that an act abolishing the State Board of Agriculture, a private corporation, and transferring its assets to another body impaired the 1851 charter in violation of the contract clause.

44. Herbert Hovenkamp, *Enterprise and American Law, 1836–1937* (Cambridge, MA: Harvard University Press, 1991), 33.

45. The commerce clause and the due process clause of the Fourteenth Amendment were also at issue. For the rate regulation controversy, see James W. Ely, Jr., *Railroads and American Law* (Lawrence: University Press of Kansas, 2001), 80–99.

See also Richard C. Cortner, *The Iron Horse and the Constitution: The Railroads and the Transformation of the Fourteenth Amendment* (Westport, CT: Greenwood, 1993).

46. Georgia Railroad and Banking Company v. Smith, 128 U.S. 174, 180 (1888) (Field, J.).

47. Chicago, Burlington, and Quincy Railroad Company v. Iowa, 94 U.S. 155, 161 (1877) (Waite, C.J.).

48. Ibid., at 155; Ruggles v. Illinois, 108 U.S. 526 (1883) (Waite, C.J.).

49. Peik v. Chicago and North-Western Railway Company, 94 U.S. 164 (1877) (Waite, C.J.); Shields v. Ohio, 95 U.S. 319 (1877) (Swayne, J.).

50. Paul Kens, *The Supreme Court under Morrison R. Waite, 1874–1888* (Columbia: University of South Carolina Press, 2010), 73–89.

51. Stone v. Farmers' Loan and Trust Company, 116 U.S. 307 (1886).

52. Ibid., at 340.

53. Ibid., at 344–346. A similar result was reached in a companion case, Stone v. Illinois Central Railroad Company, 116 U.S. 347 (1886) (Waite, C.J.), denying that broad charter language conferred rate-making power on the carrier free of state controls.

54. Benjamin F. Wright, Jr., *The Contract Clause of the Constitution* (Cambridge, MA: Harvard University Press, 1938), 135.

55. See Georgia Railroad and Banking Company v. Smith, 128 U.S. 174, 180–182 (1888) (Field, J.), declaring, "Exemption must appear by such clear and unmistakable language that it cannot be reasonably construed consistently with the reservation of the power by the State."

56. St. Louis and San Francisco Railway Company v. Gill, 156 U.S. 649 (1895).

57. Russell, "Status and Tendencies of the *Dartmouth College* Case," 352.

58. Chicago, Milwaukee, and St. Paul Railway Company v. Minnesota, 134 U.S. 418 (1890).

59. Cortner, *Iron Horse and the Constitution,* 77–124; James W. Ely, Jr., "The Railroad Question Revisited: *Chicago, Milwaukee, and St. Paul Railway v. Minnesota* and Constitutional Limits on State Regulations," *Great Plains Quarterly* 12 (1992): 121–134.

60. On occasion, however, the contract clause did figure in rate controls of other industries, such as water companies. See Santa Ana Water Co. v. Town of San Buenaventura, 56 F. 339 (Cir. Ct. S.D. Cal. 1893), holding that the 1869 contract to furnish a water system to the town and conferring on a company the right to set rates could not be impaired by a subsequent constitution provision governing rates for water.

61. Wright, *Contract Clause,* 169.

62. *O'Brien,* at 49.

63. New Jersey v. Yard, 95 U.S. 104 (1877).

64. Railroad Company v. Richmond, 96 U.S. 521 (1878) (Waite, C.J.). See also Edward L. Pierce, *A Treatise on the Law of Railroads* (Boston: Little, Brown, 1881), 456–458, noting that by virtue of the reservation of power to amend contained in charters or general laws states could impose further duties and expenses on railroad companies without running afoul of the contract cause.

65. Spring Valley Water Works v. Schottler, 110 U.S. 347, 355 (1884).

66. People ex rel. New York Electric Lines Company v. Squire, 145 U.S. 175 (1892).

67. State Board of Assessors v. Central Railroad Company of New Jersey, 48 N.J.L. 146, 286, 4 A. 578 (1886).

68. Shields v. Ohio, 95 U.S. 319, 324 (1877).

69. Detroit v. Detroit and Howell Plank Road Co., 43 Mich. 140, 147 (1880).

70. Ibid., at 148.

71. *O'Brien*, at 49–53.

72. *Spring Valley Water Works,* at 371 (Field, J., dissenting). See also Railroad Company v. Maine, 96 U.S. 499 (1877) (Field, J.).

73. See Pierce, *Treatise on the Law of Railroads,* 459, declaring that the reserved power "ought not to sanction a reckless invasion of the rights of property, or a revolution in the character and objects of the corporation."

74. In other contexts, the Supreme Court in the late nineteenth century endorsed a broad understanding of the state police power. Paterson v. Kentucky, 97 U.S. 501, 504 (1879) (Harlan, J.): "By the settled doctrines of this court, the police power extends, at least, to the protection of the lives, the health, and the property of the community against the injurious exercise by any citizen of his own rights"; Barbier v. Connolly, 113 U.S. 27, 31 (1885) (Field, J.), affirming the reach of state police power "to prescribe regulations to promote the health, peace, morals, education, and good order of the people."

75. Boyd v. Alabama, 94 U.S. 645 (1876).

76. Ibid., at 650.

77. Beer Company v. Massachusetts, 97 U.S. 25 (1878).

78. Ibid., at 32–33.

79. Fertilizing Company v. Hyde Park, 97 U.S. 659 (1878) (Swayne, J.).

80. Ibid., at 674.

81. Ibid., at 679. Justice Miller, a persistent foe of allowing states to contract away their taxing authority, nonetheless reached a conclusion similar to that of Strong. Why, he asked, if a state can surrender its power of taxation by contract can it not agree not to exercise for a time the power to remove a nuisance. He even suggested that, if the community now wishes to destroy the contract with the fertilizing company, it should turn to eminent domain and pay compensation. Ibid., at 671.

82. Ibid., at 680.

83. Tiedeman, *Unwritten Constitution,* 60, discussing "an indefinite and elastic power, called the police power, in the exercise of which it is possible for the interests of the corporation to be jeopardized."

84. Stone v. Mississippi, 101 U.S. 814 (1880).

85. See Louisiana State Lottery Company v. Fitzpatrick, 15 Fed. Cases 970 (Cir. Ct. D. La. 1879), holding that the grant of a right to draw lotteries amounted to a contract that could not be impaired.

86. See State v. Morris, 77 N.C. 512 (1877), comparing lottery grants with liquor licenses, finding them revocable at the will of the legislature, and further declaring that it was not the intention of the contract clause to restrain state police power to preserve public morals.

87. *Stone,* at 819–821.

88. Ibid., at 821.

89. Charles Warren, *The Supreme Court in United States History,* rev. ed., vol. 2 (Boston: Little, Brown, 1926), 618–620.

90. Douglas v. Kentucky, 168 U.S. 488, 502 (1897) (Harlan, J.). See also Justice v. Commonwealth, 81 Va. 209 (1885).

91. New York and New England Railroad Company v. Bristol, 151 U.S. 556, 567 (1894). Fuller also pointed out that under the corporate charter the legislature retained the right to alter or amend the grant. See also St. Louis and San Francisco Railway Company v. Mathews, 165 U.S. 1, 23–24 (1897), rejecting the contract clause challenge to a state statute imposing strict liability on railroads for damage caused by fire.

92. Chicago, Burlington, and Quincy Railroad Company v. Nebraska, 170 U.S. 57 (1898).

93. Ibid., at 72.

94. Ibid., at 74.

95. Davenport and Morris v. Richmond City, 81 Va. 636 (1886).

96. Platte and Denver Canal and Milling Company v. Dowell, 17 Colo. 37, 30 P. 68 (1892).

97. The constitutionality of this monopoly grant was upheld in the Slaughterhouse Cases, 83 U.S. 36 (1873) against arguments that such a grant violated the Fourteenth Amendment.

98. Butchers' Union Slaughterhouse and Livestock Landing Company v. Crescent City Livestock Landing and Slaughterhouse Company, 111 U.S. 747 (1884).

99. *The Nation,* August 28, 1884, 173–174.

100. *Pearsall,* at 646.

101. Wright observed that the Court in *Pearsall* apparently applied the principle that the police power cannot be contracted away, "without quite admitting that it was doing so." *Contract Clause,* 209n.70.

102. *Pearsall,* at 673–675. See Robert J. Glennon, Jr., "Justice Henry Billings Brown: Values in Tension," *University of Colorado Law Review* 44 (1973): 553, 573–574, commenting that Brown's aversion to monopoly found expression in *Pearsall.*

103. Chicago Life Insurance Company v. Needles, 113 U.S. 574 (1885).

104. See Eagle Insurance Company v. Ohio, 153 U.S. 446 (1894) (White, J.), viewing *Needles* as a police power case and upholding subsequent regulation of life insurance companies.

105. For an overview of the Supreme Court's handling of the tax exemption cases, see Wright, *Contract Clause,* 179–184.

106. Michael R. Hyman, "Taxation, Public Policy, and Political Dissent: Yeoman Disaffection in the Post-Reconstruction Lower South," *Journal of Southern History* 55 (1989): 49, 56–62.

107. Palmes v. Louisville and Nashville Railroad Company, 19 Fla. 231, 254 (1882), affirmed 109 U.S. 244 (1883).

108. See Wilmington and Weldon Railroad Company v. Alsbrook, 146 U.S. 279, 294 (1892) (Fuller, C.J.): "The surrender of a power so vital cannot be left to inference or conceded in the presence of doubt, and when the language used admits of

reasonable contention, the conclusion is inevitable in favor of the reservation of the power."

109. For Field's antagonism to tax immunities, see Charles W. McCurdy, "Justice Field and the Jurisprudence of Government-Business Relations: Some Parameters of Laissez-Faire Constitutionalism, 1863–1897," *Journal of American History* 61 (1975): 970, 990–992.

110. Bishop, *Commentaries on the Law of Contracts,* 220.

111. Ernest W. Huffcut, "Legislative Tax-Exemption Contracts," *American Law Review* 24 (1890): 399, 400–401. See also James F. Colby, "Exemption from Taxation by Legislative Contract," *American Law Review* 13 (1879): 26, 37.

112. Given v. Wright, 117 U.S. 648, 655 (1886).

113. *Stone,* at 820.

114. *Yard,* at 105.

115. *Farrington,* at 679.

116. University v. People, 99 U.S. 309 (1878).

117. Mobile and Ohio Railroad Company v. Tennessee, 153 U.S. 486 (1894).

118. Ibid., at 501–507.

119. Ibid., at 507–508.

120. Vicksburg, Shreveport, and Pacific Railroad Company v. Dennis, 116 U.S. 665 (1886) (Gray, J.).

121. Ibid., at 671.

122. *Alsbrook,* at 279 (Fuller, C.J.).

123. County Commissioners v. Colorado Seminary, 12 Colo. 497, 21 P. 490 (1889).

124. Grand Lodge v. New Orleans, 166 U.S. 143 (1897) (Brown, J.). See also Welch v. Cook, 97 U.S. 541 (1878), holding that a District of Columbia act exempting from taxation for ten years all property employed for manufacturing purposes did not create an irrevocable contract.

125. Board of Commissioners of Santa Fe County v. New Mexico and Southern Pacific Railroad Company, 3 N.M. 116 (1884).

126. See, for example, Wilson v. Gaines, 103 U.S. 417 (1880) (Waite, C.J.); Louisville and Nashville Railroad Company v. Palmes, 109 U.S. 244 (1883); Memphis and Little Rock Railroad Company v. Railroad Commissioners, 112 U.S. 609 (1884).

127. Picard v. East Tennessee, Virginia, and Georgia Railroad Company, 130 U.S. 637, 641 (1889).

128. Railroad Company v. Maine, 96 U.S. 499 (1878) (Field, J.); Railroad Company v. Georgia, 98 U.S. 359 (1878).

129. St. Louis, Iron Mountain, and Southern Railway Company v. Berry, 41 Ark. 509 (1883).

130. Tennessee v. Whitworth, 117 U.S. 139 (1886).

131. State v. Morris and Essex Railroad Company, 49 N.J.L. 193 (1886).

132. Christopher Grandy, "Can Government Be Trusted to Keep Its Part of a Social Contract? New Jersey and the Railroads, 1825–1888," *Journal of Law, Economics, and Organization,* 2 (1989): 249–269.

133. Warren, *Supreme Court in United States History,* vol. 2, 677.

134. Long Island Water Supply Company v. Brooklyn, 166 U.S. 685 (1897) (Brewer, J.).

135. In re Opening Twenty-second Street, 102 Pa. 108 (1883).

136. Keller, *Affairs of State*, 340–341.

137. For example, Syracuse Water Company v. City of Syracuse, 116 N.Y. 167, 22 N.E. 381 (1889), invoked the principle of strict construction of corporate charters and determined that an 1849 franchise to furnish water to the inhabitants of Syracuse did not confer an exclusive privilege. Consequently, there was no contractual impairment when the city authorized a competing water company.

138. New Orleans Gas Company v. Louisiana Light Company, 115 U.S. 650 (1885).

139. Ibid., at 670–673.

140. For decisions reaching the same result, see New Orleans Water Works Company v. Rivers, 115 U.S. 674 (1885) (Harlan, J.); Louisville Gas Company v. Citizens' Gas Company, 115 U.S. 683 (1885) (Harlan, J.).

141. Walla Walla City v. Walla Walla Water Company, 172 U.S. 1 (1898).

142. Ibid., at 17–18.

143. Lehigh Water Company v. Easton, 121 U.S. 388 (1887).

144. Ibid., at 392.

145. Hamilton Gaslight and Coke Company v. City of Hamilton, 146 U.S. 258 (1892) (Harlan, J.); Bienville Water Supply Company v. City of Mobile, 175 U.S. 109 (1899) (Fuller, C.J.).

146. Houston and Texas Central Railway Company v. Texas, 170 U.S. 243 (1898) (Fuller, C.J.).

147. Illinois Central Railroad v. Illinois, 146 U.S. 387 (1892). For the background of this case, see Joseph D. Kearney and Thomas W. Merrill, "The Origins of the American Public Trust Doctrine: What Really Happened in *Illinois Central*," *University of Chicago Law Review* 71 (2004): 800, 805–924.

148. *Illinois Central*, at 452.

149. Ibid.

150. For a critical appraisal of Field's reasoning, see David P. Currie, "The Constitution in the Supreme Court: The Protection of Economic Interests, 1889–1910," *University of Chicago Law Review* 52 (1985): 324, 331–334.

151. *Illinois Central*, at 454. See Paul Kens, *Justice Stephen Field: Shaping Liberty from the Gold Rush to the Gilded Age* (Lawrence: University Press of Kansas, 1997), 249–250; Kearney and Merrill, "Origins of the American Public Trust Doctrine," 926: "We can only speculate that Justice Field was incensed by what he imagined to be a power grab by a privileged corporation, shutting out all competition from potential rivals."

152. In fact, the Supreme Court had previously ruled that states held dominion over lands beneath navigable waters and could grant them to private parties as they saw fit. Hoboken v. Pennsylvania Railroad, 124 U.S. 656 (1887) (Matthews, J.).

153. *Illinois Central*, at 474.

154. Ibid. See also "The Police Power and the Lake Front Case," *Harvard Law Review* 6 (1893): 444, noting that in *Illinois Central* the issue was really monetary, "for it is here only pecuniary welfare that is affected; the community saves what constitutional confiscation would cost."

155. Ibid.

156. Shively v. Bowlby, 152 U.S. 1 (1894) (Gray, J.).

157. See Wright, *Contract Clause*, 210, declaring that the decision might have been better grounded on the police power than public trust. Compare Eric Pearson, "*Illinois Central* and the Public Trust Doctrine in State Law," *Virginia Environmental Law Journal* 15 (1996): 713, asserting that the Court's analysis in *Illinois Central* was flawed and questioning its authoritative status, with Douglas L. Grant, "Underpinnings of the Public Trust Doctrine: Lessons from *Illinois Central Railroad*," *Arizona State Law Journal* 33 (2001): 849, arguing that the case should be viewed as an application of the inalienable police power.

158. See, for example, Joseph Sax, "The Public Trust Doctrine in Natural Resource Law: Effective Judicial Intervention," *Michigan Law Review* 68 (1970): 471.

159. Murray v. Charleston, 96 U.S. 432 (1878).

160. Ibid., at 448. See also Hartman v. Greenhow, 102 U.S. 672 (1880) (Field, J.).

161. United States ex rel. Merchants' National Bank v. Jefferson County, 26 Fed. Cases 597 (Cir. Ct. E.D. Ark. 1878); United States ex rel. Carhart v. Miller, 26 Fed. Cases 1258 (Cir. Ct. E.D. Ark. 1878); United States ex rel. Foote v. Jefferson County, 26 Fed. Cases 632 (Cir. Ct. E.D. Mo. 1879); United States ex rel. Douglass v. Justices of County Court of Lincoln County, 26 Fed. Cases 670 (Cir. Ct. E.D. Mo. 1879).

162. *Merchants' National Bank*, at 603.

163. Wolff v. New Orleans, 103 U.S. 358 (1880); Louisiana v. Pilsbury, 105 U.S. 278 (1882).

164. *Pilsbury*, at 298, 300.

165. John F. Dillon, *A Treatise on the Law of Municipal Corporations* (Chicago: James Cockcroft, 1872), 157–158.

166. Mount Pleasant v. Beckwith, 100 U.S. 514 (1879).

167. Warren, *Supreme Court in United States History*, vol. 2, 663.

168. Louisiana ex rel. Elliott v. Jumel, 107 U.S. 711 (1883). The Eleventh Amendment states, "The Judicial power of the United States shall not be construed to extend to any suit in law or equity, commenced or prosecuted against one of the United States by Citizens of another State, or by Citizens or Subjects of any Foreign State."

169. *Jumel*, at 733, 740.

170. Ibid., at 740.

171. Ibid., at 769.

172. John V. Orth, *The Judicial Power of the United States* (New York: Oxford University Press, 1987), 58–89; Warren, *Supreme Court in United States History*, vol. 2, 663–671.

173. Lincoln County v. Luning, 133 U.S. 529 (1890) (Brewer, J.).

174. *Jumel*, at 727.

175. Orth, *Judicial Power of the United States*, 110–120.

176. Ibid., 90–93.

177. James Tice Moore, *Two Paths to the New South: The Virginia Debt Controversy, 1870–1883* (Lexington: University Press of Kentucky, 1974).

178. James G. Randall, "The Virginia Debt Controversy," *Political Science Quarterly* 30 (1915): 553, 560.

179. Antoni v. Wright, 22 Gratt. 833, 859 (Va. 1872). See also Clarke v. Tyler, 30 Gratt. 134 (Va. 1878) (reaffirming *Antoni*). For the political pressures on the Virginia Supreme Court of Appeals during the coupon controversy, see Margaret Virginia

Nelson, *A Study of Judicial Review in Virginia, 1789–1928* (New York: Columbia University Press, 1947), 110–120.

180. *Hartman*, at 672.

181. See C. V. Meredith, "As to Impairing the Obligation of a Contract," *Virginia Law Journal* 6 (1882): 385, arguing that the substitution of a burdensome remedy impaired the contractual rights of creditors.

182. *Antoni*, at 782. Justice Stanley Matthews concurred, citing the *Jumel* case and raising the Eleventh Amendment as a bar to a federal judicial remedy against a state for impairment of contract.

183. *Antoni*, at 791, 797. Harlan also dissented on contract clause grounds. Wright wrote that Field and Harlan took the "very reasonable ground that the new remedy, because of the expense of enforcing, alters materially the existing contract."

184. Virginia Coupon Cases, 114 U.S. 269 (1885).

185. McGahey v. Virginia, 135 U.S. 662, 694 (1890) (Bradley, J.).

186. Cuthbert v. Virginia, 135 U.S. 698, 700–701 (1890) (Bradley, J.).

187. Vashon v. Greenhow, 135 U.S. 713, 721 (1890) (Bradley, J.).

188. Douglass v. County of Pike, 101 U.S. 677, 687 (1880).

189. *Pilsbury*, at 294–295.

190. Civil Rights Cases, 109 U.S. 3, 12–13 (1883).

191. Lehigh Water Company v. Easton, 121 U.S. 388, 391–392 (1887). See also New Orleans Waterworks Company v. Louisiana Sugar Refining Company, 125 U.S. 18, 36–38 (1888) (Gray, J.), finding no federal jurisdiction where the state court did not give effect to a subsequent statute.

192. Central Land Company v. Laidley, 159 U.S. 103 (1895).

193. Ibid., at 109.

194. Conrad Reno, "Impairment of Contracts by Change of Judicial Opinion," *American Law Review* 23 (1889): 190, 199.

195. Ibid., 200.

196. Ibid., 201.

197. William H. Rand, Jr., "*Swift v. Tyson* versus *Gelpcke v. Dubuque*," *Harvard Law Review* 8 (1895): 328, 346–347.

198. James Bradley Thayer, """The Case of *Gelpcke v. Dubuque*," *Harvard Law Review* 4 (1891): 311, 319–320.

199. See Barton H. Thompson, Jr., "The History of the Judicial Impairment 'Doctrine' and Its Lessons for the Contract Clause," *Stanford Law Review* 44 (1992): 1373, 1430–1434, suggesting that the Supreme Court resolved these cases on an ad hoc basis.

200. Wright, *Contract Clause*, 238: "It is easier to believe that bondholders were being given justice than that the Supreme Court has invariably adhered to its principle that a judicial decision cannot impair the obligation of contracts under the Constitution."

201. Linda Przybyszewski, *The Republic According to John Marshall Harlan* (Chapel Hill: University of North Carolina Press, 1999), 156–157.

202. Maynard v. Hill, 125 U.S. 190 (1888).

203. See Joel Prentiss Bishop, *New Commentaries on Marriage, Divorce, and Separation*, vol. 1 (Chicago: T. H. Flood, 1891), 594–595, asserting that the contract

clause had no application to either judicial or legislative divorces. See in general Mark E. Brandon, *States of Union: Family and Change in the American Constitutional Order* (Lawrence: University Press of Kansas, 2013), 212–214.

204. For Field's approach to the contract clause, see Kens, *Justice Stephen Field*, 242–257; McCurdy, "Justice Field and the Jurisprudence of Government-Business Relations," 989–995.

205. Munn v. Illinois, 94 U.S. 113, 143 (1877) (Field, J., dissenting).

206. *Antoni*, at 801 (Field, J., dissenting).

207. James W. Ely, Jr., "The Protection of Contractual Rights: A Tale of Two Constitutional Provisions," *NYU Journal of Law and Liberty* 1 (2005): 383–388.

208. Allgeyer v. Louisiana, 165 U.S. 578, 589 (1897).

209. See, for example, David E. Bernstein, *Rehabilitating* Lochner*: Defending Individual Rights against Progressive Reform* (Chicago: University of Chicago Press, 2011); David N. Mayer, *Liberty of Contract: Rediscovering a Lost Constitutional Right* (Washington, DC: Cato Institute, 2011); Harry N. Scheiber, *The State and Freedom of Contract* (Palo Alto, CA: Stanford University Press, 1998).

210. Both federal and state courts stressed this understanding of the contract clause. *Denny*, at 489 (1888) (Miller, J.); *Squire*, at 149.

211. Hanover National Bank v. Moyses, 186 U.S. 181, 188 (1902).

212. Christopher G. Tiedeman, A *Treatise on the Limitations of Police Power in the United States* (St. Louis, MO: F. H. Thomas, 1886), 516.

CHAPTER 6. THE EARLY TWENTIETH CENTURY

1. For example, Stearns v. Minnesota, 179 U.S. 223, 232–233 (1900) (Brewer, J.); Appleby v. City of New York, 271 U.S. 364, 379–380 (1926) (Taft, C.J.).

2. "Note: The Contract Clause of the Federal Constitution," *Columbia Law Review* 32 (1932): 476, 478: "The last fifty years have witnessed a decline in the importance of the contract clause. The limelight has shifted to due process."

3. The Supreme Court of Florida, however, stressed the importance of the contract clause in Humphreys v. State ex rel. Palm Beach Company, 108 Fla. 92, 145 S. 858 (1933).

4. Pennsylvania Coal Company v. Mahon, 260 U.S. 393 (1922).

5. For the background of this important case, see William A. Fischel, *Regulatory Takings: Law, Economics, and Politics* (Cambridge, MA: Harvard University Press, 1995), 13–30; Lawrence M. Friedman, "A Search for Seizure: *Pennsylvania Coal Co. v. Mahon* in Context," *Law and History Review* 4 (1986): 1–22.

6. *Pennsylvania Coal*, at 420–421.

7. Morton Keller, *Regulating a New Economy: Public Policy and Economic Change in America, 1900–1933* (Cambridge, MA: Harvard University Press, 1990), 99–101.

8. James W. Ely, Jr., "The Progressive Era Assault on Individualism and Property Rights," *Social Philosophy and Policy* 29 (2012): 255, 264–277.

9. Richard T. Ely, *Property and Contract in Their Relation to the Distribution of Wealth*, vol. 2 (New York: Macmillan, 1914), 615–618; Ray A. Brown, "Police

Power—Legislation for Health and Personal Safety," *Harvard Law Review* 42 (1929): 866, 896–897.

10. Barbara H. Fried, *The Progressive Assault on Laissez Faire: Robert Hale and the First Law and Economics Movement* (Cambridge, MA: Harvard University Press, 1998), 16–17: "Contract terms, progressives argued, rather than being simple expressions of free will, were determined by each party's relative ability to hold out for more acceptable terms."

11. Ibid., 44. Maurice H. Merrill, "Application of the Obligation of Contract Clause to State Promises," *University of Pennsylvania Law Review* 80 (1932): 639, 664–665.

12. Muhlker v. New York and Harlem Railroad Company, 197 U.S. 544, 550 (1905) (argument for plaintiff in error).

13. "Note: Constitutionality of the New York Emergency Housing Law," *Harvard Law Review* 34 (1921): 426, 430.

14. Bradley v. Lightcap, 195 U.S. 1 (1904).

15. Hooker v. Burr, 194 U.S. 415 (1904) (Peckham, J.).

16. See State ex rel. Akerson, Gooch, and Co. v. Hurlburt, 93 Or. 34, 182 P. 169, 172 (1919): "The logic of the [*Hooker*] opinion seems, to the writer, to be questionable."

17. Smith v. Spillman, 135 Ark. 279, 205 S.W. 107 (1918); *Akerson, Gooch, and Co.*, at 169.

18. First National Bank of Turtle Lake v. Bovey, Shute, and Jackson, Inc., 419 N.D. 450, 191 N.W. 765 (1922).

19. Heritage Loan Co. v. Daykin, 56 S.W.2d 164 (Tenn. 1933).

20. Bank of Minden v. Clement, 256 U.S. 126 (1921).

21. Compare Farmers' Co-operative Creamery Co. v. Iowa State Insurance Co., 84 N.W. 904 (1900) with Smith and Marsh v. Northern Neck Mutual Fire Association, 112 Va. 192, 70 S.E. 482 (1911).

22. Sliosberg v. New York Life Insurance Company, 244 N.Y. 482, 155 N.E. 749 (1927).

23. Ibid., at 497, 155 N.E. at 755.

24. Manigualt v. Springs, 199 U.S. 473 (1905).

25. Ibid., at 480.

26. David P. Currie, "The Constitution in the Supreme Court: The Protection of Economic Interests, 1889–1910," *University of Chicago Law Review* 52 (1985): 324, 334–335. See also Benjamin F. Wright, *The Contract Clause of the Constitution* (Cambridge, MA: Harvard University Press, 1938), 211–212; Robert L. Hale, "The Supreme Court and the Contract Clause," pt. 2, *Harvard Law Review* 57 (1944): 621, 671–674.

27. Hudson County Water Company v. McCarter, 209 U.S. 349, 357 (1908). The principal argument turned upon whether water was an article of interstate commerce.

28. See Dillingham v. McLaughlin, 264 U.S. 370, 374 (1924), holding that a law limiting the business of handling small deposits to corporations did not impair prior contracts between the common law trust and individual depositors. See also Union Dry Goods Company v. Georgia Public Service Corp., 248 U.S. 372, 377 (1919), observing that "the right of private contract must yield to the exigencies of

the public welfare when determined in an appropriate manner by the authority of the state."

29. Robert M. Fogelson, *The Great Rent Wars: New York City, 1917–1929* (New Haven, CT: Yale University Press, 2013), 17–152; Keller, *Regulating a New Economy*, 178–179. See also Samuel McCune Lindsay, *Some Economic Aspects of the Recent Emergency Housing Legislation in New York* (New York: Ballou, 1924), questioning the existence of a housing shortage in New York City in 1920.

30. See Roger I. Roots, "Government by Permanent Emergency: The Forgotten History of the New Deal Constitution," *Suffolk University Law Review* 33 (2000): 259, 269–275, discussing the evolution of the emergency powers doctrine.

31. Compare "Note: Constitutionality of the New York Emergency Housing Laws" *Harvard Law Review* 34 (1921): 426, 430: "Where, however, the contract in question is an ordinary private contract, valid when made, it would seem to be going counter to the plain words of the Constitution to hold that a state, even in the exercise of the police power, could impair it" with Alan W. Boyd, "Rent Regulation under the Police Power," *Michigan Law Review* 19 (1921): 599, 606: "Why should contract rights be more sacred, where public welfare is concerned, than other property rights?"

32. New York v. LaFetra, 230 N.Y. 429, 130 N.E. 601 (1921). See also Levy Leasing Company v. Siegel, 230 N.Y. 631 (1921). See generally Fogelson, *Great Rent Wars*, 211–228.

33. See William E. Nelson, *The Legalist Reformation: Law, Politics, and Ideology in New York, 1920–1980* (Chapel Hill: University of North Carolina Press, 2001), stressing that New York courts espoused an expansive reading of the police power to encompass legislative authority to deal with emergency conditions.

34. *Levy Leasing Company*, at 640–641 (McLaughlin, J., dissenting).

35. Block v. Hirsh, 256 U.S. 135 (1921).

36. Marcus Brown Holding Company v. Feldman, 256 U.S. 170, 198 (1921). See also Edgar A. Levy Leasing Company v. Siegel, 258 U.S. 242 (1922).

37. *Block*, at 158–170 (McKenna, J. dissenting).

38. Chastleton Corp. v. Sinclair, 264 U.S. 543 (1924).

39. Ibid., at 547–549.

40. Peck v. Fink, 2 F.2d 912, 913 (Ct. App. D.C. 1924), cert. den. 266 U.S. 631 (1925). The New York legislature allowed the rent-control measures for the City of New York to lapse, effective June 1, 1929. An effort by the New York City Council to continue rent controls based on a municipal law was invalidated as exceeding the home-rule powers of the city. Although the outcome did not turn upon the contract clause, the court observed, "The relation of landlord and tenant is plainly contractual and the attempt to interfere between them after the amount of rental has been agreed upon and base it upon what the court may deem just and reasonable, is clearly a measure which alters the very essence of contract." Gennis v. Milano, 135 Misc. 209, 211, 237 N.Y.S. 432, 434 (1st Dept. 1930).

41. Ernst Freund, *The Police Power: Public Policy and Constitutional Rights* (Chicago: Callaghan, 1904), 361–368.

42. See, for example, Scott County Macadamized Road Company v. Missouri, 215 U.S. 336 (1909) (Holmes, J.); Fifth Avenue Coach Co. v. New York, 221 U.S. 467

(1911) (McKenna, J.), finding no contract between the state and the bus company regarding the right to place advertising on vehicles; Pierce Oil Corporation v. City of Hope, 248 U.S. 498 (1919) (Holmes, J.); King Manufacturing Company v. Augusta, 277 U.S. 100 (1928) (Van Devanter, J.); Kirk, Superintendent of Public Works v. Maumee Valley Electric Company, 279 U.S. 797 (1929) (Stone, J.).

43. Stearns v. Minnesota, 179 U.S. 223 (Brewer, J.).

44. Wright v. Georgia Railroad and Banking Company, 216 U.S. 420 (1910).

45. In a singular case the Supreme Court found that a state franchise tax on net income of a business corporation in effect imposed a levy on tax-exempt bonds held by the corporation and thus impaired the statutory contract by the state exempting such bonds from taxation. Macallen Company v. Massachusetts, 279 U.S. 620 (1929) (Sutherland, J.). This decision appears to have been subsequently distinguished or criticized. In Tradesmen's National Bank v. Oklahoma Tax Commission, 309 U.S. 560, 566 (1940) the Supreme Court questioned the continuing validity of *Macallen*.

46. For example, Wisconsin and Michigan Railway Company v. Powers, 191 U.S. 379, 387 (1903); Wright v. Georgia Railroad and Banking Company, 216 U.S. 420, 438 (1910).

47. See, for example, *Powers;* Seton Hall College v. South Orange, 242 U.S. 100 (1916); Troy Union Railroad Company v. Mealy, 254 U.S. 47 (1920); Clyde v. Gilchrist, 262 U.S. 94 (1923).

48. Morris Canal and Banking Company v. Baird, 239 U.S. 126 (1915).

49. See Rochester Railway Company v. City of Rochester, 205 U.S. 236 (1907), regarding assessment for paving between tracks; *Wright*, at 436–437.

50. Los Angeles v. Los Angeles City Water Company, 177 U.S. 559 (1900) (McKenna, J.).

51. Detroit v. Detroit Citizens' Street Railway Company, 184 U.S. 386 (1902).

52. Ibid., at 398.

53. For example, City of Cleveland v. Cleveland City Railway Company, 194 U.S. 517 (1904); City of Minneapolis v. Minnesota Street Railway Company, 215 U.S. 417 (1910); Detroit United Railway v. City of Detroit, 248 U.S. 429 (1919). See also Georgia Railway and Power Company v. Town of Decatur, 262 U.S. 432 (1923), holding that a decision of the state court holding that 5 cent-fare applicable to added territory beyond original corporate limits impaired the contract by adding to the burden of the street railway company.

54. See Wright, *Contract Clause of the Constitution,* 138, suggesting that the explanation may be found in "the definiteness" of the five-cent-fare provisions.

55. People ex rel. City of New York v. Nixon, 229 N.Y. 356, 128 N.E. 245 (1920).

56. Knoxville Water Company v. Knoxville, 189 U.S. 434 (1903). See also Portland Railway, Light, and Power Company v. Railroad Commission of Oregon, 229 U.S. 397 (1913), deeming a contract providing favorable fares to an outlying community subject to state control over transportation charges.

57. See Union Dry Goods v. Georgia Public Service Corporation, 248 U.S. 372, 377 (1919), stating that the public interest in electricity justified rate regulation under the police power.

58. Central Union Telephone Co. v. Indianapolis Telephone Co., 189 Ind. 21, 126 N.E. 628 (1920).

59. See Christopher G. Tiedeman, "Government Ownership of Public Utilities," *Harvard Law Review* 16 (1903): 476, 483, noting increased municipal ownership of waterworks and electric plants and contending that government ownership of public utilities might be desirable.

60. Skaneateles Water Works Company v. Skaneateles, 184 U.S. 354 (1902).

61. For example, see Bienville Water Supply Company v. Mobile, 186 U.S. 212 (1902) (Brewer, J.), holding that the franchise was granted no exclusive privilege to furnish water and that building a municipal water system did not infringe any contract; Helena Water Works Company v. Helena, 195 U.S. 383 (1904).

62. Knoxville Water Company v. Knoxville, 200 U.S. 453 (1906) (Harlan, J.). See also United Railroads v. San Francisco, 249 U.S. 517 (1919) (Holmes, J.), holding that the grant of a street railroad franchise did not restrict the city from constructing its own railway.

63. Vicksburg v. Vicksburg Waterworks Company, 202 U.S. 453 (1906) (Day, J.). See also Old Colony Trust Company v. City of Omaha, 230 U.S. 100 (1913) (Van Devanter, J.), holding that an ordinance directing the grantee of franchise to remove poles and wires transmitting electricity to private persons was arbitrary impairment of the contract granting perpetual rights.

64. Keller, *Regulating a New Economy*, 57.

65. West Chicago Street Railroad Company v. Illinois ex rel. City of Chicago, 201 U.S. 506 (1906) (Harlan, J.).

66. Northern Pacific Railway Company v. Duluth, 208 U.S. 583 (1908).

67. Chicago and Alton Railroad Company v. Tranbarger, 238 U.S. 67 (1915).

68. Missouri, Kansas, and Texas Railway Company v. Oklahoma, 271 U.S. 303 (1926).

69. Atlantic Coast Line Railroad Company v. City of Goldsboro, 232 U.S. 548 (1914).

70. Ibid., at 558.

71. Denver and Rio Grande Railroad Company v. Denver, 250 U.S. 241 (1919).

72. Texas and New Orleans Railroad Company v. Miller, 221 U.S. 408 (1911) (Van Devanter, J.).

73. Grand Trunk Western Railway Company v. City of South Bend, 227 U.S. 544 (1913).

74. Sproles v. Binford, 286 U.S. 374 (1932).

75. Ibid., at 390.

76. *Chicago and Alton Railroad*, at 77. See also Pierce Oil Corporation v. City of Hope, 248 U.S. 498 (1919) (Holmes, J.), declaring that any contract by the city to limit its power "to legislate if the public welfare should require it" would be ineffective.

77. Appleby v. City of New York, 271 U.S. 364 (1926).

78. Ibid., at 395.

79. Ibid., at 403. For a discussion of *Appleby*, see Eric Pearson, "*Illinois Central* and the Public Trust Doctrine in State Law," *Virginia Environmental Law Review* 15 (1996): 713, 739–740.

80. In a companion case Taft similarly ruled that the refusal of the city, pursuant to a later statute, to permit the landowners to fill up their underwater lots impaired the contract made with the city by covenants in the deeds. Appleby v. Delaney, 271 U.S. 403 (1926).

81. Cincinnati v. Louisville and Nashville Railroad Company, 223 U.S. 390, 400–401 (1912).

82. Pennsylvania Hospital v. City of Philadelphia, 245 U.S. 20 (1917) (White, C.J.).

83. Oshkosh Waterworks Company v. Oshkosh, 187 U.S. 437 (1903) (Harlan, J.).

84. Pittsburg Steel Company v. Baltimore Equitable Society, 226 U.S. 455 (1913) (Holmes, J.). See also Henley v. Myers, 215 U.S. 373 (1910) (Harlan, J.), upholding against a contract clause challenge a statute substituting a receiver for individual actions against stockholders of an insolvent corporation and observing: "It is a well-established doctrine that mere methods of procedure in actions on contract that do not affect the substantial rights of parties are always within the control of the State."

85. W. B. Worthen v. Kavanaugh, 295 U.S. 56, 60 (1935).

86. Houston and Texas Central Railroad Company v. Texas, 177 U.S. 66 (1900) (Peckham, J.).

87. Louisiana v. City of New Orleans, 215 U.S. 170 (1909).

88. Chicago Title and Trust Company v. Hagler Special School District, 178 Ark. 443, 12 S.W.2d 881 (1928).

89. Humphreys v. State ex rel. Palm Beach Company, 108 Fla. 92, 145 S. 858 (1933).

90. State ex rel. Sherrill v. Milam, 113 Fla. 491, 153 So. 100 (1933).

91. Larson v. South Dakota, 278 U.S. 429 (1929).

92. Snidow v. Board of Supervisors of Giles County, 123 Va. 578, 96 S.E. 810 (1918).

93. Ratcliffe v. Pulaski Turnpike Company, 69 Ark. 264 (1901).

94. Carondelet Canal and Navigation Company v. Louisiana, 233 U.S. 362 (1914).

95. Columbia Railway, Gas, and Electric Company v. South Carolina, 261 U.S. 236 (1923).

96. Ibid., at 251.

97. For the background of the debate over judicial impairments, see Chapter 3.

98. Hubert v. New Orleans, 215 U.S. 170, 175 (1909). See also *Houston and Texas Central Railroad*, at 100; *Oshkosh Waterworks Company*, at 446: "The contract clause of the Constitution of the United States has reference only to a statute of a State enacted after the making of the contract whose obligation is alleged to have been impaired"; Cross Lake Club v. Louisiana, 224 U.S. 632, 638 (1912): "This clause, as its terms disclose, is not directed against all impairment of contract obligations, but only against such as results from a subsequent exertion of the legislative power of the State"; Ross v. Oregon, 227 U.S. 150, 161 (1913), declaring that the contract clause "according to the natural import of its terms, is a restraint upon the legislative power and concern[s] the making of laws, not their construction by the courts"; Moore-Mansfield Construction Company v. Electrical Company, 234 U.S. 619, 624–625 (1914).

99. For the legal issues caused by elevated railroad construction in urban areas, see Molly Selvin, *This Tender and Delicate Business: The Public Trust Doctrine in American Law and Economic Policy, 1789–1920* (New York: Garland, 1987), 299–339.

100. *Muhlker,* at 544.

101. Ibid., at 552.

102. Justice Henry Billings Brown concurred in result but did not write an opinion.

103. For an analysis of *Muhlker* and the judicial impairment doctrine, see Wright, *Contract Clause of the Constitution,* 240–241; Barton H. Thompson, Jr., "The History of the Judicial Impairment 'Doctrine' and Its Lessons for the Contract Clause," *Stanford Law Review* 44 (1992): 1373, 1435–1436; John Martinez, "Taking Time Seriously: The Federal Constitutional Right to Be Free from 'Startling' State Court Overrulings," *Harvard Journal of Law and Public Policy* 11 (1998): 321–327.

104. *Muhlker,* at 570.

105. W. E. Dodd, "Impairment of the Obligation of Contract by State Judicial Decisions," *Illinois Law Review* 4 (1909): 27, 331.

106. Birrell v. New York and Harlem Railroad Company, 198 U.S. 390 (1905) (McKenna, J.).

107. Sauer v. City of New York, 206 U.S. 536, 556 (1907).

108. *Muhlker,* at 575.

109. Dodd, "Impairment of the Obligation of Contract by State Judicial Decisions," 327.

110. Ibid., 332.

111. James E. Babb, "Effect of Overruling Opinion of Court of Last Resort on Rights Acquired on Opinion Overruled," *American Law Review* 45 (1911): 750, 751.

112. Tidal Oil Company v. Flanagan, 263 U.S. 444 (1924).

113. Ibid., at 454.

114. Wright, *Contract Clause of the Constitution,* 242.

115. Richard A. Epstein, "Toward a Revitalization of the Contract Clause," *University of Chicago Law Review* 51 (1984): 703, 747–750; Thompson, "History of the Judicial Impairment 'Doctrine,'" 1438–1439.

116. Robert H. Skilton, "Mortgage Moratoria since 1933," *University of Pennsylvania Law Review* 92 (1943): 53, 54–55.

117. State ex rel. Cleveringa v. Klein, 63 N.D. 514, 249 N.W. 118 (1933).

118. Ibid., at 536, 249 N.W. at 128.

119. Life Insurance Company of Virginia v. Sanders, 62 S.W.2d 343 (Tex. Civ. App. 1933).

120. Ibid., at 353. See also Stewart v. Nelson, 54 Idaho 437, 32 P.2d 843 (1934), finding that a law providing that no mortgage should be enforceable after ten years from maturity of debts that secure the mortgage violated both federal and state contract clauses with respect to prior contracts and rejecting the argument that the law pertained only to the remedy.

121. State ex rel. Osage County Savings and Loan v. Worten, 167 Okla. 187, 203, 29 P.2d 1, 17 (1933).

122. Vanderbilt v. Brunton Piano Co., 111 N.J.L. 596, 169 A. 177 (1933).

123. Ibid., at 603, 169 A. at 180.

124. Adams v. Spillyards, 187 Ark. 641, 61 S.W.2d 686 (1933).

125. William L. Prosser, "The Minnesota Mortgage Moratorium," *Southern California Law Review* 7 (1934): 353, 357–358.

126. Home Building and Loan Association v. Blaisdell, 290 U.S. 398 (1934). For the background of this case, see John A. Fliter and Derek S. Hoff, *Fighting Foreclosure: The* Blaisdell *Case, the Contract Clause, and the Great Depression* (Lawrence: University Press of Kansas, 2012).

127. *Blaisdell*, at 426.

128. Ibid., at 428.

129. Ibid., at 437.

130. Ibid., at 443.

131. Ibid., at 444.

132. See G. Edward White, *The Constitution and the New Deal* (Cambridge, MA: Harvard University Press, 2000), 211–215, discussing shifting constitutional theories implicit in the Hughes opinion and commenting, "When the Supreme Court declined to apply a constitutional provision to the very situation for which it had been designed, it appeared to be making new law."

133. Samuel R. Olken, "Charles Evans Hughes and the *Blaisdell* Decision: A Historical Study of Contract Clause Jurisprudence," *Oregon Law Review* 72 (1993): 513, 591–595. See also Richard A. Maidment, "Chief Justice Hughes and the Contract Clause: A Reassessment," *Journal of Legal History* 8 (1987): 316, 326: "He was able to permit the law to stand without destroying the credibility of the contract clause and its protections."

134. *Blaisdell*, at 488.

135. Ibid., at 472.

136. Ibid., at 483. For Sutherland's dissent in *Blaisdell*, see Hadley Arkes, *The Return of George Sutherland: Restoring a Jurisprudence of Natural Rights* (Princeton, NJ: Princeton University Press, 1994), 245–247; Robert C. Palmer, "Obligations of Contracts: Intent and Distortion," *Case Western Reserve Law Review* 37 (1987): 650, commenting, "Sutherland clearly had the better historical argument." For a critical assessment of Sutherland's opinion, see Samuel R. Olken, "Justice Sutherland Reconsidered," *Vanderbilt Law Review* 62 (2009): 639, 674–676.

137. W. B. Worthen Co. v. Thomas, 292 U.S. 426 (1934). Sutherland concurred, again arguing that an emergency cannot "ever furnish an occasion for justifying, a nullification of the constitutional restriction upon state power in respect of the impairment of contractual obligations." Ibid., at 434–435.

138. *Kavanaugh*, at 56 (Cardozo, J.).

139. Treigle v. Acme Homestead Association, 297 U.S. 189 (1936) (Roberts, J.).

140. Wood v. Lovett, 313 U.S. 362 (1941) (Roberts, J.).

141. See Wright, *Contract Clause*, 111–119, picturing this line of decisions as narrowing the reach of *Blaisdell*.

142. *Wood*, at 382–383.

143. For Depression Era statutes limiting deficiency judgments, see J. Douglass Poteat, "State Legislative Relief for the Mortgage Debtor during the Depression," *Law and Contemporary Problems* 5 (1938): 517, 529–536; Geoff Walsh, "The Finger in the Dike: State and Local Laws Combat the Foreclosure Tide," *Suffolk University Law Review* 44 (2011): 139, 143–144, 148–149.

144. Richmond Mortgage and Loan Association v. Wachovia Bank and Trust, 300 U.S. 124 (1937) (Roberts, J.).

145. Ibid., at 130. See also Honeyman v. Jacobs, 306 U.S. 535 (1939) (Hughes, C.J.).

146. For example, Edward S. Corwin, "Moratorium over Minnesota," *University of Pennsylvania Law Review* 82 (1934): 311; Melvin I. Urofsky and Paul Finkelman, *A March of Liberty: A Constitutional History of the United States,* 3rd ed., vol. 2 (New York: Oxford University Press, 2011), 741: "The Court, therefore, had to look at the Contract Clause anew, in light of the current emergency and recognize that the states' higher need to protect the welfare of their citizenry justified a departure from traditional interpretations"; Peter Irons, *A People's History of the Supreme Court* (New York: Penguin, 2006), 297–298.

147. See Epstein, "Toward a Revitalization of the Contract Clause," 735–738; Douglas W. Kmiec and John O. McGinnis, "The Contract Clause: A Return to the Original Meaning," *Hastings Constitutional Law Quarterly* 14 (1987): 525, 541–542, observing that *Blaisdell* "turned the meaning of the Contract Clause on its head"; Charles A. Bieneman, "Comment: Legal Interpretations and a Constitutional Case—*Home Building and Loan Association v. Blaisdell,*" *Michigan Law Review* 90 (1992): 2534, 2535, arguing that the contract clause condemns mortgage moratoria, that *Blaisdell* was wrongly decided, and that it was "an example of cases in which a court, striving to reach a desired result, ignored the law"; Palmer, "Obligations of Contracts," 632, 672, characterizing the Hughes opinion as "result-oriented" and having "no integrity"; Rebecca M. Kahan, "Comment: Constitutional Stretch, Snap-Back, and Sag—Why *Blaisdell* Was a Harsher Blow to Liberty Than *Korematsu,*" *Northwestern University Law Review* 99 (2005): 1279.

148. Skilton, "Mortgage Moratoria since 1933," 84–89; Lee J. Alston, "Farm Foreclosure Moratorium Legislation: A Lesson from the Past," *American Economic Review* 74 (1984): 445; "Farm Foreclosure Moratoria and the Contract Clause: An Economic Analysis," *Constitutional Commentary* 3 (1986): 332.

149. See Price Fishback, Jonathan Rose, and Kenneth Snowden, *Well Worth Saving: How the New Deal Safeguarded Home Ownership* (Chicago: University of Chicago Press, 2013).

150. Des Moines Joint Stock Land Bank v. Nordholm, 271 Iowa 1313, 253 N.W. 701 (1934).

151. Ibid., at 1335, 253 N.W. at 709.

152. Ibid., at 1367, 253 N.W. at 725.

153. Russell v. Battle Creek Lumber Company, 256 Mich. 649, 650, 252 N.W. 561, 562 (1934). See also Wilson Banking Company Liquidating Corp. v. Colvard, 172 Miss. 804, 818, 161 So. 123, 127 (1935).

154. See People by Van Schaick v. Title and Mortgage Guarantee Co. of Buffalo, 264 N.Y. 69, 190 N.E. 153 (1934); Virginian Joint Stock Land Bank of Charleston v. Shaffer, 32 N.E.2d 862 (Ohio Ct. App. 936).

155. Travelers' Insurance Company v. Marshall, 124 Tex. 45, 76 S.W.2d 1007 (1934).

156. Ibid., at 78, 76 S.W.2d at 1024.

157. Ibid., at 79, 76 S.W.2d at 1025.

158. Skilton, "Mortgage Moratoria since 1933," 68–72.

159. First Trust Company of Lincoln v. Smith, 134 Neb. 84, 277 N.W. 762 (1938).

160. Ibid., at 114, 277 N.W. at 777.

161. Ibid., at 129, 277 N.W. at 784.

162. First Trust Joint Stock Land Bank of Chicago v. Arp, 225 Iowa 1331, 283 N.W. 441 (1939).

163. New York courts had no hesitation in upholding an extension of mortgage relief despite a contract clause challenge. Maguire and Company v. Lent and Lent, Inc., 277 N.Y. 694, 14 N.E.2d 629 (1938).

164. Klinke v. Samuels, 264 N.Y. 144, 190 N.E. 324 (1934).

165. Brown v. Ferdon, 5 Cal.2d 226 230, 54 P.2d 712, 713 (1936).

166. Langever v. Miller, 124 Tex. 80, 87–88, 76 S.W.2d 1025, 1029 (1934).

167. Beaver County Building and Loan Association v. Wimoweh, 323 Pa. 483, 512, 187 Atl. 489, 494 (1936).

168. Boatright v. City of Jacksonville, 117 Fla. 477, 158 So. 42 (1934). See also State ex rel. Woman's Benefit Association v. Port of Palm Beach District, 121 Fla. 746, 164 So. 851 (1935), invalidating the 1934 tax exemption under the federal contract clause. See generally Walter W. Manley II and Canter Brown, Jr., *The Supreme Court of Florida, 1917–1972* (Gainesville: University of Florida Press, 2006), 136.

169. Rieger v. Wilson, 102 Mont. 86, 56 P.2d 176 (1936).

170. See generally Lynch v. United States, 292 U.S. 571, 577 (1934) (Brandeis, J.): "Pensions, compensation allowances and privileges are gratuities. They involve no agreement of the parties; and the grant of them creates no vested right."

171. Phelps v. Board of Education, 300 U.S. 319 (1937) (Roberts, J.); Dodge v. Board of Education of Chicago, 302 U.S. 74 (1937) (Roberts, J.).

172. In some states pension schemes were not deemed contractual in nature and were therefore subject to change or revocation by the legislature until the employee retired and the pension became vested. See Roddy v. Valentine, 268 N.Y. 228, 197 N.E. 260 (1935). In response, in 1938 New York became the first state to adopt a constitutional provision declaring that participation in a state-employee retirement system "shall be a contractual relationship, the benefits of which shall not be diminished or impaired." New York Constitution, art. V, sec. 7.

173. State of Indiana ex rel. Anderson v. Brand, 303 U.S. 95 (1938) (Roberts, J.).

174. Ibid., at 109–117. See also Malone v. Hayden, 329 Pa. 213, 197 A. 344 (1938), holding that a teacher tenure act conferred a qualified contractual status on schoolteachers, subject to the authority of the legislature to abolish the act or modify its features, and finding no impairment of existing contracts.

175. See James W. Ely, Jr., "Public Employees and the Curious Mini-Revival of Contract Clause Jurisprudence," *Brigham-Kanner Property Rights Conference Journal* 2 (2013): 37, 47–56.

176. Doty v. Love, 295 U.S. 64 (1935) (Cardozo, J.).

177. *Van Schaick*, 264 N.Y. at 93–94, 190 N.E. at 161.

178. Midland Realty Company v. Kansas City Power and Light, 300 U.S. 110, 113 (1937).

179. Zeuger Milk Company v. School District of Pittsburgh, 334 Pa. 277, 5 A.2d 885 (1939).

180. Henderson Company v. Thompson, 300 U.S. 258 (1937).

181. Ibid., at 266.

182. White, *Constitution and the New Deal,* 198–236.

183. Veix v. Sixth Ward Building and Loan Association, 310 U.S. 32 (1940). The Court made an unconvincing attempt to distinguish *Treigle,* which reached the opposite conclusion on similar facts.

184. *Veix,* at 38.

185. Ibid., at 39–40. See also Robert L. Hale, "The Supreme Court and the Contract Clause," pt. 3, *Harvard Law Review* 57 (1944): 852, 886–890, tracing Supreme Court moves away from the emphasis on the existence of an emergency or the temporary nature of the legislation impairing the contract.

186. Gelfert v. National City Bank of New York, 313 U.S. 221, 235 (1941).

187. Ibid.

188. East New York Bank v. Hahn, 326 U.S. 230 (1945).

189. Ibid., at 232.

190. Faitoute Iron and Steel Company v. City of Asbury Park, 316 U.S. 502 (1942).

191. Ibid., at 511.

192. Ibid., at 516. See Hale, "Supreme Court and the Contract Clause," pt. 1, 512, 551–555, contending that because the reorganization scheme "substituted for a practically unenforceable obligation to pay a greater amount an effectively enforceable obligation to pay a smaller amount, it did not in any real sense impair the obligation"; Richard Funston, "Requiescat in Pace: A Memorial to the Contract Clause," *Texas Southern Law Review* 3 (1973): 12, 22–23, viewing *Faitoute* as an example of judicial balancing of the contract clause "against the necessities of the public welfare."

193. Atlantic Coast Line Railroad Company v. Phillips, 332 U.S. 168, 173 (1947).

194. Hale, "Supreme Court and the Contract Clause," pt. 3, 852, 890–891.

195. See Louisville Joint Stock Land Bank v. Radford, 295 U.S. 555, 589 (1935) (Brandeis, J.): "Under the bankruptcy power Congress may discharge the debtor's personal obligation, because, unlike the states, it is not prohibited from impairing the obligations of contracts."

196. Long Island Water Supply Company v. Brooklyn, 166 U.S. 685, 690–691 (1897).

197. Omnia Commercial Company, Inc. v. United States, 261 U.S. 502 (1923).

198. *Lynch,* at 579.

199. Ibid., at 580.

200. See Henry M. Hart, Jr., "The Gold Clause in United States Bonds," *Harvard Law Review* 48 (1935): 1057, 1081: "Gold clauses were not inserted in bonds, public or private, because investors wanted gold per se. They were inserted because they wanted the protection afforded by gold."

201. Gerald N. Magliocca, "The *Gold Clause Cases* and Constitutional Necessity," *Florida Law Review* 64 (2012): 1243, 1250–1253.

202. Norman v. Baltimore and Ohio Railroad Company, 294 U.S. 240 (1935).

203. Perry v. United States, 294 U.S. 330 (1935).

204. See Hart, "Gold Clause in United States Bonds," 1074, characterizing the remedial section of the *Perry* opinion as "arrant nonsense" and arguing that denial of payment in gold had "no necessary bearing upon the scope of the remedy of substituted performance"; Magliocca, "*Gold Clause Cases,*" 1271; David Glick,

"Conditional Strategic Retreat: The Court's Concession in the 1935 *Gold Clause Cases*," *Journal of Politics* 71 (2009): 800, 813: "The logic of the majority's opinion is strained."

205. See Richard H. Timberlake, *Constitutional Money: A Review of the Supreme Court's Monetary Decisions* (Cambridge, UK: Cambridge University Press, 2013), 203, asserting that the gold clauses were legitimate and should have been binding but acknowledging that the Supreme Court majority yielded to political realities and was reluctant to challenge President Roosevelt and Congress over monetary policy; Roots, "Government by Permanent Emergency," 281–283.

206. *Perry*, at 361.

207. Ibid., at 377.

208. Ibid., at 379.

CHAPTER 7. THE CONTRACT CLAUSE IN THE AGE OF REGULATION

1. See Kermit L. Hall and Peter Karsten, *The Magic Mirror: Law in American History*, 2nd ed. (New York: Oxford University Press, 2009), 308–309, noting the emergence of a "new orthodoxy of liberal liberalism" emanating from the New Deal and lasting for decades after World War II.

2. Grant Gilmore, *The Death of Contract* (Columbus: Ohio State University Press, 1974).

3. See generally Richard A. Epstein, "The Takings Jurisprudence of the Warren Court: A Constitutional Siesta," *Tulsa Law Review* 31 (1966): 643–676.

4. See Richard Funston, "Requiescat in Pace: A Memorial to the Contract Clause," *Texas Southern Law Review* (1973): 24: "Swallowed up by due process, the contract clause is no longer a subject of litigation"; Cass R. Sunstein, "*Lochner*'s Legacy," *Columbia Law Review* 87 (1987): 890–891, observing that "the clause is now for the most part a dead letter" and concluding that the Supreme Court has rendered "the contracts clause functionally identical to the due process clause."

5. City of El Paso v. Simmons, 379 U.S. 497 (1965).

6. Ibid., at 508.

7. Similarly, the Florida Supreme Court discarded the right/remedy distinction in contract clause analysis. Pomponio v. Claridge of Pompano Condominium, Inc., 378 So.2d 774, 776 (Fla. 1979).

8. Ibid., at 508–509.

9. Ibid., at 520.

10. Ibid., at 529.

11. Ibid., at 523.

12. See Matter of the Department of Buildings of the City of New York, 14 N.Y.2d 291, 200 N.E.2d 432, 437 (1964), observing, "The private interests, embodied in contracts, are made subservient to the interests of the public."

13. Globe Liquor Company v. Four Roses Distillers Company, 281 A.2d 19, 21 (Del. 1971), cert. den., 404 U.S. 873 (1971).

14. State ex rel. Builders Owners and Managers Association v. Adamany, 64 Wis.2d 280, 299, 219 N.W.2d 274, 284 (1974).

15. Portland Savings Bank v. Landry, 372 A.2d 573 (1977).

16. Yamaha Parts Distributors, Inc. v. Ehrman, 316 So.2d 557, 559 (Fla. 1975). See also Fleeman v. Case, 342 So.2d 815 (Fla. 1977), holding that a statute prohibiting rent escalation clauses in leases for recreational facilities and condominium management contracts impaired contracts in violation of both state and federal contract clauses.

17. United States Trust Company v. New Jersey, 431 U.S. 1 (1977).

18. Ibid., at 16.

19. Ibid., at 20–24.

20. Ibid., at 22.

21. Ibid., at 25.

22. Ibid., at 22–23.

23. Ibid., at 26. To bolster the adoption of a dual standard of review Blackmun cited Perry v. United States, 294 U.S. 330 (1935), one of the *Gold Clause Cases*, discussed in Chapter 6.

24. *United States Trust*, at 30–31.

25. Even this highly qualified application of the contract clause was too much for Justice William J. Brennan. In dissent, he envisioned a highly circumscribed contract clause subject to paramount state authority and accused the plurality of resuscitating a "long discarded Contract Clause doctrine." Brennan also expressed confidence that the interests of bondholders would be adequately protected by the political process. This suggestion overlooks the fact that the very purpose of a constitutional guarantee was to remove the matter from the vagaries of the political system. Ibid., at 33–62.

26. See Michael W. McConnell, "Contract Rights and Property Rights: A Case Study in the Relationship between Individual Liberties and Constitutional Structure," *California Law Review* 76 (1988): 267, 293–294: "The modern thrust of contracts clause jurisprudence is precisely backwards. . . . It is interference with private contracts that lies at the heart of the clause"; Thomas W. Merrill, "Public Contracts, Private Contracts, and the Transformation of the Constitutional Order," *Case Western Law Review* 37 (1987): 597, 609: "The modern Court has in effect turned the contract clause of both the framers and the post–*Charles River Bridge* era on its head. The prior understanding was that private contracts were protected from state interference with *more* rigor than public contracts." See also *United States Trust*, at 53n.16 (Brennan, J., dissenting), finding no historical support for applying a stricter standard when a state's own obligations are at issue; Troy, Ltd. v. Renna, 727 F.2d 287, 295 (3rd Cir. 1984), noting that, in contrast to the relaxed treatment of public contracts, "the obligation of contracts between private parties were for many years scrutinized far more rigorously."

27. Stewart E. Sterk, "The Continuity of Legislatures: Of Contracts and the Contract Clause," *Columbia Law Review* 88 (1988): 647, 687. See also Douglas W. Kmiec and John O. McGinnis, "The Contract Clause: A Return to the Original Understanding," *Hastings Constitutional Law Quarterly* 14 (1987): 525, 547: "The state

invokes the same justification for modifying public contracts and private contracts—namely, that public welfare will be advanced by the alteration—and the alteration should be reviewed under the same standard."

28. See Michael Cataldo, "Revival or Revolution: *U.S. Trust's* Role in the Contracts Clause Circuit Split," *St. John's Law Review* (2013): 1145, 1170–1178, criticizing the adoption of the dual standard of analysis for public and private contracts as a deviation from precedent and maintaining that the "less deference" standard is ambiguous and produces inconsistent results.

29. Buffalo Teachers Federation v. Tobe, 464 F.3d 362, 370 (2nd Cir. 2006), cert. den. 550 U.S. 918 (2007).

30. Allied Structural Steel Company v. Spannaus, 438 U.S. 234 (1978).

31. Ibid., at 241.

32. Ibid., at 245.

33. Ibid., at 241.

34. Ibid., at 244–245.

35. Ibid., at 246–250.

36. Multipart tests were part of the intellectual vogue of the day. Compare with the multifactor balancing formula set forth in Penn Central Transportation Company v. City of New York, 438 U.S. 104 (1987) to determine the existence of a regulatory taking of property. See Steven J. Eagle, "The Four-Factor *Penn Central* Regulatory Takings Test," *Penn State Law Review* 118 (2014): 601, analyzing the factors of the *Penn Central* test and finding them incoherent.

37. For helpful discussions of *Allied Structural Steel*, see Kmiec and McGinnis, "Contract Clause," 548–549: "*Allied Steel* reached the correct result through unprincipled reasoning"; David Crump, "The Economic Purpose of the Contract Clause," *Southern Methodist University Law Review* 66 (2013): 687, 700–701: "In terms of its principal holding, the two-stage analysis provided enough ambiguity to allow the upholding even of a contract impairment that seriously undermined investor confidence by a court that happened to be so inclined."

38. *Allied Structural Steel*, at 259.

39. See Bernard Schwartz, "Old Wine in Old Bottles? The Renaissance of the Contract Clause," *Supreme Court Review* (1979): 95–121.

40. See Earl M. Maltz, *The Chief Justiceship of Warren Burger, 1969–1986* (Columbia: University of South Carolina Press, 2000), 90, commenting that "even the revival of the Contracts Clause as a constraint on state action proved to be a matter of largely theoretical interest."

41. Energy Reserves Group v. Kansas Power and Light Company, 459 U.S. 400 (1983). For a perceptive treatment of *Energy Reserves Group*, see Crump, "Economic Purpose of the Contract Clause," 701–703.

42. *Energy Reserves Group*, at 410–413. See also General Motors Corporation v. Romein, 503 U.S. 181, 186 (1992).

43. The Eighth Circuit Court of Appeals colorfully expressed this contention: "The idea, evidently, is that if the party to the contract who is complaining could have seen it coming, it cannot claim that its expectations were disappointed." The theory, the court continued, is that "a party's evaluation of the possibility of

interference is reflected in the negotiated price." Holiday Inns Franchising, Inc. v. Branstad, 29 F.3d 383, 385 (8th Cir. 1994), cert. den. 513 U.S. 1033 (1994).

44. *Energy Reserves Group*, at 416.

45. Ibid., at 417.

46. Ibid., at 418.

47. See Kmiec and McGinnis, "Contract Clause," 559: "It is equally ironic that the Supreme Court has interpreted a constitutional provision that was designed to provide certainty to contracting parties in a manner that maximizes the unpredictability of its application." See also Leo Clarke, "The Contract Clause: A Basis for Limited Judicial Review of State Economic Regulation," *University of Miami Law Review* 39 (1985): 183, 253: "Substantial gaps and ambiguities continue to plague the contract clause doctrine."

48. Exxon Corporation v. Eagerton, 462 U.S. 176 (1983).

49. Keystone Bituminous Coal Association v. DeBenedictis, 480 U.S. 470 (1987). The four dissenters would have invalidated the law as an unconstitutional taking of property and did not address the contract clause.

50. Ibid., at 505.

51. *Romein,* at 181.

52. This was not a frivolous argument. Several state courts had held that the workers' compensation act was part of an employment contract and that legislation substantially altering the terms of the contract ran afoul of the contract clause. See, for example, Cooper v. Wicomico County, Department of Public Works, 278 Md. 596, 366 A.2d 55 (1976); Schreiner v. C. S. McClossan, Inc., 465 N.W. 2d 917 (Minn. 1991). See also Nieves v. Hess Oil Virgin Islands Company, 819 F.2d 1237 (3rd Cir. 1987), cert. den. 484 U.S. 963 (1987).

53. *Romein,* at 190.

54. Chrysler Corporation v. Kolosso Auto Sales, Inc., 148 F.3d 892, 894 (7th Cir. 1998), cert. den. 525 U.S. 1177 (1999).

55. Toledo Area AFL-CIO Council v. Pizza, 154 F.3d 307, 322 (6th Cir. 1998).

56. Equipment Manufacturers Institute v. Janklow, 300 F.3d 842, 861 (8th Cir. 2002). See also Morgan v. Kemper, 754 F.2d 145 (4th Cir. 1985), holding that retroactive application of a statute governing termination of insurance agents was unconstitutional impairment of existing contracts; *Branstad,* at 383, holding that a statute governing transfer and termination of food and hotel franchises was a substantial impairment of existing agreements not justified by a public interest; Cycle Barn, Inc. v. Arctic Cat Sales, Inc., 701 F. Supp. 2d 1197 (W.D. Wash. 2010), holding that a law requiring a franchisor to repurchase its products upon termination of the franchise substantially impaired the existing agreement and affected only a narrow class of dealers rather than serving broad public purpose.

57. *Kolosso Auto Sales,* at 892 (7th Cir. 1998); Alliance of Automobile Manufacturers v. Gwadosky, 430 F.3d 30 (1st Cir. 2005), cert. den. 547 U.S. 1143 (2006).

58. In re Workers' Compensation Refund, 46 F.3d 813, 820 (8th Cir. 1995).

59. See HRPT Properties Trust v. Lingle, 715 F. Supp. 2d 1115 (D. Hawaii 2010), pointing out that these new factors were designed to favor business tenants at the expense of the landowner.

60. Southern California Gas Company v. City of Santa Ana, 336 F.3d 885 (9th Cir. 2003).

61. United Health Care Insurance Company v. Davis, 602 F.3d 618 (5th Cir. 2010).

62. New Jersey Retail Merchants Association v. Sidamon-Eristoff, 669 F.3d 374 (3rd Cir. 2012), cert. den. 133 S. Ct. 528 (2012).

63. *Troy, Ltd.*, at 287.

64. Borman, LLC v. 18718 Borman, LLC, 777 F.3d 816 (6th Cir. 2015).

65. RUI One Corporation v. City of Berkeley, 371 F.3d 1137 (9th Cir. 2004), cert. den. 543 U.S. 1081 (2005). See Richard A. Epstein, "The Upside-Down Law of Property and Contract: Of Fannie Mae, Freddie Mac, and San Jose Pensions," *Nebraska Law Review* 93 (2015): 895–898, arguing that the city's approach in RUI was "in reality no different from a tactic whereby the city simply inserts unilaterally the added term into its leases" and contending that the municipal ordinance impaired the existing lease arrangements; Thomas E. Mitchell, "Rewriting the Terms: The Contract Clause and Special-Interest Legislation in *RUI One Corporation v. City of Berkeley*," *Harvard Journal of Law and Public Policy* 28 (2004): 691, 704–708, maintaining that the imposition of new contract terms on municipal contractors or lessees should be viewed as an impairment of the existing contractual relationship and contending that the contract clause "is designed to avoid the fundamental unfairness that would result if a government could rewrite the terms of its bargains via legislative fiat."

66. Young v. City and County of Honolulu, 639 F.3d 907 (9th Cir. 2011).

67. Hawkeye Commodity Promotions, Inc. v. Vilsack, 486 F.3d 430 (8th Cir. 2007).

68. For example, State v. All Property and Casualty Insurance Carriers, 937 So.2d 312, 323 (La. 2006); Neel v. First Federal Savings and Loan Association, 207 Mont. 376, 387, 675 P.2d 96, 103 (1984): "This Court has construed the two contract clauses interchangeably, relying on United States Supreme Court opinions to test the validity of Montana legislation under both contract clauses"; Opinion of the Justices (Furlough), 135 N.H. 625, 630, 609 A.2d 1204, 1207 (1992), finding that federal and state contract clauses "offer equivalent protections where a law impairs a contract"; Ken Moorhead Oil, Inc. v. Federated Mutual Insurance Company, 323 S.C. 532, 539, 476 S.E.2d 481, 485 (1996): "In interpreting the Contract Clause of the South Carolina Constitution, this Court has followed federal precedent construing the federal Contract Clause." See also Stuart Buck, "The Legal Ramifications of Public Pension Reform," *Texas Review of Law and Politics* 17 (2012): 25, 47: "State contracts clauses are usually interpreted and applied in parallel with that of the U.S. Constitution"; Brian R. Schar, "Note: Contract Clause Law under State Constitutions—a Model for Heightened Scrutiny," *Texas Review of Law and Politics* 1 (1997): 123, 132–133.

69. For example, Jacobsen v. Anheuser-Busch, Inc., 392 N.W.2d 868 (Minn. 1986); In the Matter of Public Service Electric and Gas Company's Rate Unbundling, 330 N.J. Supr. 65, 748 A.2d 1161 (App. Div. 2000); Seal v. Corporation Commission, 725 P.2d 278 (Okla. 1986); Shell v. Metropolitan Life Insurance Company, 181 W.Va. 16, 380 S.E.2d 183 (1989); Milwaukee Association of Commerce v. City of Milwaukee, 798 N.W.2d 287, 332 Wis.2d 459 (Ct. App. 2011). Some state courts formulate the test

slightly differently but rely on the same three factors as the basis for analysis. For example, Hageland Aviation Services, Inc. v. Harms, 210 P.3d 444 (Alaska 2009); Pierce County v. State, 159 Wash.2d 16, 148 P.3d 1002 (2006).

70. Burgos v. State, 222 N.J. 175, 183, 118 A.3d 270, 281 (N.J. 2015).

71. See Schar, "Contract Clause Law under State Constitutions," 130–131.

72. Heublein, Inc. v. Department of Alcoholic Beverage Control, 237 Va. 192, 376 S.E.2d 77, 79 (1989).

73. Earthworks Contracting, Ltd. v. Mendel-Allison Construction, 167 Ariz. 102, 804 P.2d 831, 836 (Ct. App. 1990).

74. Baytown Construction Company, Inc. v. City of Port Arthur, 792 S.W.2d 554 (Tex. Ct. App. 1990).

75. See Glen v. Christole, Inc., 582 N.E.2d 780, 783 (Ind. 1991), finding that retroactive application of a statute invalidating subdivision covenants restricting use of property for group facilities for the disabled violated the state contract clause.

76. *Pomponio*, at 774.

77. Ibid., at 779–780.

78. In re Advisory Opinion, 509 So.2d 292, 313–314 (Fla. 1987). Lower courts in Florida have grappled with whether to apply a balancing test or a per se test to ascertain a statutory impairment of contract. See, for example, Lee County v. Brown, 929 So.2d 1202 (Fla. Dist. Ct. App. 2006), discussing appropriate standard of review; Citrus Memorial Health Foundation, Inc. v. Citrus County Hospital Board, 108 So.3d 675 (Fla. Dist. Ct. App. 2013), holding that a statute imposing additional obligations on a private health facility was per se impairment of its contract with the county.

79. Chiles v. United Faculty of Florida, 615 So.2d 671, 673 (1993).

80. See Geary Distributing Company v. All Brand Importers, Inc., 931 F.2d 1431 (11th Cir. 1991), striking down the retroactive application of a beer distribution statute under the Florida contract clause.

81. See Fedway Marketplace West, LLC v. State, 183 Wash. App. 860, 336 P.3d 615 (2014), holding that a lease expressly provided for termination if the state law changed, and hence there was no longer a contract to impair when the state privatized the sale of liquor and terminated leases of property.

82. See Connecticut Education Association, Inc. v. Tirozzi, 210 Conn. 286, 554 A.2d 1065 (1989), holding that a statute invalidating permanent teaching certificates and substituting five-year renewable certificates contingent upon continuing education was a minimal impairment of teacher contracts.

83. Young Partners, LLC v. Board of Education, 284 Kan. 397, 160 P.3d 830 (2007).

84. See Ward v. Chevron USA, 123 Ariz. 208 (Ct. App. 1979), stressing absence of an emergency; Gans v. Miller Brewing Co., 560 So.2d 281 (Fla. Dist. Ct. App. 4th Dist. 1990); *Jacobsen*, at 868, holding that a law had "all the earmarks of narrow special interest legislation devoid of any broad public purpose" and violated both the federal and state constitutions; Heublein, Inc. v. Department of Alcoholic Beverage Control, 237 Va. 192, 376 S.E.2d 77 (1989).

85. Smith Insurance, Inc. v. Grievance Committee, 120 N.H. 856, 424 A.2d 816 (1980); G-H Insurance Agency, Inc. v. Continental Insurance Company, 278 S.C.

241, 94 S.E.2d 336 (1982); Insurance Financial Services, Inc. v. South Carolina Insurance Company, 282 S.C. 144, 318 S.E.2d 10 (1984); Shell v. Metropolitan Life Insurance Company, 181 W.Va. 183, 380 S.E.2d 183 (1989).

86. Federal Land Bank of Wichita v. Story, 756 P.2d 588 (Okla. 1988). See Kenneth R. Davis, "Note: Constitutional Law—Oklahoma Mortgage Foreclosure Moratoriums . . . Past, Present, and Future?" *Oklahoma Law Review* 42 (1989): 647, 652, stressing that the Oklahoma act did not protect the rights of the mortgagee during the period of the moratorium and opining that the law "clearly violated the contract clause."

87. Federal Land Bank of Wichita v. Bott, 240 Kan. 624, 732 P.2d 710 (1987); Federal Land Bank of Omaha v. Arnold, 426 N.W.2d 153 (Iowa 1988).

88. Sinclair v. Sinclair, 654 A.2d 438 (Me. 1995).

89. See Robert M. Lawless, "The American Response to Farm Crises: Procedural Debtor Relief," *University of Illinois Law Review* (1988): 1037, 1063: "Procedural relief statutes can upset market equilibrium between farm debtors and creditors, creating unforeseen economic consequences. As history demonstrates, procedural debtor relief statutes do not effectively aid farmers in the short run and actually hurt the interests of farmers in the long term."

90. Veto Message of Governor Tim Pawlenty, June 12, 2008, Senate File 3396, Minnesota Subprime Borrower Relief Act of 2008, Minnesota Senate, *Journal of the Senate*, http://www.senate.leg.state.mn.us/journals/2007-2008/200805181192pdf.

91. Builders Supply Company of Hattiesburg v. Pine Belt Savings and Loan Association, 396 So.2d 743, 745 (Miss. 1979).

92. Neel v. First Federal Savings and Loan Association, 207 Mont. 376, 675 P.2d 96 (1984).

93. Windman v. City of Englewood, 200 N.J. Super. 218, 491 A.2d 32 (App. Div. 1985).

94. Chase Manhattan Bank v. Josephson, 135 N.J. 209, 638 A.2d 1301 (1994).

95. Edgewater Investment Associates v. Borough of Edgewater, 103 N.J. 227, 510 A.2d 1178 (1986).

96. RUE-ELL Enterprises, Inc. v. City of Berkeley, 147 Cal. App.3d 81, 19 Cal. Rptr. 919 (1st Dist. 1983).

97. Anthony v. Kualoa Ranch, Inc., 69 Hawaii 112, 123, 736 P.2d 55, 63 (1987).

98. Kee v. Shelter Insurance, 852 S.W.2d 229 (Tenn. 1993).

99. State v. All Property and Casualty Insurance Carriers, 937 So.2d 313 (La. 2006). See "Recent Cases: Constitutional Law—Contracts Clause," *Harvard Law Review* 120 (2007): 844, 851, sharply criticizing *Insurance Carriers*, pointing out that the state was a major property owner that stood to benefit from the extension of the filing period and concluding that the decision "represents a failure to apply the Contracts Clause forcefully by considering the total circumstances of the State's action."

100. Crismon v. Curtiss, 785 S.W.2d 353 (Tenn. 1990).

101. Allstate Insurance v. Kim, 376 Md. 275, 829 A.2d 611 (2003). The two dissenters maintained that the law amounted to a substantial impairment of the insurance contract.

102. *Ken Moorhead Oil*, at 532.

103. Aetna Life Insurance Company v. Schilling, 67 Ohio St.3d 164, 616 N.E.2d 893 (1993); Parsonese v. Midland National Insurance Company, 550 Pa. 423, 706 A.2d 814 (1998).

104. In re Estate of DeWitt, 54 P.3d 849 (Colo. 2002); Mearns v. Scharbach, 103 Wash. App. 498, 12 P.3d 1048 (2000).

105. *Earthworks Contracting*, at 102, 804 P.2d 831 (Ariz. Ct. App. 1990).

106. Baytown Construction Company, Inc. v. City of Port Arthur, 792 S.W.2d 554 (Tex. Ct. App. 1990).

107. Brevard County v. Florida Power and Light Company, 693 So.2d 77 (Fla. Dist. Ct. App. 1997).

108. Citizens for Lee County, Inc. v. Lee County, 308 S.C. 23, 416 S.E.2d 641 (1992).

109. Seal v. Corporation Commission, 725 P.2d 278, 292 (Okla. 1986).

110. Phelps Dodge Corporation v. Arizona Electric Power Cooperative, Inc., 207 Ariz. 95, 83 P.3d 573 (Ct. App. 2004).

111. Working Waterman's Association of Virginia, Inc. v. Seafood Harvesters, Inc., 227 Va. 101, 314 S.E.2d 159 (1984).

112. See, for example, Matter of Recycling and Salvage Corporation, 246 N.J. Super. 79, 586 A.2d 1300 (1991), upholding a requirement that solid waste facilities must be certified or cease operations; General Food Vending, Inc. v. Town of Westfield, 288 N.J. 442, 672 A.2d 760 (1995), upholding an ordinance prohibiting cigarette vending machines.

113. Hageland Aviation Services, Inc. v. Harms, 210 P.3d 444 (Alaska 2009).

114. Metropolitan Milwaukee Association of Commerce, Inc. v. City of Milwaukee, 332 Wis.2d 459, 798 N.W.2d 287 (Ct. App. 2011).

115. Tuttle v. New Hampshire Medical Malpractice Joint Underwriting Association, 159 N.H. 627, 655, 992 A.2d 624, 646 (2010). But see *Ken Moorhead Oil*, at 545, 476 S.E.2d at 488 (1996), limiting reduced deference to situations in which the state was a contracting party and expressing concern that under a "broad construction of the term 'self-interest,' virtually every state statute that impairs a purely private contract would be subject to heightened scrutiny." Recall that critics of the dual standard of review make this very point in arguing the state's interest is involved whenever it abridges a contract, and thus there is no persuasive rationale for treating public and private agreements differently.

116. See Pierce County v. State, 159 Wash.2d 16, 148 P.3d 1002 (2006), finding violations of state contract clause. See also George D. Hardin, Inc. v. Village of Mount Prospect, 99 Ill.2d 96, 457 N.E.2d 429 (1983), finding impairment of special assessment bonds in violation of both the federal and state constitutions.

117. See Lower Village Hydroelectric Associates, L.P. v. City of Claremont, 147 N.H. 73, 78, 782 A.2d 897, 902 (2001), finding violations of state contract clause.

118. *Tuttle*, at 627, 992 A.2d 624 (2010).

119. *Citizens for Lee County*, at 30, 416 S.E.2d 641, 645 (1992): "The general purpose of the Contract Clause is to encourage trade and credit by promoting confidence in the stability of contractual obligations."

120. William J. Brennan, "State Constitutions and the Protection of Individual Rights," *Harvard Law Review* 90 (1977): 489.

121. Kelo v. City of New London, 545 U.S. 469, 489 (2005).

122. City of Norwood v. Horney, 110 Ohio St.3d 353, 853 N.E.2d 1115 (2006); Board of County Commissioners of Muskogee County v. Lowery, 136 P.3d 639 (Okla. 2006); Benson v. State, 710 N.W.2d 131 (S.D. 2006). See also County of Wayne v. Hathcock, 471 Mich. 445, 684 N.W.2d 765 (2004). For an excellent analysis of the post-*Kelo* treatment of "public use" by state courts, see Ilya Somin, *The Grasping Hand*: Kelo v. City of New London *and the Limits of Eminent Domain* (Chicago: University of Chicago Press, 2015), 181–203.

123. See Schar, "Contract Clause Law under State Constitutions," 140–147, urging that state courts apply heightened scrutiny to contract clause claims.

124. In 2015 the Supreme Court of Michigan, in a case arising from legislative efforts to trim public-sector employee benefits, specifically noted that the claimant did not argue that the contract clause in the state constitution afforded greater protection than its federal counterpart. Yet the court stressed that with respect to taking jurisprudence it construed the "public use" limitation on the exercise of eminent domain more broadly than did the Supreme Court. AFT Michigan v. State, 497 Mich. 197, 217n.9, 866 N.W.2d 782, 794n.9 (2015). See also Carlstrom v. State, 103 Wash.2d 391, 394, 694 P.2d 1, 3 (1985), pointing out that neither party argued that "our state constitution should be construed differently from the federal contract clause."

125. See, for example, Debra Brubaker Burns, "Too Big to Fail and Too Big to Pay: States, Their Public-Pension Bills, and the Constitution," *Hastings Constitutional Law Quarterly* 39 (2011): 253, 267: "First, many states over-promised benefits to employees during the financially flush 1990s. Second, many states have projected unrealistic amounts of funding resources or rates of return for current and future pension investments"; Ernest A. Young, "Its Hour Come Round at Last? State Sovereign Immunity and the Great State Debt Crisis of the Early Twenty-first Century," *Harvard Journal of Law and Public Policy* 35 (2012): 593, 617–620, discussing the severe debt crisis in several states and pointing out that "states have failed to set aside money to fund future obligations for healthcare costs and pensions."

126. For an overview of contract clause litigation with respect to public employee benefit reforms, see James W. Ely, Jr., "Public Employees and the Curious Mini-Revival of Contract Clause Jurisprudence," *Brigham-Kanner Property Rights Conference Journal* 2 (2013): 37–60. See also T. Leigh Anenson, Alex Slabaugh, and Karen Eilers Lahey, "Reforming Public Pensions," *Yale Law and Policy Review* 33 (2014): 1, 33, observing that "reform measures face the most serious challenge from state and federal constitutional contract clauses."

127. David A. Skeel, Jr., "States of Bankruptcy," *University of Chicago Law Review* 79 (2012): 677, 711: "With the exception of layoffs and furloughs, a state's tools for addressing unsustainable contracts with its public employee unions ordinarily apply only to future contracts."

128. See Pennie v. Reis, 132 U.S. 464, 471 (1889) (Field, J.); Brown v. City of Highland Park, 320 Mich. 108, 114, 30 N.W.2d 798, 800 (1948), holding that the pension granted by public authority was not a contractual obligation; Mell v. State ex rel. Fritz, 130 Ohio St. 306, 308, 199 N.W. 72, 73 (1935): "A pension is generally defined as a gratuity, at all times subject to the will of the donor. It is a creature of law rather

than contract, and the pensioner has no vested right in the continuance of a gratuitous allowance."

129. Alston v. City of Camden, S.C., 322 S.C. 38, 471 S.E.2d 174 (1996). See also AFT v. State, 497 Mich. 197, N.W.2d (2015), holding that an instructional brochure explaining retirement benefits available at the time of publication did not constitute a legal obligation to provide such benefits in the future.

130. Fraternal Order of Police v. Prince George's County, 608 F.3d 183 (4th Cir. 2010). See also Washington Education Association v. Washington Department of Retirement Systems, 181 Wash.2d 233, 332 P.3d 439 (2014), holding that the legislature expressly reserved the right to modify or repeal a cost-of-living adjustments (COLA) scheme, and hence law repealing legislation granting future COLA did not impair any contract.

131. See Burgos v. State, 222 N.J. 175, 212–213, 118 A.3d 270, 292–293 (2015), cert. den. 2016 WL 763251 (February 29, 2016), holding that the state constitution prohibited the legislature from making a binding contract to annually appropriate contributions to various pension funds; San Diego City Firefighters Local 145 v. Board of Administration of San Diego City Employees Retirement System, 206 Cal. App. 4th 594, 141 Cal. Rptr. 3d 860 (4th Dist. 2012).

132. Madison Teachers, Inc. v. Walker, 358 Wis.2d 1, 851 N.W.2d 337 (2014). See also Professional Fire Fighters of New Hampshire v. State, 167 N.H. 188, 107 A.3d 1229 (2014), holding that public employees have no contractual right to a fixed contribution rate. Compare with Valdes v. Cory, 139 Cal. App. 3d 773, 189 Cal. Rptr. 212 (1983), holding that rescission of the state's obligation to make monthly contributions to a retirement fund substantially impaired the government contract.

133. Maine Association of Retirees v. Board of Trustees of Maine Public Employees Retirement System, 758 F.3d 23 (1st Cir. 2014). See also Rhode Island Council 94 v. Rhode Island, F. Supp. 2d 165 (D.R.I. 2010), invoking the unmistakability doctrine and rejecting the contract clause challenge to changes in the state's retiree health benefit scheme.

134. Justus v. State, 336 P.3d 202 (Colo. 2014); Bartlett v. Cameron, 316 P.3d 889 (N.M. 2014); American Federation of Teachers v. State, 111 A.3d 63 (N.H. 2015).

135. Scott v. Williams, 107 So.3d 379 (Fla. 2013).

136. In addition to New York, Alaska, Arizona, Hawaii, Illinois, Louisiana, and Michigan have constitutional provisions pertaining to public employee pensions. Florida, Kentucky, and Wisconsin have statutes declaring that participation in a state retirement system constitutes a contract.

137. Unified Government of Athens-Clarke County v. McCrary, 280 Ga. 901, 635 S.E.2d 150 (2006); Denning v. Kansas Public Employees Retirement System, 285 Kan. 1045, 180 P.3d 564 (2008).

138. See United Automobile, Aerospace, Agricultural Implement Workers of America v. Fortuno, 633 F.3d 37, 44 (1st Cir. 2011): "Even when the state impairs its own contractual obligations, the state's judgment that the impairment was justified is afforded meaningful deference"; Buffalo Teachers Federation v. Tobe, 464 F.3d 362, 370 (2nd Cir. 2006), cert. den. 550 U.S. 918 (2007); Baltimore Teachers Union v. Mayor and City Council of Baltimore, 6 F.3d 1012, 1019 (4th Cir. 1993), cert. den. 510 U.S. 1141 (1994): "While complete deference is inappropriate, however, at least some

deference to legislative policy decisions to modify these contracts in the public interest must be accorded."

139. *Fortuno*, at 43 (1st Cir. 2011). See also *Buffalo Teachers' Federation*, at 373: "No one questions the existence of a very real fiscal emergency in Buffalo"; In the Matter of Subway-Surface Supervisors Association v. New York City Transit Authority, 44 N.Y. 101, 113, 375 N.E.2d 384, 389 (1978), noting "the financial distress under which the city was laboring and which threatened to overwhelm it."

140. *Baltimore Teachers' Union*, at 1022.

141. *Buffalo Teachers Federation*, at 371. For decades the Supreme Court's decision in *Lochner v. New York*, 198 U.S. 45 (1905), has been assailed as a poster child of judicial activism in support of business interests and has served as a punching bag for constitutional theorists of various stripes. In recent years a number of revisionist historians have defended the ruling as a vindication of individual liberty and assailed the conventional account as inaccurate and politically inspired. See David E. Bernstein, *Rehabilitating* Lochner*: Defending Individual Rights against Progressive Reform* (Chicago: University of Chicago Press, 2011).

142. For example, see State of Nevada Employees Association v. Keating, 903 F.2d 1223 (9th Cir. 1990), holding that elimination of the right to withdraw pension fund contributions was not necessary and unconstitutionally impaired the state's contract; Chiles v. United Faculty of Florida, 615 So.2d 671 (Fla. 1993), holding that the state failed to demonstrate the lack of a reasonable alternative to abrogation of pay raises in a collective bargaining agreement and violated the state contract clause; Carlstrom v. State, 103 Wash.2d 391, 694 P.2d 1 (1985), holding that the legislative cancellation of a salary increase provided for in a union agreement was unconstitutional impairment of the contract.

143. For example, see University of Hawaii Professional Assembly v. Cayetano, 183 F.3d 1096, 1107 (9th Cir. 1999), emphasizing that the state "knew of the budgetary crisis at the time the collective bargaining agreement was negotiated" and ruling that imposition of a "pay lag" law was not reasonable; Massachusetts Community College Council v. Commonwealth, 420 Mass. 126, 649 N.E.2d 708, 716 (1995), noting that state's fiscal problems "were reasonably foreseeable when collective bargaining agreements were signed," and thus impairment was not reasonable; *Carlstrom*, at 397, 694 P.2d 1, 6 (1985): "Since the State was fully aware of its financial problems while negotiating and prior to signing the Agreement, it cannot now be permitted to avoid the Agreement based on those same economic circumstances."

144. American Federation of State, County, and Municipal Employees v. City of Benton, 513 F.3d 874, 882 (8th Cir. 2008).

145. *Cayetano*, at 1107; *Opinion of the Justices (Furlough)*, at 636, 609 A.2d at 1211 (1992): "The legislature has many alternatives available to it, including reducing non-contractual State services and raising taxes and fees."

146. Welch v. Brown, 551 Fed. Appx. 804, 812 (6th Cir. 2014).

147. See *United Faculty of Florida*, at 675 (Overton, J., dissenting), noting that by holding that the state could not eliminate a pay raise in a collective bargaining agreement without violating the contract clause the court majority left lawmakers the sole option of eliminating jobs when faced with a revenue shortfall.

148. *AFT Michigan*, at 215, 866 N.W.2d at 792–793 (2015).

149. *Alston*, at 38, 471 S.E.2d 174, 179 (1996).

150. *Cayetano*, at 1107; Nila M. Merola, "Judicial Review of State Legislation: An Ironic Return to Lochnerian Ideology When Public Sector Contracts Are Impaired," *St. John's Law Review* 84 (2010): 1179, 1211, asserting that "enormous public interest . . . demands that strict scrutiny be applied to laws that impair public sector labor contracts" and declaring that "public sector employees deserve the utmost protection."

151. Illinois Constitution, art. XIII, sec. 5. For a study of this provision, see Eric M. Madiar, "Is Welching on Public Pension Promises an Option for Illinois? An Analysis of Article XIII, Section 5 of the Illinois Constitution," *John Marshall Law Review* 48 (2014): 167–323.

152. Kanerva v. Weems, 12 N.E.3d 1228 (Ill. 2014). A dissenting judge argued that the constitutional measure safeguarded only retirement income and did not extend to nonpension benefits. Ibid., at 1245–1252.

153. In re Pension Reform Litigation, 32 N.E.3d 1, 27 (Ill. 2015). In July of 2015 an Illinois circuit court voided a Chicago pension reform plan on the same ground.

154. Jones v. Municipal Employees' Annuity and Benefit Fund of Chicago, 2016 WL 1137984 (Ill. 2016).

155. Fields v. Elected Officials' Retirement Plan, 234 Ariz. 214, 219, 320 P.3d 1160, 1164–1165 (2014).

156. Hanover National Bank v. Moyses, 186 U.S. 188 (1902).

157. See In re City of Detroit, Michigan, 504 B.R. 97 (Bankr. Ct. E.D. Mich. 2013), brushing aside the contention that the contract clause and the pension clause in the state constitution protected contractual pension rights from modification in bankruptcy.

158. In re City of Stockton, California, 526 B.R. 35, 56 (Bankr. Ct. E.D. Cal. 2015).

159. Compare Pontiac Retired Employees Association v. Schimmel, 751 F.3d 427, 431 (6th Cir. 2014), considering whether emergency manager's orders were legislative in character, and Welch v. Brown, 551 Fed. Appx. 804, 809–810 (6th Cir. 2014), finding emergency manager's actions to be legislative and subject to contract clause scrutiny, with Taylor v. City of Gadsden, 767 F.3d 1124, 1133 (11th Cir. 2014), holding that the city's exercise of an option available under state law did not constitute legislative action.

160. See New Orleans Waterworks Company v. Louisiana Sugar Refining Company, 125 U.S. 18, 30–31 (1888), declaring that the contract clause "is aimed at the legislative power of the State, and not . . . administrative or executive boards or officers" but adding that "any enactment, from whatever source originating, to which a State gives the force of law, is a statute of the State."

161. For a helpful analysis of the delegation issue, see Rodney W. Harrell, "Comment: The Contract Clause of the Constitution and the Need for 'Pass Any Law' Rehabilitation in the Age of Delegation," *George Mason Law Review* 22 (2015): 1317–1348.

162. United States v. Winstar Corporation, 518 U.S. 839, 876 (1996).

163. Ibid., at 883. Three justices concurred, agreeing that the federal government violated its contractual obligation to provide the claimants with favorable accounting treatment.

EPILOGUE

1. Joseph Story, "Discourse upon the Inauguration of the Author, as Dane Professor of Law in Harvard University, August 25th, 1829" in *The Miscellaneous Writings, Literary, Critical, Juridical, and Political, of Joseph Story* (Boston: James Munroe, 1835).

2. James W. Ely, Jr., *The Guardian of Every Other Right: A Constitutional History of Property Rights,* 3rd ed. (New York: Oxford University Press, 2008), 156–166. For more recent developments, see Ilya Somin, "Two Steps Forward for the 'Poor Relation' of Constitutional Law: *Koontz, Arkansas Fish and Game,* and the Future of the Takings Clause," *Cato Supreme Court Review* (2013), 215–234; Horne v. Department of Agriculture, 135 S. Ct. 2419 (2015), emphasizing that the takings clause applies to both personal and real property and holding that seizure of raisins by the government under a marketing order amounted to a compensable taking.

Bibliography

PRIMARY SOURCES

Books

Garfield, James A. *The Future of the Republic: Its Dangers and Its Hopes.* New York: George F. Nesbitt, 1880.

Lindsay, Samuel McCune. *Some Economic Aspects of the Recent Emergency Housing Legislation in New York.* New York: Ballou, 1924.

Maine, Henry Sumner. *Ancient Law.* New York: Charles Scribner, 1864.

———. *Popular Government.* New York: Henry Holt, 1886.

Miller, Samuel Freeman. *Lectures on the Constitution of the United States.* Preface by J. C. Bancroft Davis. New York: Banks and Brothers, 1891.

Scott, William A. *The Repudiation of State Debts.* New York: Thomas Y. Crowell, 1893.

Shirley, John M. *The* Dartmouth College *Case and the Supreme Court of the United States.* St. Louis, MO: G. I. Jones, 1879.

Tyler, Samuel. *Memoir of Roger Brooke Taney.* Baltimore, MD: J. Murphy, 1872.

Legal Treatises

Bishop, Joel Prentiss. *Commentaries on the Law of Contracts.* Chicago: T. H. Flood, 1887.

———. *New Commentaries on Marriage, Divorce, and Separation.* Chicago: T. H. Flood, 1891.

Cooley, Thomas M. *A Treatise on the Constitutional Limitations Which Rest upon the Legislative Power of the States of the American Union.* Boston: Little, Brown, 1868; reprint, New York: DaCapo Press, 1972.

———. *A Treatise on the Constitutional Limitations Which Rest upon the Legislative Power of the States of the American Union.* 2nd ed. Boston: Little, Brown, 1871.

———. *A Treatise on the Constitutional Limitations Which Rest upon the Legislative Power of the States of the American Union.* 4th ed. Boston: Little, Brown, 1878.

Dillon, John F. *Treatise on the Law of Municipal Corporations.* Chicago: James Cockcroft, 1872.

Freund, Ernst. *The Police Power: Public Policy and Constitutional Rights.* Chicago: Callaghan, 1904.

Kent, James. *Commentaries on American Law.* 3 vols. New York: O. Halsted, 1827–1828.

———. *Commentaries on American Law.* 5th ed. 4 vols. New York: Printed for the Author, 1844.

———. *Commentaries on American Law.* 6th ed. New York: William Kent, 1848.

Parsons, Theophilus. *The Law of Contracts.* 3rd ed. 2 vols. Boston: Little, Brown, 1857.

Pierce, Edward L. *A Treatise on the Law of Railroads.* Boston: Little, Brown, 1881.

Rutland, Robert A., and Charles F. Hobson, eds. *The Papers of James Madison.* Vol. 10. Chicago: University of Chicago Press, 1977.

———. *The Papers of James Madison.* Vol. 11. Charlottesville: University of Virginia Press, 1977.

Sedgwick, Theodore. *A Treatise on the Rules Which Govern the Interpretation and Application of Statutory and Constitutional Law.* New York: John Voorhies, 1857.

———. *A Treatise on the Rules Which Govern the Interpretation and Application of Statutory and Constitutional Law.* 2nd ed. New York: Baker, Voorhies, 1874.

Story, Joseph. *Commentaries on the Constitution of the United States.* Boston: Hilliard, Gray, 1833; reprint, Durham, NC: Carolina Academic Press, 1987.

Syrett, Harold C., ed. *The Papers of Alexander Hamilton.* Vol. 6. New York: Columbia University Press, 1962.

Tiedeman, Christopher G. *A Treatise on the Limitations of Police Power in the United States.* St. Louis, MO: F. H. Thomas, 1886.

———. *The Unwritten Constitution of the United States.* New York: G. P. Putnam's Sons, 1890.

Walker, Timothy. *Introduction to American Law.* Philadelphia, PA: Nicklin and Johnson, 1837; reprint, New York: DaCapo Press, 1972.

Wharton, Francis. *Commentaries on Law.* Philadelphia, PA: Kay and Brothers, 1884.

Documents and Pamphlets

Allen, W. B., and Gordon Lloyd, eds. *The Essential Antifederalist.* 2nd ed. Lanham, MD: Rowman and Littlefield, 2002.

Bailyn, Bernard, ed. *The Debate on the Constitution.* Part 2: *Debates in the Press and Private Correspondence.* New York: Library of America Press, 1993.

Charge of Judge William Paterson to the Jury in the Case of Vanhorne's Lessee against Dorrance. Philadelphia, PA: Samuel H. Smith, 1796.

Elliot, Jonathan, ed. *The Debates in the Several State Conventions on the Adoption of the Federal Constitution.* 2nd ed. 4 vols. Philadelphia: Published under the Sanction of Congress, 1836–1859; reprint, Salem, NH: Ayer, 1987.

Farrand, Max, ed. *The Records of the Federal Convention of 1787*, rev. ed. New Haven, CT: Yale University Press, 1937.

Ford, Paul Leicester, ed. *Pamphlets on the Constitution of the United States.* Brooklyn, NY: 1888; reprint, New York: DaCapo Press, 1968.

Gobel, Julius, Jr., and Joseph H. Smith, eds. *The Law Practice of Alexander Hamilton.* Vol. 4. New York: Columbia University Press, 1980.

Godkin, E. L. "The Labor Crisis." *North American Review* 105 (1867).

Hall, Kermit L., and Mark David Hall, eds. *Collected Works of James Wilson.* Vol. 1. Indianapolis, IN: Liberty Fund, 2007.

Thorpe, Francis Newton, ed. *The Federal and State Constitutions.* 7 vols. Washington, DC: Government Printing Office, 1909.

Webster, Noah. *A Collection of Essays and Fugitiv Writings on Moral, Historical, Political, and Literary Subjects.* Boston: I. Thomas and E. T. Andrews, 1790.

Webster, Pelatiah. *An Essay on Credit in Which the Doctrine of Banks Is Considered.* Philadelphia: Eleazer Oswald, 1786.

Articles

Black, H. Campbell. "Legislation Impairing the Obligation of Contracts." *American Law Register* 34 (1886): 81–97.
Colby, James F. "Exemption from Taxation by Legislative Contract." *American Law Review* 13 (1879): 26–39.
Doe, Charles. "A New View of the *Dartmouth College* Case." *Harvard Law Review* 6 (1892): 161–183.
Gray, Morris. "The Coupon-Legislation of Virginia." *American Law Review* 23 (1889): 924–945.
Harper, Robert Goodloe. "The Yazoo Question" (August 3, 1796), *American Law Journal* 5 (1814).
Hill, Clement H. "The *Dartmouth College* Case." *American Law Review* 8 (1874): 189–239.
Hornblower, William B. "Conflict between Federal and State Decisions." *American Law Review* 14 (1880): 211–228.
Huffcut, Ernest W. "Legislative Tax-Exemption Contracts." *American Law Review* 24 (1890).
Hutchinson, R. "Laws Impairing the Obligation of Contracts." *Southern Law Review* 1 (1875): 401–432.
Meredith, C. V. "As to Impairing the Obligation of a Contract." *Virginia Law Journal* 6 (1882): 385–402.
Morrison, John M. "The Legislative History of the Ordinance of 1787." *Proceedings of the American Antiquarian Society*, New Series, 5 (1889): 331–332.
"The Police Power and the Lake Front Case." Editorial. *Harvard Law Review* 6 (1893): 444–445.
Rand, William H., Jr. "*Swift v. Tyson* versus *Gelpcke v. Dubuque.*" *Harvard Law Review* 8 (1895): 328–351.
Reno, Conrad. "Impairment of Contracts by Change of Judicial Opinion." *American Law Review* 23 (1889): 190–207.
Russell, Alfred. "Status and Tendencies of the *Dartmouth College* Case." *American Law Register* 30 (1896): 321–356.
Sewall, Samuel E. "On a National Bankruptcy Law." *American Jurist* 1 (1829): 35, 39–40.
Thayer, James Bradley. "The Case of *Gelpcke v. Dubuque.*" *Harvard Law Review* 4 (1891): 311–320.
Thomas, J. H. "Homestead and Exemption Laws of the Southern States." *American Law Register* 19 (1871): 137–150.
Tiedeman, Christopher G. "Government Ownership of Public Utilities." *Harvard Law Review* 16 (1903): 476–490.

SECONDARY SOURCES

Books

Allen, Austin. *Origins of the* Dred Scott *Case: Jacksonian Jurisprudence and the Supreme Court, 1837–1857*. Athens: University of Georgia Press, 2006.

Arkes, Hadley. *The Return of George Sutherland: Restoring a Jurisprudence of Natural Rights.* Princeton, NJ: Princeton University Press, 1994.

Balleisen, Edward J. *Navigating Failure: Bankruptcy and Commercial Society in Antebellum America.* Chapel Hill: University of North Carolina Press, 2001.

Beard, Charles A. *An Economic Interpretation of the Constitution of the United States.* New York: Macmillan, 1913.

Bernstein, David A. *Rehabilitating* Lochner: *Defending Individual Rights against Progressive Reform.* Chicago: University of Chicago Press, 2011.

Brandon, Mark E. *States of Union: Family and Change in the American Constitutional Order.* Lawrence: University Press of Kansas, 2013.

Cadman, John W., Jr. *The Corporation in New Jersey: Business and Politics, 1791–1875.* Cambridge, MA: Harvard University Press, 1949.

Clarkson, Paul S., and R. Samuel Jett. *Luther Martin of Maryland.* Baltimore, MD: Johns Hopkins University Press, 1970.

Coleman, Peter J. *Debtors and Creditors in America: Insolvency, Imprisonment for Debt, and Bankruptcy, 1607–1900.* Madison: State Historical Society of Wisconsin, 1974.

Conley, Patrick T., Jr., ed. *Liberty and Justice: A History of Law and Lawyers in Rhode Island, 1636–1998.* Providence: Rhode Island Publication Society, 1998.

Cortner, Richard C. *The Iron Horse and the Constitution: The Railroads and the Transformation of the Fourteenth Amendment.* Westport, CT: Greenwood, 1993.

Corwin, Edward S. *John Marshall and the Constitution: A Chronicle of the Supreme Court.* New Haven, CT: Yale University Press, 1919.

Davis, Joseph Stancliffe. *Essays in the Earlier History of American Corporations.* 2 vols. Cambridge, MA: Harvard University Press, 1917; reprint, New York: Russell and Russell, 1965.

Dodd, Edwin Merrick. *American Business Corporations until 1860.* Cambridge, MA: Harvard University Press, 1954.

Ellis, David Maldwyn. *Landlords and Farmers in the Hudson-Mohawk Region.* Ithaca, NY: Cornell University Press, 1946.

Ely, James W., Jr. *The Chief Justiceship of Melville W. Fuller, 1888–1910.* Columbia: University of South Carolina Press, 1995.

———. *The Guardian of Every Other Right: A Constitutional History of Property Rights.* 3rd ed. New York: Oxford University Press, 2008.

———. *Railroads and American Law.* Lawrence: University Press of Kansas, 2001.

Ely, Richard T. *Property and Contract in Their Relation to the Distribution of Wealth.* 2 vols. New York: Macmillan, 1914.

Ernst, Robert. *Rufus King: American Federalist.* Chapel Hill: University of North Carolina Press, 1968.

Fairman, Charles. *Reconstruction and Reunion, 1864–1888.* New York: Macmillan, 1971.

Fischel, William A. *Regulatory Takings: Law, Economics, and Politics.* Cambridge, MA: Harvard University Press, 1995.

Fishback, Price, Jonathan Rose, and Kenneth Snowden. *Well Worth Saving: How the New Deal Safeguarded Home Ownership.* Chicago: University of Chicago Press, 2013.

Fliter, John A., and Derek S. Hoff. *Fighting Foreclosure: The* Blaisdell *Case, the Contract Clause, and the Great Depression.* Lawrence: University Press of Kansas, 2012.

Fogelson, Robert M. *The Great Rent Wars: New York, 1917–1929.* New Haven, CT: Yale University Press, 2013.

Foner, Eric. *Reconstruction: America's Unfinished Revolution, 1863–1977.* New York: Harper and Row, 1988.

Frank, John P. *Justice Daniel Dissenting: A Biography of Peter V. Daniel, 1784–1860.* Cambridge, MA: Harvard University Press, 1964.

Fried, Barbara H. *The Progressive Assault on Laissez-Faire: Robert Hale and the First Law and Economics Movement.* Cambridge, MA: Harvard University Press, 1998.

Friedman, Lawrence M. *American Law in the 20th Century.* New Haven, CT: Yale University Press, 2002.

———. *A History of American Law.* 3rd ed. New York: Touchstone, 2005.

Gerber, Scott Douglas, ed. *Seriatim: The Supreme Court before John Marshall.* New York: New York University Press, 1998.

Gilmore, Grant. *The Death of Contract.* Columbus: Ohio State University Press, 1974.

Graham, D. Kurt. *To Bring Law Home: The Federal Judiciary in Early National Rhode Island.* DeKalb: Northern Illinois University Press, 2010.

Greve, Michael S. *The Upside-Down Constitution.* Cambridge, MA: Harvard University Press, 2012.

Hall, Kermit L., and Peter Karsten. *The Magic Mirror: Law in American History.* 2nd ed. New York: Oxford University Press, 2009.

Hall, Mark David. *The Political and Legal Philosophy of James Wilson, 1724–1798.* Columbia: University of Missouri Press, 1997.

Hamilton, Daniel W. *The Limits of Sovereignty: Legislative Property Confiscation in the Union and the Confederacy during the Civil War.* Chicago: University of Chicago Press, 2007.

Higgs, Robert. *Crisis and Leviathan: Critical Episodes in the Growth of American Government.* New York: Oxford University Press, 1987.

Hobson, Charles F. *The Great Chief Justice: John Marshall and the Rule of Law.* Lawrence: University Press of Kansas, 1996.

———. *The Great Yazoo Land Sale: The Case of* Fletcher v. Peck. Lawrence: University Press of Kansas, 2016.

Horton, John Theodore. *James Kent: A Study in Conservatism, 1763–1847.* New York: D. Appleton-Century, 1939; reprint, New York: DaCapo Press, 1969.

Horwitz, Morton J. *The Transformation of American Law, 1780–1860.* Cambridge, MA: Harvard University Press, 1977.

Hovenkamp, Herbert. *Enterprise and American Law, 1836–1937.* Cambridge, MA: Harvard University Press, 1991.

Howe, Daniel Walker. *What Hath God Wrought? The Transformation of America, 1815–1848.* New York: Oxford University Press, 2007.

Huebner, Timothy S. *The Southern Judicial Tradition: State Judges and Sectional Distinctiveness, 1790–1890.* Athens: University of Georgia Press, 1999.

———. *The Taney Court: Justices, Rulings, and Legacy.* Santa Barbara, CA: ABC-CLIO, 2003.

Hunt, Robert S. *Law and Locomotives: The Impact of the Railroad on Wisconsin Law in the Nineteenth Century.* Madison: State Historical Society of Wisconsin, 1958.

Hunting, Warren B. *The Obligation of Contracts Clause of the United States Constitution.* Baltimore, MD: Johns Hopkins University Press, 1919.

Hurst, James Willard. *Law and Markets in United States History.* Madison: University of Wisconsin Press, 1982.

———. *Law and the Conditions of Freedom in the Nineteenth-Century United States.* Madison: University of Wisconsin Press, 1956.

Huston, Reeve. *Land and Freedom: Rural Society, Popular Protest, and Party Politics in Antebellum New York.* New York: Oxford University Press, 2000.

Irons, Peter. *A People's History of the Supreme Court.* New York: Penguin, 2006.

Johnson, Herbert A. *The Chief Justiceship of John Marshall, 1801–1835.* Columbia: University of South Carolina Press, 1997.

Keller, Morton. *Affairs of State: Public Life in Late Nineteenth-Century America.* Cambridge, MA: Harvard University Press, 1977.

———. *Regulating a New Economy: Public Policy and Economic Change in America, 1900–1933.* Cambridge, MA: Harvard University Press, 1990.

Kelly, Alfred H., Winfred A. Harbison, and Herman Belz. *The American Constitution: Its Origins and Development.* 7th ed. 2 vols. New York: Norton, 1991.

Kens, Paul. *Justice Stephen Field: Shaping Liberty from the Gold Rush to the Gilded Age.* Lawrence: University Press of Kansas, 1997.

———. *The Supreme Court under Morrison R. Waite, 1874–1888.* Columbia: University of South Carolina Press, 2010.

Kutler, Stanley I. *Privilege and Creative Destruction: The* Charles River Bridge *Case.* New York: J. B. Lippincott, 1971.

Lang, Meredith. *Defender of the Faith: The High Court of Mississippi, 1817–1875.* Jackson: University of Mississippi Press, 1977.

Lawrence, Alexander A. *James Moore Wayne: Southern Unionist.* Chapel Hill: University of North Carolina Press, 1943.

Leuchtenburg, William. *The Supreme Court Reborn: The Constitutional Revolution in the Age of Roosevelt.* New York: Oxford University Press, 1995.

Levy, Leonard W. *The Law of the Commonwealth and Chief Justice Shaw.* Cambridge, MA: Harvard University Press, 1957.

Magrath, C. Peter. *Yazoo: Law and Politics in the New Republic: The Case of* Fletcher v. Peck. Providence, RI: Brown University Press, 1966.

Main, Jackson Turner. *The Sovereign States, 1775–1783.* New York: New Viewpoints, 1973.

Maltz, Earl M. *The Chief Justiceship of Warren Burger, 1969–1986.* Columbia: University of South Carolina Press, 2000.

Manley, Walter W., II, and Cantor Brown, Jr. *The Supreme Court of Florida, 1917–1972.* Gainesville: University of Florida Press, 2006.

Mayer, David N. *Liberty of Contract: Rediscovering a Lost Constitutional Right.* Washington, DC: Cato Institute, 2011.

McCurdy, Charles W. *The Anti-Rent Era in New York Law and Politics, 1839–1865.* Chapel Hill: University of North Carolina Press, 2001.

McDonald, Forrest. *Novus Ordo Seclorum: The Intellectual Origins of the Constitution.* Lawrence: University Press of Kansas, 1985.

Mintz, Max M. *Gouverneur Morris and the American Revolution.* Norman: University of Oklahoma Press, 1970.

Moore, James Tice. *Two Paths to the New South: The Virginia Debt Controversy, 1870–1883.* Lexington: University Press of Kentucky, 1974.

Morgan, Donald G. *Justice William Johnson: The First Dissenter.* Columbia: University of South Carolina Press, 1954.

Morris, Richard B. *Witnesses at the Creation: Hamilton, Madison, Jay, and the Constitution.* New York: Holt, Rinehart, and Winston, 1985.

Nadelhaft, Jerome J. *The Disorders of War: The Revolution in South Carolina.* Orono: University of Maine Press, 1981.

Nedelsky, Jennifer. *Private Property and the Limits of American Constitutionalism: The Madisonian Framework and Its Legacy.* Chicago: University of Chicago Press, 1990.

Nelson, Margaret Virginia. *A Study of Judicial Review in Virginia, 1789–1928.* New York: Columbia University Press, 1947.

Nelson, William E. *The Common Law in Colonial America.* Vol. 1: *The Chesapeake and New England, 1607–1660.* New York: Oxford University Press, 2008.

———. *The Legalist Reformation: Law, Politics, and Ideology in New York, 1920–1980.* Chapel Hill: University of North Carolina Press, 2001.

Nevins, Allan. *The American States during and after the Revolution, 1775–1789.* New York: Macmillan, 1924.

Newmyer, R. Kent. *John Marshall and the Heroic Age of the Supreme Court.* Baton Rouge: Louisiana State University Press, 2001.

———. *Supreme Court Justice Joseph Story: Statesman of the Old Republic.* Chapel Hill: University of North Carolina Press, 1985.

Niven, John. *Salmon P. Chase: A Biography.* New York: Oxford University Press, 1995.

Orth, John V. *The Judicial Power of the United States: The Eleventh Amendment in American History.* New York: Oxford University Press, 1987.

Pratt, Walker F., Jr. *The Supreme Court under Edward Douglas White, 1910–1921.* Columbia: University of South Carolina Press, 1999.

Przybyszewski, Linda. *The Republic According to John Harlan Marshall.* Chapel Hill: University of North Carolina Press, 1999.

Reid, John Phillip. *Chief Justice: The Judicial World of Charles Doe.* Cambridge, MA: Harvard University Press, 1967.

———. *Constitutional History of the American Revolution: The Authority of Rights.* Madison: University of Wisconsin Press, 1986.

Ross, Michael A. *Justice of Shattered Dreams: Samuel Freeman Miller and the Supreme Court during the Civil War Era.* Baton Rouge: Louisiana State University Press, 2003.

Ross, William G. *The Chief Justiceship of Charles Evans Hughes, 1930–1941.* Columbia: University of South Carolina Press, 2007.

Saunders, Robert, Jr. *John Archibald Campbell: Southern Moderate, 1811–1889.* Tuscaloosa: University of Alabama Press, 1997.

Scheiber, Harry N., ed. *The State and Freedom of Contract.* Palo Alto, CA: Stanford University Press, 1998.

Selvin, Molly. *This Tender and Delicate Business: The Public Trust Doctrine in American Law and Economic Policy, 1789–1920.* New York: Garland, 1987.

Silver, David M. *Lincoln's Supreme Court.* Urbana: University of Illinois Press, 1956.

Smith, Page. *James Wilson: Founding Father, 1742–1798.* Chapel Hill: University of North Carolina Press, 1956.

Somin, Ilya. *The Grasping Hand:* Kelo v. City of New London *and the Limits of Eminent Domain.* Chicago: University of Chicago Press, 2015.

Stanley, Amy Dru. *From Bondage to Contract: Wage Labor, Marriage, and the Market in the Age of Slave Emancipation.* Cambridge, UK: Cambridge University Press, 1998.

Stites, Francis N. *Private Interest and Public Gain: The* Dartmouth College *Case, 1819.* Amherst: University of Massachusetts Press, 1972.

Street, Alfred B. *The Council of Revision of the State of New York.* Albany, NY: William Gould, 1859.

Summers, Mark Wahlgren. *The Ordeal of the Reunion: A New History of Reconstruction.* Chapel Hill: University of North Carolina Press, 2014.

Thompson, Elizabeth Lee. *Reconstruction of Southern Debtors: Bankruptcy after the Civil War.* Athens: University Press of Georgia, 2004.

Timberlake, Richard H. *Constitutional Money: A Review of the Supreme Court's Monetary Decisions.* Cambridge, UK: Cambridge University Press, 2013.

Unger, Irwin. *The Greenback Era: A Social and Political History of American Finance, 1865–1879.* Princeton, NJ: Princeton University Press, 1964.

Urofsky, Melvin I., and Paul Finkelman. *A March of Liberty: A Constitutional History of the United States.* 3rd ed. 2 vols. New York: Oxford University Press, 2011.

Warren, Charles. *Bankruptcy in United States History.* Cambridge, MA: Harvard University Press, 1935.

———. *The Supreme Court in United States History.* Revised edition. 2 vols. Boston: Little, Brown, 1926.

White, G. Edward. *The Constitution and the New Deal.* Cambridge, MA: Harvard University Press, 2000.

———. *History of the Supreme Court of the United States: The Marshall Court and Cultural Change, 1815–1835.* New York: Macmillan, 1988.

Wood, Gordon S. *The Radicalism of the American Revolution.* New York: Knopf, 1992.

Wright, Benjamin F. *The Contract Clause of the Constitution.* Cambridge, MA: Harvard University Press, 1938.

Articles and Chapters

Ackerman, Bruce. "Constitutional Politics/Constitutional Law." *Yale Law Journal* 99 (1989).

Alston, Lee J. "Farm Foreclosure Moratorium Legislation: A Lesson from the Past." *American Economic Review* 74 (1984): 445–457.

Anenson, T. Leigh, Alex Slabaugh, and Karen Eilers Lahey. "Reforming Public Pensions." *Yale Law and Policy Review* 33 (2014): 1–74.

Aumann, F. R. "Some Constitutional Aspects of War Rent Regulation Measures." *Kentucky Law Review* 18 (1930): 354–372.

Babb, James E. "Effect of Overruling Opinion of Court of Last Resort on Rights Acquired on Opinion Overruled." *American Law Review* 45 (1911): 750–759.

Bieneman, Charles A. "Note: Legal Interpretation and a Constitutional Case—*Home Building and Loan Association v. Blaisdell*." *Michigan Law Review* 90 (1992): 2534–2564.

Boyd, Alan W. "Rent Regulation under the Police Power." *Michigan Law Review* 19 (1921).

Boyd, Julian P. "Connecticut's Experiment in Expansion: The Susquehanna Company, 1753–1803." *Journal of Economic and Business History* 4 (1931–1932).

———. "William Paterson: Forerunner of John Marshall," in *The Lives of Eighteen from Princeton.* Edited by Willard Thorp. Princeton, NJ: Princeton University Press, 1946, 1–23.

Boyd, Steven R. "The Contract Clause and the Evolution of American Federalism." *William and Mary Quarterly* 44 (1987): 529–548.

Brennan, William J. "State Constitutions and the Protection of Individual Rights." *Harvard Law Review* 90 (1997): 489–504.

Brophy, Alfred L. "'Necessity Knows No Law': Vested Rights and the Styles of Reasoning in the Confederate Conscription Cases." *Mississippi Law Journal* 69 (2000): 1123–1180.

Brown, Ray A. "Police Power—Legislation for Health and Personal Safety." *Harvard Law Review* 42 (1929): 866–898.

Bruchey, Stuart. "The Impact of Concern for the Security of Property Rights on the Legal System of the Early American Republic," *Wisconsin Law Review* (1980): 1138–1140.

Buck, Stuart. "The Legal Ramifications of Public Pension Reform." *Texas Review of Law and Politics* 17 (2012): 25–96.

Burns, Debra Brubaker. "Too Big to Fail and Too Big to Pay: States, Their Public-Pension Bills, and the Constitution." *Hastings Constitutional Law Quarterly* 39 (2011): 253–295.

Butler, Henry N., and Larry E. Ribstein. "The Contract Clause and the Corporation." *Brooklyn Law Review* 55 (1989): 767–808.

Campbell, Bruce A. "*Dartmouth College* as a Civil Liberties Case: The Formation of Constitutional Policy." *Kentucky Law Review* 70 (1982): 643–706.

———. "John Marshall, the Virginia Political Economy, and the *Dartmouth College* Decision." *American Journal of Legal History* 19 (1975): 40–65.

Cataldo, Michael. "Note: Revival or Revolution—*U.S. Trust*'s Role in the Contracts Clause Circuit Split." *St. John's Law Review* 87 (2013): 1145–1192.

Cayton, Andrew R. L. "The Northwest Ordinance from the Perspective of the Frontier," in *The Northwest Ordinance, 1787: A Bicentennial Handbook.* Edited by Robert M. Taylor, Jr. Indianapolis: Indiana Historical Society, 1987.

Clarke, Leo. "The Contract Clause: A Basis for Limited Judicial Review of State Economic Regulation." *University of Miami Law Review* 39 (1985): 183–255.

Clinton, Robert L. "The Obligation Clause of the United States Constitution: Public and/or Private Contracts." *University of Arkansas at Little Rock Law Journal* 11 (1988): 343–367.

Collier, Christopher. "Article III, Section 2, and the Bloody Background of *Van Horne's Lessee v. Dorrance.*" In *Constitution Day*. Edited by Patrick T. Conley, Jr. Providence: Rhode Island Publications Society, 2010, 157–181.

Corwin, Edward S. "Moratorium over Minnesota." *University of Pennsylvania Law Review* 82 (1934): 311–316.

Crump, David. "The Economic Purpose of the Contract Clause." *Southern Methodist University Law Review* 66 (2013): 687–709.

Currie, David P. "The Constitution in the Supreme Court: Contracts and Commerce, 1836–1864." 1983 *Duke Law Journal* (1983): 471–513.

———. "The Constitution in the Supreme Court: The Protection of Economic Interests, 1889–1910." *University of Chicago Law Review* 52 (1985): 324–388.

Dam, Kenneth W. "The *Legal Tender Cases*." *Supreme Court Review* (1981): 367–412.

Davis, Kenneth R. "Note: Constitutional Law—Oklahoma Mortgage Foreclosure Moratoriums . . . Past, Present, and Future?" *Oklahoma Law Review* 42 (1989): 647–662.

Dirck, Brian R. "Prosperity's Blush: Civil Liberties, Property Rights, and Property Confiscation in the Confederacy." *Civil War History* 48 (2002): 237–256.

Dodd, W. E. "Impairment of the Obligation of Contract by State Judicial Decisions." *Illinois Law Review* 4 (1909): 155–173.

Dougan, Michael B. "The Doctrine of Creative Destruction: Ferry and Bridge Law in Arkansas." *Arkansas Historical Quarterly* 39 (1980): 136–158.

Dowd, Morgan D. "Justice Story, the Supreme Court, and the Obligation of Contract." *Case Western Reserve Law Review* 19 (1968): 493–527.

Duffey, Denis P. "The Northwest Ordinance as a Constitutional Document." *Columbia Law Review* 95 (1995): 929–968.

Eagle, Steven J. "The Four-Factor Penn Central Regulatory Takings Test." *Penn State Law Review* 118 (2014): 601–646.

Ely, James W., Jr. "American Independence and the Law: A Study of Post-Revolutionary South Carolina Legislation." *Vanderbilt Law Review* 26 (1973): 939–971.

———. "Economic Liberties and the Original Meaning of the Constitution." *San Diego Law Review* 45 (2008): 673–708.

———. "Homestead Exemption and Southern Legal Culture." In *Signposts: New Directions in Southern Legal History*. Edited by Sally E. Hadden and Patricia Hagler Minter. Athens: University of Georgia Press, 2013: 289–314.

———. "The Marshall Court and Property Rights: A Reappraisal." *John Marshall Law Review* 33 (2000): 1023–1061.

———. "The Progressive Era Assault on Individualism and Property Rights." *Social Philosophy and Policy* 29 (2012): 255–282.

———. "Property Rights and the Supreme Court in the Gilded Age." *Journal of Supreme Court History* 38 (2013): 330–344.

———. "The Protection of Contractual Rights: A Tale of Two Constitutional Provisions." *NYU Journal of Law and Liberty* 1 (2005): 370–403.

———. "Public Employees and the Curious Mini-Revival of Contract Clause Jurisprudence." *Brigham-Kanner Property Rights Conference Journal* 2 (2013): 37–60.

———. "'To Pursue Any Lawful Trade or Avocation': The Evolution of Unenumerated Economic Rights in the Nineteenth Century." *University of Pennsylvania Journal of Constitutional Law* 8 (2006).

———. "The Railroad Question Revisited: *Chicago, Milwaukee, and St. Paul Railway v. Minnesota* and Constitutional Limits on State Regulations." *Great Plains Quarterly* 12 (1992): 121–134.

———. "Whatever Happened to the Contract Clause?" *Charleston Law Review* 4 (2010): 371–394.

Epstein, Richard A. "The Takings Jurisprudence of the Warren Court: A Constitutional Siesta." *Tulsa Law Review* 31 (1996): 643–676.

———. "Toward a Revitalization of the Contract Clause." *University of Chicago Law* Review 51 (1984): 703–751.

———. "The Upside-Down Law of Property and Contract: Of Fannie Mae, Freddie Mac, and San Jose Pensions." *Nebraska Law Review* 93 (2015): 869–900.

Ewald, William. "James Wilson and the Drafting of the Constitution." *University of Pennsylvania Journal of Constitutional Law* 10 (2008): 901–1009.

Farber, David A. "Justice Bushrod Washington and the Age of Discovery in American Law." *West Virginia Law Review* 102 (2000): 735–807.

"Farm Foreclosure Moratoria and the Contract Clause: An Economic Analysis." *Constitutional Commentary* 3 (1986): 331–345.

Feller, A. H. "Moratory Legislation: A Comparative Study." *Harvard Law Review* 46 (1933): 1061–1085.

Festa, Matthew J. "Property and Republicanism in the Northwest Ordinance." *Arizona State Law Journal* 45 (2013): 409–470.

Finkelman, Paul. "John McLean: Moderate Abolitionist and Supreme Court Politician." *Vanderbilt Law Review* 62 (2009): 519–565.

Friedman, Lawrence M. "A Search for Seizure: *Pennsylvania Coal Co. v. Mahon* in Context." *Law and History Review* 4 (1986): 1–22.

Funston, Richard. "Requiescat in Pace: A Memorial to the Contract Clause." *Texas Southern Law Review* 3 (1973): 12–24.

Gates, Paul W. "Tenants of the Log Cabins." *Mississippi Valley Historical Society* 49 (1962): 3–31.

Glennon, Robert J., Jr. "Justice Henry Billings Brown: Values in Tension." *University of Colorado Law Review* 44 (1973): 553–603.

Glick, David. "Conditional Strategic Retreat: The Court's Concession in the 1935 *Gold Clause Cases*." *Journal of Politics* 71 (2009): 800–816.

Gordon, Sarah Barringer. "The Landscape of Faith: Religious Property and Confiscation in the Early Republic." In *Making Legal History: Essays in Honor of William E. Nelson*. Edited by Daniel J. Hulsebosch and R. B. Bernstein. New York: New York University Press, 2013, 13–48.

Graham, Robert A. "Note: The Constitution, the Legislature, and Unfair Surprise—Toward a Reliance-Based Approach to the Contract Clause." *Michigan Law Review* (1993): 398–437.

Grandy, Christopher. "Can Government Be Trusted to Keep Its Part of a Social Contract? New Jersey and the Railroads, 1825–1888." *Journal of Law, Economics, and Organization* 5 (1989): 249–269.

Grant, Douglas L. "Underpinning of the Public Trust Doctrine: Lessons from *Illinois Central Railroad.*" *Arizona State Law Journal* 33 (2001): 849–885.

Grant, J. A. C. "The 'Higher Law' Background of the Law of Eminent Domain." *Wisconsin Law Review* 6 (1931): 67–85.

Griffin, Christopher, Jr. "Connecticut's Legal Liability for Modifying Public Pension Benefits." Connecticut Policy Institute, November 12, 2014, 1–13.

Hale, Robert L. "The Supreme Court and the Contract Clause." Part 1, *Harvard Law Review* 57 (1944): 512–557; Part 2, *Harvard Law Review* 57 (1944): 621–674; Part 3, *Harvard Law Review* 57 (1944): 852–892.

Harrell, Rodney. "Comment: The Contract Clause of the Constitution and the Need for 'Pass Any . . . Law' Rehabilitation in the Age of Delegation." *George Mason Law Review* 22 (2015): 1317–1348.

Hart, Henry M., Jr. "The Gold Clauses in United States Bonds." *Harvard Law Review* 48 (1935): 1057–1099.

Heckman, Charles A. "Establishing the Basis for Local Financing of American Railroad Construction in the Nineteenth Century: From *City of Bridgeport v. the Housatonic Railroad Company* to *Gelpcke v. City of Dubuque.*" *American Journal of Legal History* 32 (1988): 236–264.

Holton, Woody. "Equality as Unintended Consequence: The Contracts Clause and the Married Women's Property Acts." *Journal of Southern History* 81 (2015): 313–340.

Horton, Wesley W. "The Pre-Civil War Connecticut Supreme Court." *Connecticut Law Review* 34 (2002): 1209–1231.

Huebner, Timothy S. "Encouraging Economic Growth: Joseph Henry Lumpkin and the Law of Contract, 1846–1860." *Georgia Journal of Southern Legal History* 1 (1991): 357–375.

Hyman, Michael R. "Taxation, Public Policy, and Political Dissent: Yeoman Disaffection in the Post-Reconstruction Lower South." *Journal of Southern History* 55 (1989): 49–76.

Hynning, Clifford C. "Constitutionality of Moratory Legislation." *Chicago-Kent Review* 12 (1934): 182–211.

James, F. Cyril. "The Bank of North America and the Financial History of Philadelphia." *Pennsylvania Magazine of History and Biography* 64 (1940): 56–87.

Kahan, Rebecca M. "Comment: Constitutional Stretch, Snap-Back, and Sag—Why *Blaisdell* Was a Harsher Blow to Liberty Than *Korematsu.*" *Northwestern University Law Review* 99 (2005): 1279–1313.

Kainen, James L. "The Historical Framework for Reviving Constitutional Protection for Property and Contract Rights." *Cornell Law Review* 79 (1993): 87–142.

Kauper, Paul G. "What Is a 'Contract' under the Contracts Clause of the Federal Constitution?" *Michigan Law Review* 31 (1932): 187–205.

Kearney, Joseph D., and Thomas W. Merrill. "The Origins of the American Public Trust Doctrine: What Really Happened in *Illinois Central.*" *University of Chicago Law Review* 71 (2004): 799–931.

Klarman, Michael J. "How Great Were the 'Great' Marshall Court Decisions?" *Virginia Law Review* 87 (2001): 1111–1184.

Kmiec, Douglas W., and John O. McGinnis. "The Contract Clause: A Return to the Original Understanding." *Hastings Constitutional Law Quarterly* 14 (1987): 525–560.

Kull, Andrew. "The Enforceability after Emancipation of Debts Contracted for the Purchase of Slaves." *Chicago-Kent Law Review* 70 (1994): 493–538.

Lawless, Robert M. "The American Response to Farm Crises: Procedural Debt Relief." *University of Illinois Law Review* (1988): 1037–1066.

Leonard, Gerald. "*Fletcher v. Peck* and Constitutional Development in the Early United States." *University of California, Davis Law Review* 47 (2014): 1843–1857.

Lynch, Joseph M. "*Fletcher v. Peck:* The Nature of the Contract Clause." *Seton Hall Law Review* 13 (1982): 1–20.

Madiar, Eric M. "Is Welching on Public Pension Promises an Option for Illinois? An Analysis of Article XIII, Section 5 of the Illinois Constitution." *John Marshall Law Review* 48 (2014): 167–323.

Magliocca, Gerald N. "The Gold Clause Cases and Constitutional Necessity." *Florida Law Review* 64 (2012): 1243–1277.

Maidment, Richard A. "Chief Justice Hughes and the Contract Clause: A Reassessment." *Journal of Legal History* 8 (1987): 316–329.

Martinez, John. "Taking Time Seriously: The Federal Constitutional Right to Be Free from 'Startling' State Court Overrulings." *Harvard Journal of Law and Public Policy* 11 (1998): 297–345.

McConnell, Michael W. "Contract Rights and Property Rights: A Case Study in the Relationship between Individual Liberties and Constitutional Structure." *California Law Review* 76 (1988): 267–295.

McCurdy, Charles W. "Justice Field and the Jurisprudence of Government-Business Relations: Some Parameters of Laissez-Faire Constitutionalism, 1863–1897." *Journal of American History* 61 (1975): 970–1005.

Mendelson, Wallace. "B. F. Wright on the Contract Clause: A Progressive Misreading of the Marshall-Taney Era." *Western Political Quarterly* 38 (1985): 262–275.

Merola, Nila M. "Judicial Review of State Legislation: An Ironic Return to Lochnerian Ideology When Public Sector Contracts Are Impaired." *St. John's Law Review* 84 (2010): 1179–1217.

Merrill, Maurice H. "Application of the Obligation of Contract Clause to State Promises." *University of Pennsylvania Law Review* 80 (1932): 639–669.

Merrill, Thomas W. "Public Contracts, Private Contracts, and the Transformation of the Constitutional Order." Case *Western Reserve Law Review* 37 (1987): 597–630.

Mitchell, Thomas E. "Rewriting the Terms: The Contract Clause and Special Interest Legislation in *RUI One Corp. v. City of Berkeley.*" *Harvard Journal of Law and Public Policy* 28 (2004): 691–712.

Moreno, Paul D. "'The Legitimate Object of Government': Constitutional Problems of Civil War–Era Republican Policy." In *Constitutionalism in the Approach and Aftermath of the Civil War.* Edited by Paul D. Moreno and Johnathan O'Neill. New York: Fordham University Press, 2013, 160–180.

Nelson, William E. "Authority and the Rule of Law in Early Virginia." *Ohio Northern University Law Review* 29 (2003): 357–360.

———. "The Eighteenth-Century Background of John Marshall's Constitutional Jurisprudence." *Michigan Law Review* 76 (1978): 893–960.
"Note: Constitutionality of the New York Emergency Housing Law." *Harvard Law Review* 34 (1921): 426–430.
"Note: The Contract Clause of the Federal Constitution." *Columbia Law Review* 32 (1932): 476–493.
Olken, Samuel R. "Charles Evans Hughes and the *Blaisdell* Decision: A Historical Study of Contract Clause Jurisprudence." *Oregon Law Review* 72 (1993): 513–602.
———. "Justice Sutherland Reconsidered." *Vanderbilt Law Review* 62 (2009): 639–693.
Palmer, Robert C. "Obligations of Contracts: Intent and Distortion." *Case Western Reserve Law Review* 37 (1987): 631–673.
Pearson, Eric. "*Illinois Central* and the Public Trust Doctrine in State Law." *Virginia Environmental Law Journal* 15 (1996): 713–741.
Porter, Mary Cornelia. "That Commerce Shall Be Free: A New Look at the Old Laissez-Faire Court." *Supreme Court Review* (1976): 135–159.
Poteat, J. Douglas. "State Legislative Relief for the Mortgage Debtor during the Depression." *Law and Contemporary Problems* 5 (1938): 517–544.
Powe, L. A., Jr. "Rehearsal for Substantive Due Process: The Municipal Bond Cases." *Texas Law Review* 53 (1975): 738–756.
Priest, Claire. "Creating an American Property Law: Alienability and Its Limits." *Harvard Law Review* 120 (2006): 408–458.
Priest, George L. "Law and Economic Distress: Sangamon County, Illinois, 1837–1844." *Journal of Legal Studies* 2 (1973): 469–492.
Prosser, William L. "The Minnesota Mortgage Moratorium." *Southern California Law Review* 7 (1934): 353–371.
Randall, James G. "The Virginia Debt Controversy." *Political Science Quarterly* 30 (1915): 553–577.
"Recent Cases: Constitutional Law—Contracts Clause." *Harvard Law Review* 120 (2007): 844–851.
Roots, Roger I. "Government by Permanent Emergency: The Forgotten History of the New Deal Constitution." *Suffolk University Law Review* 33 (2000): 259–292.
Sax, Joseph. "The Public Trust Doctrine in Natural Resources Law: Effective Judicial Intervention." *Michigan Law Review* 68 (1970): 471–566.
Schar, Brian A. "Note: Contract Clause Law under State Constitutions—a Model for Heightened Scrutiny." *Texas Review of Law and Politics* 1 (1997): 123–147.
Schwartz, Bernard. "Old Wine in Old Bottles? The Renaissance of the Contract Clause." *Supreme Court Review* (1979): 95–121.
Secunda, Paul M. "Constitutional Contracts Clause Challenges in Public Pension Litigation." *Hofstra Labor and Employment Law Journal* 28 (2010): 263–300.
Sherry, Suzanna. "The Founders' Unwritten Constitution." *University of Chicago Law Review* 54 (1987): 1127–1177.
———. "Natural Law in the States." *University of Cincinnati Law Review* 61 (1992): 171–172.
———. "The Ninth Amendment: Righting an Unwritten Constitution." *Chicago-Kent Law Review* 64 (1988): 1001–1014.

Siegel, Stephen A. "*Lochner*-Era Jurisprudence and the American Constitutional Tradition." *North Carolina Law Review* 70 (1991): 1–11.
———. "Understanding the Nineteenth-Century Contract Clause: The Role of the Property-Privilege and 'Takings' Clause Jurisprudence." *Southern California Law Review* 60 (1986): 1–108.
Skeel, David A., Jr. "States of Bankruptcy." *University of Chicago Law Review* 79 (2012): 677–735.
Skilton, Robert. "Mortgage Moratoria since 1933." *University of Pennsylvania Law Review* 92 (1943): 53–90.
Somin, Ilya. "Two Steps Forward for the 'Poor Relation' of Constitutional Law: *Koontz, Arkansas Game and Fish,* and the Future of the Takings Clause." *Cato Supreme Court Review* (2012–2013): 215–243.
Sterk, Stewart E. "The Continuity of Legislatures: Of Contracts and the Contract Clause." *Columbia Law Review* 88 (1988): 647–722.
Sunstein, Cass R. "*Lochner*'s Legacy." *Columbia Law Review* 87 (1987): 873–919.
Thies, Clifford. "Repudiation in Antebellum Mississippi." *Independent Review* 19 (2014): 191–208.
Thompson, Barton H., Jr., "The History of the Judicial Impairment 'Doctrine' and Its Lessons for the Contract Clause." *Stanford Law Review* 44 (1992): 1373–1466.
Trimble, Bruce R. "Chief Justice Waite and the Limitations on the *Dartmouth College* Decision." *University of Cincinnati Law Review* (1935): 41–66.
Walsh, Geoff. "The Finger in the Dike: State and Local Laws Combat the Foreclosure Tide." *Suffolk University Law Review* 44 (2011): 139–191.
White, G. Edward. "John Marshall Harlan I: The Precursor." *American Journal of Legal History* 19 (1975): 1–21.
Wilson, Janet. "The Bank of North America and Pennsylvania Politics, 1781–1787." *Pennsylvania Magazine of History and Biography* 66 (1942): 3–28.
Wood, Gordon S. "The Origins of Vested Rights in the Early Republic." *Virginia Law Review* 85 (1999): 1421–1445.
Woody, R. H. "Some Aspects of the Economic Condition of South Carolina after the Civil War." *North Carolina Historical Review* 7 (1930): 346–364.
Young, Ernest A. "Its Hour Come Round at Last? State Sovereignty and the Great State Debt Crisis of the Early Twenty-first Century." *Harvard Journal of Law and Public Policy* 35 (2012): 593–622.

Index of Cases

Index

www.ingramcontent.com/pod-product-compliance
Lightning Source LLC
Chambersburg PA
CBHW051257200926
51612CB00003B/68/J
9780700623075